THE CAMBRIDGE COMPANION TO HISTORICAL ARCHAEOLOGY

The *Cambridge Companion to Historical Archaeology* provides an overview of the international field of historical archaeology (c. AD 1500 to the present) through seventeen specially commissioned essays from leading researchers in the field. The volume explores key themes in historical archaeology including documentary archaeology, the writing of historical archaeology, colonialism, capitalism, industrial archaeology, maritime archaeology, cultural resource management and urban archaeology. Three special sections explore the distinctive contributions of material culture studies, landscape archaeology and the archaeology of buildings and the household. Drawing on case studies from North America, Europe, Australasia, Africa and around the world, the volume captures the breadth and diversity of contemporary historical archaeology, considers archaeology's relationship with history, cultural anthropology and other periods of archaeological study, and introduces alternative conceptions of the field. This book is essential reading for anyone studying or researching the material remains of the recent past.

DAN HICKS is Lecturer in Archaeology and Anthropology at the University of Bristol, where he is Director of the MA in Historical Archaeology. He is a member of the Council for Post-Medieval Archaeology and has written widely on world historical archaeology.

MARY C. BEAUDRY is Professor of Archaeology and Anthropology at Boston University. She is the editor of *Documentary Archaeology in the New World* (Cambridge, 1988) and the author of *Findings: The Material Culture of Needlework and Sewing* (2006) and over 70 articles on historical archaeology.

THE CAMBRIDGE COMPANION TO

HISTORICAL ARCHAEOLOGY

EDITED BY

DAN HICKS AND MARY C. BEAUDRY

 CAMBRIDGE
UNIVERSITY PRESS

CAMBRIDGE UNIVERSITY PRESS
Cambridge, New York, Melbourne, Madrid, Cape Town, Singapore, São Paulo

Cambridge University Press
The Edinburgh Building, Cambridge CB2 2RU, UK

Published in the United States of America by Cambridge University Press, New York

www.cambridge.org
Information on this title: www.cambridge.org/9780521619622

© Cambridge University Press 2006

First published 2006

Printed in the United Kingdom at the University Press, Cambridge

A catalogue record for this publication is available from the British Library

ISBN-13 978-0-521-85375-0 hardback
ISBN-10 0-521-85375-3 hardback

ISBN-13 978-0-521-61962-2 paperback
ISBN-10 0-521-61962-9 paperback

DH
For Chris Currie MIFA, FSA
1952–2005

MCB
In memory of my sister, Faye M. Beaudry
'Life is a beach'

Contents

viii   Contents

Figures

Table

Contributors

DAVID BARKER is Senior Archaeologist at Stoke-on-Trent City Council

MARY C. BEAUDRY is Professor of Archaeology and Anthropology at Boston University

ELEANOR C. CASELLA is Senior Lecturer in Archaeology at the University of Manchester

MATTHEW D. COCHRAN is a doctoral student in Material Culture Studies at the University College, London

BARRY CUNLIFFE is Professor of European Archaeology at the University of Oxford

LU ANN DE CUNZO is Professor of Anthropology at the University of Delaware

JULIE H. ERNSTEIN is Assistant Professor of Anthropology and Heritage Resources at Northwestern State University, Louisiana

JOE FLATMAN is Lecturer in Maritime Archaeology at University College, London

DAN HICKS is Lecturer in Archaeology and Anthropology at the University of Bristol and Research Fellow in the Department of Archaeology, Boston University.

CORNELIUS HOLTORF is Assistant Professor at the Institute of Archaeology and Ancient History, University of Lund, Sweden

AUDREY HORNING is Lecturer in Archaeology at the University of Leicester

WILLIAM GRAY JOHNSON is Associate Research Professor at the Desert Research Institute, California

ROSEMARY A. JOYCE is Professor of Anthropology at the University of California, Berkeley

JULIA KING is Associate Professor in Anthropology at St Mary's College of Maryland

SUSAN LAWRENCE is Senior Lecturer in Archaeology at La Trobe University, Melbourne

GAVIN LUCAS is Lecturer in Archaeology at the University of Iceland and member of the Board of Directors, Institute of Archaeology, Reykjavik

TADHG O'KEEFFE is Senior Lecturer in Archaeology at University College, Dublin

TERESITA MAJEWSKI is Director of the Historic Division and Principal Investigator at Statistical Research, Inc., Tucson, Arizona

RANDALL McGUIRE is Professor of Anthropology at Binghamton University, New York

JOHN SCHOFIELD is Research Fellow in Archaeology at the University of Bristol and Head of Military Programmes at English Heritage

NICK SHEPHERD is Senior Lecturer in the Centre for African Studies at the University of Cape Town

MARK STANIFORTH is Associate Professor in Maritime Archaeology at Flinders University, Adelaide

JAMES SYMONDS is Executive Director of the Archaeological Research and Consultancy at the University of Sheffield

LAURIE A. WILKIE is Assistant Professor of Anthropology at the University of California, Berkeley

HOWARD WILLIAMS is Lecturer in Archaeology at the University of Exeter

REBECCA YAMIN is Principal Archaeologist with John Milner Associates, Philadelphia

Acknowledgements

We would like to thank all our contributing authors for their excellent contributions, speedy responses, and good humour as the volume took shape. We are also indebted to our editor Simon Whitmore and his colleagues at Cambridge University Press for the vision for this book, and for constant encouragement, and to four anonymous reviewers for their comments. Dan would also like to thank Olivia, Eva and Iris for all their support and patience during the project. The later stages of the editing were supported by a grant from the Faculty of Arts at the University of Bristol, to whom thanks are due.

We are grateful to Victor Buchli, Fiona Campbell, Stefan Claesson, Kate Clark, Claire Dempsey, Claire Doherty, Roberta Gilchrist, Kate Giles, Chris Gosden, Mark Horton, Matthew Johnson, Mark Leone, Laura McAtackney, Janet Miller, Joshua Pollard, Adrian and Mary Praetzellis, Andrew Sherratt, Athena Tadakis, Sarah Tarlow, Jonna Ulin and our graduate students past and present for inspiring us to think about historical archaeology in new ways.

Abbreviations

ACO	Archaeological Contracts Office
AIA	Association for Industrial Archaeology
ARCUS	Archaeological Research and Consultancy at the University of Sheffield
BIAS	Bristol Industrial Archaeology Society
CBA	Council for British Archaeology
CC	cream-coloured
CEO	Chief Executive Officer
CRM	Cultural Resource Management
CSRF	Cultural Sites and Resources Forum
DRI	Desert Research Institute
EIC	East India Company
GAMA	Ground-launched cruise missiles alert and maintenance area
GIS	Geographical Information System
HABS	Historic American Buildings Survey
HAER	Historic American Engineering Record
HLC	Historic Landscape Characterisation
HOC	Hands off Committee
nd.	no date
NRIM	National Record of Industrial Monuments
NTS	Nevada Test Site
NTSHF	Nevada Test Site Historical Foundation
pers. com.	personal communication
RCHME	Royal Commission on the Historical Monuments of England
SAHRA	South African Heritage Resources Agency
scuba	self-contained underwater breathing apparatus
SFRG	Special Focus Reference Group
SHPO	State Historic Preservation Office
TICCIH	The International Committee for the Conservation of Industrial Heritage

UCT	University of Cape Town
UWC	University of Western Cape
VOC	Dutch East India Company
WAC	World Archaeological Congress
WAMM	Western Australia Maritime Museum
WPA	Work Projects Administration

CHAPTER I

Introduction: the place of historical archaeology

Dan Hicks and Mary C. Beaudry

Historical archaeology – a phrase used by archaeologists to describe the archaeology of the period from around AD 1500 up to and including the present – is unusual in its emergence as a new field of enquiry since the 1950s. This collection of contrasting chapters aims to capture the energy and diversity of contemporary anthropological historical archaeology, and to open up this material, which remains virtually unmentioned in conventional accounts of archaeological thought (e.g. Trigger 1990), to a wider archaeological and interdisciplinary readership. For some, the notion of 'historical archaeology' will appear tautological. Archaeology is often seen as the search for the remains of distant, prehistoric societies, or of Classical or Near Eastern civilisations. For others, the fact that archaeologists have neglected the most recent past – the periods studied most commonly by other disciplines, and from which massive quantities of materials survive – will appear perverse. Our commitment to this editorial project, however, derives from our understanding of archaeology as a contemporary project with a distinctive bundle of methods and practices, which works on the material remains of human societies from all periods.

The volume is offered as an open-minded and varied contribution to those interested in the role of material things in human social life, and in what survives from the recent past. We view the diversity of anthropological historical archaeology as a principal strength of the field, and therefore do not wish in an introduction to summarise the complex, sophisticated and sometimes contrasting arguments and approaches of our contributors. Instead, in this short introductory chapter we want to present some brief thoughts that have emerged during twelve months of editorial exchanges between the American east coast and the English west country. From this partial perspective, we consider how 'the place of historical archaeology' looks from here, underlining the creative and hybrid nature of this field that freely crosses disciplinary boundaries and provides distinctive insights into the study of the material world.

***

A note on that phrase *historical archaeology* is a necessary starting point. It raises the field's potential location in interdisciplinary environments. Some archaeologists, among them John Moreland (2001), define historical archaeology by the presence of written documents in the society being investigated. This perspective draws upon a strong tradition of thought in archaeology and anthropology that has marked out literate societies, and especially those that write their own histories, as special subjects of enquiry. Thus, anthropologist Jack Goody has considered the importance of writing, first recorded in the urbanising societies of the second half of the fourth millennium BC in south-west Asia and Egypt (see Houston 2004: 1), as a material dimension of the human development of language and as a relatively uncommon phenomenon until the closing centuries of the second millennium AD. He observed how 'written cultures were' for most of the past 5000 years 'minority cultures' (Goody 2000: 134). Goody has argued that the presence of writing affected the whole of society regardless of whether all its members could write, changing senses of time and conceptions of temporality.

Separating out cultures with traditions of writing, especially of writing histories, as the subject matter of historical archaeology is problematic. As Laurie Wilkie (this volume) acknowledges, while the presence of documents offers unique opportunities for historical archaeologists, written sources represent simply another, albeit distinctive, form of material culture rather than a revolutionary change in the human past. In both literate and non-literate situations, oral traditions often produce deep senses of temporality, history and ways of recounting. As Eric Wolf (1982) observed, there is a political imperative to rejecting models of non-western or non-literate societies as being 'without history'. For many historical archaeologists, then, the presence of written documents does not define a special field of archaeological study. African historical archaeologists, for example, have long relied upon oral tradition and oral history as a key element in their study of precolonial, colonial, and postcolonial African societies of the past 500 years (see e.g. DeCorse 1996; Schmidt 1978). Rather than claiming that historical archaeology is the study of 'people with history' (Little 1994), in this volume we use the term *historical* to refer broadly to the post-1500 period, strongly resisting any attempt to separate the field from the archaeology of earlier periods.

Of course, historical archaeology works on the material remains of situations from which no written records survive as often as it does at sites for which rich documentary sources exist. In all cases, historical archaeologists bring an awareness of how much of daily life remains undocumented, unspoken, and yet is far from insignificant and often leaves material traces. Historical archaeologies are different from the work of our prehistorian colleagues only in the sheer diversity and quantities of materials that survive, and in the relative proximity of the material to the present: both of which bring distinctive opportunities rather than essential differences.

Concerns with the excess and temporal contiguity of the material remains of the recent past that we study in the present have often led to a certain nervousness over the status of the field (Hicks 2004). In the United Kingdom, this has been most visible in debates over terminology, where the alternative merits of the appellations *post-medieval archaeology, industrial archaeology, later historical archaeology*, etc. have been considered (e.g. Tarlow 1999a), in contrast with the term in international usage, 'historical archaeology', used in the present volume. Post-medieval archaeology has traditionally been defined as the archaeology of the period between c. AD 1450–1750, with later material being left to 'industrial archaeologists'. While many British 'post-medievalists' increasingly work beyond the mid-eighteenth century, this division is still visible in many places. Such terminologies derive in part from a definition of the period from the mid-eighteenth century in Europe as 'industrial society', but also from the fact that the material remains of industrial manufacturing sites have been a principal focus of archaeological interest in this period since the 1950s and 1960s. Meanwhile, debates over the relationships between 'medieval' and 'post-medieval' archaeology have also proceeded, especially in relation to models of an 'age of transition' (Gaimster and Stamper 1997). While such 'transition' is as much a product of contemporary institutional divisions as of any significant historical shifts (Courtney 1997), the archaeology of this neglected period is now receiving more attention – for instance through archaeological studies of the reformation (Gaimster and Gilchrist 2004).

Relationships between historical archaeology and the material remains of the most recent past have been approached in a number of contrasting ways. Some have aimed to bound off the field through 'cut-off' points, where archaeological attention must stop. For example, in his overview of 'the historical archaeology of Britain', Richard Newman argues that

The end of the Victorian Age makes much sense as a terminus. We are probably too close to the twentieth century's cultural detritus to be able to focus on the nature of its archaeology. Moreover, the development of the telegraph, the telephone, photography and, at the end of the nineteenth century, the internal combustion engine, all had profound effects on material culture and everyday life. (Newman 2001: 8)

Alternatively, in their edited volume *The Familiar Past? Archaeologies of Later Historical Britain*, Sarah Tarlow and Susie West seek to take up 'the challenge that American historical archaeology offers to British post-medieval archaeology' by producing 'theoretically informed and inclusive accounts of the recent past' (West 1999: 2). They argue that archaeologists mistakenly assume that they know and understand the recent past, and define a principal goal of contemporary historical archaeology as 'de-familiarising' the recent past (Tarlow 1999a: 264). However, here the 'familiar' past is limited to British material, and is actively distinguished from alternative traditions of historical archaeology, especially those developed in North America.

A third approach, and the one adopted in assembling and editing this volume, defines historical archaeology as a contemporary and creative practice, rather than trying to imagine recent pasts that are distanced, made unfamiliar, before being interpreted. By extending the limits of archaeology into the twentieth century (e.g. Buchli 1999; Schofield and Johnson this volume) and the contemporary world (e.g. Buchli and Lucas 2001a), historical archaeologists have been at the vanguard of archaeological contributions to the awareness of the contemporary nature of our work on material remains. In the reflexive study of the 'contemporary past' (Buchli 2002b; Buchli and Lucas 2001c; Lucas 2001; Olivier 2001), the contemporary dimensions of archaeological practice are emphasised, and any firm, linear narratives dividing 'history' from 'prehistory' are broken down (cf. Hodder 1999: 80–104). A scepticism towards models of the uniqueness of 'modernity' or of rupture from an archaic past emerges. By studying material culture to discern more complex situations – like others working to 'gather up dark, discarded scraps and peer into them' (Bennett 2001: 7) – historical archaeologists have developed approaches that problematise suggestions of a 'great divide' between premodern and modern, modern and contemporary, scholar and object (cf. Latour 1993: 10–12). Archaeologists no longer, as Bill Rathje has put it, have to wait until 'after the dust settles' (Rathje 2001: 67).

By underlining how they work in the present on what survives from the past, historical archaeologists are increasingly able to move beyond traditional arguments over the distinctive contribution of historical archaeology. In the United Kingdom, for instance, a focus upon objects and their production dominated 'post-medieval archaeology' into the 1990s, mainly because the individuals involved were often museum professionals or employed in urban rescue archaeologies. This led to sustained attempts to contribute material illustrations of normative economic histories. Thus, in his

introduction to the major synthetic work in British post-medieval archaeology, David Crossley observed how

Without doubt, the economic history of the three centuries from 1450 is dominated
by demographic recovery after the late-medieval epidemics, to which changes in
agriculture, industry and trade as well as in individual wealth and status are related.
The archaeological record provides ample material evidence for these developments. (Crossley 1990: 3)

   While Crossley aimed to illustrate and supplement broad economic histories, in the United States historical archaeology's relationship with cultural
anthropology led to an emphasis on cultural evolution, adaptation, cultural differentiation, shifting world views, and capitalism (e.g. Deetz 1977;
Leone 1999; South 1977a). Attracted to the generalising traditions of mod-
ernist anthropology, which aimed to address what were seen as the 'big questions' about culture and culture change, historical archaeologists emphasised
studies of global contexts. Trying to say something of broader use, such
contributions to grand narratives in economic or social history, especially
through 'archaeologies of capitalism', have primarily focused upon normative accounts of the recent past (e.g. Leone 1999). Through their interest in
themes such as meaning, ideology and structure, in critical theory and structural Marxism, and in theorists such as Foucault, Bourdieu and Giddens,
scholars associated with the 'Archaeology in Annapolis' project drew inspiration from the 'postprocessualism' of Ian Hodder, Daniel Miller, Michael
Shanks and Christopher Tilley (Shackel 2000b: 769). Meanwhile, a recipro-
cal process occurred, through which work of Annapolis archaeologists came
to the attention of a new British audience (see e.g. M. Johnson 1996; Tarlow
1999b). The influence of the Annapolis school, especially through the work
in the 1990s of Mark Leone and Charles Orser, has for some become 'so
pervasive that many archaeologists and non-archaeologists alike have come
to consider historical archaeology synonymous with the archaeology of capitalism' (Wilkie and Bartoy 2000: 748). The repercussions of this work will
be felt by the reader in this volume's repeated punctuation by discussions
of Annapolis.
   However, alternatives to such normative accounts have developed across
the field, and Marxist archaeologists (McGuire this volume) and some of
those associated with Archaeology in Annapolis (Leone 2005; Matthews
2002; Palus 2005) have developed more nuanced studies of capitalism.
Such shifts have been driven especially by the emergence of 'interpretive' historical archaeologies out of interpretive and critical anthropologies
(Beaudry 1995, 1996; cf. Geertz 1973; Hymes 1972; Marcus and Fischer 1986;

Rabinow and Sullivan 1987), and the rejection of the 'totalising' approaches within processualism, structuralism and structural Marxism – rather than simply illustrating or supplementing other disciplines, as 'handmaiden to history' or sociocultural anthropology (Noël Hume 1964).

Interpretive historical archaeologists have focused upon the close relationships between people and things in the past, revealing 'the intimate and unheralded details of day-to-day life' (Beaudry 1996: 496) in a similar fashion to anthropological studies of consumption and material culture (Douglas and Isherwood 1979; J. Hoskins 1998; D. Miller 1987; see Cochran and Beaudry this volume). Such approaches are particularly visible in studies of households (King this volume; O'Keeffe and Yamin this volume), of gender, sexuality, ethnicity and of children (Gilchrist 2005; Wilkie 2003), in studies of the contingency of archaeological knowledge upon situated engagements with what material remains happen to survive (Hicks and Horning this volume; Holtorf and Williams this volume), or in studies that explore storytelling as an interpretive practice (Joyce this volume).

***

The power of such studies does not, however, simply derive from the imaginative and theoretically sophisticated work of interpretive scholars: it emerges from a bundle of distinctive archaeological attitudes, methods and practices in relation to materiality. As Barker and Majewski (this volume) point out, descriptive and typological work in ceramic studies continue to construct strong empirical foundations for broader interdisciplinary studies. Indeed, we suggest that it is this combination of interpretation and method, developed especially in this hybrid field that goes unmentioned in so many archaeological textbooks, that distinguishes the place of historical archaeology.

In many fields of the arts, humanities and social sciences, a refocusing upon the material dimensions of social life is taking place. Material things are increasingly discussed in cultural geography (P. Jackson 2000), visual studies (Edwards 2002: 69), social theory (Pels et al. 2002; cf. Latour 2000a), economics (Fine 2004: 337), or literary theory (B. Brown 2001), bringing, in the words of one historian, a 'material turn' (Joyce 2001, quoted by Spicksley 2003: 87). Contemporary artists like Cornelia Parker explore the transformations of material objects (J. Pollard 2004). Historical anthropologists revisit notions of fetishism and reification (Pels 1998), cultural geographers increasingly emphasise the importance of heterogenous materialities (Whatmore 2002), and increasing attention is paid to early work in science and technology studies which 'underline[d] the importance of material elements' (Latour and Woolgar 1979: 238), 'material constraints' (Star 1983: 206), or 'the wide range of things' (Zenzen and Restivo 1982: 457; see also Schlecker and Hirsch 2001: 82, note 11).

Often, these developments have involved the 'appropriation' of ethnographic practice by scholars working outside social anthropology (Strathern 2004: 554), or its extension in historical archaeology (Beaudry 1995). For many, the attraction of material and ethnographic approaches lies in their potential of simultaneously putting into practice a reflexive awareness of the situatedness of sociological knowledge (Clifford and Marcus 1986; Haraway 1991; Strathern 1991) while also moving beyond the post-structural concerns with 'reading meaning'. Where an almost exclusive focus upon the immaterial and the ideational accompanied many incarnations of the 'cultural turn' of the 1980s, in historical archaeology critiques of an emphasis upon textual meaning have emerged (Buchli 1995; Graves-Brown 2000; Olsen 2003; cf. Boivin 2004). In what Victor Buchli and Gavin Lucas have termed 'critical empiricism' (Buchli 1999: 11; Buchli 2002b: 133; Buchli and Lucas 2001d; Lucas 2001), historical archaeologists have aimed to bring together scientific method and interpretive practice. Unlike some fields of archaeology, in historical archaeology scientific, processual or 'new' archaeology has persisted alongside more interpretive approaches, which have developed since Geertz (1973), and especially since Hodder (1986). Rather than 'two cultures' – a materials-based science and an interpretive, theoretical field concerned with meaning – historical archaeology has, unusually perhaps, remained a hybrid field (cf. A. Jones 2002, 2004: 329). As such, and especially through its 'unfolding' into broader archaeologies of the contemporary past (Hicks 2003), historical archaeology is in a unique position to combine 'material' and 'immaterial' concerns: folding together broader narratives (geographical or temporal) with rich and nuanced local stories, and exploring the permeabilities between human and material worlds.

***

We wish to conclude with a note on 'companionship'. This volume has emerged from many conversations, excavations, conferences and friendships. We wanted to introduce the reader to the energy and richness of historical archaeology around the world, through a variety of themes that have been important in the emergence of the field. The overwhelming potentialities of archaeologies of the recent past have led us to underline, indeed to celebrate, the partiality of the snapshot presented here: presenting a series of coherent themes as essentially provisional and contestable. This is a volume of passionate and personal essays rather than contributions to 'adequate archaeological theory', or periodisation. Such an approach is a necessary response to the material complexities of the recent past, and the

Figure 1.1 Idris Khan's *Every . . . Bernd and Hilla Becher Gable Sided House* (2004)
(courtesy of Idris Khan and the Victoria Miro Gallery www.victoriamiro.com).

contemporary and political nature of archaeological practice. In editing *The Cambridge Companion to Historical Archaeology*, then, we wanted to place 'companionship' at the heart of the volume. The term nicely combines *collegiality* with *journeying*. Collaboration lies at the heart of all archaeology; the collegiality developed through excavations, field trips and post-excavation research in groups spills over into conferences and lecture theatres, teaching and administrative practices and communication and partnerships with non-archaeological groups of all kinds (cf. Finn and Henig 2001). At the same time, archaeology is always itinerant; it demands in the words of W. G. Hoskins, as Hicks and Horning (this volume) remind us, that we 'look over hedges'. Through fieldwork, the archaeologist engages with materials and place in a distinctive manner – travelling to sites, excavating or surveying. As Thomas Yarrow has observed, in these processes the features and finds that are recorded or discovered 'modify the thoughts and actions' of the archaeologist (Yarrow 2003: 69; cf. Chadwick 2003; Edgeworth 2003). Our combination of collaboration with itinerancy brings creative iterations, as we repeatedly apply archaeological methods in new contexts. We want to illustrate our point with reference to the photographic practice of visual artist Idris Khan.

In his series *'Every . . .'*, Khan takes photographs of every image from a particular body of work, and combines them in a single photograph. He photographs every page of his father's Koran, every stave from his mother's copy of Frederick Chopin's nocturnes for the piano and every William Turner postcard from Tate Britain. Most vividly, he photographs every gable-sided house, spherical-type gasholder and prison-type gasholder previously photographed by Bernd and Hilla Becher in their documentation of European and American industrial buildings (Figure 1.1; Becher and Becher 2004). These layered images aim to encourage the viewer to spend 'a long time unravelling . . . ambiguity and . . . authorship' (Khan 2004). A part of their quality lies in the temporality of the process of photographing each image, developing, combining, and presenting. Most striking, though, is their vivid depiction of how adding up 'every' image results in quite the opposite of a neat, uniform depiction: the photographs instead are richly textured.

Similarly, historical archaeology's repeated engagements, investing long periods of time in applying its methods in the contexts of households, industrial landscapes or its many other themes and places, result in complex and evocative stories, rather than neat, closed accounts of prime movers. We hope that this volume will inspire yet more open-minded, creative and collaborative explorations of the material remains of the recent past and to the place of historical archaeology.

PART I

Archaeology and history

CHAPTER 2

Documentary archaeology

Laurie A. Wilkie

Documentary archaeology is an approach to history that brings together diverse source materials related to cultures and societies that peopled the recent past. Documentary archaeological interpretations offer perspectives and understandings of the past not possible through single lines of evidentiary analysis. The term 'documentary archaeology' was introduced to the literature by Mary Beaudry (1988a: 1), who in the introduction to her edited volume *Documentary Archaeology in the New World* argued that 'historical archaeologists must develop an approach towards documentary analysis that is uniquely their own' (Beaudry 1988a: 1).

Historical archaeologists' willingness to blend oral historical, textual and material sources about the past into their interpretive narratives creates unique challenges for practitioners. The temporal and scalar resolution that each body of evidence provides into past lives may vary radically. Using two sites associated with African-American families, I will provide examples of scalar and temporal resolution as they are related to the integration of diverse evidentiary lines in archaeological interpretation. Finally, using evidence drawn from a late nineteenth to early twentieth-century fraternity house, this chapter will provide a case study demonstrating how documentary records and archaeological findings can be quilted together to understand individual past lives as they connect to issues of race, class and gender. Documentary archaeology has developed a particularly strong tradition in the United States, and the discussion will focus most heavily on Americanist practice.

THE ARCHIVE

While documentary archaeology shares an essential database, the documentary record, with historians, the two are distinct in their focus, practice, and gaze. Historians, although they may use oral historical or material evidence, usually see the documentary record as the primary window available for gazing into the past. Documentary archaeologists see their 'archive' as including written records, oral traditions, and material culture – from both archaeological and curated sources. These additional windows may provide overlapping, conflicting, or entirely different insights into the past. The challenge for archaeologists is to use these independent but complementary lines of evidence to construct meaningful, fuller, understandings of the past.

Archaeologists have experimented with alternative ways of 'excavating' the resources of the documentary record with increasingly sophisticated results (e.g. Beaudry, Cook and Mrozowski 1991; Buchli and Lucas 2001a; Tarlow and West 1999). How the relationship between documents and materials might be conceptualised has been a source of debate and innovation within the field. For archaeologists, texts are not only sources of information, but are also artefacts that have been produced in particular cultural–historical contexts for specific reasons.

Early collections of papers in documentary archaeology focused upon ways that archaeologists could use particular kinds of texts in specific ways (e.g. Beaudry 1988b; Little 1992a). Barbara Little's (1992b) volume built upon the notion of the archive available to historical archaeologists by including discussions of ethnohistory (Cleland 1992) and oral history (Purser 1992). Little's choice of 'text-aided' to describe archaeology demonstrates a slightly different orientation from the interpretive practice of historical archaeology. Little's terminology suggests that texts serve archaeology rather than the reverse as argued by an earlier generation of historical archaeologists such as Ivor Noël Hume (1969). More recently, historical archaeologists have become increasingly concerned by approaches that juxtapose texts and artefacts as separate bodies of evidence. For example, Martin Hall (2000: 16) observes how, 'Both artefacts and literary texts make use of images; those who read their meaning did not respect the disciplinary boundaries of the practitioners who would one day seek to understand their minds.' Hall (2000: 16) dismisses the notion that the archival and archaeological records are distinct and instead employs the concept of 'transcripts' in his interpretive work, recognising that each are the products of the same cultural context. Drawing strongly on Michel Foucault, Hall suggests that the experiences of subaltern peoples can be found through an understanding of the colonial transcripts of the dominant classes, and by examining the ways that rulers react in material and text to the day-to-day acts of resistance by subjugated peoples.

John Moreland (2001: 110–111) has critiqued historical archaeologies as falling into two camps: those who are too quick to embrace the authority of documents, and those too quick to dismiss their reliability. In both cases, he argues, archaeologists miss the role of writing as a tool of oppression and power. Moreland proposes that archaeologists need to see 'the Object, the Voice and the Word' (2001: 119) as tools that past societies used to create systems of power. Moreland doubts that historical archaeologists can, as they currently practise, offer any real insights into the lives of the subaltern as long as they fail to recognise writing and access to it as a distinct and unique circumstance in the construction of inequality. I shall return to these issues shortly.

Documentary archaeology also shares a complementary agenda and knowledge base with historical anthropology. For Americanist archaeologies in particular, it is an anthropological gaze that shapes our work. Through our interpretations, documentary archaeologists produce historical ethnographies. As defined by cultural anthropologists Jean and John Comaroff (1992: 35), 'a historical ethnography must always go beyond literary traces, beyond explicit narrative, exegesis, even argument. For the poetics of history lie also in mute meanings transacted through goods and practices, through icons and images dispersed in the landscape of the everyday.' The Comaroffs see the sources and evidence for historical anthropology as any of the fragments of the past, be they literary or otherwise, that are available for our consideration. Their integrated use of text, word, and thing, complements Hall's colonial transcripts.

Historical anthropologists increasingly share documentary archaeologists' attention to the active roles and life histories of objects in historical process. For example, in his study of exchange and gifting between Europeans and Pacific Islanders during the nineteenth and twentieth centuries, anthropologist Nicholas Thomas (1991) attempts to understand the transformations in objects' meanings and values in ways that echo documentary archaeological studies of cultural interaction and exchange, and the discipline's interest in commodities and the spread of global capitalism (e.g. M. Johnson 1996; Lydon 2003). By focusing on the role of objects in social life, such work complements the social–historical studies of personal-material culture, especially through the analysis of probate inventories, which have shaped documentary archaeologies (e.g. Shammas 1990; Weatherill 1988).

While documentary archaeology has been influenced by the practice of history, the field is distinctive in its approach to historiography. Essential to historiography is the role of the 'historical imagination', which the writer draws upon to make meaningful interpretive connections between source materials, or evidence (Collingwood 1994 [1946]). In documentary archaeology, a central aim is for our historical imagination to be guided by both our anthropological perspective and our attention to materiality. These distinctive, archaeological perspectives profoundly affect the kinds of documentary sources that archaeologists rely upon.

USING DOCUMENTS ARCHAEOLOGICALLY

As documentary archaeology becomes a global endeavour, it becomes increasingly difficult to categorise meaningfully the range of documents used in our practice, with certain types of documents being important for some scholars, and of little use to others. Barbara Little (1992a: 3) provided perhaps the most comprehensive account of the range of documents used in American archaeology, and should be consulted by those hoping for a more exhaustive treatment. For the purposes of this discussion, I shall provide a bare-bones overview and refer to some particularly illustrative case studies. Archaeologists use documents primarily in three ways: to identify the people who once lived at a particular site; to understand the social–cultural context in which the site was occupied, and to understand the social meanings and lives of the objects they recover.

Finding people

Historical archaeologists often carry out a great deal of archival research in order to identify the individuals or collectivities that inhabited a site in the past. Identifying the people who inhabited or used the places that we excavate in this way allows archaeologists to create finer-grained and more nuanced archaeological interpretations. While often the people who resided at the sites that we study are not represented in the manuscript sources curated at archival repositories, there are some occasions when one is fortunate to work on a site where personal papers, either curated in an archive or held by individual families, are available. The letters, diaries, photographs, and even mundane financial accountings that can be found in personal paper collections provide an intimate textual perspective on the persons whose excavated material culture archaeologists study. Anne Yentsch's (1994) archaeological study of the Calvert family of Annapolis, Maryland, provides a powerful example of how family papers, in conjunction with archaeological remains, can lead to the construction of richly detailed understandings of lived lives. Typically, these kinds of primary sources are not available, and instead we track actors through a range of administrative records, maps, city directories, court records, census roles, church registers, vital statistics and oral histories.

Mundane sources such as plat maps (showing original land partitions), conveyance records (title transfers, mortgage or rental agreements), assessor's records (property taxes), or crown grants are often the most helpful sources for archaeologists wishing to identify who owned particular properties at particular points in time. At the level of the household, maps can be used to situate individuals or to understand the mosaic of families that inhabited an area. Even in colonial settings, different forms of census records are available for many areas and can be used to tie particular people to particular places, be it as precise as the level of the household, or to a particular estate or community. Census records can provide important glimpses into the demographic make up of a study area. Although most North American cities did not have directories of occupants published much prior to the 1850s, directories allow researchers to identify neighbours, resources and services available in an area and were often published every year or two.

A striking example of the potential of cartographic studies for archaeologists is Donna Seifert's (1994) study of prostitution in nineteenth-century Washington, DC, which used Sanborn fire insurance maps and census records to look at changing neighbourhood compositions and the distribution of brothels through time. The Sanborn fire insurance maps are widely consulted in the United States by documentary archaeologists because they show the outlines of structures (with descriptive notations) and property boundaries. Seifert was able to trace how the neighbourhood in question transitioned from a mixed working-class neighbourhood to a red-light district.

A fruitful body of court records for North American archaeologists has been probate inventories, which are an accounting of an estate's belongings and value following the owner's death. The probate or his agent would physically enter the domicile of the house and make, in the best examples, a room-by-room accounting of the person's belongings. These records provide the same kind of evidence we recover from the ground – provenance and associations. We see in what rooms items were found, and with what other objects they belonged. The comparative study of probates provides us with a sense of how spaces inside houses were organised, of the objects which are not represented in the archaeological record and of differential distributions of wealth within a community; while also providing insights into the emic terms used for the objects we find in the archaeological record (e.g. Beaudry et al. 1988; Deetz 1977; Leone 1988a).

Understanding times and places

As demonstrated in the discussion of probate inventories, documentary sources provide important insights into the historical contexts in which our sites were situated. While the secondary sources produced by historians provide archaeologists with important insights, there is a range of rich documentary resources that archaeologists have used to understand the social, political and economic contexts in which sites were situated. Travel accounts, newspapers, court transcripts, photographs, maps and personal paper collections are only a few of the documents used productively to appreciate context.

Archaeologists identify contexts at a number of levels – ranging in scale from household to nation. In her study of convict households in late eighteenth- to early nineteenth-century Sydney, Australia, Grace Karskens (2003) used court records and coroners' inquests to explore how people thought about the physical organisation of household spaces and how those thoughts situated them in larger shifts in social consciousness that accompanied colonisation, such as the growing influence of the notion of individualism. While Karskens' work demonstrates how documentary analysis can be used to situate sites into global contexts, Barry Higman's (1998) work at Montpelier, Jamaica, is an excellent example of documents being used to understand local communities. Higman used British Colonial Office records, Jamaican parliamentary records and slave registries, published travel accounts and proscriptive literature and estate records to present a detailed picture of the competing forces that shaped the lives of enslaved Jamaicans. While his focus is Montpelier's community, through his thick description Higman succeeds in illuminating the experiences of people throughout the African diaspora.

Situating things

While a great deal of documentary research by archaeologists is focused on understanding the lives of the people we study, an equal amount of time is spent studying documents for understandings of material histories and the contexts where materials were used. Archaeologists, working with manufacturers', customs and other trade records, have created detailed histories of different artefactual materials, including glasswares, ceramics, cans, coins, firearms and a range of other materials (e.g. Gates and Ormerod 1982; O. Jones 1986; Noël Hume 1969). Susan Henry (1987) demonstrated in her study of late nineteenth-century ceramics from house sites in Tucson,

Arizona, that consumer catalogues, like those of Montgomery Ward and Sears, Roebuck and Company, provide the opportunity to explore the socioeconomic contexts of materials we recover. Using the catalogues' price lists and product pictures and descriptions, Henry developed a typology of ceramic types based on relative cost for consumers. The typology presents a way of comparing how households differentially invested in different commodities. In the United States, demand by collectors has led to a number of consumer catalogues being reprinted and widely available.

ORAL HISTORY

Oral traditions are another powerful source for documentary archaeology. Oral traditions are histories that are transmitted from generation to generation through word-of-mouth. Many oral traditions are part of formalised storytelling practices. Historians and archaeologists alike have demonstrated that oral traditions should be seen as a legitimate source of historical insight (e.g. Sahlins 1985; Schmidt 1978; Stahl 2001; Vansina 1985). Oral traditions include origin stories, folktales, or accounts of individuals' lives. In a particularly powerful example of the use of oral history, J. Douglas McDonald et al. (1991) used Cheyenne oral traditions in conjunction with archaeological remains to critically re-evaluate US government accounts of a nineteenth-century massacre that occurred in Nebraska in 1879.

Oral history has been most used in African-American archaeology. Archaeologists such as Theresa Singleton (1991) and Ywone Edwards-Ingram (2001) have recognised the testimony of formerly enslaved people as providing an alternate view of enslavement. The slave narrative collection of the Work Projects Administration (WPA) federal writers project has been a particularly influential source. As part of Roosevelt's New Deal, the Federal Writers Project during the late 1930s and early 1940s collected first-hand accounts of enslavement from the people who endured it. In an early innovative work, historical archaeologists Robert Ascher and Charles Fairbanks (1971) used excerpts from the ex-slave narratives alongside artefact descriptions from a Georgia slave cabin to create an interpretive narrative that aimed to highlight the voices of African-Americans. While oral history has been extensively used in African-American archaeology, it has been fruitfully used in other contexts. Margaret Purser (1991) used newspaper social columns and oral-history interviews to understand how women's social networks served to create economic dependencies among several Californian mining communities, and Julia Costello (2000) used oral histories from New Orleans' red-light district to make a powerful presentation of materials from a Los Angeles brothel. Since the 1960s, large numbers of oral-history archives have been created, particularly in the United States. Documentary archaeologists may take advantage of materials housed in these repositories, or may interview informants themselves (e.g. Perks and Thomson 1998).

SEEING THROUGH ARCHIVAL LENSES

Having provided a brief overview of the materials used by documentary archaeologists, I want to consider how these sources illuminate one another. Like Jean and John Comaroff (1992) and Martin Hall (2000), I see oral history, materials and texts as all traces of the past that can and should be considered together in the interpretive process. The archaeological, oral-historical, and documentary records are distinct sources of evidence that have been shaped by varied circumstances of creation and preservation. On a practical level, in integrating these materials we need to consider these differences when using sources.

Part of the craft of documentary archaeology lies in recognising different scales of temporal and social resolution offered in our data. Once we have interrogated each evidentiary line for insights it offers, then we can proceed with making connections among our sources. To illustrate this, I want to discuss two sites associated with African-American women and their families who lived during the second half of the nineteenth century and into the first part of the twentieth. They are Silvia Freeman (Wilkie 2000) of Oakley Plantation (West Feliciana Parish, Louisiana), and Lucrecia Perryman (Wilkie 2003), of Mobile, Alabama (Figure 2.1).

SILVIA FREEMAN AND LUCRECIA PERRYMAN

Siliva Freeman was born into enslavement in Virginia in 1855. Like other enslaved Virginians of the time, she may have been sold to Louisiana as a result of the failing tobacco market. It is unclear whether she had kin in Louisiana other than her husband, Lewis Freeman, and her children. Silvia Freeman appeared only once in the West Feliciana courthouse records. Lewis and Silvia were one of the few African-American couples in the parish to pay the marriage license fee, doing so on 5 June 1875. There is no death certificate for Lewis or Silvia Freeman, no record of where their burials took place, and no probate or succession either. Most records concerning Silvia's life date not to the time of her marriage, but to her widowhood.

The documents most helpful for understanding Freeman's life are US census records for 1870–1900 and records kept by her employer, Isabelle

Figure 2.1 Locations of sites in the USA discussed in Chapter 2.

Matthews. From the census we learn that Silvia was living on Oakley with her husband in 1870 and 1880. In 1900, the last census in which she appears, Freeman is described as a widowed cook. Unfortunately, the entire 1890 manuscript census was nearly completely consumed in the 1906 San Francisco earthquake and fire, so there is a twenty-year gap in census records. It is the period from 1886 to 1903 when Freeman appears in the plantation journal of her employer, Isabelle Matthews. The Matthews journal includes information such as Freeman's salary, her monthly purchases from the plantation commissary, her cash advances, maintenance done to her home, and items loaned to Freeman from the Matthews' kitchen.

Lucrecia Perryman, who lived in a city and was married to a landowner, is more visible in the documentary record than Freeman. Like Freeman, what we understand of Perryman's antebellum life comes from census records. She was born in North Carolina, and had at least five children during her period of enslavement. In 1870, she is listed as married to Marshall Perryman and living in Mobile with five children. The couple had been together since at least 1866. City records show that Marshall had purchased a small parcel of land that year. Marshall continued to purchase property until his death in 1885. Through the Mobile city directories it was possible to identify when Lucrecia became a midwife around 1890, and when she retired, around 1911.

While helpful, any of the documents connected to these women must be viewed critically. Government records can be particularly biased or poorly completed when involving African-American subjects. Even vital statistics records can be extremely problematic – on her death certificate, Lucrecia Perryman is checked off as a man. A critical tool for any historian is scepticism.

Oral history

While working at Oakley Plantation, I interviewed several former tenants. One former tenant, Bob Cummings, was ninety-eight years old in 1991. He spoke to me for three hours, during which time I learned a great deal about his experiences and about different people who lived on the plantation. Mr Cummings identified our excavations as being at the location of the cook's house, and recalled Silvia Freeman and her daughters. Other interviews and documentary evidence agreed with this identification. Oral history at Oakley provided important contextual information about social dynamics within the plantation population, as well as helping to identify the occupants of particular sites within the plantation.

The oral history collected for the Perryman project was the opposite, providing specific insights into the personality of Lucrecia Perryman rather than broader contextual information. Three of Lucrecia Perryman's great-grandchildren had been raised in part by Perryman's eldest daughter, Caroline, who had been born in 1855. They were able to relate two of Caroline's observations about her mother to me. Caroline told them that Lucrecia had been a much harsher parent during slavery than she was after. This characterisation aligns with recollections from the slave narratives that emphasise that to protect them, African-American mothers had to be stern with their children, particularly in training them to understand how to navigate the terrains of racism. Emancipation brought with it greater freedom for African-American women to mother their children on their own terms. Caroline also noted that her mother hated to have her hair cut after freedom – that she had resented having others control how she wore her hair and chose to wear long braids. The surviving photographs of Perryman conform to this. Although the two photographs from her later years show her wearing a head wrap, it is clear, particularly from the last photograph, that the wrap was tied in a way that could accommodate long hair. These two anecdotes provide a brief but humanising insight into the unique personhood of Lucrecia Perryman.

Archaeology

Excavations at Oakley Plantation were conducted in 1991 and 1992 as part of my doctoral research. Archaeologically, I was able to identify the structure in which the Freemans lived. They were the second identifiable occupation of the house. Changes in soil colour and texture allowed us to distinguish three different occupations – that of an antebellum African-American family, that of Silvia Freeman, and that of her daughters, Eliza and Delphine. In each soil level were items that had been discarded outside of the house and swept along fence lines or under the structure, which was raised on brick piers. Under the house, we were able to find artefacts that had slipped through the gaps between sagging floorboards. This combination of primary and secondary deposits associated with architectural remains tells us a great deal about the activities the families were involved in, and the ways they used the space in and around their home.

The archaeological site associated with Lucrecia Perryman was discovered during grading for a new baseball field in Crawford Park, Mobile. The architectural remains of the Perryman house had been destroyed during the creation of Crawford Park in the 1920s. What was discovered archaeologically were two pits filled with trash. The pits were filled quickly at two different times. The first dated to about 1885, around the time Marshall Perryman died, and may have been related to a house cleaning following his death. The second feature was an old well that was filled around 1911. Not only did this correspond to the time when Lucrecia retired from midwifery, it is also when indoor plumbing became established in the city. Wells were dangerous to have standing open, and were popular trash receptacles. There was no chronological difference between the materials at the top of the well and the bottom. The well was filled quickly.

Resolution and integration

For both the Freeman and Perryman families there are documents, oral accounts and material culture available to us. The kinds of interpretive insights they provide are very different. Silvia Freeman is visible in the texts of her employers during the 1880s and 1890s, listed in the census records from 1870–1900, vaguely remembered in an oral-history interview, and has a rich archaeological record associated with her home life between 1880 and about 1910. The divergent databases converge to provide multiple lines of evidence about the last half of her life. The resolution for this period of her life is sharp. Because the archaeological materials were recovered from continuously deposited contexts, we do not see changes in her life during this period through the lens of material culture. Instead, we see continuities in her family's lives. The documentary record is largely quiet about the last years of her life, and even her death. The evidence allows us to see

L. A. Wilkie

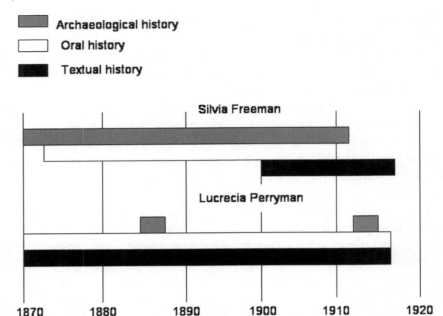

Figure 2.2 Illustrative depiction of the temporal insights into the lives of Lucrecia Perryman and Silvia Freeman provided through the lenses of archaeology, oral history and textual sources.

Silvia Freeman in middle age, with an emphasis on the continuities of her existence rather than the changes. Her youth and her married life are lost to us. What I have learned about her life provides an important counterpoint to the narrative histories of tenancy provided by white planters.

Lucrecia Perryman also has a rich textual and archaeological narrative associated with her, as well as some oral historical evidence (Figure 2.2). As a function of her family's landholdings and duration of tenancy, the textual evidence is wider sweeping for Perryman than Freeman. The textual evidence related to Lucrecia's life spans from 1870 until her death in 1917, illuminating her life from her 30s through her 80s. The textual history of Perryman allows us to see the ups and downs, the victories and tragedies that were part of her experience. This is not to say that the narrative is exhaustive, but it is richer than that available for many African-American women. The archaeological record associated with Perryman provides two important material windows into her life: at the close of what was, based on limited documentary evidence, a loving marriage, and at the close of a long midwifery career. While the archaeology does not provide a continuum, as is the case for the life of Silvia Freeman, the two temporally succinct deposits allow us to see changes, not just continuities. The oral history associated with Perryman, though not abundant, is very evocative. Through documents, materials and the memories of her family, we get a very strong sense of this woman's individuality.

Given the nature of the archive, how do we merge these very different lines of evidence that show different scales of resolution? Archaeologists often must integrate seemingly incompatible evidence, whether bringing together lithic and ceramic evidence, or textual evidence with fragments of bottle glass. In this sense, documentary archaeology is no different from any other archaeological endeavour, assembling diverse material sources of evidence. The perspectives of Alison Wylie (1989), a philosopher of science, upon archaeological theory and practice are useful here. Wylie suggests that archaeology cannot be fully objective, yet, because it is grounded in a web of empirical data, it cannot be an entirely subjective endeavour either. Instead, she argues, archaeological interpretations gain strength by moving back and forth between multiple lines of evidence, a process she refers to as 'tacking'. The diversity of sources at play in documentary archaeology is its unique strength. The documentary, oral historical or archaeological data for a particular area may not be comprehensive on its own, and through the integration of these resources we can construct more holistic histories. Moreover, the integration of these databases provides an opportunity to play to the differences in resolution inherent in the materials. 'Tacking back and forth' between sources involves a movement between social scales – the individual, the family, the community – as well as a movement back and forth between scales of time. A final advantage of this approach is that it allows for the possibility of multiple interpretations of the historical past. The measure of which interpretation is best is which interpretation involves the greatest integration of evidentiary lines. Now, let me provide a brief example of a documentary archaeology with an example from a University of California fraternity.

A DOCUMENTARY ARCHAEOLOGY OF MASCULINITY

The last third of the nineteenth century was a time when gender roles were being redefined in American society. Men pursued a primal masculinity shaped by men like Buffalo Bill Cody, Teddy Roosevelt, and athletes such as Jim Jeffries, the boxer, which greatly contrasted with the civilised manhood of the Victorians. This new masculinity was constructed as part of a discursive, and sometimes antagonistic, relationship with the rapidly developing new womanhood. As women demanded rights equal to those of men, declared themselves the moral centre of their households, and sought out the benefits of exercise and education, the male response was to create a robust manhood whose appetites and pursuits were beyond women's reach (Bederman 1995).

The shift in masculine identity is seen in a number of social arenas during the last quarter of the nineteenth century. Fraternal orders became extremely popular at this time. Men demonstrated their dislike for the new woman by avoiding marriage, leading to the largest nationwide population of bachelors in the country's history during the 1890s. Bachelors were so prevalent as to be seen by some as a threat to American social fabric (Chudacoff 1999). Athletics – encouraged by the revival of the Olympics in 1896 and the development of collegiate and professional teams – became important pastimes for American men. Boxing and bodybuilding also drew fanatical followers (H. Green 1986).

It was during this transformation in masculinity that the Iota Chapter of Zeta Psi Fraternity was founded in 1870, building their first house on the University of California, Berkeley, campus in 1876 (Figure 2.1; Blue and Gold 1880). The men of Zeta Psi occupied this first house until 1910, at which time they found their house to be falling short of the standards of newer, competing fraternities. The first house was moved back on the lot and became a rental property. A greater, finer structure was built on the same location as the first house in 1911 (Figure 2.3; *Oakland Tribune*, 1910). The fraternity occupied the house until 1959, at which time the university seized the property in order to complete the vision of its 1957 campus masterplan, and relocated the fraternity members to a parcel of land on the edge of campus (City of Berkeley Liaison Committee 1957), where the fraternity still resides.

The national tensions that characterised gender relations between men and women at this time were pronounced at the University of California. The campus had a remarkably large and politically engaged population of women from the earliest days of the school. In 1900, Phoebe Apperson Hearst donated money and a structure for a women's gym on campus (*Daily Californian* 1900) following a protest by campus women objecting to the collection of athletic fees when no facilities were available to them. Women earned degrees in fields such as astronomy, and women faculty from Stanford and other institutions were brought to lecture on campus (*Daily Californian* 1902). A cartoon depicting weightlifting women from the 1880 Blue and Gold Yearbook (which incidentally was edited by Zeta Psi) demonstrates some unease by the fraternity men with images of the new woman. The quest for suffrage, pursuit of education and careers, and

Figure 2.3 Photograph of the 1911 Zeta Psi fraternity house, as it appears today.

athleticism, were all features of the new womanhood that threatened to obscure the new masculinity.

I directed excavations at the fraternity in 1995 and 2001 (Wilkie 2001). In 1995, a prohibition-period bottle pit was found during the construction of an annex to the adjacent law school. Materials were collected, the edge of the pit defined, and one small excavation unit was placed in a remnant of the pit. More extensive excavations were undertaken in 2001 as part of the seismic retrofit of the 1911 structure. During this time, excavations focused on an area that had once been an open courtyard, but had been sealed under asphalt and enclosed by the university. Distinct strata associated with the first house, the construction of the second house and the occupation of the second house were found and excavated.

The Zeta Psi site provides an interesting opportunity to study a community of young men at a time when what it was to be a man was in flux. The members of Zeta Psi were also members of two broader communities, that of their fraternity and its associated chapters, and that of the university campus. Through documentary archaeology it is possible to come to an understanding of how these different identities were constructed and maintained in fraternity life. Maintaining a sense of brotherhood, or fictive kinship, was an essential part of fraternity life. The Victorian middle-class household became the model that fraternity life emulated.

Fraternities were a form of household, and as such, had a range of domestic tasks that needed to be undertaken. For an all-male community of the late nineteenth century to early twentieth century, this offered a particular difficulty. The domestic sphere and all its associations had been marked by the Victorians and their immediate descendants as the realm of the feminine (Wall 1994). For elite women, caring for the domestic sphere required the management of servants. Less-well-to-do women found themselves undertaking these tasks themselves, while the least-well-to-do found themselves working at these tasks for others. The brothers of Zeta Psi were confronted with both realities – that of managing labour, and that of doing it themselves. Alumni indicate that these tasks were left to the lower classmen, who had housekeeping duties and served as hosts for the 'mothers club' that advised the men on decorating and housekeeping. The senior classmen served as the patriarchs of the household. They sat at the head of the dining-room table, where they were served first, and, with alumnae, made the financial and ritual decisions for the household (Hal Forkner 1995, pers. com.).

The 1876–1910 fraternity occupation demonstrates that fraternity meal-time was strongly shaped by elite dining practices of the time. Tablewares were simple white ironstones, represented by a wide range of vessels. Meals were served family-style with the elaborate table settings familiar to Victorians (Wall 1994). Butter dishes, tureens, a range of plate and bowl sizes, and coffee and teawares were all represented. Through the use of established material expressions of the spiritual importance of family life, the brothers reinforced their bonds to one another. A sense of family was also built through the shared consumption of beer. Prior to prohibition, beer was a beverage seen as healthful, even by temperance advocates as radical as Carrie Nation (Armstrong and Armstrong 1991). It was typically produced and consumed within the home by family. In a circa 1891 Zeta Psi photograph, beer was consumed socially around the dinner table, in this instance, accompanied by wheels of cheese and biscuits (Iota Chapter 1890–1893). Archaeological remains demonstrated that beer drinking remained an important expression of fictive kinship for the second household occupation, where even during Prohibition, brothers continued to consume non-alcoholic 'near-beers' (as identified from bottle embossing) in addition to bootlegged liquor.

During the occupation of the first house, Zeta Psi brothers were among the few fraternities on campus. Contemporary photographs demonstrate

```
1876

VINCENT HOOK
L. A. JORDAN
C. B. OVERACK
J. H. WILKINS
C. J. WRIGHT


1939

SAMUEL L. ABOTT JR.
STEVEN T. BARBER
HOBART S. LEONARD
C. S. LINCOLN
F. E. SHINE
GORDON L. ONSTOTH
```

Figure 2.4 Example of the engraved redwood panels showing Zeta Psi brothers by pledge year. These panels were begun in the first house, moved to the second, and then turned inwards by the University of California.

that the first house was similar to other domestic structures of the time, with only a stained-glass window bearing Greek letters to distinguish it. Construction of the second house was prompted by brothers' desire to reassert their prominence on campus. The second house was designed by a Zeta Psi alumnus. At a groundbreaking ceremony covered by the *Oakland Tribune* (1910), an alumnus declared that the new house should 'rise like a temple to Zeta Psi'. The house, with its Greek revival architecture, mimics a Greek temple. There are structural continuities in the layout of space between the first and second house, based on period descriptions (*Berkeleyan* 1880). In both houses, the room north of the entrance was the parlour, while the dining room was located to the south. In the first house, the tradition of engraving the names of pledges by year in redwood panels was begun (Figure 2.4). The panels were moved to the second house and discovered during the retrofit. The panels include pledge classes from 1870 through 1957, when the university forced the fraternity out. The movement of these planks from the first to second house served as an important link for the different generations of the fraternity.

While sharing some similarities with the old house, the new house was specifically designed for fraternity life. Shaped as a 'C', the building mimics the 'Big C' located on a hillside of the campus. Ceiling woodwork in the parlour is painted with California's colours, blue and gold. The basement of

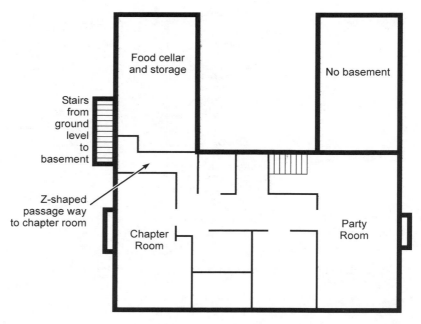

Figure 2.5 Layout of the basement of the 1911 fraternity house. Note both the C-shape of the building and the Z-shaped hallway leading to the chapter room.

the building features a chapter room for ceremonial use that was approached by pledges through a Z-shaped hallway (Figure 2.5). Zs, denoting Zeta Psi, seem to be hidden throughout the building, in crests, in brickwork, in the split-level second floor and in the ways that bodies move through space. The identities of 'Zeta Psi brother' and 'Cal student' were ritually enacted in the embodied experience of moving through the structure.

The archaeological remains from this later house also indicate that the concern for demonstrations of prestige may have influenced changes in dining. In 1918, the brothers ordered a new set of porcelain china from the Onondaga Pottery Company (now Syracuse China). The new set featured a white body with a dark green annular band, and the Zeta Psi crest (Figure 2.6). Green was one of the official fraternity colours, thus its selection was not random. Plainwares were rapidly falling from favour, and ornate French and German porcelain dining sets were the rage (Montgomery Ward 1924). The introduction of decalcomania decorations facilitated the production of personalised dining sets featuring monogrammed initials and logos for élite households, restaurants and hotels, or organisations like the fraternity.

Figure 2.6   Example of Zeta Psi ceramic produced by Onondaga Pottery Company
(now Syracuse China).

Syracuse China's records demonstrate that a broad range of vessels was
ordered by Zeta Psi (Syracuse China 1918; Table 2.1). From the archaeological record, we see that these vessels were also used . . . or at least regularly
broken. From the 1923 bottle pit we recovered dinner plates, bread plates,
berry bowls, serving bowls, teacups, demitasse cups and saucers. The price
list also indicates that the tablewares rivalled the prices of expensive porcelain sets, as suggested by a comparison with Sears and Montgomery Ward
Catalogues from 1909, 1924 and 1927 (Mirkin 1970; Montgomery Ward
1924). The set continued to be supplemented with additional purchases until
1957.

To brothers dining together, the image of the fraternity crest reinforced
a sense of community and brotherhood, providing a visual reinforcement
of their ties together. The imagery in the crest represents the stages of

Table 2.1 *Prices for Zeta Psi specialty tablewares,
1918 (Source: Syracuse China Archive. All prices are
per dozen vessels)*

Teacups and saucers	$5.35
Coffee cups and saucers	$4.80
6$\frac{1}{4}$ inch plates	$2.50
7$\frac{1}{2}$ inch plates	$3.60
8 inch plates	$3.80
5$\frac{3}{8}$ inch plates	$4.20
9 inch soup plate	$2.40
Round oatmeal	$4.50
8 inch baker	$13.20
12$\frac{1}{2}$ inch chop dish	$28.80
15$\frac{1}{4}$ inch dish	$32.40
2 pint 8 oz. jug	$13.20
5$\frac{3}{4}$ inch fruit saucer	$4.40

initiation and fraternal life that the pledges and initiates experienced. For those outside of the fraternity's membership, the crest would have reminded visitors whose hospitality they were enjoying as well as underscoring their position as outsiders.

I want to turn now to the ways that the brothers positioned themselves within the new masculinity. In the archaeological assemblages from both houses there was evidence that at least some of the brothers were involved in hunting fowl and game, and the courtyard area of the second house contained several makeshift hearths (barbeque pits). Yearbooks demonstrate that some brothers were consistently members of the university rifle club (Blue and Gold 1880–1920). For the men of Zeta Psi, hunting would have been part of a gentlemanly pursuit, not driven by subsistence needs. Teddy Roosevelt, and images of his safari-hunting expeditions, glamorised hunting as a manly endeavour (H. Green 1986). Documents and oral histories related to the fraternity demonstrate that the men of Zeta Psi embraced the new interest in team sports, participating in crew (team rowing), baseball and football.

We can see, even in this short summary of work at the fraternity, how documents and materials feed into one another in the interpretation of fraternity life. Using architecture, artefacts, texts and oral histories, we see how the men of Zeta Psi used the notions and materiality of Victorian domesticity to create a sense of family life at the same time they were distancing themselves from Victorian masculinities.

CONCLUSIONS

Documentary archaeology is still a young field. As archaeologists continue to develop their own historiographic methods and philosophies, documentary archaeology will become an increasingly important avenue for understanding the past. Documentary archaeologists face two primary challenges in their practice: how to understand the relationship between different source materials, and how in practice to integrate diverse sources into meaningful narratives about the past. In the first case, the discipline is marked by lively and creative debates that are challenging our understandings of the relationship between past and present and the nature of the past. Regarding the latter, students entering the field can find the prospect of integrating the data of archaeology with other source materials intimidating. The practices of history and historical ethnography provide some guidance, but ultimately, documentary archaeology is creating new intellectual and disciplinary spaces in the study of the past. I have proposed here that attention be paid to how source creation and issues of temporal and scalar resolution can provide a general framework for evaluating what research questions are appropriate to ask of our source materials. As evidenced by the diversity of case studies cited throughout this chapter, the strength of documentary archaeology is that by its very nature it defies the imposition of narrow theoretical or methodological boundaries. Instead, it is a discipline whose boundaries and potentials are limited only by the creativity and innovation of its practitioners.

CHAPTER 3

Historical archaeology and time

Gavin Lucas

The concept of time in archaeology has, until recently, been relatively under-theorised and discussed. In the past few years, however, a number of volumes dedicated to the topic have emerged (Karlsson 2001; Lucas 2005; Murray 1999), while time-related issues such as social memory in the past have also been the subject of research (e.g. Van Dyke and Alcock 2003). On the whole, this work has focused upon prehistoric and medieval periods, although the first theoretical critique of time in archaeology was by an American historical archaeologist, Mark Leone. Leone (1978) raised the importance of both past people's perception of time and the archaeologist's view of time, and in many ways these two strands have remained at the heart of all subsequent discussion. In particular, Leone's own work has exposed the ideological nature of the archaeological presentation of the past at places such as Colonial Williamsburg (Leone 1981a). While recognising the importance of these twin strands, they are to a great extent inseparable so I have preferred to organise this chapter in terms of several connected themes. Accordingly, this chapter addresses five key aspects of time in historical archaeology.

The first is chronology. Historical archaeology is distinct insofar as it can utilise historical dates in archaeological research, not only at a general level but also at a methodological level – from the dating of makers' marks on pottery to quantitative techniques of 'mean ceramic dating' (cf. Barker and Majewski this volume). Historical archaeologists have developed unique methods of dating deposits and sites, integrating historical records with archaeological data, and this section will discuss these approaches and the role of chronology in general in historical archaeology, highlighting problems as well as advantages. The second issue concerns change: how historical archaeologists can explore – partly due to the chronological capabilities just mentioned – shifts over both long-term and everyday scales of time. Historical archaeologists can examine the relations between events at very close timescales and larger-scale processes, although these have often been studied independently. Thirdly, debates on historicity and critiques of 'totalising' narratives will be discussed, outlining various alternative approaches such as genealogies and biographies. A fourth theme is the past perception of time in the historical period, and this will be explored through concepts such as 'aging' of objects as well as more obvious material evidence of temporal consciousness such as clocks. The fifth and final issue concerns the broader theoretical implications of historical archaeology for our understanding of time. Historical archaeology brings into sharp relief the temporal tension between the present and the past. In doing so it raises critical issues about archaeological conceptions of time, and archaeological modes of time or temporalisation.

HISTORICAL ARCHAEOLOGY AND CHRONOLOGY

For all archaeologists, questions such as 'How old is it?' or 'What date is it?' are a fundamental part of research, and it is no different in historical archaeology. When excavating a site or surveying a building or landscape, establishing chronological parameters for parts or the whole is a central element in the interpretive process. Historical archaeologists determine chronologies in many of the same ways that archaeologists working on prehistoric sites do – they use techniques developed since the beginning of the discipline, such as interpreting the stratigraphy of layers or the seriation of objects (e.g. Orser and Fagan 1995: 95–108). Such techniques establish relative sequences. Where historical archaeologists start to diverge from prehistorians is in terms of absolute dating, since prehistory relies heavily on various radiometric techniques, most commonly the analysis of C14 calibrated against dendrochronology. C14 is an isotope of carbon found in all living organisms and occurs at a more or less constant level while the organism is alive. After death however, C14 decays at a constant and measurable rate, and so recording the amount remaining in any organic sample such as plant seeds or animal bone recovered from an archaeological deposit will give a date at which the organism died. However, there is a glitch: this 'more or less' constant level is just that, as various factors affect the amount of C14 in the biosphere, which has resulted in long- and short-term fluctuations of the decay curve. Fortunately, these fluctuations can be accounted for by calibrating the curve against tree-ring growth. Dendrochronology uses annual growth rings in trees to provide a date. Starting from the present and working backwards, a series of tree-ring sets can be stitched together to provide a long chronology from which C14 samples can be tested to provide the calibration. Moreover, should suitable samples of wood be recovered from archaeological sites or standing buildings, dendrochronology can also be used directly as a dating method (bearing in mind that the date will refer to the cutting of the tree and not necessarily the construction of a building).

In contrast, C14 is of more limited use to historical archaeologists both because it has a cut-off of c. AD 1800 (due to increased fossil fuel contamination in the biosphere) and because its precision is often exceeded by documentary and artefactual sources. While dendrochronology remains a useful tool, especially for standing buildings where thick timbers survive, historical archaeology generally makes most use of other resources to provide absolute dates: documents, paintings, photographs or even dated inscriptions on the objects themselves.

Because historical archaeologists are working in a period where there is a calendrical system to which documentation is linked, sites, buildings or artefacts can usually be dated quite closely. Documentation about the founding or abandonment of sites may exist, providing very precise chronological parameters; however, even for historical periods, many sites have no such accompanying documentation, and even on sites that do, many events and changes will have been unrecorded. More commonly, historical archaeologists rely on the documented dating of artefacts or types of artefacts. Many objects will have direct dating information, such as coins, stamped pipe bowls and marked pottery, which provide either a specific year or span of years. Alternatively, and more commonly, documentary sources will indicate a known or estimated production span for a type of artefact, such as scratch-blue white salt-glazed stoneware, or onion-shaped wine bottles. These work in much the same way as prehistorians use 'type-finds' dated through radio-carbon, though usually with much tighter chronological resolution.

Historical archaeologists have been constructing these chronologies from artefacts since the 1950s, particularly though the pioneering studies of Ivor Noël Hume (1969; 1983). With the emergence of 'New archaeology' during the 1960s, statistical methods were inevitably introduced to try to supplement or regulate dating methods. Given that dating of a site or assemblage is often based on an unarticulated yet still informed interpretation, archaeologists like Stanley South developed the concept of *formula dating*. Although formula dating was applied to various types of artefact (e.g. Carillo 1974), the two most common examples were the *pipe stem formula* and the *mean ceramic formula*. The pipe stem formula was constructed by Lewis Binford using data collected by J. C. Harrington, which showed that English clay-pipe stem-bore diameters gradually decreased over time (Harrington 1978) during the seventeenth and eighteenth centuries. Binford constructed a formula that accounted for Harrington's data, and that could be extended to date an excavated assemblage of pipe stem fragments from an otherwise undated site or context (Binford 1978). Stanley South's mean ceramic dating method was similar; producing a formula for calculating the median date of an assemblage or site by taking into consideration the median production date of key ceramic types within the assemblage – the median dates for each ceramic type being based on the estimates and research of Noël Hume (South 1977a). Both studies generally used known production dates to infer occupation dates. Indeed, South explicitly argued that because breakage and replacement rates might be presumed to be high, and since only a few pieces would have been curated as heirlooms, the statistical nature of the mean ceramic formula meant that time lag between production and use or deposition was insignificant (1977a: 206). Yet while he found that the variation between the documented median date and ceramic median date was only around four or five years, it has also been pointed out that South often calculated time lag into his initial data, in that the date ranges of several ceramic types were not so much known production spans, but modified spans that reflected ranges of currency on North American historical sites (W. H. Adams 2003: 45–46).

While this question of time lag is particularly significant in historical archaeologists' analysis of chronologies because of the relatively high chronological resolution available to the field, its significance also raises various interpretive questions about objects such as their frequency of use, availability of replacement, or personal attachment (W. H. Adams 2003; Hill 1982). In other words, time lag is not simply a question of economic supply and demand, but entwined with issues of cultural valuation. Time lag forces historical archaeologists to relate chronology to processes of consumption and discard, understanding chronology as not just a basic framework within which more high-level interpretations can operate, but as directly implicated within such interpretations.

HISTORICAL ARCHAEOLOGY, TIMESCALES AND CHANGE

As observed above, historical archaeology often has much closer chronological resolution available in its studies of material remains than the archaeology of prehistoric periods. Historical archaeologists can often discuss changes on the scale of years, and certainly decades – a possibility which many prehistorians may envy. Consequently, much historical archaeology focuses on detailed micro-histories. The availability of documentary sources, with their localised temporal scale, has no doubt encouraged this, and many studies now combine rich, fine-grained textual data with material remains to tell stories about individuals or households (cf. Wilkie this volume).

However, this does not mean that historical archaeology is only concerned with such micro-historical interpretation; as part of the general discipline of archaeology, its concern for larger scales of analysis is equally strong. In particular, given its ability to deal with both micro- and macro-historical scales, the field is perhaps in an unusual and privileged position, not just within archaeology but the social sciences in general.

It is not surprising therefore that several archaeologists have eagerly adopted Braudel's multi-scalar approach to history, encapsulated in the distinction between the long term (*longue durée*) and the event (*événement*), mediated by a middle term of social structure (*conjuncture*; Braudel 1980). In particular, Barbara Little and Paul Shackel were among the first to argue explicitly for the importance of addressing all three levels, which they called long-term history, social time and individual time (Little and Shackel 1989). In their study, later expanded in Shackel's book *Personal Discipline and Material Culture*, they studied dining etiquette through these three scales (Little and Shackel 1989; Shackel 1993): exploring the broad development of dining customs in Europe and colonial North America from medieval to modern times, through etiquette manuals and ceramic change; considering medium-scale development through probate data and ceramic standardisation from Annapolis, Maryland; and finally studying the records and archaeology of the household of an Annapolis printer, Jonas Green. All three scales were articulated in terms of social power relations, as Shackel focused upon how dining etiquette was used by elites as a strategy of exclusion and separation. Ultimately, the various scales of change in etiquette were seen through transformations in the nature of consumption in Western society, and its links to capitalism. Drawing on such a multi-scalar approach, similar to that of the *Annales* school of social historians, might seem to be the most useful way to articulate relations between micro- and macro-histories, but there is often an ambiguous tension within *Annales* history that tends to privilege *either* enduring structures *or* event-based narratives. One only has to compare the works of *Annales* historians Braudel and LeRoy Ladurie to see these opposing tendencies in practice (Braudel 1972; LeRoy Ladurie 1979; 1980) – and it is perhaps unsurprising that the same tension is dominant within historical archaeology. Little and Shackel's study of etiquette largely avoids this privileging, and while they end by affirming the key importance of long-term history they are clearly aware of the dangers of a normative structuralism accruing to such studies (Little and Shackel 1989: 507–508).

At stake here are historical archaeologists' conceptions of historical process and the role of material culture in this. The primary danger of a

Braudelian-derived approach is that it tends to encourage a top-down model of history, with long-term structures forming the framework within which to situate smaller-scale changes. Thus a recurrent theme among historical archaeologists who either explicitly or implicitly situate their work in a 'long-term' perspective is how the temporality of everyday material culture is enmeshed within the broader development of capitalism (e.g. M. Johnson 1996; Leone and Potter 1999; Orser 1996). This predominance given to capitalism has recently been criticised for perpetuating a eurocentric view of history, and even of what historical archaeology 'should' be (Funari et al. 1999). More generally, an over-emphasis on a single historical process – such as capitalism – privileges the kind of 'grand narrative' approach to history that came under intense criticism in the 'postprocessual' archaeology of the 1980s (M. Johnson 1999b). Such visions of a 'total history' certainly form a core part of Braudel's version of *Annales* history as well as other related approaches, most notably Immanuel Wallerstein's (1995) 'world systems analysis', which was partly inspired by Braudel.

For historical archaeology, the danger in producing 'totalising' histories lies not only in a privileging of European perspectives, but also in the attendant flattening out of local diversity and particular histories. And yet an equal danger lies in shifting to another extreme – rejecting grand narratives, and conducting archaeologies that only produce highly specific, localised narratives whose broader relevance is missing. Historical archaeology is not just local history. One should not lose sight of the importance of the key questions of how sites and practices, objects and people are enchained into patterns that constitute a recognisable historical process. There may be many ways to answer these questions, and surely they need to be constantly mediating the general and particular; however, if there is no single history to be told, no one story (cf. Joyce this volume), then to what extent are questions of timescales relevant? It is not that different stories cannot be told on different temporal scales, but rather that connecting different scales together, as part of a single story, is no longer an issue. Historical archaeology invites new approaches to time and historical interpretation, that map the temporalities of specific traditions, communities, or things.

OTHER STORIES: GENEALOGIES AND BIOGRAPHIES

Two of the most common alternatives to 'totalising' histories first explored by historians and anthropologists have influenced studies of prehistory rather than historical archaeology. The first, what might be called a genealogical approach, derives largely from Foucault (and his interpretation of

Nietzsche), who used the term as a way to historicise ontology – that is, in his particular work, to look at the constitution of human subjectivity in historical rather than universal terms. Almost all of Foucault's works can be seen as attempts to explore this historical ontology of the subject in relation to three different domains: *truth, power* and *ethics* (Foucault 1983). In archaeology, the term 'genealogy' has been adopted to refer to an approach that actively resists producing a totalising representation of the past in favour of tracing specific practices, where the narrative could change according to the starting point and the trajectory followed (e.g. Gosden 1994: 140). As the everyday meaning of the term implies, a genealogy – like a family tree – is a network of connections with a temporal basis, and tracing different paths along this network produces different histories. Just as there can be no total family tree – its very construction depends on a specific starting point (ego), so there can be no total genealogy.

The genealogical approach – as explicitly cited – had a certain circulation of use in archaeology in the 1990s, mostly in prehistory, though Matthew Johnson employed the term occasionally in one of his key works to refer to specific trajectories of capitalism and the Georgian Order (Johnson 1996: 206–212). However, the failure of the term to gain wider currency probably reflects a certain fracture between its broad connotation and more specific usage: while archaeologists freely used the term to refer to non-totalising histories, they found it far harder to produce a specific example of an archaeological genealogy as opposed to just any particularising narrative. Part of the problem may be that the everyday meaning of the term just cannot be stretched to incorporate such specificity in another context. However, there may be potential in reviving it by bringing it back closer to its everyday meaning. Because of the availability of rich textual sources, historical archaeology could – and to some extent already has – developed a genealogical approach, which conjoins with more conventional family-history. While typically eschewed by historians as amateur or trivial history, family-history research has the potential to explore detailed histories which, when combined with more 'respectable' social and economic research, has been shown to be greatly rewarding. Developed particularly by feminist historians (e.g. Davidoff and Hall 2002; but also see Gye 2005), this approach, when combined with archaeological research, has even greater potential – and moreover provides materials which can engage with local communities at a much more personal level.

The second major alternative to 'totalising history' has been to construct archaeological biographies. There are two discernible strands here. The first is similar to the genealogical approach just mentioned, concerning the biographies of individuals or households. This approach has been very popular in recent years, particularly in North American historical archaeology, where it is closely associated with new styles of archaeological narrative (e.g. A. Praetzellis 1998; Yamin 2001; cf. Wilkie this volume). Because of the rich documentary sources, especially from the nineteenth century onwards, quite detailed connections can be drawn between specific people and their material remains, allowing a unique interpretive approach, which has been justly exploited – despite the problems that do exist when connecting archaeological remains to documented households (e.g. see Groover 2001; Mayne and Murray 2003). Such narratives are often very personal and human accounts that, while still raising broader themes, can present them through a highly particular perspective. Indeed, such narratives can address important dimensions such as the life cycles of individuals or households, and a number of studies have done just this (e.g. see Gilchrist 2000; Sofaer Deverenski 2000; Wilkie 2003). The other strand of archaeological biography is focused more on material culture than on people. While of course much traditional archaeological work is concerned with the chronology of a site through stratigraphy and phasing/periods, or the life cycle of an artefact through attention to formation processes, the particular emphasis of this biographical approach is on the changing cultural *meanings* of sites and objects. Inspired by anthropological studies of consumption and material culture (Appadurai 1986; J. Hoskins 1998), it is prehistoric archaeologists who have adopted this biographical approach more than historical archaeologists (e.g. Bradley 2002). Nevertheless, given the traditional nature of archaeological methodology and its focus on site sequence and artefact analysis, this latter biographical approach also offers a lot of scope for historical archaeologists, especially where the ability to gain finer temporal resolution ought to make it more viable.

Such biographical perspectives have the potential for connecting rather disparate studies in historical archaeology, which are currently practised largely by two different groups. On the one hand, there is the strong tradition of artefact studies that focus upon details of production and chronology. While these form the backbone of much archaeological work, they have recently been marginalised in theoretical debate in favour, on the other hand, of studies on consumption and how such objects were used and what they meant. This schism between two approaches – what one might also characterise as the traditional/descriptive versus the contemporary/interpretive schools of historical archaeology – is potentially damaging. Adopting a biographical perspective on material culture means that archaeologists need to develop more sophisticated theoretical frameworks that can conjoin traditional studies of production with more recent research on consumption. In fact greater emphasis needs to be given to the temporal connection between the multiple contexts through which objects travel: production sites (e.g. factories), distribution sites (e.g. warehouses, ships, retail shops), consumption sites (e.g. households) and discard sites (e.g. middens). One already established model for exploring such connections is the 'commodity chain'. Analysis of commodity chains largely developed out of economics and focused mainly on the producer–consumer interface or systems of provision – i.e. how goods get from the factory to the household (Leslie and Reimer 1999) – but can be extended across the whole life cycle of a commodity, including use within the household and subsequent discard or recycling. Moreover, commodity chains can (and no doubt should) be studied in two ways – as temporal chains connecting different sites/contexts in the movement of objects and as geographical chains where different objects are connected at certain sites (e.g. factories, middens, shops). Given that archaeologists and those studying modern material culture tend to be site oriented, rather more attention has been directed at the latter. However, a more multi-sited archaeology, and one with more attention to the temporal nature of material culture and its movement, could not only provide a new set of stories to tell but could also offer a fruitful way of exploring more general historical processes that mediates the current schism between different fields of historical archaeology (Hicks 2003; cf. Marcus 1995).

MATERIAL CULTURE AND THE CONSTRUCTION OF TEMPORALITY

Looking at the biography of sites and objects also has the potential to develop our understanding of past people's perception of time. Examining qualities of objects such as their 'age' in any particular context, in both a chronological and cultural sense, can help archaeologists to explore the different ways in which time and a sense of the past was constructed during the modern period through material culture. Notions of durability and decay – how objects remain in circulation and the temporal properties associated with them – are important here. Can archaeologists understand how people in the past regarded different elements of their material world in terms of 'oldness' or 'newness', and if so, what can this tell us about past people's perception of time? A good example is the widespread replacement of pewter tableware by industrial ceramics in late eighteenth-century Virginia (Lucas 2005: 89–92). One of the curious things about the archaeological record of the seventeenth and eighteenth centuries in England and Virginia is the lack of a major type of artefact used for the table in homes and taverns everywhere: pewter. This material is fairly hardy, yet it is rarely ever found, despite being a major component of domestic-tableware assemblages in the form of plates, tankards and other items, as probate inventories testify (A. Martin 1989). A large part of the reason for this is undoubtedly due to its durability and recyclability. If you drop it, at most it acquires a dent, and if it starts to look too battered or is no longer wanted, it can be sold for scrap or recast. For this reason, it makes for a good material as tableware. Yet towards the end of the eighteenth century and into the first decades of the nineteenth century, its role was completely supplanted by ceramics – which were eminently breakable and non-recyclable. Why?

Some reasons undoubtedly relate to cost – the new industrial refined earthenwares such as creamwares and pearlwares, were vastly cheaper (a third to a quarter of the cost). Also, the widespread adoption of drinking hot beverages such as tea and coffee made pewter impractical. Pewter was also limited in terms of its decorative potential, unlike the 'white canvas' of pottery. At the heart of these changes is the larger issue of the changing nature of consumption. We may not think of pewter in the same league as 'family silver', but in the seventeenth century it certainly carried connotations of status and wealth, and was often on display in homes. As Ann Smart Martin (1989) points out, it took quite a long time for the introduction of mass-produced ceramics to replace pewter in homes, a lag which cannot be due to financial reasons. Instead, I want to suggest that the transformation from pewter to ceramics was related to shifts in people's relations with objects and time, visible in changes in consumption. A key concept here is that of *patina* (McCracken 1990).

Patina is that quality of an object that indicates age, the signs of longevity – gloss on old wood, spots on old silver or pewter, general wear and tear. In medieval and early modern England, the patina of household possessions was an important symbol of the family's status and honour, chiefly aristocratic families but more generally any household that owned what might called heirlooms (McCracken 1990: 31–43; also see Shackel 1993: 163–164). Pewter, unlike ceramics, carried 'patina' *because* of its durability, and thus it had the power to invoke family history. Ceramics, though they are potentially durable and repairable, are also more disposable and cheaply replaceable. The transformation from pewter to ceramics would seem therefore to be linked to major changes in the nature of consumption and what it signified. This change occurred in the later eighteenth century as the so-called 'consumer revolution' swept England (McKendrick et al. 1982). Suddenly wealth and status was marked by new material culture; rather than patina or age acting to signal status, now it was novelty – the latest design, the latest fashion helped to accrue status. Ceramics were a much better material for the new style of consumption than pewter because of these qualities, and this is why they replaced pewter as the primary element of tableware.

The explosion of ceramic tablewares in the archaeological record in the late eighteenth and early nineteenth century tells us not just about new patterns of consumption, but whole new ways of perceiving the world which included time. The notion of tablewares having family history, that every time you sit down to eat you are also using objects with personal historical meaning, was completely altered by the replacement of pewter by ceramics. This example suggests that material culture, and in particular its temporal properties, holds information about a society's perception of time: that how a society creates or breaks links with the past through the *aging* of material culture provides a window into its perception of time.

Such a study of a particular type of artefact can be linked with more obvious evidence for the perception of time in the modern period. Around the same time as these changes in consumption, evidence of a new time awareness in material culture in terms of marking time is also visible. The more common archaeological examples include coins, where from the sixteenth century in Europe, dates started to appear marked on the coin face – prior to this, there was usually only 'proxy' dating, in the form of the reigning monarch's name. Similarly, from the seventeenth century, some pottery vessels (especially tin-glazed earthenware and later, industrial white-wares) were occasionally marked with years, or even specific dates – often commemorating particular events. The use of dates on coins and other objects paralleled the adoption, from the sixteenth century, of the Gregorian calendar in Europe, which was primarily established to regulate the cycle of festivals and holidays, and consequently helped to create more standardised conceptions of time. Thus, dated objects are not just useful chronological tools for the archaeologist: they also tell us something about the changing perception of time among the populations such coins circulated. Both of these brief examples – and more could no doubt be found – indicate changes in conceptions of time during the modern period, the role of objects in such changes and, more specifically, that time and change have been increasingly 'domesticated'. Such 'domestication' of time was bound up with the development of consumerism, and perhaps made novelty or fashion a normal and acceptable part of everyday life, by accentuating a linear perception of time.

The emergence and circulation of dated objects and calendars among society was just one aspect of this domestication of time; the other, and perhaps even more pervasive innovation was the clock. Clocks in the form of public-church and tower clocks became fairly widespread from the fourteenth century in European towns and cities, where until the seventeenth and eighteenth century this was most people's experience of clocks. It was only from the late seventeenth and especially eighteenth century that domestic or interior clocks started to become at all common in upper-, then middle-class, and later working-class homes in Europe or the New World, as well as inside public rooms such as taverns or workshops. This increase in the numbers of clocks as items in the household marked a changing use of clocks by the majority of the population from marking time to reading the time; a difference that can may be observed by looking more closely at the design of clocks (Lucas 1995).

An important aspect of the medieval tower clocks was the presence of a striking mechanism. For most people, it was the sound of the bell striking that indicated a certain time, rather than people actually reading the clock face to see what time it was, and bells of course had a much longer history as time indicators in European culture, being an important part of both monastic and urban life, and used to mark events such as daily mass or festivals (Cipolla 1967; North 1975). Clocks in medieval and early modern Europe, for most people then, did not represent a time-reading system but simply time indication. Nevertheless, reading clocks is something that did develop among the mass population, and this process probably started to take place during the late seventeenth century. This is evident in the gradual and widespread appearance of domestic or interior clocks at this time, and also changes in the design of the clock face (Lucas 1995). In particular, from the eighteenth century, the way in which time is marked and divided on the clock face went through various stages of development – from increasing subdivisions of the hour with just an hour hand to, after the mid-eighteenth century, a switch across to two main divisions: the hour and the minute with two hands. These changes can be said to relate to different ways of reading the time, specifically marking an awareness of smaller division of time than previously. They coincided with changes in the industrial organisation of labour and the role clocks played in factory production (Thompson 1967), but at the same time by enabling the mass of people to read time clocks brought a new time consciousness that pervaded a number of areas of social life, including people's relations with material culture, such as through consumption.

HISTORICAL ARCHAEOLOGY AND THE CONTEMPORARY PAST

The new mode of time consciousness discussed in the previous section, which was engendered by and through changes in material culture between the seventeenth and nineteenth centuries, is of course also entwined with the understanding of time used by archaeologists in the present. Most obvious is the use of the same, standardised, calendrical chronology: when one thinks of the archaeological concept of time, chronology is likely to be what most comes to mind, and indeed the present chapter began with issues of chronology and dating. However, chronology is just one particular type of time, and as subsequent sections in this chapter revealed, there are other aspects of time that archaeologists can and should explore. Moreover, it could be argued that one of the reasons why archaeology for so long has sought total histories is because the model of history derives from the chronological model of time: time as a linear, singular and universal container for events, which needs to be filled out (Lucas 2005: 13–14). Such a linear and singular model has also affected the way in which the discipline of archaeology has been practised – e.g. subdivided by discrete periods, however one defines them: e.g. prehistory and historical archaeology, medieval and post-medieval periods, colonial and native. Such divides – into which students are educated and on which careers are made – are often obstructive, and it is no surprise that in the past few years, archaeologists have been trying to break these borders down through cross-period conferences and publications (e.g. Gaimster and Stamper 1997). A more genealogical or biographical approach helps to traverse these boundaries, which are, after all, a construction based purely on a notion of total history. Such periodisations must be viewed as contingent and multiple rather than absolute and singular. This is not to deny that there are major historical transitions, which affect a deep structural transformation on societies and cultures, and that consequently broad period specialisations within archaeology are inevitable. But nor should these boundaries be drawn too firmly.

Furthermore, there is a deep irony in the use of chronology to define archaeological time, in that while chronology actually serves to connect the past to the present through a single system, archaeology routinely separates the present from the past in order to construct its object. It feels the contradiction most acutely when it tries to put a date to when archaeology 'stops'; not so long ago, post-medieval archaeology in England frequently cut off at AD 1750, and most heritage management systems in Europe have a moveable minimum year rule which stipulates what constitutes archaeology (e.g. thirty years, a century). Theoretically of course, this is absurd, and it highlights the tension between a double temporality in archaeology: an explicit one of chronology where the past is connected to the present through a universal timeline, and a concealed one where the past is separated from the present (Lucas 2004). Recent work on diverse themes such as garbage, forensics, or family history has been pushing at this tension via an archaeology of the present – or 'contemporary past' (e.g. Buchli and Lucas 2001a; Campbell and Hansson 2000; Olivier 2001; Rathje and Murphy 1992). Such studies have helped to foster what Dan Hicks has called 'the loss of antiquity', that is, a rejection of definitions of the archaeological past as necessarily distant (Hicks 2003: 316–17). But more than that, they question the very distinction between present and past, and thus the very nature of *the archaeological.*

To what extent is there still a difference between such 'archaeologies of the contemporary past' and historical archaeology? From one perspective, the only difference is a chronological one and therefore any boundary is as fluid or as tight as that between, say, post-medieval and medieval archaeology. However, a more radical position would argue that there is more than a chronological distinction here. Victor Buchli and Gavin Lucas have suggested that while the temporal distance between the subject and object of study is preserved within mainstream historical archaeologies, it is no longer present when conducting archaeologies of the contemporary past (Buchli and Lucas 2001c: 8–9). Consequently, any pretence of detachment, which might be mobilised through a rhetoric of time, becomes implausible, and the role of archaeology as a cultural practice in the present is thoroughly foregrounded. None of this is any less true, of course, of the archaeology of the recent or distant past (cf. Shanks 2004b), but perhaps it is most easily seen in archaeologies of the contemporary past, situating such an archaeology in a unique position to develop the social role of archaeology. Ultimately, the concept of archaeology is bound up with the concept of time: by rethinking time, we rethink archaeology. Historical archaeologies, and particularly archaeologies of the contemporary past, play perhaps the most pivotal role in this process – precisely because they throw into relief the tensions inherent in the abiding double temporality of all archaeological endeavours.

CHAPTER 4

Writing historical archaeology

Rosemary Joyce

The way that we write our archaeological accounts is as much constitutive of our field as are the questions we think are significant and the ways we think those questions should be addressed (Joyce 2002). In writing, we seek to persuade others of our understandings, and to evoke from them a response. Whether the response we get is affirmative or contests our arguments, it is in the reception of our writing that we see ourselves connected to others in our discipline. It is through the engagement of scholars in exchanges that a body of accepted knowledge is produced. Through the same engagement, writers recognise themselves and are recognised as parts of a community of scholarship.

In this I consider how historical archaeology is shaped by particular forms of writing. Historical archaeology has produced some of the most sustained experiments in writing in the discipline of archaeology as a whole. I will be concerned particularly with the placements of the writer in relation to the subject that is typical in historical archaeological writing. I will suggest that what most distinguishes historical archaeology in writing is that the imaginary third party toward whose approval a text is oriented is distinct from those typical of other forms of archaeology.

Writing by historical archaeologists shows far more explicit engagement with problems of narrative and representation than most such work in other traditions of archaeology. Part of the reason for this difference may be a greater sense of the real historically situated persons whose lives and actions writers attempt to represent, created by the ability of historical archaeologists to engage with their subjects through documents as well as other forms of material culture. Another source of that sensibility undoubtedly is the routine engagement of historical archaeologists with living human beings who are often descendants of those whose life histories archaeology intersects. But it is not simply the existence of living people who will be affected by what they say that gives historical archaeologists a strong sense of responsibility for representation. More fundamental may be the fact that in their encounters with the contradictions between words and things, historical archaeologists always live with the knowledge that there is no single story that can adequately account for the phenomena they study. This predisposes them to prefer accounts that deal meaningfully with all the richness of the material at hand, rather than explanations which reduce that richness to a few main points that may have broader explanatory power. In the memorable phrase of James Deetz (1977), historical archaeologists are concerned with 'small things forgotten', and the texts they create are densely populated with these things. The multiplicity of voices that is required to account for these things creates in the texts of historical archaeology a multivocality that distinguishes writing in historical archaeology as a whole, even in the less self-consciously experimental technical reports that still, of course, predominate.

BEGINNING POINTS OF REFERENCE

This chapter considers how the writing of historical archaeology, by scholars who habitually publish in journals such as *Historical Archaeology* and *The International Journal of Historical Archaeology*, might have a distinctive contribution to make to transdisciplinary studies of writing and representation, and in particular, their relationship to the study of human beings. The formulation of the human subject as an object for scientific study is, of course, one of the hallmarks of Enlightenment scholarship. The objectivity this made possible sustained nineteenth- and twentieth-century scholarship, including the formation and development of anthropology and archaeology. In the second half of the twentieth century, persistent concerns were raised in history and anthropology about writing and representation. The questions raised have particular importance for historical archaeology as it engages with both material and textual evidence.

In his studies of historiography and narrative, literary critic Hayden White (1987) argued that there were dominant sensibilities at different periods which led to the construction of historical narratives in forms specific to a time and place. It is important to distinguish between the kind of doubts White and others expressed about the possibility of creating objective histories, constructed purely as if a disinterested viewer watched through a glass screen as events unfolded in front of him, and an assertion that all historical accounts are equally good. As he wrote,

this is not to say that a historical discourse is not properly assessed in terms of the truth value of its factual (singular existential) statements taken individually and the logical conjunction of the whole set of such statements taken distributively. For unless a historical discourse acceded to assessment in these terms, it would lose all justification for its claim to represent and provide explanations of specifically real events. (H. White 1987: 45)

His argument was that historians constructed accounts that made sense of all the materials available to them, but within a form that incorporated assumptions about causality that were themselves products of particular historical times and places.

Because the historian is actually connected to the events that he or she wants to explain, he or she can never occupy a position entirely outside of what happened. There will always be more than one perspective in any analysis; at a minimum, there will be the perspective of the scholar connected to the events described (primarily concerned with understanding what happened), and the perspective that the same scholar takes on his or her own engagement (a more distanced perspective that explicitly acknowledges the points of connection that orient a writer to his or her subject).

The late twentieth-century discussion of writing in history is of direct relevance to archaeology because both disciplines seek to understand and represent subjects who are not directly observed, but related debates in Americanist sociocultural anthropology are also pertinent here. Many of these works proposed that ethnographers needed to promote multivocality, to provide a way for the voices of living subjects to be recognised in their texts and to represent more clearly the situated perspectives of the ethnographer, no longer claiming a distanced objectivity (Behar and Gordon 1995; Clifford and Marcus 1986).

The concern expressed by ethnographers over representation of the experiences of others has special resonance for archaeologists. Archaeologists may be the only party today speaking for certain past subjects. As we represent past realities, we also claim that our representations are reliable. Archaeologists need to make sure that the way they speak for past subjects does not assume too broad an authority in the service of dehumanising or 'totalising' narratives. As in ethnography, one tool available to contemporary archaeologists is reflexivity: the acknowledgement in the text of the situated position of the archaeologist–writer commenting on past human subjects.

Where these two strands of 'writing about writing' converge is in an emphasis on the way that textual rhetoric represents the scholar and the authority he or she claims. One of the key issues we can explore is the way that a writer's own position is represented, how the role of the writer as narrator is acknowledged or obscured.

For H. White (1987: 2–3) historical narrative is an account represented as that of an apparently objective speaker telling what really happened in chronological order represented as cause and effect. He claimed that the 'objectivity of narrative is defined by the *absence* of all reference to the narrator' (H. White 1987: 2–3, my emphasis). White based his analysis on distinctions sketched out earlier by French literary critic Gérard Genette between story (narrated events), narrative (the oral or written discourse that tells events), and narration (the act of telling events) (1988: 13–14). Genette (1988: 14–15) argued that in historical narrative 'the actual order [of creation] is obviously *story* (the completed events), *narrating* (the narrative act of the historian), *narrative*'. While this would appear to position historical narratives as defined by virtue of their relation in time to events, this was not the central difference identified between historical and fictional narratives. Instead, Genette distinguished between these in terms of substantiation by a listener or reader:

the typically modal query 'How does the author know that?' does not have the same meaning in fiction as in nonfiction. *In nonfiction, the historian must provide evidence and documents.* (1988: 15, my emphasis)

In other words, narratives that claim to be truthful (as do all archaeological works, even those most sceptical about objectivity) rely on specific kinds of relations between readers and writers. Rom Harré argues that in technical articles this trust is founded on an acceptance of the written work as reliable for other scientists to use in making their own arguments. 'One trusts that making use of a claim to know originated by one of one's fellow scientists will not let one down in a debate' (1990: 83). Harré notes that 'to publish abroad a discovery couched in the rhetoric of science is to let it be known that the presumed fact can safely be used in debate, in practical projects, and so on. Knowledge claims are tacitly prefixed with a performative of trust' (1990: 97). Harré identifies this 'performative of trust' (1990: 82) as embedded in the rhetoric of scientific articles, where there is an implied phrase 'I know' before statements that are presented as facts: an omitted claim of specific individual knowledge that invites the reader to identify as a member of the community of scientists by substituting the implied phrase 'we [scholars] know'.

The text can only be completed in this way by those who can reinstate in their own minds the missing pieces, particularly the procedures that would be necessary to create reliable data to back up the knowledge claim. But these knowledgeable members of the scholarly community in fact take on faith that the commonly accepted procedures have been carried out in a way that ensures the implications are reliable. 'We know' because the author implies he or she knows, and does so in a way that suggests the author applies the same approaches to create and evaluate data as we would.

We can take as an example almost any published article, and interpolate the missing 'performative of trust':

[We know that] archaeological analyses of household wealth differentials at Cebu and Tanjay (as measured in densities of foreign porcelain, elaborate earthenware, metal goods, glass beads, and other presumed 'prestige goods') show that household status display becomes more finely graded and continuously varied by the fifteenth–sixteenth centuries. (Junker 1998: 310)

This example, with its scrupulous stipulation of the procedure that underwrites the assertion (measures of densities of prestige goods) shows how acceptance of the claim assumes understanding what is implied in measuring densities of prestige goods. Even the term 'prestige goods' requires a certain degree of expertise to understand, and accepting it as meaningful binds a reader to the writer as members of a single rhetorical community.

This is not a critique of archaeologists for talking about prestige goods; technical language like this is a necessary and appropriate part of the contemporary project of creating archaeological meaning, of communication among archaeologists (Little 2000: 11). But as archaeologists, like ethnographers and historians, realise, the meanings that make sense to us today are not the same as the meanings that made sense to our human subjects in their time and place. What is interesting for the purposes of an account of how historical archaeology is being written today is the fact that archaeologists are sometimes, more or less self-consciously, reshaping their use of language so that the texts they produce may possibly be meaningful simultaneously for other archaeologists and for non-archaeologists, and might even represent something closer to a statement that a past subject might have made.

A number of authors have offered critical analyses of the way archaeology in general is written that form part of the context for the writing of historical archaeology. These discussions concern three kinds of writing: works in which archaeologists reflect on their own experiences autobiographically, or those of others biographically (Givens 1992; Schrire 1995); works in which archaeological practices or findings are considered by non-archaeologists (Finn 2004; Jameson, Finn and Ehrenhard 2003); and more general studies of the ways in which archaeologists write about their understandings of the past, whether for specialists or broader audiences. While this chapter is concerned primarily with the third of these forms of writing archaeology, the broader contexts provided by the other works cited are worth serious consideration by anyone concerned with writing in archaeology.

Contemporary concern with rhetoric and representation in archaeology predates postprocessualism, but gained greater urgency in the critical response to processualism in the 1980s and 1990s. Recognition of the status of archaeological narratives as exercises of power required critical self-consciousness about writing (Baker, Taylor and Thomas 1990; Shanks and Tilley 1987; Sinclair 1989). Contrasting a late eighteenth-century archaeological field report with its late twentieth-century descendants, Ian Hodder (1989) called for archaeologists to reflect on their writing practices, as ethnographers and historians were then already doing. Many of the late eighteenth-century reports he discusses were in the form of letters. By the late nineteenth and early twentieth century, the first-person narrator was banished. Hodder (1989) drew attention to the fact that late twentieth-century archaeological reports presented conclusions without representing any of the actual debate and discussion through which those contingent understandings were obtained. He called for a return of the narrator's voice, of the narration of a sequence of events, and the incorporation of more of the real dialogue among participants in research in the written text.

Subsequent discussion of narrative in archaeology invoked tropological analysis and the structure of folktales (Hodder 1993, 1995; Pluciennik 1999; J. Terrell 1990). The popularity of these frameworks of analysis suggests that much archaeological writing can be considered as either historical narrative (a story told about what happened) or variants on hero-quest tales (the story of the archaeological project). Once the narrative nature of archaeological representation was acknowledged, the way was cleared for experiments in writing that went far beyond simply telling what the archaeologist thought had happened, or how the archaeologist gained the prized knowledge. One of the earliest and most widely cited archaeological experiments with writing was Janet Spector's *What This Awl Means* (1993). She listed among her goals that she 'wanted to communicate in an easily accessible way' what she had learned about a nineteenth-century Wahpeton Dakota village through the study of a single artefact (Spector 1993: 17). Her narrative was an externalisation of the imaginative work which she had to accomplish during her archaeological practice, but which is not normally represented in conventional archaeological writing (Spector 1993: 18).

A third form of narrative writing characteristic of archaeology, the dialogue between archaeologist and real or imagined others, is centrally concerned with making public such processes of imagination (Bapty 1989, 1990;

B. Bender 1998; Flannery 1976; Hodder 1992, 1999; Johnson 1999a). In some dialogues the characters are fictional constructs who stand in for stereotypes, such as Flannery's (1976) Real Mesoamerican Archaeologist, Sceptical Graduate Student, and Great Synthesiser, or Matthew Johnson's character Roger Beefy 'an undergraduate student at Northern University, England' (1999a: 3). The characters, contemporaries of the archaeologist narrator, are generic 'stand-ins' for the actual interlocutors with whom the archaeologist talks things out in the field, the lab, and the classroom. Other dialogues give voice more openly to the internal uncertainties of the archaeologist (Bapty 1990; Hodder 1992). Many archaeological dialogues may be seen as projections of multiple perspectives that the archaeologist narrator can adopt, including voices of contrast (e.g. Hodder 1999: 64–65): an approach dramatically used in historical archaeology by Adrian and Mary Praetzellis in a paper discussed below (A. Praetzellis and M. Praetzellis 1998).

The possibilities for contrasting perspectives may be most forcefully represented in dialogues that transcribe words uttered by real people other than the archaeologist, although even here the author controls the citation and thus contextual understanding of what was said (B. Bender 1998: 11). Hybrid dialogues, combining real quotations and those composed by the archaeologist–author, have had a particularly critical role in historical archaeology. Mary Beaudry (1998) created a four-part dialogue combining some actual journal entries with others she imagined. Remarking on the absence of women's journals from her documentary record, she decided to provide them, stating that, 'I've often thought how marvellous it would be if other people . . . had left us journals recording their observations and the details of their day-to-day lives' (Beaudry 1998: 20). Another of the narratives she presents combines 'real' and 'imagined' journal entries by another person.

Even the choice of words used in writing conventional archaeological accounts has rhetorical significance (Fotiadis 1992; N. Hamilton 2000). The normative language of archaeological excavation reports was self-consciously selected by early practitioners to express relations of hierarchical authority and organisation of 'campaigns' seen as parallel to military expeditions (Joyce 2002: 18–26). Less self-conscious adoption of tropes of the 'cowboy' also shaped the understanding of what archaeology is and who effectively really was a genuine archaeologist (Gero 1985). Language choices like these help shape our understanding of who speaks the truth of archaeology, understandings clearly reflected in citation practices that favour broader claims over more particularistic studies (Beaudry and White 1994). Language choices also serve to delimit a community of reception of archaeological writing, consisting of specialists who understand the terms used. Thus it is not surprising that one of the other ways contemporary archaeological writing has been transformed is through explicit engagement with non-archaeologist readers.

Adrian Praetzellis (2000, 2003) takes the impulse to tell a story for those outside the discipline to its fullest expression in his textbooks in the form of mystery novels. But most such writing is in sometimes ephemeral media addressed to non-specialists: visitors to sites and the public in general (F. Jameson 1997; Joyce 2002: 127–129). For example, a series of five interpretive booklets published by the University of New England and the Yarrawarra Aboriginal Corporation reproduce 'stories from Aboriginal people, archaeology, oral history, maps, and photographs', intending 'to make visible some of the stories of this landscape that have not been previously visible to non-indigenous people' (Somerville et al. 1999: 5). The booklets use different typefaces to represent distinct voices, which are also signed and dated. The voices of archaeologists and community elders are juxtaposed and create a cumulative effect of multiple stories.

Writing archaeology is self-evidently more than a form of neutral representation of facts, arranged in a storyline that makes some kind of sense. It is an act of communication, with its own rhetorical forms shaped by the orientations of writers to their assumed audiences. By claiming a position in the text as narrator, many contemporary historical archaeologists introduce into their texts a specific speaking voice, the first step in constructing polyphony, the sound of multiple voices.

POLYPHONY IN HISTORICAL ARCHAEOLOGY

Narrators speak from a defined time and place. Archaeologists narrate from multiple positions, both those of the contemporary speaker – the writer – and those of past speakers, the subjects about whom they write. Many historical archaeologists grapple with the problem of representation that the claim of speaking for another poses by introducing into their texts a multiplicity of languages: a '*heteroglossia*' which Mikhail Bakhtin (1981: 288–293 and *passim*) proposed necessary to achieve polyphony.

I have suggested elsewhere that archaeologists can draw on the work of Bakhtin to understand writing as communication with a specifically ethical dimension, created by our responsibility for the representation of often-voiceless past subjects (Joyce 2002). Bakhtin paid particular attention to the central dilemma which objectivism posed for scholars whose object of study was other human beings, noting that any object of knowledge (including [a human being]) can be perceived and cognized as a thing. But a subject as such cannot be perceived and studied as a thing, for as a subject it cannot, while remaining a subject, become voiceless, and consequently, cognition of it can only be *dialogic*. (1986: 161)

For Bakhtin, dialogue meant more than an exchange between two speakers. His concept of dialogue requires a society of speakers and the listeners they address in expectation of receiving a response, which always evaluates, critiques, confirms, contests, or reinflects the received utterance (1981: 276). Bakhtin accordingly described the task of social scientists as

the transcription of a special kind of dialogue: the complex interrelations between the *text* (the object of study and reflection) and the created, framing *context* (questioning, refuting, and so forth) in which the scholar's cognizing and evaluating thought takes place. This is the meeting of two texts – of the readymade and the reactive text being created – and, consequently, the meeting of two subjects and two authors. (1986: 106–107)

For archaeological authors, perhaps the most crucial implication of Bakhtin's arguments is his insistence that we cannot simply place ourselves in the position of the other. He characterises attempts to do this as transforming other subjects into mere mirrors for our self, 'pretender-doubles' or 'soul-slaves'. Because he is concerned with precisely the tension between the work authors do and the degree to which they can, in that work, absorb other subjects, Bakhtin's approach provides a useful way to evaluate archaeological narratives according to new criteria grounded in concern for representational responsibility, the central concern expressed by historical archaeologists otherwise sympathetic to experiments with narrative (K. Lewis 2000: 8; Little 2000: 11; Majewski 2000: 19; L. McKee and Galle 2000).

Historical archaeologists routinely employ texts contemporary with the sites they study as a significant body of evidence, juxtaposed with other materials (Wilkie this volume). Sometimes these texts even record statements attributed to speakers known to have been present when other materials were created, used, or discarded. The texts that historical archaeologists create often incorporate such historical voices. In this respect they conform closely to literary texts in which 'indirect speech' – statements attributed to speakers by the writer citing them – introduces heteroglossia into the text (Bakhtin 1981: 428). Heteroglossia can be intentionally employed in texts to convey nuances of meaning through the way things are said, not just what is said (Bakhtin 1981: 288–296). Heteroglossia is an 'internal stratification' of language specific to a particular place and time, the presence of multiple social dialects, characteristic group behaviour, professional jargons, generic languages, languages of generations and age groups, tendentious languages, languages of the authorities, of various circles and of passing fashions, languages that serve the specific socio-political purposes of the day, even of the hour. (Bakhtin 1981: 262–263)

To represent another time and place in a responsible way, a writer needs to introduce into his or her texts the heteroglossia, the stratified language, of that time and place.

In experimental writing in historical archaeology, the use of contemporary documents as models addresses this requirement. Acknowledging that he could not imagine spoken dialogue for seventeenth-century Virginia, historical archaeologist Daniel Mouer wrote an experimental narrative in the form of a document because of the existing models of petitions and court papers whose 'language is conventional, somewhat formal, and immediately familiar to any who have spent much time reading papers of the period' (Mouer 1998: 12). Mary Beaudry (1998: 27) constructed a completely convincing blend of real and imagined journal entries, basing the voice of one male character on a preserved letter, and those of women on contemporary diarists.

While these are self-consciously innovative texts, they develop out of traditional approaches in historical archaeology, in which indirect cited speech drawn from texts and oral histories forms a counterpoint for the voice of the modern archaeologist. Rebecca Yamin's (2002) discussion of the historical archaeology of children's toys in Paterson, New Jersey and New York's Five Points neighbourhood provides a good example of what it means to introduce the stratified languages of a time and place into a text not conceived or presented as an experiment in writing. She opens with a passage from a novel, originally published in 1914, that describes working-class parents providing toys for their children for Christmas. This quotation instantly places us in a different time and place through the use of language, with the toys specifically named – locomotive engines, Japanese dolls, tea service, drawing slate, and rag dolls – both materially and linguistically of another time. The language used by the author of this novel, which includes quoted speech from his working-class protagonists, is distinct from the words later used by the archaeologist to describe the toys in the archaeological assemblages: from 'frozen charlotte' dolls to miniature tea sets described, following archaeological classifications, as hand-painted or moulded porcelain, gilded, and spatter-painted whiteware. Terms like these are, as Barbara Little (2000: 11) reminds us, necessary jargon that

allows archaeologists to 'avoid spending their whole lives explaining single
complex things to each other'.

Yamin's text mixes these technical terms with other languages drawn
from fiction and contemporary journalism to create a text in which the past
subjects are polyphonically present through heteroglossia. The distancing
effect of the specialist language used in describing the 'material culture
of working-class play' (Yamin 2002: 114) opens up a space reminding the
modern reader of the difference between her (and the archaeologist author
whose perspective she is invited to share) and the represented parents of that
former time. As Yamin notes in her descriptions of the two sites, children in
these neighbourhoods were workers in factories or trades. She cites the words
of parents of working children in Paterson in the 1830s, who complained
that the hours of work made it impossible 'for poor children who had to
work in the mills, with barely time to sleep, and hardly time to eat a meal's
victuals in peace [to] get educated' (Yamin 2002: 115). She juxtaposes these
to the claims of middle-class critics of the nineteenth-century working poor
who 'accused workers of "compelling their children to go to the mills"',
introducing a diversity of class-based languages dealing with the challenges
which these children faced.

Yamin also demonstrates how in archaeological texts objects create other
dialogues and add to the mix of stratified languages. She describes children's
cups, inscribed with names or moral messages, recovered from the Five
Points neighbourhood (Yamin 2002: 121). She notes that when these are
part of middle-class assemblages, they are interpreted as instructions in the
importance of respecting private property. Yamin suggests that 'at Five Points
they may simply have been a parent's attempt to provide a child with an
item that was specially theirs'. But she goes on to cite the interpretation by
another archaeologist of similar objects in a working-class neighbourhood
in Sydney as possibly

evidence of mothers' efforts to educate their children in ways that countered the
claims of men like the City Health Officer 'who blamed women in particular
for poor domestic conditions, flatly declaring they were "dirty mothers" with no
parenting skills or notions about hygiene' (Yamin 2002: 121)

This is a remarkable sentence, from the perspective of the stratification of
language it achieves. Yamin does not clearly claim this position as her own;
instead, she introduces the opinion of Australian historical archaeologist
Grace Karskens in dialogue with her own statement, both in turn engaging
with the dominant interpretation of these objects in middle-class contexts.
By choosing to cite Karskens citing an anonymous city health officer, Yamin

represents the language of authority in working-class Sydney in the nineteenth century; the implied response by working-class women at that time and place; an implied response by contemporary working-class women in Five Points to unvoiced, implicit critiques of the same kind by unnamed city officials; and the indirectly cited middle-class women of the same time. These languages of represented subjects are revoiced by a variety of modern archaeologists who engage through these selective citations in distinct dialogues with the simple material remains, objects which also represent the presence, if not the voices, of nineteenth-century children.

Immediately following these passages Yamin presents an analysis of marbles recovered from the two sites, in comparison with a third site in Brooklyn where the residents were middle class. The comparative presentation uses the common archaeological visual trope of frequency bar graphs, something that can only be seen as a visual form of professional jargon, based on conventions that are quite opaque to those outside our discipline. This conventional scientific presentation is followed by a description of the game(s) of marbles that culminates in an extraordinary introduction of polyphony when the writer abandons the passive voice ('any outdoor hard or semi hard surface was suitable for play') for an engaging passage in third person narrative:

Marbles, like cards, is an internally interesting game, and although it is a game of skill, there is also an element of luck. *Sometimes you win and sometimes you don't.* Sometimes you're up (with a pocketful of marbles to click the way some men jangle change) and sometimes you're down. Importantly, you are expected to keep playing in marbles, to stay in the game long enough to give your opponents a chance to win back what they have lost. The excitement of winning and the disappointment of losing are shared experience – players can feel each other's ups and downs (Robin Stevens, personal communication). There is a sense of commonality and solidarity in the game just as there was in the tenements where everyone's troubles, as well as their triumphs, were visible to everyone else, and there was an ebb and flow of good times and bad. (Yamin 2002: 122–123, emphasis added)

The insistent use of the word 'you' here, implicating the reader as participant, injects into the text a totally unexpected conversational quality that, added to the previous speakers so carefully introduced, populates the text with the multiplicity of voices that Bakhtin called polyphony. The citation in the midst of this stream of direct address of a personal communication reinforces the sense that here we are dealing with indirect cited speech, a conversation which we are invited to overhear. The switch in address comes abruptly in the second sentence (italicised above), from the passive 'there is also an element of luck'. We move from outsider to insider, from observer to player. The personal communication marks a shift back, as the passive voice ('there is a sense of commonality and solidarity') reintroduces the observer's perspective – now not solely observing a game which transcends the temporal context of the working-class children and the modern archaeologist, but directly engaging in description of the nineteenth-century scene 'in the tenements'.

Yamin's article may be an unusually rich example of the ways in which historical archaeologists create polyphony, and also includes carefully selected visual images that create further dialogues whose analysis is outside the scope of this paper. It is the product of an accomplished writer who has discussed her own self-conscious understanding of the way narrative works: 'the telling of a story is more than a style of presentation; it becomes a way of knowing. By having to order facts in a plot . . . the historian comes to understand' (Yamin 1998a: 84). But there are many other examples of the routine introduction of a plurality of languages resulting in the rich polyphony typical of historical archaeology.

An otherwise routine discussion of a colonial gun from Uganda provides an example. The authors propose early on that 'a physical examination of the artefact itself and an extensive search of the relevant documentary sources suggest that *there is a remarkable story attached to it*' (Connah and Pearson 2002: 59, emphasis added). The stories that archaeologists tell about things, of course, are not literally tied to these objects; but for historical archaeologists, there routinely are already existing narratives, published and unpublished texts and oral histories about the specific or generic things under study. Graham Connah and David Pearson (2002: 64) connect the specific gun to a general documentary history but also to 'its own individual history which resulted in its survival in Uganda'. They write that

the story of the Kampala gun provides an interesting example of the interplay of documentary and physical evidence. Written sources alone give only a patchy account of its historical significance but, when these are combined with an examination of the weapon itself, its context within both the technological history of gun manufacture and the history of European colonialism in East Africa becomes apparent. (Connah and Pearson 2002: 67, emphasis added)

The narrative that these authors present is repeatedly characterised as a story, constructed by the juxtaposition of voices captured in text and recorded by the modern authors. Even in this article, which is clearly not offered as an experiment, polyphony is consciously introduced:

while one of the writers (GC) was examining it, he was approached by two schoolboy visitors to the Museum who wanted to know what this (at that time) unlabelled object was and why it was worth looking at. When its technological and historical significance was explained to them, they were surprised and interested: clearly they regarded this object as belonging to their history as well as to that of the British who had manufactured and used it. (Connah and Pearson 2002: 67–68)

This is an extraordinarily interesting narrative move. The opinions of the authors, their acknowledged motivation for writing the article, are put in the mouths of other speakers (members of a descendant community) who are represented as in dialogue with the archaeologist author. The dialogues imagined in fact extend far further, and the final sentence of the article suggested that 'artifacts like the Kampala gun have a story to tell, a story in which both colonizers and colonized came to understand both themselves and each other better than formerly' (Connah and Pearson 2002: 67).

TELLING STORIES IN HISTORICAL ARCHAEOLOGY

These more or less conventional articles, already polyphonic and dialogic, form the background for a substantial body of more self-conscious experiments in narrative form. This kind of experimentation has a far longer tradition in historical archaeology than in archaeology in general: indeed an article published in 1971 exhibited many of the characteristics of more recent work, including employing direct address to the reader:

Here is an interpretation of what was found in the ruins of a slave cabin . . . Our presentation includes a soundtrack and pictures. The soundtrack is composed from eye-witness accounts, slave narratives, and other sources. *You are encouraged to sound out the words*; the soundtrack selections are based on their auditory value and on their connection with the archaeological findings . . . You are invited to reassemble the components to best suit yourself. (Ascher and Fairbanks 1971: 3–4, my emphasis)

The 'soundtracks' are first-person quotations from documents and published works juxtaposed with first-person (plural) statements by the authors like 'We think that some of the people just named lived in the excavated cabin' (Ascher and Fairbanks 1971: 5). Like Connah and Pearson, Yamin, and others discussed here, Ascher and Fairbanks understood there to be stories embedded in the archaeological site itself: 'an outline history of the cabin . . . told in its stratigraphy and soils' (Ascher and Fairbanks 1971: 6). By choosing narrative labels drawn from the lived experience of the people who inhabited this cabin, rather than taxonomies, discussion of excavated materials 'for holding liquids', 'for holding food' and 'for preparing food', while still intelligible to an archaeologist, is also accessible to other readers and arguably closer to the experience of the people whose lives this script represents (Ascher and Fairbanks 1971: 9–10).

More recent attention to alternative forms of narrative was sparked by a series of sessions at the annual meetings of the Society for Historical Archaeology, beginning in 1996. The published papers from the first such session actually exemplify a variety of experiments, most of them less stories or 'interpretive historical fiction' (Gibb 2000) that present the narrative structure beginning–middle–end, than 'vignettes' (Yamin 1998a), often constructed as dialogues (A. Praetzellis and M. Praetzellis 1998), journals, letters or other documents (Beaudry 1998; Mouer 1998), or oral histories (Cook 1998a; Costello 1998; Ryder 1998). Lu Ann De Cunzo (1998) has described this process as proceeding from the formulation of narratives to the construction of stories that were suggested by the incongruities between received histories and the materials present at the archaeological sites she was attempting to understand. These diverse ways of introducing an explicit narrative voice into the technical literature require a more complex framework than the simple dichotomy story (or narrative)/technical report.

As Mark Pluciennik (1999: 667) notes, the majority of archaeological narratives employ 'a characteristic narrative chronological position and tense – that of hindsight offered as a sequential story of, rather than in, the past'. This characteristic representation of a unified temporal stream in which the writer stands looking back and picking out the sequence of events that caused the final creation of the archaeological site is what Bakhtin (1986) called a chronotope, a 'form-shaping ideology' that underlies differences in genre. Form shaping, because it determines the tense adopted, allows for and even demands certain kinds of rhetoric and rules out other rhetorical tropes: the archaeologist in this relation to his or her subjects cannot directly address them or be addressed by them, for example. Ideological, because the construction of causal arguments always foregrounds certain kinds of causation, proposing that certain relations and actions were ultimately important, while others were ephemeral or inconsequential.

Some experiments use chronotopes that are well-established literary forms. Beaudry's (1998) narrative, mixing fictive and actual journal entries, mirrors one of Bakhtin's classic examples of chronotopes, the epistolary novel, in which the inclusion of letters addressed to another character within the story allows narrative in direct address to stand in for the reader, otherwise impossible without changing the relative position in time of subject, writer, and reader. In a particularly rich example, interruptions in the delivery of a conventional academic paper at the annual meeting of the Society for Historical Archaeology by a nineteenth-century merchant and lawyer Josiah Gallup were imagined by Adrian and Mary Praetzellis, placing the archaeologists in direct dialogue with the subject about whom they are writing (A. Praetzellis and M. Praetzellis 1998).

This kind of dialogue troubles the sequence (story/narrating/narrative) and substitutes for it an equation (narrating=narrative=story); all three happening at once, not in a past at which we gaze with perfect vision, but in a present in which our grasp of things is open to contestation.

In other experimental writing in historical archaeology, time–space relations are reformulated as a kind of 'heterotopia' – a place where multiple places are juxtaposed (Foucault 1986b). Thus Mary and Adrian Praetzellis invoke the Los Vaqueros Reservoir as a place where multiple timeframes are present simultaneously, not arranged in a causal narrative:

in the absence of people, what gives time depth to a landscape such as this? In the absence of people, might all time overlap and have existence simultaneously? (M. Praetzellis and A. Praetzellis 1998: 55)

Such place-based non-causal narratives, often in the form of what Rebecca Yamin (1998a) calls 'vignettes', communicate a sense of the fragmentary nature of archaeological understanding while representing the density of detail available for individual intervals of time. Like writers of fiction, archaeologists who succeed in constructing such compelling narratives draw on small details to show, rather than tell (following Gass 1970: 55–76), to let an object condense meaning: 'the key to good stories, as to good scholarship, is details – an object, an action, a thought, a look' (De Cunzo 1998: 43).

Many of the features of contemporary writing in historical archaeological discussed above are evident in Laurie Wilkie's *The Archaeology of Mothering: An African-American Midwife's Tale* (2003). The book presents narratives of multiple kinds, including direct address by the author to contemporary readers including other specialists in the field: 'Let us have a brief word about the context and materials of the two archaeological deposits associated with the Perrymans' (Wilkie 2003: 89). The conversational tone counterbalances presentation, using standardised vocabulary, conventional graphic representations, and numerical tables, summarising the contents of two features whose rich contextualisation occupies the book. There are many performatives of trust: '[I know that] the probable production of home remedies by Perryman is also supported by the large number of knapped glass scrapers recovered from the well' (Wilkie 2003: 127). But the abundant instances of narrative direct address make clear that it is the author–narrator whose interpretations we are asked to accept.

Like other historical–archaeological writing, this book uses extensive quotations from published works contemporary with the occupation of the site, as well as quotations from later oral histories. These introduce heteroglossia and create polyphony. Especially effective are the juxtapositions throughout the text of official discourses on mothering with the words of former midwives, as in divergent views on feeding infants. A medical doctor wrote that 'the successful combating of infant mortality can only be brought about by the education of the mothers in the essential facts of the science of the nourishment of the infant' (Wilkie 2003: 190). His endorsement of breastfeeding in the language of science was a far cry from that of a midwife, exclaiming 'mother's milk is always better for a baby! And then it makes you closer to your baby when you nurse your baby' (Wilkie 2003: 195). Through the citation of a wide variety of voices – of midwives, doctors, leaders of the African-American middle class, and other commentators on the contemporary scene – Wilkie introduces a variety of understandings of the objects recovered from the site of Lucrecia Perryman's home (cf. Wilkie this volume). Provided with two limited windows into the occupation of the site, she fleshes out each to give a sense of lived experience at these two points in time without providing an artificial coherence to the story she can tell.

To these stories Wilkie adds an additional layer of imagined narratives that take the book beyond the limits inherent in the archaeological data, providing readers with a way of connecting the archaeologist to the text. In a series of 'narrative interludes' she provides dialogues through a proxy for herself, Hazel Neumann, who is placed as an interviewer gathering exslave narratives for the Work Projects Administration (WPA). Like Beaudry (1998), Wilkie imagines extensions to an existing genre of text that does not quite cover all the topics she would like to know about. By using the real WPA narratives as a warrant for the voices she presents, she is able to give a convincing sense of other characters that in turn reflects on her imagination of Lucrecia Perryman. Attentive to the problematic issues involved in putting imagined words in the mouth of a real person, she does not include in the subjects of these ex-slave narratives her real historical persons, but instead creates people like them.

Responding to concerns about reflexivity, Wilkie uses letters written by Hazel Neumann to her husband to embed reflexivity in the text. Her alter ego is provided with the situated perspective of a pregnant woman, whose interest in what her interview subjects have to say about mothering grows because of her own biographical situation. These narratives position the reader with the archaeologist and the interviewer, outside the lived experience of the interview subjects and the people who created the archaeological deposits, but connected to them by a particular orientation that guides the understanding of the materials in the archaeological features. By positioning this alter ego after the fact – interviewing subjects about their past – Wilkie creates a sense of multiple timeframes that are joined to each other only by retrospective narration. This may well be a third viable chronotope for new writing, one in which the archaeologist looks back not with hindsight creating a causal narrative, but in the fragments of personal recollection that might be sparked by the kinds of objects that survive to be recovered by an archaeologist.

WRITING AND TRUTH

Such experiments in writing historical archaeology are, I would suggest, not that far removed from more commonly accepted archaeological ways of writing. Even apparently neutral technical writing is narrative in form, embodied in a particular rhetoric that appeals to the scientific community for validation. Imagined narratives with clearly identified narrators can more clearly situate the writer and introduce the polyphony of actual lived experience. As Hayden White noted,

the nonnarrative manner of speaking common to the physical sciences seems more appropriate for the representation of 'real' events. But here the notion of what constitutes a real event turns, not on the distinction between true and false . . . But rather on the distinction between real and imaginary . . . How else can any past, which by definition comprises events, processes, structures, and so forth, considered to be no longer perceivable, be represented in either consciousness or discourse except in an 'imaginary' way? Is it not possible that the question of narrative in any discussion of historical theory is always finally about the function of imagination in the production of a specifically human truth? (1987: 45)

In historical archaeology, the juxtaposition of text and material remains entails juxtapositions of real things and utterances with imagined ones. Whether this is understood and acknowledged in the written product of scholarship, all such texts are based in imagination, and simultaneously in real, material facts. The assemblage of these real and imagined facts takes place in the present, but the relationship constructed to the past is by no means automatic. By actively managing the way in which specific representations of the temporal and spatial relations of story, narrating, and narrative are connected, writers broaden the scope of interpretation and representation, and denaturalise the taken-for-granted stories of historical archaeology.

PART II

Key themes in historical archaeology

CHAPTER 5

Historical archaeology and colonialism

Susan Lawrence and Nick Shepherd

Colonisation involves the expansion of one state or polity into the territory of another and the establishment of settlements subject to that parent state. Expansion may be accomplished by conquest or by trade, and includes political, economic, social, cultural and psychological dimensions. Colonialism is the process by which new societies emerge in both the new territories and the core because of colonisation, and the new systems of relationships that result. Colonial sites might be defined culturally as those occupied during the first generation or two of colonisation, or politically as any from the period that precedes independence from the homeland. Colonialism appears as a complex, layered process, whose implications extend to the writing and practice of history and archaeology, and our understanding of the past. As the South African anti-apartheid activist and writer Steve Biko commented: 'the colonists were not satisfied merely with holding a people in their grip and emptying the Native's brain of all form and content, they turned to the past of the oppressed people and distorted, disfigured and destroyed it' (Biko and Stubbs 1978: 29). The notion of postcolonialism is a contested term, which describes a surprisingly wide range of subject positions, professional fields and critical enterprises (Slemon 1995). In one usage it refers simply to the period since independence. A potentially more productive usage is to understand it as being primarily an oppositional term, used to describe a set of anti-colonial projects and ideas. In some cases these may be coeval with colonialism itself. Neocolonialism refers to economic and other ties that outlive formal political independence, and serve to perpetuate colonial forms and relations (Hewitt 2002).

Colonialism and postcolonialism are characteristics of the modern world, but the process has deep historical roots and has been of interest to archaeologists for some time. The major state-based societies in the ancient world, such as the Romans, Greeks, and Mayas, incorporated colonialism of some form (Gosden 2004; Lyons and Papadopoulos 2002). Processes of colonisation may explain patterns of social, economic, and political development in early agricultural societies (Frankel 2000; Frankel and Webb 1998), while the archaeological literature on empires, the state systems that drive colonialism, is substantial (S. Alcock et al. 2001; Sinopoli 1994, 1995).

Historical archaeology has a particular relationship with colonialism that consists of two principal strands. The first lies at the heart of how historical archaeology has conceptualised itself. Based on the North American origins and subject matter that dominated historical archaeology for the second half of the twentieth century, James Deetz defined the field as 'the archaeology of the spread of European cultures throughout the world since the fifteenth century, and their impact on and interaction with the cultures of indigenous peoples' (Deetz 1977: 5). While this understanding has been challenged more recently by scholars from outside North America (e.g. Courtney 1999; Funari et al. 1999; Tarlow and West 1999), who point to its exclusion of both other historical periods and the archaeology of those who remained in Europe during this period, it continues to have considerable influence. Significantly, this definition places the emphasis on European expansion, and by extension, the colonisation of the non-European world and the development of colonies. As Courtney (1999) has noted, other disciplines that have embraced postcolonial studies have found significant influence of colonial expansion upon Europe. Historical archaeology is likewise in a position to profit from returning the colonial gaze to the metropole.

Historical archaeologists from the beginning have been interested in sites associated with early colonial settlement, be they forts, trading posts, missions, farms, villages, or cities. However, the main subject of these studies has generally been the European colonists, with interest in indigenous peoples and the slaves forced to migrate against their will being of secondary consideration. Most studies have been of settlements where Europeans were present, and until recently there has been little interest in contemporaneous sites occupied exclusively by indigenous or enslaved peoples.

The eurocentric perspective of much of historical archaeology is linked to the second principal strand in the relationship between historical archaeology and colonialism. The archaeological study of European colonies and the societies that resulted can be understood more generally as bound up with the colonisation process itself. Until quite recently most archaeologists, including historical archaeologists, have been the descendants of settler groups in the once-colonised territories. They have been employed in institutions that were established by colonial governments and their successors, under a particular regime of knowledge production. Excavation of indigenous and slave sites associated with colonial settlement was largely carried out without the involvement of or consultation with descendant communities, that is, those claiming genetic or cultural affiliation with the occupants of the sites. It has been argued persuasively (McDavid and Babson 1997; Potter 1991) that this constitutes a further extension of European hegemony over these groups.

Historical archaeologists have become increasingly aware of this second aspect of their discipline, and have belatedly begun to engage much more closely with members of indigenous and descendant communities. In part this has been a result of activism and organisation on the part of groups affected by archaeological activities, and in part because of developments within the discipline itself. Organisations like the World Archaeological Congress (WAC) have played an important advocacy role. The subdisciplines of Indigenous Archaeology and community archaeology have made an impact as they seek to contest prevailing power/knowledge relations. Significant aspects of archaeological work are now guided by protocols such as the Vermillion Accord and the WAC First Code of Ethics (World Archaeological Congress 1989, 1991).

Colonial sites provide the basis for exploring a number of themes of significance in archaeology. Indeed, the availability of written documents, images, maps and oral history means that historical archaeology is ideally situated to shed light on archaeological approaches to colonialism more broadly. Historical archaeologists interested in colonial sites are using all of these resources to provide insight on questions of power, status, domination, resistance, ethnicity and gender. Issues of identity in the past and in the present are also intimately associated with the study of colonialism and colonial sites. Historical archaeologists are also well placed to study the international reach of colonial systems and to compare sites in different parts of the world. Indeed, archaeologist Chris Gosden (2004: 3) has suggested that colonialism is best understood as a material phenomenon, wherein the power lies in new sets of material culture and practices associated with a symbolic centre. Historical archaeology provides the opportunity to test such assertions, and has much to contribute to the study of the archaeology of colonialism in any period of human history.

THEMES IN THE HISTORICAL ARCHAEOLOGY OF COLONIALISM

One of the earliest themes to emerge in the study of colonial sites was that of acculturation and adaptation, as new arrivals from Europe imported and altered their familiar ways of doing things while they learned about the New World. Many archaeologists have sought to delineate the nature of colonial experiences at different places and times. Exemplifying such research is James Deetz's (1977) study of New England colonists, which revealed some of the fundamental changes to culture and worldview that are part of colonialism. Deetz argued that numerous classes of material culture, including food, tableware, houses and headstones shared a similar underlying 'grammar', and that this grammar changed over time as the first English colonists became Americans. According to Deetz's scheme, the world of the seventeenth-century settlers was organised according to a traditional, late medieval worldview that was organic and communal. Meals consisted of single dishes that combined several meat and vegetable elements. They were shared from a few central vessels with a minimum of individual implements. Houses contained few rooms, which were multi-purpose and provided for little personal privacy. Headstones, which reflected views of death and the afterlife, emphasised warnings to the community of the living. By the eighteenth century, several generations of people had been born and died in the American colonies, and the Enlightenment was also having an effect. Meals became segmented and were served on individual place settings. Houses became externally balanced and symmetrical, and internally were divided into a series of single-purpose, private spaces. Spirituality as reflected in headstones emphasised individual salvation rather than a community of souls. Deetz identified this latter system as the 'Georgian World View', and it quickly became widespread as a way of describing colonial America.

Other archaeologists have studied the effect of colonisation on foodways and on industry. Charles Cheek (1999), for example, has used a combination of sources including faunal remains, ceramics and cookbooks to compare the regional cooking traditions of New England and the Chesapeake in North America. He argues that the preference in New England for baking, especially pies, and in the Chesapeake for puddings is a direct result of the origins and traditional backgrounds of the English migrants who settled the two regions. The New England settlers were mainly from eastern England, where baking was most common. In contrast, the Chesapeake settlers were mainly from the south and west of England where frying was more usual. This study highlights the significance of regional variation in both the Old and New Worlds, and the problems associated with assuming a monolithic culture in either place.

Industry similarly underwent a process of experimentation and change as people attempted to implement familiar processes in new environments. Warwick Pearson's (1996) study of water-powered flour mills in Australia illustrates some of the difficulties faced by the nineteenth-century British migrants there. For centuries British flour mills had exploited the abundant natural waterways as a power source, and British migrants brought this technology with them to Australia. However, Australia is a much drier continent and many of its waterways are dry for part of the year, or have a substantial seasonal variation in flow. As a result, the traditional water-powered mills that were initially built failed and new technology was called for. The colonists quickly turned to steam, and the Australian landscape is littered with the remains of abandoned water-powered mills.

Along with adaptation, one of the markers of settler societies that has been explored by historical archaeologists is the range of ethnic groups represented, and the emergence of new forms of interaction. Colonialism is not simply a matter for the colonists and the colonised: it precipitates the creation of whole new groups and social categories, including the off-spring of unions between settlers and indigenous people, and also the slaves and indentured labourers for whom migration was less than voluntary. The notion of 'creolisation' – the creation of new identities in colonial situations – has been used by historical archaeologists, especially in the island Caribbean and the Spanish colonies in the New World. The work of Kathleen Deagan and her colleagues at St Augustine, Florida (Deagan 1983, 1985, 1996) has been particularly influential. St Augustine was settled by the Spanish in 1565 as a military garrison and mission, and has been contin-uously inhabited ever since. Deagan began with the premise that it was a 'Creole' community, not just a Spanish one. It included both Spanish-born and Spanish-American people, as well as large groups of Guale Indians, African and African-American people, and mestizo, or mixed-blood people of Spanish, Guale, and African heritage. Individual life experience in this already complex society was further mediated by the factors of gender and social status. The archaeological record is a rich testimony to how this diver-sity was negotiated on a day-to-day basis in the food, furnishings, dress and architecture of households within St Augustine at different times.

Other historical archaeologists have focused explicitly on the experience of colonisation from the perspective of the colonised, especially through the local consumption of European mass-produced material culture. Indigenous colonial sites include those associated with the fur trade in North America, with religious missions, war and conflict, and traditional indigenous settle-ments or camps occupied during the colonial period. Archaeologist David Burley (Burley 1989) has studied Metis wintering camps, temporary, sea-sonal villages established annually, and particularly the social and symbolic dimensions of the ceramic teawares recovered there. The Metis of western Canada are the descendants of native peoples and French, English, and Scottish fur traders. By the middle of the nineteenth century many Metis

lived as communal and migratory bison hunters who travelled and worked
in family groups. Fragile and distinctive European ceramic teawares initially appeared out-of-place in an otherwise austere and limited archaeological record. Burley has argued that the teawares had a symbolic rather
than strictly functional role, and that the drinking of tea was a central part
of Metis social interaction. Among an intensely social people, the shared
activity of taking tea was a key component of integration and information exchange. Its significance was such that it warranted the use of fragile
ceramics even by impoverished and migratory bison hunters.

Oral history and oral traditions within contemporary indigenous communities can be a potent way of gaining further insight into archaeological
sites and what took place there. Janet Spector (1993) worked closely with
the descendants of the Wahpeton Dakota who had occupied the site of
Little Rapids, Minnesota in the 1830s and 1840s. One result of her interviews, archival research and excavation, was to highlight the role of gender
in structuring the lives of those at the site, and the resulting archaeological
record. Little Rapids was a traditional Dakota settlement occupied over the
summer months. Prominent in the archaeological record were the tools and
items associated with women's hide-processing activities. Spector was able
to decode the social and symbolic meaning of these otherwise functional
objects during the course of her research, and to track the ways in which
European trade goods were integrated into Dakota lifeways and belief systems. The image she presents is far more dynamic and active than what
has sometimes been suggested by the more typical archaeological practice
of statically listing and enumerating 'native' objects versus 'trade' objects.

A distinguishing feature of colonialism is the presence of unequal power
relationships, and historical archaeologists have often emphasised these in
their studies of colonialism. The material record is particularly able to shed
light on those less able to exercise overt power, and investigating agency
among the dispossessed has been a prominent theme in the archaeology of
colonialism. Studies of domination and resistance have examined both the
efforts of the elite to exert power, as in the case of Mark Leone's (1996 [1984])
study of William Paca's garden in eighteenth-century Annapolis, Maryland,
and the power of 'subaltern' individuals and classes to resist. Leland Ferguson's (1991) study of African-American foodways in colonial South Carolina
demonstrates the persistence of African traditions of preparing and eating
food, even under the severe constraints of plantation slavery. Ferguson argues
that because the African-American slaves provided much of their own food
and supplies, they were able to create for themselves an African material
world of locally made folk pottery, carved wooden bowls, gourds, baskets,

and cuisine. This strengthened their identities as Africans, and constituted a significant form of non-violent resistance to the slave-owners' moves to dehumanise them.

In a South African context, Martin Hall and Carmel Schrire have both been concerned with examining the material imprint of first Dutch, and later British, colonialism at the Cape. Hall has used James Scott's (1985) notion of public and hidden transcripts to argue for evidence of slave resistance (Hall 2000). Schrire's important book, *Digging Through Darkness; Chronicles of an Archaeologist* (Schrire 1995) combines autobiography and fiction with archaeological analysis to paint a picture of life at the Dutch military outpost of Oudepost on the Cape west coast.

Insights gained from examples in the modern world have proven useful models in the archaeology of colonialism. The selectivity with which new goods were adopted, the ability of subaltern groups to resist domination and to continue to follow traditional ways of life, and the ways in which settler society adapted and changed all suggest alternative ways of viewing the archaeological record of Roman colonisation in Britain (Hingley 1999, 2000). New lessons from the recent colonial past are also being learnt as non-archaeologists and descendant communities begin to take a greater interest in how colonial sites are studied.

To illustrate the distinctive contribution of historical archaeology to the study of colonialism during the past 500 years, we provide two case studies: from York Town, Australia and from Cape Town, South Africa, below.

YORK TOWN, AUSTRALIA

One of the ways in which European colonisation operated was through the spread of its institutions. While some colonies were conceived as independent, private affairs outside the ambit of political intervention, such as New England's Plymouth colony, others were overtly political from the start. Spanish, French, Dutch, Russian and Portuguese colonies all existed to further the interests of their respective governments, as did many British colonies. Military and religious institutions were critical to this success. The Spanish presence in North America was characterised by Catholic missions supported by garrisons of soldiers (Deagan 2003; D. Thomas 1990). The Cape colony at the tip of Africa functioned according to the administrative bureaucracy of the Dutch East India Company or VOC (Markell et al. 1995; Schrire 1995), while Australia began as a penal colony dependent for survival on the convict system (Connah 1994). One study of the latter illustrates the ways in which historical archaeologists can examine how bureaucratic intentions shaped colonial experience, and the global dimension of colonialism in the modern world.

York Town was established in 1804, the second British settlement in Van Diemen's Land (Tasmania). Both it and Hobart, established the previous year, were outposts of the settlement at Sydney, the main British colony in Australia, established in 1788. Like Sydney, York Town and Hobart were penal settlements and comprised convicts and the soldiers detailed to guard them, with very few free settlers. York Town was inhabited for less than five years, and the majority of the population of around 300 people had relocated to the nearby site of Launceston by 1807 (Robson 1983). Although sold into private ownership, the land at York Town has not been substantially reoccupied, and considerable archaeological evidence of the settlement remains. It became the subject of archaeological investigation in 2003 when the local historical society and descendents of the first settlers initiated plans to establish an interpretive centre at the site (Sansom et al. 2004). The location of York Town and the architecture and layout of the settlement are all reflective of its role in a greater colonial plan, and of the government's increasing experience in administering penal colonies.

The significance of York Town in furthering imperial ambitions is demonstrated by its location, which is better suited to strategic agendas rather than agendas of settlement. York Town is situated at the head of the western arm of the Tamar River, the major river draining northern Tasmania. The Tamar is a broad, winding, tidal river, much of which becomes mudflats at low tide. Although York Town was located on high ground between two creeks, fresh water is not abundant and the soil is poor and rocky. Neither grazing nor the growing of crops was particularly successful, which led to the ultimate abandonment of the site and the relocation to Launceston at the head of the Tamar. Significantly, it was known from previous exploration in the Tamar that the area around Launceston was both well watered and had excellent grazing land (MacKnight 1998). Settling at York Town was thus not an unfortunate mistake but a calculated decision, and one that makes plain that the establishment of a self-sufficient farming colony was not the first or only objective of the settlement. Indeed, Lt Governor William Paterson, in charge of the settlement, was well aware of the multiple roles his party was expected to fulfil. Certainly, self-sufficiency was desirable: in 1805 a herd of cattle from Bengal was imported at great expense to the government, and six months later the colonists nearly starved when a shipment of stores was hijacked. However, the colonists were convicts, not free settlers with farming skills and the desire to colonise, and the settlement was intended as a place of punishment rather than prosperity. The primary reason for establishing a new colony on the north coast of Tasmania was strategic, and part of the British government's overall design for imperial power in the Pacific.

Until the 1790s, Tasmania was thought to be attached to mainland Australia. As far as the British were concerned, the colony at Sydney thus secured sovereignty over the entire east coast of the continent. In 1797–1798 a voyage to chart the coast of Australia confirmed that Tasmania was a distinct land mass, separated from the mainland by what became known as the Bass Strait. This quickly became the preferred shipping route around the south of the continent because it cut valuable weeks off the voyage from Europe and the Cape of Good Hope. It also exposed a weakness in British territorial claims, something of which the governments in both Sydney and London were acutely conscious. The French had already been exploring Australia's west and south coasts in the early 1790s, and in 1801 they returned. Although both expeditions were ostensibly scientific, Britain and France were at war at this time, and the French presence around Australia made the British uneasy and suspicious. In addition, the Spanish, who claimed the Pacific as a result of the 1494 Treaty of Tordesillas, had also sent an expedition to the Australian coast in 1793 (Frost 2003: 235–242; A. Johnson 2003). The colonial administration in London moved quickly to counteract the perceived threat, and by 1804 new British colonies had been established in southern Tasmania at Hobart and in northern Tasmania at York Town.

Political aims were uppermost in Paterson's mind when he and his party arrived at the Tamar, and when he surveyed its reaches for a likely spot to settle (Historical Records of Australia 1921 *Vol. I:* xxxi; MacKnight 1998: 72–73, 102). The first landing place, Outer Cove, immediately inside the Heads, was judged inadequate because of lack of water. Launceston admirably met the requirements of settlement, but did not meet the strategic needs of the colony. It was 40 kilometres (about 25 miles) up river, much too far to maintain a vigil for the French and the Spanish, and the river itself was difficult to navigate with many shallow, shifting sandbanks. York Town then was the place of compromise: enough water and level ground for a settlement, but close enough to the open sea to mount an effective guard. The convict settlers simply had to cope as best they could.

The layout of the settlement they built has been reconstructed from documentary and archaeological sources (Sansom et al. 2004). It indicates that time-honoured understandings of rank and hierarchy were more important in structuring the settlement than were arbitrary, preconceived plans. The most important places were situated in the centre of the settlement, where Government House (Paterson's residence and the administrative centre), the flag pole and parade ground, the soldiers' barracks, and the guardhouse were all clustered together. This was also the highest ground in the settlement, ensuring that there could be effective surveillance of those of lesser rank. The huts housing married soldiers occupied the ground immediately next to and below the administrative precinct, while the convict huts were both most distant and on the lowest ground. Industrial activities were relegated to the margins of the settlement, where a brickfields and kiln, a saw pit, a mill, a public oven, gardens and a stockyard were established.

Status and rank determined access to space in the settlement. A small elite included Paterson and his second in command, Captain Anthony Fenn Kemp, as well as members of the small civil establishment such as Alexander Riley, the storekeeper and Joseph Mountgarrett, the surgeon. Kemp, Riley, and Mountgarrett all received grants of land on which to establish farms, and all lived in private houses on their land. They were also assigned convict servants, and Kemp and Riley were accompanied by their wives. This grant-ing of land to the upper ranks was common practice in British colonies, and one of the inducements to free settlement. Mountgarrett had already been granted land at Hobart, where he had previously been stationed, while Kemp and Riley had extensive land holdings around Sydney. More junior members of the military were also allowed plots for homes and gardens, and these formed the basis of the soldiers' camp. However, the plots were much smaller and were not considered freehold, nor were the soldiers given convict servants. Some of the convicts were also permitted plots on a similar basis, but in a different part of the settlement.

Gender and family formation also played a significant role in structuring space. Women were always a minority in the settlement (approximately 50 of the nearly 300 settlers in 1806), but they had an important advantage. Entitlement to a private dwelling, rather than a shared barracks, was a privilege essentially granted to women. While the 'ownership' of the huts went to men, they were generally restricted to men with families, so it was the woman who was the key player in acquiring additional private space. Almost all of the women at York Town, both free and convict, were married or in a common-law relationship, and thus permitted a private home. The soldiers' camp, mentioned above, was distinguished from the barracks not only by the individual houses but also by the presence of women and children. It was a neighbourhood of families. Likewise, in the convict camp families also had separate households, as they did in other convict settlements such as Sydney and Hobart, where for several decades convict families lived lives not easily distinguishable from their free counterparts (Karskens 1997, 1999).

Kinship also shaped the spaces occupied by the upper ranks. Elizabeth Kemp, whose husband Anthony was the second-highest officer at York Town, was the sister of Alexander Riley, the storekeeper. The Rileys' cottage, near the store, and the Kemps' cottage, near Government House, were on the same side of the settlement. In contrast, Surgeon Joseph Mountgarrett, who was single, lived at his farm on the far side of the settlement.

British territorial aspirations determined the location of the colony. British scientific aspirations helped shape some of the activity there. Paterson was a Fellow of the Royal Society in England and a regular correspondent with Sir Joseph Banks (Serle, 1949: 1804). He had trained in botany before joining the army and was sent to Africa as a botanical collector. He had also spent time in India, and while serving on Norfolk Island he compiled a list of the plant life there. Both Paterson and Banks saw his service in Australia as the ideal opportunity to 'advance natural history', and once in York Town Paterson set about doing just that. One of the first things he did was to establish an official Botanical Garden; he also collected local specimens of plants and animals for Banks and was the first to record the existence of the now-extinct Tasmanian tiger *Thylacinus cynocephalus*. Natural history also governed his approach to the Aboriginal Tasmanians around York Town. It has been estimated that between 100 and 200 people of the Port Dalrymple tribe lived on the western side of the Tamar at the time of British arrival (Ryan 1996: 30–32). Although there are few accounts of contact, in January 1805 Paterson wrote that 'the natives are still shy, but are constantly in the neighbourhood' (Historical Records of Australia 1921: 621). There were a few recorded incidents of violence where either settlers were speared or Aboriginal people were shot, but there must be much that was left unsaid, for a year after arrival Paterson was able to send to Banks 'a very perfect Native's Head' (Historical Records of Australia 1921: 643), amongst a collection of plant and animal specimens. For this Enlightenment scientist, indigenous people were worthy of attention as specimens to be observed and collected rather than as fellow human beings.

York Town and the people who lived there were typical of British colonisation of the period. After the loss of the American colonies, British imperial attention turned to building a new empire, and Asia and the Pacific were to play a major role. The Bass Strait sea route was a vital link between British possessions at the Cape of Good Hope, in India and Southeast Asia, and in Australia and the Pacific. York Town was strategically important and given every possible official stimulus to succeed. Notably, it was an official colony, staffed by government employees responding to government directives. Historical archaeology, by turning attention to the physical evidence of the settlement, is able to highlight the importance of that official dimension. Spatial analysis of the archaeological remains reveals the priority given to strategic rather than colonising aims. It also highlights the more personal and intimate influence of factors of rank, gender and kinship that ultimately mediated the individual experience of colonisation.

PRESTWICH STREET, CAPE TOWN, SOUTH AFRICA

Implicit in the account so far has been the potentially unstable nature of historical archaeology given its ambiguous relation to colonialism on the one hand, and on the other hand, to the descendants of groups of people who were themselves the objects of archaeological scrutiny and colonial collecting practices. Historical archaeology appears as both a field of knowledge production concerned with the objective record of colonial occupation, and as a form of social practice in contemporary society, deeply implicated in issues of heritage, memory and identity. A recent case study in Cape Town, South Africa, serves to highlight some of these tensions and instabilities.

Green Point is a suburb of Cape Town strategically located between the central business district and the new waterfront development at Cape Town's harbour. For much of the seventeenth and eighteenth centuries it lay outside the formal boundaries of the settlement, a marginal zone that was the site of the gallows and a place of torture (situated on a prominent sand dune). It was also the site of a number of graveyards, including the graveyards of the Dutch Reformed Church and the military, and of numerous undocumented, informal burials. Those buried outside the official burial grounds would have made up a cross-section of the underclasses of colonial Cape Town: slaves, free blacks, artisans, fishermen, sailors, maids, washerwomen and their children, as well as executed criminals, suicide deaths, paupers and unidentified victims of shipwrecks (Hart 2003). In the 1820s Green Point was subdivided and sold as real estate, in time becoming part of the densely built urban core. In the late 1960s and early 1970s black and coloured residents of Green Point were forcibly removed, and relocated to the bleak townships of the Cape Flats, a series of events that have entered popular imagination via the fate of the residents of District Six on the other side of the city (Jeppie and Soudien 1990). Green Point is currently undergoing a process of rapid gentrification, driven by sky-rocketing property prices.

In mid-May 2003 in the course of construction activities at a city block in Green Point bordered by Prestwich Street, human bones were discovered. The developer notified the South African Heritage Resources Agency (SAHRA) in accordance with the newly passed National Heritage Resources

Act (Anon 1999), and construction was halted. Also in terms of the Act, the developer appointed the Archaeological Contracts Office (ACO), a University of Cape Town (UCT) affiliated contract archaeology unit, to do the archaeological investigation. The ACO applied for and was issued a permit by SAHRA for a 'rescue exhumation of human remains'. The Act provides for a 60-day notification period, and for a public consultation process. Antonia Malan, a historical archaeologist based at the University of Cape Town, was appointed to run the public consultation process, which she did in the name of the Cultural Sites and Resources Forum (CSRF), an advocacy organisation with a track record of involvement in heritage issues.

On 11 June 2003 exhumation of the bodies began. Seven weeks later, on 29 July, a public meeting was held at St Stephen's Church in central Cape Town. At this point the remains of approximately 500 individuals had been exhumed, at a density of approximately one body per square metre. The site was fenced with wire-link fencing and was open to public view. Estimates of the total number of bodies stood at 1200 (up from an initial estimate of 200). In the meantime, a Special Focus Reference Group (SFRG) had been set up, mainly of UCT-based archaeologists and human biologists. Taking total exhumation as a given, Malan and the SFRG framed the agenda for the public meeting in terms of consultations regarding the relocation of the bodies and the memorialisation of the site. Judith Sealy, an archaeologist in the SFRG, presented a proposal that envisaged reinterment of the bodies 'in individual caskets, in a crypt or mausoleum'. This would be a place where 'one could honour the dead' while allowing 'access to the skeletons for careful, respectful, scientific study by bona fide researchers' (Sealy 2003: 1).

The response was immediate, vociferous and angry. The minutes of the meeting record a 'general feeling of dissatisfaction, disquiet and disrespect'. Questions were asked as to why the demolition permit had been approved without the requirement of an archaeological survey, why the exhumations had continued through the 60-day notification period, and why the first public meeting had come so late in the process. Yvette Abrahams, a University of the Western Cape (UWC) based historian asked: 'Is this a public participation process or a rubber stamping exercise . . . How can [a] permit be given for the bodies to be dug up before I am consulted?' Opposition to the exhumations came from several quarters: community leaders, many of whom had been active in the struggle against apartheid; Christian and Muslim spiritual leaders; academics from the historically black UWC (UCT is an historically white institution); heritage-sector NGOs; and Khoisan representatives. The minutes also record comments by a number of unnamed individuals:

Woman at back: On what basis does SAHRA decide on exhumation? Issues of African morality and African rights . . .

Man in green shirt: Developer contacted SAHRA and did marketing strategy for this evening. I don't buy these ideas . . . Archaeologists can go elsewhere to dig . . .

Rob (Haven Shelter [a night shelter for homeless people]): Many questions come from black people who hang around the site. Why are white people, and white women, scratching in our bones? This is sacrilege . . .

Zenzile Khoisan, leaving hall: Stop robbing graves – stop robbing graves! (Malan 2003)

On 1 August SAHRA announced an 'interim cessation' of archaeological activity on the site until 18 August, to allow for a wider process of public consultation. This was later extended to 31 August. On 16 August the CSRF convened a second public meeting, as well as collecting submissions by telephone, email and fax. Between 25 and 29 August SAHRA convened a series of 'Special Focus Group' meetings with 'interested and affected groups'. At a meeting with the Cape Metropolitan Council it emerged that the delegation of powers between SAHRA and the City was in question, and that the City was 'acting illegally on some of [its] duties' (SAHRA 2003: 3). On 29 August SAHRA convened a third public meeting at St Andrew's Church in Green Point 'to wind up the public participation process' (Hands Off Committee 2003a). A feature of this period appears to have been a growing anxiety on the part of SAHRA over the cost of expropriation, and the possibility of legal action on the part of the developer. A leaked internal memo to SAHRA's Archaeology, Palaeontology, Meteorite and Heritage Object Committee (the permit-issuing committee in this case) expressed the concern that should the site be conserved as a heritage site it would have 'disastrous consequences for the developer who will presumably appeal against the decision and may instigate litigation against SAHRA and the city'. The Committee was informed that it was 'imperative that a responsible decision be made by SAHRA and the city . . . The matter is urgent, as the apartments in the development have been pre-sold and every delay means that the expenses are increasing' (Hands Off Committee 2003a).

On 1 September, despite a clear weight of opinion at the third public meeting opposed to the exhumations, Pumla Madiba, the CEO of SAHRA, announced a resumption of archaeological work at the site. In a statement to the press she said: 'Many of the people who objected were highly emotional and did not give real reasons why the skeletons should not be relocated' (Kassiem 2003). On 4 September the Hands Off Prestwich Street Ad Hoc Committee (HOC) was launched. At this point opposition to the exhumations shifted outside the officially mandated process of public consultation, to civic society and the politics of mass action. Central figures in the HOC were Michael Wheeder and Terry Lester, both Anglican Church ministers whose families had been victims of forced removals. On 12 September the HOC lodged an appeal with SAHRA calling for a halt to the exhumations and 'a full and extended process of community consultation'. The appeal document noted that '[for] a large section of Cape Town's community, whose existence and dignity has for so long been denied, the discovery and continued preservation of the Prestwich Street burial ground can symbolically restore their memory and identity'. It continued,

[the] needs of archaeology as a science seem to have been given precedence over other needs: the needs of community socio-cultural history, of collective remembering and of acknowledging the pain and trauma related to the site and this history that gave rise to its existence. (Hands Off Committee 2003b: 2)

In opposing the exhumations it argues that

[exhumation] makes impossible a whole range of people's identifications with that specific physical space in the city. Such a removal echoes, albeit unintentionally, the apartheid regime's forced removals from the same area. (Hands Off Committee 2003b: 2)

The 23 October was set as the date for tribunal hearing to consider the appeal. In the run up to the hearing the HOC organised regular candle-lit vigils at the Prestwich Street site on Sunday evenings and erected a billboard outside St George's Cathedral, a symbolic site of anti-apartheid protest, with the slogan: 'Stop the exhumations! Stop the desecration!' Lunchtime pickets were held in the city centre. The SAHRA-convened appeals committee handed down a written ruling on 19 November. The excavation permit awarded to the ACO was revalidated and the rights of the developer upheld. The HOC reconvened as the Prestwich Place Project Committee to launch an appeal directly to the Minister of Arts and Culture. A letter of appeal was lodged with the Ministry on 12 January 2004. By this time all the human remains on the original site had been exhumed and were in temporary storage in Napier House, a building on the adjacent block, itself to be demolished as part of the Prestwich Place development.

Through the course of events at Prestwich Street a clear polarisation emerged, with those arguing for exhumations doing so on the basis of the scientific value of the remains as a source to access 'hidden histories'. The proposal circulated by the SFRG at the first public meeting states:

These skeletons are also – literally – our history, the ordinary people of Cape Town, whose lives are not written in the official documents of the time. They did not leave possessions or archives. If we want to recover their history, then one of the most powerful ways to do so is through the study of their skeletons. (Sealy 2003: 1)

The semantic slide from 'our' to 'their' precisely captures the ambiguity around notions of agency and constituency that characterised so much of the discipline's involvement in the process. A number of tropes emerged and were recycled by archaeologists throughout the process. At the second public meeting Belinda Mutti argued in favour of exhumation 'to give history back to the people'. Liesbet Schiettecatte argued that '[leaving] bones leaves information unknown. Studying them brings them back to life'. Mary Patrick argued to '[continue the] exhumation – otherwise half a story is being told' (Malan 2003: 13). At a public level this desire to 'give history back to the people' and 'bring the bones to life' was mediated by the technical discourse of cultural resource management, with its rituals of 'public consultation', and its circumscribed notions of value, need and interest.

In opposition to this discourse, the HOC emphasised the language of memory and personal reminiscence. They sought to articulate an alternative set of values (African values, spiritual values), and alternative notions of space–time (the notion of the site as a heritage site or a site of conscience, and in one memorable intervention, the notion of 'time for the dead'). They insisted on recalling a more recent past of apartheid and forced removals, as well as a deep past of slavery and colonialism. More generally, they sought to insert the events at Prestwich Street into a prevailing debate in post-apartheid society around notions of truth, reconciliation and restitution (a debate which had its most public expression in the workings of the Truth and Reconciliation Commission).

Ultimately, the story of Prestwich Street is a story of failure. The appeal to the Minister was turned down and development went ahead. Little remains of the burial site and its shadowed history. The transformation of the humble block on Prestwich Street into the luxury apartments envisaged by the developer is currently in process. These events may yet emerge as a 'teaching moment' as the HOC put it in their appeal document. If there is one thing to be learned, then it is the need for archaeology to come to terms with what might be characterised as the necessary entanglements of race, culture and identity in the post-colony. Archaeology in South Africa (and elsewhere) has a long history of shying away from such entanglements, of regarding them as extraneous to the core business of the discipline. In fact, the case study of Prestwich Street suggests that it is precisely through engaging with the complex play of contemporary forces and interests that historical archaeology finds a place for itself in the post-colony, confronts the full complexity of its knowledge objects, and deals with the legacies of its colonial past.

CONCLUSIONS

In the introductory section of this paper we suggested that colonial sites provide the basis for exploring a number of topics of significance for archaeology as a whole, including issues of power, identity, domination, resistance, ethnicity and gender. In the second part of the paper we listed a number of themes and studies that seem to us to be central to defining the intellectual terrain of historical archaeology. In the first place, these include the theme of acculturation and adaptation in classes of material culture. Deetz's (1977) classic study of the material culture of colonial New England was used as an example. In the second place, the theme of creolisation and the creation of new and hybrid societies was explored, citing the work of Kathleen Deagan (1983, 1985, 1996). In the third place, we explored the experience of colonialism from the perspective of the colonised, for example in David Burley's (1989) study of Metis wintering camps, and Janet Spector's (1993) work with the descendants of the Wahpeton Dakota. Finally, we examined briefly the theme of power and resistance, citing Mark Leone's (1996 [1984]) study of William Paca's garden in eighteenth-century Annapolis, Leland Ferguson's (1991) study of African-American foodways in South Carolina, and Martin Hall's (2000) study of slave resistance in colonial Cape Town.

Our two case studies have aimed to provide a working out of these themes. The site of York Town in Australia exemplifies the spread of the institutions of colonialism, and the manner in which bureaucratic intentions shaped the colonial experience. The strategic and territorial interests of Britain, and of imperial power in the Pacific, together with imperatives relating to the nature of the penal colony as an institution, served to determine both the situation and the nature of the settlement. Particular emphasis was placed on notions of hierarchy, surveillance and control, and on the role of rank, gender and kinship in determining settlement patterns. As in other colonial contexts, notions of science and various associated collecting practices played a significant role in mediating the colonial encounter.

The site of Prestwich Street in Cape Town provides an example of the contested contexts of historical archaeological work in the post-colony. The exhumation of an early colonial burial ground occasioned the interplay of a complex set of interests, including those of the developer, the state via SAHRA, city planners, a group of pro-exhumation archaeologists and human biologists who made a case for the scientific value of the remains, and civil society activists who identified themselves as being part of a wider descendant community and insisted on the symbolic value of Prestwich Street as a site of memory and a reminder of a neglected history.

What unites these two studies is the manner in which past and present social relations are made powerfully present in material culture, whether in the form of settled landscapes or via the remains of colonial underclasses themselves. If we follow Gosden's (2004) contention that colonialism is best understood as a material phenomenon linked to the circulation of new sets of material culture and practices, then historical archaeology offers a unique insight into the working out of social and historical processes associated with colonialism and postcolonialism. It also offers an important site for thinking through the manner in which archaeology remains a contested field of practice in the present.

CHAPTER 6

Urban historical archaeology

Tadhg O'Keeffe and Rebecca Yamin

Studies of the historical geographies of the towns and cities of the recent past through their material remains have developed within a broad multi-disciplinary context. Ethnographers, cultural geographers, sociologists and others have examined the historical built environment within a spectrum of behavioural, spatial and historical sciences, while archaeologists have studied the development and abandonment of urban places across five millennia and around the world from a great range of perspectives. Many key themes in the contemporary social sciences, including capitalism, colonialism and the politics of identity, are implicated in the development of modern urban places. Over the past forty years historical archaeologists have aimed to contribute to the cross-disciplinary exchange, both by developing distinctive perspectives on towns and cities and by engaging with contemporary urban communities as they negotiate their urban heritages, whether standing buildings and landscapes or buried remains.

This chapter aims to explore the practical and intellectual contributions of the diverse traditions of urban historical archaeology. It places the historiography of urban historical archaeology within its wider cross-disciplinary context and provides a detailed case study, drawn from New York and Philadelphia, that explores how historical archaeologists have researched streetscapes, buildings and backyards. The chapter concludes with reflections on how archaeological practice and archaeological knowledge shape contemporary living within urban environments.

CHANGES IN ARCHAEOLOGICAL CONCEPTIONS OF HISTORICAL TOWNS

The archaeological analysis of urban space is complex. There are two principal practical challenges. First, cities are vast archaeological sites. Urban landscapes extend across hundreds, and often thousands, of square miles. 'Historic cores', as conventionally defined, tend to be relatively small, but they are still among the most complex of all archaeological sites in their histories of development, and significantly larger in area and stratigraphic depth. Moreover, the extensive settled areas that stretch out beyond such 'historic cores' are also of interest, and these have complex histories in their own right. The second challenge derives from the fact that almost all cities established or occupied within the post-1500 period are still occupied. Cities that were founded in more ancient times but were still flourishing in the sixteenth century are virtually all also living places today; and abandoned urban settlements of relatively recent foundation, such as Santa Fe la Vieja in Argentina – the sixteenth-century predecessor to Buenos Aires – are exceptional and rare. Continuous occupation has generated deep stratigraphic records, but they are more often than not buried below modern pavements or sidewalks that are still in daily use. While the redevelopment of urban sites sometimes provides opportunities for developer-funded archaeological investigation, especially in those countries that have legislation that requires that such investigations take place, contemporary use and occupation means that archaeologists rarely can choose the specific sites within urban environments that they wish to explore. Moreover, the most recent layers of the record are often most seriously disturbed simply because they are 'high up' in the stratigraphy (cf. Carver 1987).

These problems notwithstanding, historical archaeology has made, and continues to make, a contribution to the study of historic urban places. One contribution has been the retrieval, using such familiar techniques as survey and excavation, of the raw data necessary for writing narratives of spatial and structural development and change for individual cities or groups of cities. However, historical archaeology's contribution to urban research extends far beyond the acquisition of structural and material data (cf. Cameron and Tomka 1996; Fletcher 1995). The field is also concerned with documenting and explaining how cities are simultaneously local and global places, how they accommodate juxtapositions of polite and vernacular architecture and their associated cultures, and how they operate as places of opportunity and innovation, but also of oppression.

These dual interests, concerns not only with the historical development of individual cities but also with cities as social–material phenomena, are reflected in the published literature. Detailed accounts of archaeological work within individual historical cities are legion. All too often these belong within the realm of 'grey literature' – reports that are accessible and intelligible to professional practitioners but make little concession to the interests and needs of interdisciplinary or public readerships. In other instances the detailed work is fed into more popular, though no less scholarly, narratives of urban redevelopment in specific places. Cantwell and Wall's (2001) study of New York is a good example from the United States. In Europe, the results of archaeological investigations are factored into the atlas fascicles of the International Commission for the History of Towns, some 500 of which have already been published (International Commission for the History of Towns 2005). Archaeologists of historical urban places have, however, shied away from producing sequential and cross-cultural syntheses of the kind associated with urban historians over the past forty years or so (for example, Kostoff 1991; 1992; A. Morris 1979; Mumford 1961).

Much urban historical archaeological literature is dominated by multi-thematic case studies in which the empirical data are collated and analysed alongside explicit delineations of the practical and intellectual methodologies of the research, and sometimes even of the politics of archaeology. The Archaeology in Annapolis project, begun in 1981 and directed by Mark Leone, is probably the best-known urban historical archaeological study of this kind. A partnership between the Department of Anthropology at the University of Maryland (College Park) and the Historic Annapolis Foundation, it involves the investigation of places, as they become available, within a living city in the Chesapeake area. Using an explicitly 'critical' approach, the project interpreted the city's past through its material remains, and presented this understanding to its contemporary population and especially to visiting tourists (Leone and Potter 1996 [1984]; Potter 1994; Shackel et al. 1998). The work at Annapolis was not unique in this regard: a similar programme of opportunistic investigations of vacant lots, married to a research vision for the urban area in question and executed with the help of a similar coalition of trained archaeologists, volunteers and students, has guided archaeological work within the city of Alexandria in Virginia (Alexandria Archaeology Museum nd.) for example, and within an area of Melbourne, Australia ('Little Lon') which was notorious in the nineteenth century as a red-light district (Mayne and Lawrence 1998).

Archaeology in Annapolis stands out as having generated an awareness of the politically engaged nature of historical archaeology, within the urban sphere and without (see McGuire this volume). The project's political agenda was contained in its particular conceptualisation as a project of 'public archaeology', pursuing two aims. The first was to show, through the study of its historical material remains, that such inequality is not an inevitable feature of human existence. The second aim was to give voice to those in the urban past, such as working-class people and African-Americans, whose voices are generally silent in the historical sources themselves and whose urban experiences are consequently under-represented in the historiography of urbanism (see Goings and Mohl 1996 for attempts to rectify this for African-Americans at least). Archaeology in Annapolis thus aimed to respond to contemporary needs in its manifesto of inclusion both in the past and in the present.

This emphasis on allowing the material culture to speak for otherwise silent voices in some ways qualifies Archaeology in Annapolis as a more conventionally archaeological project than other projects in 'interpretive' archaeology in other urban areas. Those other projects, however, have come closer to the centre of the cross-disciplinary currents to which we referred at the beginning of the chapter. We might compare, for example, the study of Victorian Sacramento in California by archaeologists Adrian and Mary Praetzellis (1987, 1998) with the recent study of Victorian Philadelphia by historian John Henry Hepp (Hepp 2003), or indeed with historian Gary Nash's study of Philadelphia up to and including the Victorian era (Nash 2001). Hepp's study uses buildings and material objects alongside more conventional historical source materials such as diaries and newspapers to study Victorian 'taxonomies' of time and space, and one could easily envisage his goal being pursued within the context of interpretive archaeological research. By taking two cities and probing their Victorian personalities, these authors, in turn, are as close in intellectual spirit to authors of detailed sociospatial biographies of cities, such as geographer James Lemon and urban historian Peter Hall (Hall 1998; Lemon 1996), as they are to Mark Leone at Annapolis. There is, by the same token, both intellectual and methodological convergence between, say, Alan Mayne's work on the representation of late Victorian and early Edwardian slums in the popular press (Mayne 1993), and the more conventional archaeological work on slums presented in the volume on urban-slum landscapes that he co-edited with Tim Murray (Mayne and Murray 2001).

Boundaries between interpretive urban historical archaeology and other fields in the humanities and social sciences that are concerned with urbanism are clearly very difficult to identify. This is not an accident. These fields have converged knowingly, if not intentionally, around a set of core concerns and methodologies. For example, one could reasonably shelve Christine Finn's radical and explicitly titled archaeology of the people and their débitage in the built-up technological landscape of Silicon Valley (Finn 2001) alongside Edward Soja's conceptual work on Los Angeles, or Dolores Hayden's work on the 'power of place' within the same city (Hayden 1995; Soja 1996). It is not the relative proximity of Silicon Valley and Los Angeles that prompts this view: rather, these studies spring from a common understanding of the social, material and spatial complexities of contemporary urbanism, and the intellectual challenges associated with their study.

However, the contribution of historical archaeologists to this urban research – even historical urban research – remains largely unrecognised, if only to judge by the infrequency with which the word 'archaeology' appears in two of the most significant web-based resource guides for urban studies (http://vlib.iur.it/history/topical/urban.html; www.h-net.org/~urban/, consulted 14 March 2005). Changing this may require greater advocacy by archaeologists themselves, and in particular by underlining how archaeology links the urban past with the urban present (Symonds 2004: 43).

COMPLEXITY IN URBAN ARCHAEOLOGIES

Archaeologists, urban historians and other specialists are generating increasingly complex stories of urban development around the globe over the past few centuries (cf. Murray 2003). We now possess a good stock of comparative knowledge at different spatial and geopolitical levels, and we have the capacity to engage in cross-cultural analysis should we choose to. That knowledge is far too extensive to be summarised here; readers seeking an understanding of the city as a global spatial–cultural phenomenon might begin by consulting Spiro Kostoff's great surveys (Kostoff 1991; 1992). Instead, in this section we have chosen two related themes within the urban sphere – notions of visible and hidden 'performance' – and we present brief commentaries on them in order to demonstrate the material complexities of the urban environment on the one hand, and the type of historical narrative that can be written on the other.

City as theatre

One of the repercussions of the so-called 'cultural turn' in the social sciences during the 1980s has been an increasing emphasis upon notions of culture, and especially material culture, as 'performed' (C. Nash 2000; cf. J. Butler 1993; Thrift 1996, 2000). As human beings that live communally, we are endlessly engaged in social and material performance, both as 'actors' ourselves and as monitors of others. Archaeologists and anthropologists have emphasised how human relationships are built through participation in public performances. Where processual archaeologies of the 1960s and 1970s studied built environments solely in terms of narrowly defined functions, spatial arrangements, and stylistic and structural sequences, more recently historical archaeologists have begun to broaden their interests, sometimes exploring the means by which built environments encourage or permit the enactment and observation of social performances. In other words, some archaeologists have come to examine built spaces not as artefacts that are incidental to the social world but as actively involved in the performance of social life (cf. Pearson and Shanks 2001). The city, a built environment, is stage *par excellence*, and archaeology's material focus and access to long-term histories of cities provides distinctive perspectives upon the interdisciplinary study of urban performativity.

The idea of the city as theatre, as a place of spectacle, is not new. It has informed urban planning around the world from ancient times to the present, linking classical cities like Rome to 'modern movement' cities like Brasilia. The specific ideas of theatrical urban planning that emerged in mainland western Europe in the decades around 1500 – the age that is described as the *Renaissance*, the age of rebirth – dominated much of the thinking on new urban-landscape design up to the nineteenth century. These ideas and the landscapes that they inspired fall squarely within historical archaeology's remit.

Briefly, fourteenth- and fifteenth-century European towns, especially those of the Hanseatic League around the Baltic and North Seas, had been hotbeds of merchant capitalism, facilitating and effecting that transformation in social–political organisation that is customarily, if rather simplistically, described in terms of the end of medieval feudalism and the rise of early modern capitalism. These towns retained medieval plans even as new spaces and architectures of economic specialisation and sociopolitical differentiation, such as exchanges (Harreld 2003) and guildhalls (Crossick 1997; Giles 1999), were incorporated within them. Then, from around 1500, the new concept of urban planning brought new European streetscapes designed with carefully regulated geometries, and often with vistas focused on new neo-Classical buildings. The first such project was the Via Nuova in Genoa in 1470, even though Florence's urban landscape had been transformed by new building projects earlier that century.

Rome was transformed under papal patronage in the sixteenth century. The Eternal City's first straight Renaissance street, the Via Guilia, was created by Julius II (papacy 1503–1513), but the greatest project was the axial and monumental reordering of Rome under Sixtus V (papacy 1585–1590). Long straight streets were laid out between selected landmarks, such as key ancient sites, new town squares with their re-erected Egyptian obelisks (preserved from ancient Roman campaigns), and major contemporary churches. The theatrical dimension is self evident: the city's dwellers were enrolled in a historicised, counter-reformation choreography of great visual sophistication.

Various buildings were even cleared away so that these vistas would be uncluttered and their messages unambiguous. While the Catholic credentials of this new type of urban scheme are indisputable, the template spread beyond the geographical limits of Mediterranean Catholicism. Paris, for example, was substantially redesigned as a Rome-like city under the patronage of Henry IV, a Protestant who came to power in 1589. The new formal plans of communal urban spaces were not just about the religious ideologies that underpinned contemporary political power: pleasure was as much a motivation, as witness the way in which the formal plans of cities like Versailles and Karlsruhe converged conceptually with the formal plans of the great gardens of the contemporary social–political élite (Rogers 2001: 194–220).

The vista element of neo-Classical urban design that originated in the sixteenth century survived the age of reformation and counter-reformation, remaining central to the conceptualisation of the urban landscape in much of Europe right up to the period of industrialisation. There is scope for exploring the neo-classical roots of industrial cityscapes: new or redesigned urban landscapes of the industrial age were no less formal than those of the sixteenth century, and while their formality – and the formality of the industrial architecture itself – might be understood in terms of simple practical convenience it was no less imbued with ideological content than the formality of Renaissance and later cities.

Such material performativity was not confined to the boulevards and grand buildings of preindustrial urban centres. These centres were initially bounded by the physical barriers – town walls – that separated the urban and rural spheres, but in the later sixteenth and seventeenth centuries those barriers were themselves incorporated into the performative schemes. Whereas the medieval urban boundaries had often been walls in the most literal sense, from around 1500 urban boundaries were often vast starbursts of low stone walls, earthen ramparts, and dry or water-filled fosses. Ostensibly designed as practical measures against artillery attack, a point underscored by the occasional presence of a specially designated fort or citadel along their circuit, the aesthetic co-intent of these so-called 'star-shaped' defenses is unmistakable. The 'walls' were often organised with careful geometric regularity, especially in towns that were newly founded in this period, and the street layout was often tied into their symmetry, as is strikingly the case in such famous places as Palma Nova in Italy, founded in 1593, and Neuf Brisach in France, founded around 1700. The water-filled fosses and walled ramparts of the cities came to resemble the artificial ponds and parterres of contemporary pleasure gardens, just as the access-ways of the cities resembled

the vista-ways of the gardens. The fact that the star-shaped ramparts of Louis
XIV's early seventeenth-century Paris were used by citizens for leisurely –
and strategically elevated – perambulations tells its own story (compare
Mukerji 1997).

These changes to European cityscapes in the sixteenth and seventeenth
centuries were contemporary with the development of European exploration and colonisation in the New World. There was no causal connection
between these developments, but it is clear that a deeply embedded ideology of Christian imperialism connected the process of urban redesign in the
homelands of the overseas colonisers to the process of new urban generation
in the colonies themselves. The etymological link between the words 'city'
and 'civilisation' reminds us of the historical connections between urban
foundations and notions of 'civilising' processes (cf. Gosden 2004: 126–127).
Such connections were alive as late as the 1800s, as David Hamer has shown
in his study of the 'urban frontier' in Australia, New Zealand, and the
United States (Hamer 1990). In some situations, then, the reproduction of
the monumental order of the Renaissance town plan in the overseas colonies
represented the *civilising* of the natives under God. Although Columbus'
town of La Isabela, the first European settlement in the Americas,
followed a conventional medieval form, colonial towns overseas such as
Santo Domingo, founded in 1502, had regular street patterns reflective of
those in European cities. Indeed, the failure of La Isabela as a settlement
may actually have provoked the Spanish crown to insist on more rigorously designed urban plans in its overseas colonies (Deagan and Cruxent
2002). Elsewhere, the European model was worked out differently. As Henry
Miller (1988b) has shown through a combination of meticulous archaeological research and historical documentation, St Mary's City, the state of
Maryland's first capital, was laid out on Baroque principles in the mid-
seventeenth century, as was Annapolis thirty years later.

The close morphological relationships between 'home' and colonial
urbanisms are especially apparent in colonial South America, where Iberian
city forms were knowingly replicated: sixteenth- and seventeenth-century
Spanish urban design at home and abroad was orderly, with regularly laid-
out streets and squares, and with carefully positioned public buildings, while
the contemporary cities of Portugal and its South American colony (Brazil,
as it became known) were less formally planned. Sandra Low's suggestion
that not all towns in the Americas with grid-plans and central plazas need
to be regarded as solely European in origin (1993: 76) does, however, introduce a timely note of warning: our thinking on global historical urbanism

is eurocentric, and we ignore indigenous patterns and processes of urban formation at our peril.

The city as non-theatre

So far we have concentrated on the macro-scale level of the town plan and on how the emergence and development of town plans, with their constituent buildings, can be understood in terms of spectacle and performance. Such perspectives demonstrate how important it is for urban historical archaeologists to think beyond the simple categories – style structure, form, sequence, function – of traditional archaeology. City-as-theatre, as presented here, is however only a small part of a complex story: one useful way of approaching the materiality of urban histories. Other stories – city-as-economy, city-as-power, city-as-ruin, city-as-imagined space, and so on – can also be told.

In the present context, perhaps the most interesting 'other' story might be the city as a place of 'non-theatre': a place of hidden performance or covert actions, a place occupied by people who are not 'on stage', either by their own choice or by the design of others, and whose buildings and built spaces are concealed and invisible rather than displayed, and which may appear 'immaterial'. Such relatively silent urban spaces are sometimes products of segregation or discrimination. For example, urban sites of homosexual interaction are commonly marginal or concealed within cities: documented sites in London, Amsterdam, Paris, Lisbon, Moscow, San Francisco, and Rio do Janeiro sometimes include urban parkland, transport stations, and public baths and toilets (Higgs 1999). While racial and cultural segregation, by contrast, often found highly visible institutional embodiment in the fabrics and constitutions of many colonial cities – whether physical and spatial separation of natives and Europeans, of 'blacks' and 'whites', as in sixteenth- and seventeenth-century Hispanic South America, eighteenth-century North America, or in the nineteenth-century British Raj in India – the acknowledgement of the reduced visibilities or shrouded materialities is just as pressing.

We may explore such concerns further by turning our attention to the archaeology of urban luminosities. The invention of the glass-paned street lantern meant that night-time Paris had artificial light in 1667, Amsterdam in 1669, and forty-one other northern European cities by 1700 (Koslofsky 2002). The illumination of the night created a visual separation of the central city space from everything else; one need only look out of an aeroplane window at night to see this. It shifted the temporal dimensions of the same space: the day lasted longer thanks to the use of artificial light. And it created a social separation: it disenfranchised those members of urban society whose illicit activities required natural nocturnal darkness, so that they either resisted from within (by breaking street lights – a serious crime) or they relocated to darker situations. One can easily extend into more recent contexts this idea of cities as bounded places of differential time and accentuated surveillance. The street lanterns of early modern Paris and elsewhere belong at the head of a genealogy of urban furniture that today includes the sensor-controlled lights, the security camera, and the barbed-wire fence. But the main point remains: acknowledging the performance of less visible, hidden, or secret materialities in urban studies needs to run alongside emphases of theatre or spectacle. As Kathryn Denning has put it, archaeologists have much to learn from the 'artist's axiom that when one draws the dark, the light emerges' (Denning 2003).

EXCAVATING URBAN BIOGRAPHIES

The idea of the city as being a place of the hidden, the covert, the non-theatrical, as much as the overtly enacted, finds much resonance in the 'performance' of fieldwork in urban archaeology. The living urban landscape is perhaps the most secretive of all landscapes because it hides traces of its many transformations beneath layers of concrete and reconfigured spaces. In this section, we consider these, often hidden, 'biographies' – of cities themselves, and the people who inhabited them in the past.

Even in the supermodernity of New York, physical remnants of the past lie buried under city streets, cellar floors, deep deposits of fill, and the labyrinths of utility trenches that it takes to support urban living. But it is, as we have noted, more than an occasional crumbling fragment of wall foundation that urban archaeology brings to the surface. The layered depth of the material and the complexity of the spaces uncovered capture something of what urban historian Sam Bass Warner called 'cityness' (Stave 1974: 92; cf. Salinger 1992: 330). The past landscape revealed through excavation in the midst of the contemporary city suggests the dynamic nature of urban life, the energy that comes from many different kinds of people living and working in close quarters and the theatricality of it all. While the study of documents such as census records, city directories, church records, deeds, diaries and tax lists is essential to urban archaeology, it is the materiality of an urban site that breathes life into a city's past, illuminating its relationships with its present. It is the same physicality that makes urban living different from rural, or even suburban, living.

The act of peeling back the layers of concrete that cover the city's past is itself dramatic. Huge mechanical excavators break up concrete and remove the fill that covers former building foundations and backyards under archaeologists' directions. On the Courthouse Block in lower Manhattan, for instance, eighteen tenement foundations lay beneath a parking lot. Parking lots are often the site of urban investigations because they are the only open space available for development. The tenement foundations enclosed the remains of earlier buildings and backyards, although the yard surfaces had been scraped away when the basements for the tenements were excavated. Beneath the basement floors were the truncated features that had been backyard privies, wells and cisterns. Fifty were found on the Courthouse Block, distributed among fourteen historic properties. Those features, used as trash receptacles by tenants who did not have the luxury of garbage collection, produced nearly a million artefacts, the possessions of the waves of immigrants who lived in this once-overcrowded working-class neighbourhood that in the present is the site of a gleaming new courthouse, the newest addition to Foley Square, New York City's judicial district.

The development of this particular neighbourhood, known as Five Points in the nineteenth century, is not untypical of other nineteenth-century working-class neighbourhoods in other North American cities. It began on land that was outside the city proper, even outside the wall that separated the settled city from its hinterland to the north. Eighteenth-century maps show a large pond dominating the landscape. On one side was rough terrain used as a 'negroes' burying ground' and on the other was a foul-smelling industrial area of tannery yards, breweries and rope walks, which spewed industrial by-products into the pond and along its shoreline. The area hardly seemed a likely residential enclave, but as the city absorbed more and more workers in the nineteenth century the need for affordable housing increased, and once-uninhabitable places became the very places that workers lived. The earliest residents at Five Points were free blacks and newly arrived immigrants who either worked in the local industries or set up shop as independent artisans. Besides day labourers, there were tanners, bakers, brewers, carpenters and tailors, many with German surnames. They lived and worked on the same premises; their houses were small and probably overcrowded and the atmosphere was thick with the smells of the various industries. In spite of the conditions, some of the residents maintained Old World elegance. Tobias Hoffman, a baker who set up business on Pearl Street just east of the pond in the 1790s, and his family served meals on floral-decorated Chinese porcelain plates, they drank from delicately etched goblets and Tobias smoked a German-style porcelain pipe.

The pond, eventually filled and converted into saleable real estate, became the heart of a neighbourhood that absorbed one immigrant group after another. Eastern-European Jews had settled in the subdivided houses on one of the bounding streets of the Courthouse Block by the 1830s, making their livings as second-hand clothing dealers, tailors and shoemakers. In the 1840s Irish immigrants fleeing the potato famines at home and seeking work in the rapidly industrialising United States filled four- and five-storey tenements along the other side of the block. Creating distinct worlds on different sides of the block, and thus creating what Peter Hall (1998) describes as the urban 'cultural crucible', these residents left no written record of their lives, but they did leave a material record, the record urban archaeologists 'read' to see how immigrants adjusted to life in New York.

Archaeological evidence, especially artefacts and food remains found in the features associated with these different groups suggest that ethnic identities continued to be important in the urban context. The Irish appear to have used their limited incomes to buy Staffordshire tewares that were identical to those used in Ireland, and sets of the familiar Willow ware. While fish would have been less expensive, they favoured a diet of pork and the many pig's feet recovered may have been left over from a characteristically Irish dish made of pigs' feet cooked in wine and spices. They drank more wine than beer in the privacy of their homes and treated their aches and pains (many were manual labourers) with a variety of patent medicines. The Jewish population, who were mainly tailors and second-hand clothing dealers (this was New York's first garment district) appear to have consumed more fish than meat, favouring lamb over pork or beef, and to have owned different and fewer dishes. They also preferred wine to beer but drank relatively little and also consumed significantly less medicine than their Irish neighbours. Most interesting of all were the two groups' different choices of smoking pipes. The Irish avoided pipes with patriotic symbols, choosing instead the plainest (fluted) and least expensive pipes available. The German and Polish populations, however, owned pipes decorated with stars and eagles, symbols that were used by the Nativist political party to signify their status as native-born members of society. Nativists were notoriously prejudiced against the Irish and while the Eastern Europeans may have been comfortable identifying with Nativist imagery the Irish appear to have intentionally avoided it.

As these results indicate, historical archaeology can produce an intimate view of the urban process. Our stories are told 'from the inside out' (Beaudry et al. 1991: 284). From excavated trash, we see how people coped with the overcrowding that is so characteristic of urban living, how they maintained their identities in new circumstances, and how neighbourhoods changed as one group moved out and another moved in. The stories come not just from these artefacts, but also from spatial arrangements. On the Courthouse Block the space became increasingly constricted. The backyards behind the original small houses shrank significantly when the tenements were built on the fronts of the lots, and shrank even further when additional tenements were built on the backs of the lots sometimes leaving as little as 20 by 20 feet (about 6 metres square) of open space between the front and back buildings and sometimes leaving no space at all. These changes are recorded on nineteenth-century insurance maps, which in the United States are the urban archaeologist's basic tool when approaching a site slated for investigation. But such maps do not show the jerry-rigged plumbing facilities that filled the backyards, nor do they reveal the lives that were lived inside the walls of the houses and tenements that lined the streets. Even contemporary observers failed to see the reality of life on the Courthouse Block. As outsiders, they saw the block as part of the notorious Five Points, New York City's mythic nineteenth-century slum (see Cook 1998b for a discussion of the Five Points myth).

The mythic slum, what historian Alan Mayne calls the 'imagined slum' (Mayne 1993), is a good example of how easy it is to misunderstand an urban neighbourhood from the outside (Fitts 2000; Yamin 1997, 1998c), but it is also an example of how the façades of urban neighbourhoods can mask what goes on inside. A contrast between public and private is characteristic of urban places. They are not transparent, and that lack of transparency is one of the things that gives them their 'cityness'. A city's many myths and stories are part of its identity and to deny them is to deny a fundamental component of the urban cultural landscape (Chisholm and Brazeau 2002). While urban archaeology may dig into the private lives of past residents, it misses the complexities of urban life if it does not also take the public side of life into account. In the case of the Courthouse Block, the results of the archaeological analysis were more, not less, interesting because the public and private views of what life was like for nineteenth-century workers in New York City were woven together.

THE POLITICS OF EXCAVATING URBAN BIOGRAPHIES

Given this urban interplay of the visible and the unseen it is perhaps not surprising that archaeological discoveries in towns and cities often reveal aspects of the past that generate enormous interest in the present. In New York an eighteenth-century African burial ground was identified nineteen feet below the present ground surface during the construction of a federal office building (LaRoche and Blakey 1997). The discovery ignited the interest of the African-American community which did not want its ancestors treated cavalierly (about 400 burials were excavated). Ultimately the project and associated long-term education programme made people infinitely more aware of the role of slavery in eighteenth-century New York than had been the case before and set a standard for including a descendant community in a sensitive situation (see also Lawrence and Shepherd, this volume). A practical example of a development-led archaeological project in Philadelphia nicely illustrates some of the same political issues, although the circumstances were very different.

Philadelphia's urban plan was developed in 1683 by Thomas Holme for William Penn, and remains largely intact. Four open squares anchor the north–south, east–west grid system, and remain as open land. A fifth square, in the middle, holds the city's ornate Second Empire city hall. Large town houses line the major residential streets in the city's core and smaller row houses line the intervening alleys. This designed urban fabric, with its built-in hierarchical implications, is in great part still visible – with one major exception. In 1950 the three blocks in front of Independence Hall, where the country's Declaration of Independence was signed, were cleared to create what was considered a more appropriate (and more fireproof) context for the Hall. Patriotic fervour in the post-World War II era had elevated Independence Hall as a symbol of freedom and the surrounding blocks, also cleared, became Independence National Historical Park. No archaeological investigations were conducted on the three blocks (now known as Independence Mall) in front of Independence Hall although some were conducted elsewhere in the park. The redesign of Independence Mall in the 1990s, however, did require archaeology and the excavation on the site of a new building to house the Liberty Bell produced, among other things, an archaeological feature in the backyard of the house where George Washington and John Adams lived during their presidencies while the fledgling federal government was seated in Philadelphia from 1790 to 1800.

The feature measured 13.5 feet (4.1 metres) in diameter, and was an eight-sided, stone-lined pit built to hold ice. The superstructure had clearly been removed when the house on the property was demolished in 1832. It seemed to the archaeologists involved in the excavation that the icehouse feature would be a useful focal point for discussing the work that was done by enslaved Africans and indentured servants to support the elite presidential residence. They recommended that the National Park Service incorporate the feature into the new landscape. For a variety of reasons the Park Service did not find that possible, and they arranged for the feature to be filled with gravel and buried it. The archaeologists proceeded to excavate other backyard features within the Liberty Bell Center site, although none related to the President's House.

Not long after the icehouse was buried, a major historian, in league with a local researcher, began to campaign for including a discussion of George Washington's slaves in the interpretive materials presented in the new Liberty Bell Center. The researcher claimed that George Washington had converted a smoke house between the kitchen and stables into slave quarters (Lawler 2002) and members of the local African-American community began to call for an excavation. Unfortunately the house and all other structures except the stone-lined octagonal hole in the ground had been destroyed in 1832 and replaced with three commercial buildings with basements. No archaeology had been conducted at the former location of the slave quarters because it lay outside the development area, and there was no evidence that any remains of the slave quarters survived. The only feature that could have served their purpose already lay partially buried beneath the Liberty Bell Center. It is clear that if the icehouse feature had been retained in the landscape it would have been a powerful link to an unremembered past: a practical example of how past and present are bound up together in the everyday practice of urban archaeology.

CLOSING THOUGHTS

The excavations, debates and absences at Independence Mall remind us that urban historical archaeology is always public and political. Often publicly funded as part of construction projects, its operations take place alongside construction workers and in full view of a general public that, in its increasing demand for accountability, is often invited to visit and view the ongoing performances of excavations. Communication is not always easy and it takes time, but these contemporary engagements are part of the distinctive perspectives that historical archaeology brings to urban studies.

Throughout this paper, we have aimed to highlight the complexities of urban archaeology. Its indelicate field methods often involve working with large machines and their operators to strip away fill and building rubble that covers evidence of earlier occupations, harvesting thousands upon thousands of artefacts from deep deposits of unpleasant-smelling nightsoil, and figuring out stratigraphy that is more often than not riddled with modern disturbances. It is almost always expensive, and sometimes dangerous.

Equally intensive are the post-excavation analytical methods – the mending of glass and ceramic vessels in order to estimate sets, the identification of thousands of pieces of bone, miniscule seeds, and parasite eggs, and the generation of complex sequences of site formation.

The strongest urban historical archaeologies place the weaving together of the documentary and material records (buried and above ground) at the heart of their research designs and practices. Such work can result in new stories about cities in the past, illuminating life in the urban past (Beaudry 1998; M. Praetzellis and A. Praetzellis 2004; Yamin 1998b, 2001), and addressing material conditions in different ways from other disciplines. Most powerful, however, for historical archaeologists are the material remains themselves, both in the ground and out, which evoke the complexities of urban life. Urban historians' concern with the 'power of place' (Dubrow and Graves 2002; Hayden 1994, 1995) has relevance here. Hayden (1994: 466) has argued that while urban landscapes may contain traces of earlier landscapes 'intertwined with its current configuration', they rarely preserve 'the spatial history of ordinary working people and everyday lives' or other untold histories (e.g. Sandercock 1998). While this may sometimes be true above ground (but see Hicks and Horning this volume for a more optimistic view), it is certainly untrue in the archaeological analysis of subsurface remains. Although fragmentary, the buried urban archaeological record reveals the constant process of change that is a fact of urban life. Above all, urban historical archaeologies reveal people, both remembered and not remembered, and connect them to the present.

We have confined our discussion here to the built urban environments in (and of) 'the West', by which we mean the western hemisphere, and we therefore want to end with a comment on the notion of 'global historical archaeology'. We are cognisant that the corollary of our emphasis is the under-representation of archaeologies of indigenous, non-European (and non-Europeanised) urbanism in, say, parts of Africa, South America, Asia or Australasia (e.g. Karskens 1999; Lydon 1999a; Reid and Lane 2004; Schávevelzon 1999; Sinclair et al. 1993). The archaeology of Islamic towns and cities (cf. Insoll 1999, 2003), for example, is virtually absent from our account. Western narratives of global urban history have, of course, always privileged western-hemisphere cities, especially with respect to the period after the 'discovery of the New World'. Importantly, historical archaeology holds the potential to offer alternative accounts, using undocumented material from non-western situations to critique such conventional accounts (Funari et al. 1999).

Our choice here, to limit our discussions, has been for two reasons. Firstly, we have aimed to discuss aspects of a particular interpretive body of literature in historical archaeology that has emerged in western urban contexts, in order to describe its potential to tell new stories about towns and cities in the past. But secondly, and as western writers, we are also aware that some calls for global perspectives in historical archaeology belie an uncritical use of the western concept of the 'global', which has arguably originated in western exploration and colonisation of the New World (Trouillot 2003).

Had generalisation been our aim, we could have used the extensive secondary literature on non-western urbanism to provide generalisations. Many writers on urban history have achieved such projects, promoting crosscultural, global syntheses. But in the treatment of Islamic urbanism and its domestic architecture by A. Morris (1979) and Schoenauer (2000: 156–8), respectively, non-western situations are marginalised and presented as alien. Instead, we have emphasised the contextual studies to which we feel historical archaeology is particularly suited. In keeping with the aims of this volume, we have aimed to provide a 'partial' perspective upon urban historical archaeology (Hicks and Beaudry this volume). We hope that the opportunities opened up by the literature discussed here will in coming years be further explored in new situations, exploring the geographical and material complexities of visible and hidden urban pasts.

CHAPTER 7

Archaeology, heritage and the recent and contemporary past

John Schofield and William Gray Johnson

For the first time, those concerned for the historic environment are taking decisions not only about the management and interpretation of ancient and historic monuments, buildings and landscapes, but also about those of the recent and 'contemporary past' (Buchli and Lucas 2001c); about those places that we ourselves have created, or whose creation is remembered, and whose form and character we continue to influence in our everyday lives and social practices. Furthermore, such decisions are being influenced by a wider range of people and groups than at any time since conservation practice first gained legislative support, in the late nineteenth century in England's case and the early twentieth century in the United States. Decisions are now the result of dialogue and participation involving not only national organisations and government at local, regional and national levels, but also – significantly – local communities. As Roger Thomas (2004: 191) has said, 'today, people are less ready to accept the "authorized" view of the archaeological past, preferring to choose for themselves what kind of past they wish to believe in.'

This is especially the case where the past is close, and involves people's direct experience and memory – a past in other words to which people have strong attachment. In Silicon Valley, northern California, for example, the present has very quickly become the past: here memory, place and progress are closely interwoven in a complex social and cultural–technological landscape (Finn 2001). In Detroit, sense of place and the city's heritage is recognised in various ways, not least through its music: the origins of Motown in the 1960s, and techno in the 1980s and 90s, are both reflections of the city's mean streets and industrial ambiance; the distinctive rhythms a result – some say – of the clattering mechanical beat of its assembly lines (Connell and Gibson 2003: 99). Both examples demonstrate the diversity of recent

Acknowledgements: Some sections of this chapter were originally presented by John Schofield at the Institute of Field Archaeologists conference, Liverpool (England), April 2004, and at the DELTA workshop on Compatible Uses of Heritage, Valletta, Malta, December 2004. We are grateful to the editors of this volume for their comments on an earlier draft of this chapter.

and contemporary material culture and the importance of place for existing communities. They each demonstrate also the close proximity of past and present, and the challenge of this proximity for researchers, curators and local communities.

In this chapter we explore approaches to managing the material legacy of the recent and contemporary pasts (broadly the period AD 1900 to the present), asking specifically: why does the recent and contemporary past matter, and how can we make decisions about such recent and familiar places and times in an informed and objective way, given their recency and the fact that many of the places are valued for their social significance; for their personal attachments and sense of place? The chapter develops a review of the literature relating to the management of change in this historic environment and provides three case studies concerning: the informed conservation and protection of recent buildings and monuments (World War II sites in England); the role of characterisation (the English landscape, 1950–2000); and interpretation and presentation of recent events and material culture (the Nevada Test Site and the Atomic Testing Museum in Las Vegas, USA). In general terms the chapter considers the methods and theory that determine our approach to managing this modern material culture. But more specifically, it explores how we seek to balance the maintenance of 'historic character' with the dynamic state that has created the landscape we have today. Although most of the concepts and examples presented here are from England, work is more widespread, the recent and contemporary pasts being a focus of attention in the United States (Slaton and Shiffer 1995) and Australia (D. Jones 2002) for example. Examples of a diversity of projects exploring the recent and contemporary pasts can be found on the web pages of an English Heritage initiative examining the later twentieth century – *Change and Creation*: www.changeandcreation.org.

BACKGROUND

I was born in the fifties, was a child in the sixties, a teenager in the seventies, married in the eighties, divorced in the nineties. The second half of the twentieth century is my whole life. And you know, when I go back none of the places from that part of my life exist anymore. My parents' house was bulldozed and replaced with townhouses twenty years ago. The schools I went to have both been demolished. Even the service stations where I worked part-time are gone. It's as if my life is being erased in my wake. (Stropin and Marsden 2001: 3)

This quotation describes loss, social significance and sense of place. It is a relatively commonplace description of some of the material changes experienced during a lifetime. But it is a rather nostalgic and negative view: suggesting that 'what was there has now gone', and portraying twentieth-century developments as having destroyed what existed before. Historical archaeologists might draw three pertinent observations from this account. Firstly, the cultural resources (artefacts, buildings, sites, and landscapes) of the twentieth century often 'matter' and there will be some that we wish to keep. Secondly, the material remains of this period encourage a recognition that change and creation are quite natural and reasonable processes, and we should no longer view the twentieth century merely as a pollutant that has devalued or destroyed what went before. Thirdly, the archaeological analysis of material culture offers a unique perspective upon modern life.

Historical archaeologists' views of the twentieth century, and how best to address its material record, have changed markedly in the past few years. The wider processes of 'change and creation' are now better understood for the recent and contemporary pasts, and the methods for dealing with them are better established (Bradley et al. 2004). Historical archaeologists increasingly adopt broader views of landscape rather than starting with specific – and usually what many consider to be 'special' – places (Fairclough 2003). Such approaches enable the study of landscape to be holistic, taking account of longer-term processes and their impact (Clark et al. 2004). They also give recognition to the fact that through archaeology we participate in processes of material change (Buchli and Lucas 2001a). Many assume that because the recent and contemporary pasts are so modern, we know all we need to know about them, either from documents, first-hand accounts or from personal experience (Schofield 2005a), but as Graves-Brown (2000: 1) has argued, examining the materiality of the modern world opens up distinctive new perspectives.

Such approaches are very different to previous uses of the archaeology of recent periods as the basis for understanding human behaviour of the more distant past. The 'ethnoarchaeology' of the 1970s and early 1980s studied modern society in order to learn lessons about the formation of the archaeological record, and then to apply those lessons to conventional archaeological contexts. This process of using the present to interpret the past can also be seen in reverse: one reader commented that an article about the Cold War peace camp at Greenham Common (Schofield and Anderton 2000) could only have been written as it was by someone with a grounding in early prehistoric archaeology (Nicholas James, pers. com.)! But historical archaeologies of the modern period now also stand alone, for their own sake. William Rathje's 'garbology' project is one of the best-known examples of this modern archaeology, in which excavations of landfill sites and domestic refuse in people's back yards have begun to demystify aspects of contemporary domestic consumption (Rathje 2001). Rathje's 'first principle of food waste', for example, demonstrated how less food is wasted when fewer variations in food use occur. This explains why in the results of the study, regular sliced bread was wasted at a rate of less than 10 per cent of purchase, while speciality breads are wasted at more than 35 per cent. It also explains why during a sugar shortage the waste of sugar and sweets doubled, despite both being more expensive and in short supply. This knowledge is applicable to shopping and meal planning, as well as the design of prepared foods and packaging. The archaeology of conflict similarly provides evidence for the relevance of this modern archaeology: the work of the American missing-in-action teams (Hoshower-Leppo 2002), for example, reveals how excavation may be undertaken for reasons of memory, commemoration and in some instances to provide a proper burial; but in the case of Argentina's disappeared (Crossland 2002) sometimes it is for retribution or justice and to provide evidence for war-crimes tribunals.

That said, there are systems in place that allow us to accommodate modern material culture within mainstream heritage-management practice. In the United Kingdom, for example, there is no 'fifty-year rule', meaning that sites of any date can be given official recognition. A fifty-year rule does exist in the United States, but this may be set aside for properties that demonstrate exceptional importance. Thus, in the United States and in the United Kingdom, there is the option to preserve recent sites where they have particular significance, and – in the United Kingdom at least – where such designation will serve a specific purpose. In the United States, the National Register of Historic Places in 1994 listed 2,025 properties that had achieved their significance in the past 50 years. Of these, 464 reflected some aspect of history since 1950 and 77 since 1974 (Shull and Savage 1995: 3). But there are often complications.

In England the remains of the Cold War cruise missile alert and mainte-nance area (GAMA) at Greenham Common were scheduled less than ten years after it went out of use. That decision was uncontested. Conversely, the award of an historic 'blue plaque' (representing a formal recognition of the cultural significance of a place or person) to the house in London where rock musician Jimi Hendrix lived was contested, albeit unsuccess-fully, despite the existence of a plaque marking the former residency by the classical composer Handel of the house next door. Why did people consider the Hendrix blue plaque a 'dumbing down' of heritage practice? And why was a stone monolith, constructed by roads protestors on Twyford Down in the 1990s, not accepted for protection despite that being English Heritage's recommendation (Schofield 2005b)? The archaeology of the 'contemporary past' is full of such challenging contradictions, which go to the heart of our definitions of archaeological material.

THEORY AND PRINCIPLES

Differences exist between countries and states in their approach to managing the historic environment, though there is much common ground (see Archaeologia Polona 2000 for a review of European approaches). In England, for example, cultural resources are managed separately from the natural. At government level there is legislation, covering ancient monuments, historic buildings, historic or conservation areas and marine archaeology including wrecks (Hunter and Ralston n.d.). These 'acts' are enforced by the relevant government departments, mainly the Department of Culture, Media and Sport. In addition to legislation there is planning guidance, formal advice issued by government departments to planning authorities on a variety of matters, including (separately) archaeology and the historic environment. Archaeology is now a material matter within the planning system in England – it must be accommodated where encountered or predicted.

English Heritage has a major role within this legislative and planning framework. The Department of Culture, Media and Sport – and specifically the Secretary of State in that Department – has responsibility for enforcing the legislation; but English Heritage advises the Department on which sites to protect, on government policy, and on the granting of consent for works to protected buildings and monuments. Local authority staff take decisions at a local level, albeit within the wider context of government advice and guidance, specifically in strategic and spatial planning, and where planning applications have an archaeological or historic environment implication. These local officers also now increasingly contribute to national debate and decision-making, often encouraging participation of local communities and special-interest groups.

In the United States, much historic preservation is in the hands of the individual states. Each state has a State Historic Preservation Office (SHPO) that oversees the preservation efforts of government entities. In turn, these offices report to the federal government through the United States Department of Interior, National Park Service. Generally, archaeological sites, historic buildings, historic landmarks and traditional cultural properties (T. King 2003) are evaluated case-by-case. The largest number of these is evaluated because an undertaking initiated by a government agency has potential to affect cultural resources that may be eligible for listing on the National Register of Historic Places. While it is the agency's responsibility to determine the significance of all cultural resources affected by an undertaking, it is a consultation process with the SHPO that produces a determination of eligibility. If the consultation process fails, the agency or the SHPO can turn to a federal agency (the Advisory Council on Historic Preservation) for resolution. In very rare cases, the Keeper of the National Register may be called into the process to make a determination of eligibility. In addition to this process, there are local efforts in historic preservation that vary widely: some communities invest in their past with historic districts and/or conservation areas, and others regularly sacrifice their past to make room for the future. Many of these community efforts that support historic preservation may be aided by the SHPO but are not necessarily under their oversight.

These, in outline, are the frameworks that exist in England and the United States. Similar approaches exist in Australia where twentieth-century resources have been the subject of considerable thought and conservation effort (e.g. D. Jones 2002), and elsewhere in the world. There are common factors in all of these approaches, informed by the increasingly international field of heritage studies and practice, and in this general section we will briefly review the literature and current management frameworks through seven interrelated themes: understanding, significance, management, protection, outreach, research and partnership. We will use three case studies to explore their relevance specifically to the recent and contemporary past.

Understanding

'Informed conservation' refers to the research, analysis, survey and investigation necessary to understand the significance of a building and its landscape and to inform decisions about repair, alteration, use and management (Clark 2001: 9). This principle operates at various levels. At a national level for example, Cold War sites or Roman villas can be assessed to determine which to retain, which society can afford to lose, and which can be adapted to new uses, but perhaps retaining their plan form, fabric or façade. It can also operate at a more detailed level, for example in assessing the redecoration or retention of Cold War-era wall art on an American Air Force hangar wall. Here paint research may be needed to determine what damage may occur, and how best to mitigate against it, for example through minimal surface preparation or masking surviving historic paint; research may be needed to determine the type of paint originally used, and the method of application; and it may involve attempting to identify and locate the artist (Cocroft et al. 2006; English Heritage 2004).

How this informed conservation approach works on a thematic level can be seen in the approach towards World War II sites in England. In 1994 English Heritage embarked on a programme of research into World War II and later military sites in England, including for example anti-aircraft batteries, radar sites, coast batteries, airfields, army and prisoner-of-war camps. Commissioned from historians and specialists in this period, the work sought to document for all major classes of twentieth-century military sites: their typology, their distribution and population, as well as the strategies underpinning the various deployments (see Dobinson et al. 1997). This project was largely based on documentary evidence. A second project used wartime and contemporary aerial photographs to determine how many of those original sites now survive (Anderton and Schofield 1999; Schofield 2002b). For World War II radar stations for example, only 14 of the 242 sites deployed survive in their original form, with original plan form still legible and the buildings recognisable, at least from the air. In all, 105 of the 242 sites have been removed, leaving no trace on the ground, 60 years after they went out of use. For anti-aircraft gun sites the survival figures are worse: only 10 of the 981 heavy anti-aircraft sites survive intact, while 790 have been removed, largely the result of post-war suburban expansion (see Dobinson 2001 for examples of surviving sites). A further project has studied Cold War sites (Cocroft 2001; Cocroft and Thomas 2003), and another has used results from the national Heritage Lottery funded Defence of Britain Project to provide an assessment of the 67 areas in England where anti-invasion defences survive in a legible form in landscapes largely unmodified since they were defended in 1940–1941 (Foot 2004).

The methodologies developed in this programme of research have relevance to further studies of the recent and contemporary past. Documentary evidence will often exist, as will contemporary aerial photographs, sometimes in digital form that can be examined rapidly and in close detail. By studying one (to determine what was built), and then the other (to establish survival, both by monument class, and of buildings on individual sites), detailed information can be provided, documenting how many sites survive of the original population, where those sites are, what form they take, and whether they are currently at risk. From the study of World War II sites it has been possible to establish national policy for the selection of these sites for statutory protection, and to consider drawing up conservation plans for a few, based on their rarity and the condition of surviving buildings. But there are wider implications too. The fact that such large numbers of World

War II sites, sites that were heavily built and substantial settlements, have been removed from view in just sixty years has relevance to our approach to managing other categories of site and landscape types from the twentieth century, and earlier periods also. Presumably we can assume an equivalent scale of loss for World War II sites in other developed European countries, representing a major loss of material culture related to arguably the most significant event of world history. A strategy for managing loss in the future needs now to be addressed at this broader geographic scale.

Significance

It seems to be widely accepted now that heritage brings benefit to society (Little 2002) – the question 'who cares?' is now rarely asked. In 2000 English Heritage published *Power of Place: the Future of the Historic Environment* (English Heritage 2000). Building on the results of an opinion poll, this report – presented by English Heritage to the British government – noted that most people place a high value on the historic environment. The poll showed that 87 per cent of people in England think its right that there should be public funding to preserve it, 85 per cent think it is important in the regeneration of our towns and cities, and 77 per cent disagree that we preserve too much. It is seen as a major contributor to the quality of life. In the United States a survey in 1999 drew similar results. Almost all respondents (99 per cent) said that archaeological sites have educational and scientific value, 94 per cent recognised aesthetic or artistic value, and 93 per cent saw value related to personal heritage. In all, 69 per cent of respondents believed public funding should be used to preserve historic sites (Ramos and Duganne 2000). Returning to *Power of Place*, it is clear that

For most people the historic environment represents the place where they live. They value it for the quality of life it can afford them. For others, it is the place they visit and value, for the inspiration and enjoyment that it offers. For the people that welcome and serve those visitors, it is a source of livelihood, a powerful generator of wealth and prosperity. (English Heritage 2000: 4)

In England some sites are recognised as having 'national importance' – and sites must meet stringent criteria if they are to be declared as such. Only nationally important sites can be protected through scheduling, an ancient and rather draconian legislative power that tends now to be applied only to monuments in the strict sense, that is monuments out of everyday use. We shall return to this theme below, but it is clear that the problem with national importance is that this can give the impression that other sites have less value or significance, or even no value at all; these are sites we can afford

to lose, some say and in some cases without adequate record. Of course
that is not generally the case, but it is the perception. In Australia valuable innovative work has been undertaken on the issue of significance, and
specifically social significance – recognising that both historic and contemporary places and landscapes will mean different things to different people,
but that everywhere has the potential to hold value for somebody (Byrne et
al. 2001). Some places are valued by particular groups in society (Schofield
2004b), or – uniquely for the recent and contemporary past – by individuals
for whom they have some personal connection (P. Read 1996). Sometimes
that personal connection has no material manifestation, a point discussed
by Denis Byrne (1999), who notes that for post-coup Bali, c. 1965, material
traces are almost entirely absent and memory provides the only link between
a painful recent past and the present:

> The way people signify things and landscapes, privately, locally, intimately, ani-
> mates them in ways that are likely to be invisible to outsiders. This invisibility, this
> localised activity taking place 'below the thresholds at which visibility begins,' to
> use Michel de Certeau's words, can be a form of resistance in the face of larger,
> national narratives which aim to impose their own ultra-visible truth claims. While
> not suggesting that memory is static or immune to decay, or not changed with every
> recall, it is nevertheless possible to see how the memory of individuals can preserve
> an account of events subversive to the official version. Not available to surveil-
> lance, these private memories constitute a type of 'noise' in the officially imposed
> silence. (Byrne 1999: 47–48)

Government-led policy on the designation of heritage sites tends only to
recognise cultural value in a restricted way, a white, middle-class way in England's case. But there are other views, and other values. An example is Tower
Hamlets in the East End of London where there exists a large Bangladeshi
community, the subject of Monica Ali's recent best-selling novel (2003).
Within this community are buildings that have been given protection (have
been 'listed'). Yet these buildings mean little to the present Bangladeshi
community that for the past few decades has made up 90 per cent of the
population in this area; and those buildings which do matter to the community – mosques and community centres for example – have no protection
because they do not meet national criteria (Gard'ner 2001). The advantage
of the approach being developed in Australia is that it recognises this fact,
and takes account of different perceptions and different values. A recently
completed project in Sydney for example sought first to understand and then
to accommodate the views of minority groups concerning national parks
and their use of these open spaces (M. Thomas 2001). The Macedonian
community brought with them to Australia a cultural tradition of large

open-air picnics, which they hold at weekends and public holidays in the wooded parks around the city. They are noisy and often boisterous affairs, which have offended other users of the parks. But rather than just ban these events, a project was undertaken to first document and understand the social significance of the events, and balance that with the needs of other users (M. Thomas 2001). By adopting a conciliatory approach, solutions become possible.

The historic environment therefore matters, but it is often the most familiar places that mean most, for reasons of personal attachment and memory. These places can be obvious, monumental structures, or the personalised spaces, such as a gateway through which a child or lover was glimpsed for the last time. As Byrne suggests, would this gateway not be imprinted thereafter, for those left behind, with intimations of loss (1999: 47)? Michael Bell talks of the 'ghosts of place', amidst a concern that such talk may be deemed unscientific, referring to the presence of those who are not physically there. But there is a valid point here, especially where we are discussing places of loss and conflict:

Although the cultural language of modernity usually prevents us from speaking about their presence, we constitute a place in large measure by the ghosts we sense inhabit and possess it. The meaning of a place, its *genius loci*, depends upon the geniuses we locate there. (M. Bell 1997: 813)

Attachment is keenly felt, and arguably it is this attachment that contributes most to the meaning and significance of place. The sense of those no longer physically there can be a key part of that equation.

Management

It is unrealistic to seek to protect everything that survives from the past, and nor should we try. This is especially clear for the remains of the recent past. A rigorous approach, based on contemporary social significance, and the things that give a place its distinctive qualities, is therefore desirable. Our third theme concerns how we can manage the historic environment as a whole, without having to focus only on some of the special places within it, but recognising the need to maintain its defining and dynamic qualities. Quoting again from *Power of Place*:

Although people value the historic environment, this does not represent resistance to change. On the contrary, most people believe change is necessary and desirable. But, they see change taking place in the context of the historic environment. Keeping the best from the past provides a powerful justification for gracing our surroundings with the very best of the new. Good new buildings, high quality design, thoughtful planning, intelligent land-use, are desirable objectives in their own right. With proper understanding of the historic environment, clarity of purpose and sensitivity to the quality of place, excellent new building and design will both complement and enhance the historic environment. (English Heritage 2000: 4).

But how can we decide what is appropriate? What is the framework within which change can be managed rather than resisted? What are we using as our benchmark? One answer to this is characterisation, which has been undertaken now across most of England, and in parts of Europe (English Heritage 2005; Fairclough and Rippon 2002). Characterisation within English Heritage has three main strands: historic landscape characterisation (HLC); urban characterisation work; and thematic programmes, such as its work on World War II, the Cold War, industrial heritage and so on (this thematic work was described earlier, through the example of World War II sites).

HLC and urban characterisation have much in common. They were each developed in the 1990s partly in reaction to changing views of the traditional designation system, a system that in England has proved effective for over fifty years for buildings and over a hundred years for monuments. This system does not work well for the wider historic landscape however. One option was to create landscape 'registers', as was done in Wales (Cadw 2003). But drawing lines around only 'special' parts of the historic landscape can devalue the areas outside those lines, just as it can with scheduling; also, it is not always clear what registers achieve, other than simply highlighting interest with perhaps the view that further change in these 'special' areas should be resisted. More than any other part of the historic environment, landscape is characterised and enriched by centuries of change and modification. If we are to celebrate the result of past change, we must logically accept further change, especially as so many areas depend on living, shifting, ever-changing and often semi-natural patterns of use. We surely need landscape to change so that it continues to be cultural, and a dynamic inheritance for our successors.

Characterisation enables this dynamic process to occur, while recognising what matters from the past. It uses attributes such as field morphology, place names, boundary loss, historic environment and modern land-use data to create a geographical information system (GIS)-based view of the landscape. In towns the same principles apply, recognising the significance of plan-form components, and their interrelationships. Analysis of these attributes produces characterisation maps which can be interrogated through GIS at a variety of spatial scales. Each distinct area has its own defining characteristics, which provide the framework within which the characterisation can be used in a variety of ways. These can include planning for new development, or informing agri-environment policies, as well as partnership, learning and outreach initiatives.

Similarly, urban characterisation is not intended to prevent development, but rather to guide it, perhaps towards areas where particular types of development are more in keeping with the character of that area, or will be less damaging to buried archaeological remains.

Characterisation does not replace designation therefore, but it is a way of managing change in a dynamic way, allowing historic character and fabric to influence future development. A new project that extends these principles of characterisation to the later twentieth century has the title *Change and Creation: Historic Landscape Character 1950–2000*, and this forms the subject of our second case study. This project takes characterisation to a new level, recognising our own contemporary landscape, and the values people attach to it (see also Hayden 2004 for a characterisation of contemporary urban, periurban and industrial landscapes in the United States). It makes the point that landscape is by definition a fluid and dynamic thing; that until recently change and new development has been cast in a negative light, damaging/destroying what went before. *Change and Creation* presents a different view: that what we ourselves have created is every bit as much a part of the landscape as Roman roads and medieval fields. It may be more recent, more familiar, we may hate it . . . but it is there, and it is now part of the landscape we must pass on to future generations. Often in the past we have waited too long before recording historic sites, or seeking to protect them, and by the time that stage is reached much of the resource has been removed (e.g. the World War II sites discussed above).

The aim of *Change and Creation* is therefore to characterise the contribution to England's landscape made between 1950–2000 through a range of public engagements including a website (www.changeandcreation.org), which poses a series of questions on which opinions are sought, and specifically (the booklet states), 'not only from academics, government organisations and heritage managers' (Bradley et al. 2004: 11). Questions include:

• What do you remember most clearly about the twentieth century? How are those events and activities still represented in the landscape?
• What do you appreciate, dislike or miss about the later twentieth-century landscape?
• What do you think about change and creation? Would you prefer our landscape to be more like it was in the early twentieth century?
• What can, and what should we do with modern landscape character? What should we be recording now for the future? (Bradley et al. 2004: 11)

As Bradley et al. state (2004: 7), *Change and Creation* borrows from the ideas of contemporary archaeology. It challenges and reviews established conservation and cultural resource management theories and principles that are taken too much for granted. The programme contributes to developing philosophies of archaeological resource management, as well as to our understanding and treatment of later twentieth-century landscape. The choices we face are not now whether to have a cut-off date, nor how to incorporate recent change into perceptions of landscape since this already happens. What we need to do now is to find ways of doing so consciously and transparently, and to debate the process (Bradley et al. 2004).

Protection

While recognising that the historic environment is dynamic, and that even its most valued historic components may be able to support significant changes of use, some sites will need to be protected, either to ensure they remain as monuments, or sometimes to ensure that stringent consent procedures that accompany designated sites are available to prevent unnecessary damage. Currently in England there are two main forms of statutory protection (although the system is currently under review and this may change): scheduling for monuments out of everyday use; and listing for historic buildings where a future in use is considered both likely and appropriate. Military buildings are an interesting example. Many military buildings and sites have now fallen out of use, and some of those have been disposed of by the Defence Estate and are now privately owned. Some of these sites and buildings are clearly of national importance, but just leaving them empty and unused is not really an option. These buildings were intended to be used, and would generally be best served if an appropriate new use could be found for them. Some can and do become museum facilities; some find occasional use as exhibition and gallery spaces, for works of art often on the theme of militarisation. The control tower at the former airbase at Greenham Common for example is being kept in the hope that funding can be found to use it for interpretation of the wider site; but for now it is in occasional use as a gallery, including recently for a sound installation. Buildings have also often been converted into offices. In Swindon, former railway buildings were converted to become English Heritage's National Monument Record Centre.

Outreach

Engagements with the public in historical archaeology are often contested, and always complex (Shackel 2000a; cf. Hodder 2004). Yet, returning to the opinion poll referred to earlier, most English people are interested in the historic environment – it is as we have seen an 'incomparable source of information' (English Heritage 2000: 4) – we just need to make that information more widely available, and open to comment and critique. An example of outreach, and one that makes good use of new technology, is the Hackney Building Exploratory, East London. This is the first such centre in the United Kingdom, exploring the local area by means of hands-on exhibitions and bringing resources focused on the local environment together under one roof. Set up in one of the poorest boroughs in the country as a prototype for community education, the Exploratory provides local people with information about the local area through interactive exhibits. These help people develop a sense of place and encourage them to express their views about the neighbourhood. Residents are therefore better informed about their community and better able to participate in decisions about change and improvement (DCMS 2001: 29).

So far our examples have been drawn from England, but managing the recent past is increasingly a matter of global concern, as our next case study shows. Alongside the popular media and in particular television, interpretive facilities and museums have the most significant role to play in conveying meaning to those that seem increasingly aware of modern material culture. A new facility is that in Las Vegas, documenting the history and material legacy of atomic testing programmes in the state. This forms the subject of our final case study.

For most US citizens, 'old' buildings or sites are hundreds of years old: exotic oddities that conjure images of the past as a foreign country, in contrast with the contemporary world. The idea that the remains of atomic testing activities deserved special recognition for their importance in history was therefore at first viewed suspiciously by many. Now that the Atomic Testing Museum is built and open to the public, it is increasingly appreciated for its unusual approach to a time period most young adults associate with their parents and grandparents (Figure 7.1).

While Cold War historians have existed in the United States for decades, it is only since the 1990s that Cold War archaeologists have become indispensable. One reason is because so much of what remains from the Cold War is ruinous. Another is the technological nature of the remains. Both reasons justify archaeological examination in a way that works well with the process of determining significance. This case study examines the Nevada Test Site (NTS) as an agency-owned and operated site dedicated to dealing with the country's highest, most-sensitive technologies throughout its entire existence. Even now, the test site supports multiple high-end technology

Figure 7.1   The Atmospheric Testing Gallery at the Atomic Testing Museum, Nevada.

programmes as it stands in readiness should the United States ever return to nuclear weapons testing. But it also has a long history of recognising the value of its archaeological resources.

The NTS was established in late 1950 from land that was already under federal-government control. In January 1951, the first nuclear-weapon test was conducted. From then until October 1992, a total of 928 nuclear-test weapons were exploded. Other non-explosive nuclear research was also conducted at the site including the nuclear-rocket development programme, dosimetry experiments, and fallout studies. While these and other programmes were underway, the NTS had an archaeologist examining archaeological sites as early as 1963 (Worman 1969). These studies were expanded after the passage of the Historic Preservation Act of 1966 to include work at the Central Nevada Test Area (Brooks 1968; Edwards and Johnson 1994). By 1978, the Desert Research Institute (DRI) had established a long-term archaeological programme on the NTS that continues to the present day. It was in the late 1980s that one of the DRI archaeologists recognised the significance of the buildings, towers and other structures from the atomic weapons and non-explosive nuclear research programmes and began a quest for funding historic research at these sites. Then, in 1991, the first of these sites was evaluated by a team that included archaeologists and an architectural historian (Goldenberg and Beck 1991a, 1991b). These studies expanded to the establishment of two historic districts (Johnson and Edwards 2000; W. Johnson et al. 2000) as well as numerous historical evaluations, surveys and other preservation documentation. Research has also now been conducted at Peace Camp, immediately outside the test site's main entrance (Beck et al. n.d.; Schofield 2000).

Parallel with these developments, local citizens who worked on the NTS recognised the need to organise a non-profit corporation in order to preserve the history of the site and tell its story to the public. On 15 April 1998 the Nevada Test Site Historical Foundation (NTSHF) was granted its not-for-profit status and began the process of establishing the Atomic Testing Museum. The paths of the DRI historic-preservation programme and the NTSHF museum crossed resulting in a synergy that brings us to the opening of the museum.

The Atomic Testing Museum is located near the famed Las Vegas Strip and expects that it will be visited by tourists or locals who have an interest in this history. The museum promotes cultural, educational, and scientific programmes to encourage the development and public exchange of views regarding the NTS and its impact on the nation. The Museum occupies an 8,000-square-foot (800m^2) permanent exhibit space, a 2,000-square-foot (200m^2) exhibit hall for travelling exhibits and a 400-square-foot (40m^2) museum store. Featured artefacts include a copy of Einstein's letter to President Roosevelt urging the United States of America to consider development of nuclear weaponry, a 10-foot-diameter (3m) decoupler representative of similar artefacts used for underground testing in tunnels and recording stations from the Fizeau test conducted on 14 September 1957. Approximately 40 per cent of the museum's content is in multimedia formats.

What will the reaction of the public be to this museum? If successful, the museum will enhance the public's understanding of the Cold War – both in its technological developments and the social concerns that grew from it. In order to maintain public interest, the museum's 2,000-square-foot (200m^2) exhibit space has hosted 'A Cold War Sampler' (the Francis Gary Powers U-2 Incident, Mount Charleston Cold War Commemoration and Cold War Archaeology), Dr Peter Goin's, photographic essay, 'Nuclear Landscapes', and 'EG&G: Together Again' highlighting the work of Harold 'Doc' Edgerton, Kenneth Germeshausen and Herbert E. Grier, founders of 'EG&G' Technical Services, Inc.

EG&G, founded over fifty years ago, is foremost in the memory of NTS veterans as the company that designed, built and operated the equipment that armed, timed, fired, photographed and acquired performance data on almost every nuclear test at the NTS and in the Pacific. Edgerton's 'Seeing the Unseen' features high-speed photographic images and graphics. Germeshausen's patent drawings and Grier's hand-crafted engine models complete this historical exhibit. In addition, the museum has hosted a variety of authors, lecturers and artists since October 2003. One of the museum's first speakers was Sergei Khrushchev, son of former Soviet Chairman Nikita Khrushchev, who managed to humanise his father in a way that no one in the audience expected. Former Secretary of the Air Force Thomas C. Reed spoke on his experiences gained through his many Cold War-era roles and about his new book *At the Abyss: An Insider's History of the Cold War*.

Research

We need to constantly keep abreast of the subjects that we work with, the values we attribute to our historic resources, and the motivations we have for managing them. Our views now are very different – very much more inclusive – than they were even ten years ago. Characterisation now exists as a methodology, for example, transforming perceptions and approaches. But above all, decisions have to be well informed, and part of that concerns knowing both what we know, and what we do not know. What are the gaps in our understanding of the recent past? What do we most urgently need to find out, and how can the study of material remains assist us in these enquiries? What opportunities might be available to pursue these research agendas? Many published agendas do now exist, some thematic and some regional. But all need to be kept under constant review, and there is always the danger that they will be interpreted in too prescriptive a way by curators and heritage managers. *Modern Military Matters* (Schofield 2004a) is a recently published agenda: it reviews what we now know of twentieth-century military material culture, where the gaps in our understanding lie, and by what means we can best address them.

Agendas are also now required for further aspects of the recent and contemporary pasts, and not just the more conventional and accepted topics such as military and industrial remains. It is also now timely to critically review the methodologies for studying this period, and the theoretical frameworks for understanding and interpreting it. These are initiatives best considered at a pan-European or even a global scale, given the increasing trend towards globalisation during the modern period, and through interdisciplinary research programmes (see Schofield and Cocroft n.d. for an example of how this can be achieved, in this case through studies of material culture of the Cold War era).

Partnership

It is often easy to remain fragmented, with special interest groups, professional bodies, even professions, working in isolation. The real gains in researching the recent and contemporary pasts are to be had through integration and partnership, however, and we are reminded of something the biologist E. O. Wilson said (1998): that transdisciplinary projects have the benefit of bringing a diversity of views and perspectives to a subject, and that thinking quite a long way across established disciplinary boundaries is generally needed in order to achieve that. This tendency towards what Wilson calls 'consilience' is an important new development and one that will bring great benefit to all concerned for the historic environment, and for its continued relevance to and enjoyment by the many and diverse communities that occupy it.

CONCLUSIONS

This chapter has provided an overview of cultural-resource management practices, mostly in the United Kingdom and the United States, where work on the recent and contemporary pasts is well advanced. The projects described are necessarily diverse but combine to recognise the values we attach to familiar places, and the different ways that significance is expressed, through tangible and intangible remains: buildings and monuments, for example; musical styles and scenes; but also the subtle traces of human activity – often the things that contribute most to a place's character, and the feel of the landscape, its distinctive qualities and aura. These are all true for earlier periods as well, but for the recent and contemporary pasts they are most strongly felt.

It is also an area of work that presents very particular challenges. Perhaps the most perplexing issue for archaeologists working with the recent and contemporary past is the cultural bias introduced into any decision on preservation of recent material culture by our participation in free-market economies. We remember well the stark contrast in the material culture between East and West Berliners when the Wall came down. Most shocking was the self-introspection it caused for many of us to realise the disdain we held for 'apparently' out-dated technologies and the 'rightness' of free-market economies to keep technologies on the cutting edge. At the same time, a somewhat schizophrenic state of mind exists for many of us as we subscribe to the eco-friendly paradigm gripping most modern-day countries that views today's disposable world negatively. This is a view however that masks the plethora of material goods surrounding each of us. It is precisely that materiality which leads to the difficulty of managing the recent and contemporary past.

CHAPTER 8

Marxism and capitalism in historical archaeology

Randall H. McGuire

Marx's theory of capitalism has found its strongest following in Anglo-American archaeology among those scholars who study the modern world. Currently Marxists represent a major school of thought in historical archaeology in North America, the United Kingdom, and Australia. This should not be surprising because Marx's analysis of class is plainly applicable to the deep-seated class exploitation found in the modern history of the West. Moreover, archaeologists studying capitalism are themselves embedded in capitalist class relations. These archaeologists define historical archaeology as the archaeology of capitalism (Leone and Potter 1999). Contemporary historical archaeologists working in the Marxist tradition have by and large rejected a 'totalising' notion of Marxism: they instead use class and Marxist analyses as entry points for studies that also consider race, gender, and ethnicity as loci of oppression.

MARXISM

Karl Marx did not create Marxism. In fact, in a famous reaction to the development of a 'Marxist' workers' party in France he said, 'If anything is certain, it is that I myself am not a Marxist' (Engels 1992). Marxism is a tradition of thought, a philosophy, and a mode of theoretical production that began with Marx's ideas and writings. Many intertwined and sometimes conflicting lines of theory have developed from this origin. Marx pondered the basic questions of social life in order to formulate a critical theory of capitalism. His attempts to understand the social world were tentative, dynamic, and often paradoxical. Modern social thinkers cannot escape the basic questions he raised: much like biologists rereading Darwin, they return to Marx. For social science in general, and for historical archaeology in particular, this tradition is a rich source of insights, theories, concepts, and ideas about the nature of cultural change.

All well-founded Marxist approaches strive for three goals: to gain knowledge of the world, to critique the world, and to transform the world. The tension between these objectives warns scholars away from a sterile scholasticism, a nihilistic scepticism, or politically self-serving illusions. In order to change the world, people must have accurate knowledge of the world, since action based upon incorrect or flawed knowledge can only result in failure and error. Accurate knowledge does not, however, exist independently of the social consciousness of the individual. Knowledge is not something simply waiting to be discovered in the world. People produce knowledge in a complex dialectic between the reality that they observe and the consciousness that they bring to that observation. Knowledge for knowledge's sake is usually self-serving or trivial. Knowledge becomes meaningful and important when the process of gaining knowledge is intimately interconnected both with social concerns and with the social position and interests of social agents. Accurate knowledge, therefore, is only possible from a critical stance. If people do not question the ethics, politics, epistemology, and reality behind their knowledge, then their actions in the world will be unsound and likely to result in unanticipated, harmful, and/or counterproductive consequences. Marxist critiques challenge how people use the reality of the world, the social context in which they exist, and their own interests in creating knowledge. These critiques question different visions or interpretations of knowledge, and lead to a self-examination of Marxist perspectives. Critique must, however, ultimately rest in the reality of the observable world. If it does not engage reality, it will only lead to self-delusion and fantasy. By the same token, critique should lead to social action. Critique without reality generates self-delusion; critique that does not lead to social action produces only nihilism and despondency. Many communist states transformed Marxism into little more than an ideology to legitimate their exercise of political power. Ideology lacks the tension between knowledge, critique, and action. Without this tension Marxism became a source of alienation, domination, exploitation, and repression (Klejn 1991: 70; Trigger 1995: 326).

Many scholars have embraced a 'totalising' theory of Marxism (Cohen 1978; Gilman 1998, 2001). They argue that Marxism can explain the totality of society through its analysis of class struggle. From this totalising and sometimes totalitarian position class struggle creates inequalities based in gender, race, or ethnicity. The feminist notion of entry point, however, offers an alternative to these totalitarian ideas (A. Wylie 1991). A totalising theory of Marxism never took hold in historical archaeology and contemporary Marxist historical archaeologists take the diversity and the complexity of oppression seriously. They recognise that exploitation derives from many relationships including those of gender, class, race, and ethnicity. Each of these relationships provides an entry point to the study of social relations and of oppression. Marxist historical archaeologists enter the study of the social world with the analysis of class, and from this entry point examine the complex relationships between class, gender, race, and ethnicity in the construction of oppression. As long as scholars seeking a radical transformation of the social world recognise that that transformation must include relations of gender, class, race, and ethnicity (hooks 2000), then theories using class, gender, race or ethnicity as entry points can be compatible and complementary.

POLITICAL ECONOMY

A Marxist approach to archaeology begins with Marx's study of *Political Economy* (Marx 1906). His political economy was an integral and original approach that entailed its own logic, theory, and method; that is, a dialectical logic, a theory of capitalism, and the method of class analysis. Marxists apply this logic, theory, and method to the study of society as a dynamic whole. A Marxist political economy focuses on the historical reality of lived conditions and on how these conditions produce and are products of social action.

There is no simple or unambiguous way to describe the *dialectic*. Different approaches to Marxism define the dialectic in different ways. But all definitions share a few general principles. The dialectic views society as a whole: as a complex interconnected web within which any given entity is defined by its relationship to other entities. Thus, you cannot have teachers without students, as each social entity exists because of the existence of its opposite. If such interconnectedness is broken the opposites dissolve away, or more properly, are transformed into something else. By this same token, causes do not exist free of their effects and no variable is ever independent. This social world has an intrinsic dynamic because change in any part of the world alters the whole of the relations, sustaining all elements forever in flux.

In the dialectic the entities that make up the social whole are not expected to fit comfortably together. They may fit, but the dynamics of change are not to be found in these functional relations. Rather, they lie in relational contradictions that spring from the fact that social categories are defined by and require the existence of their opposite. Thus, slavery defines both the master and the slave. For one to exist so too must the other, and yet as opposites they are potentially in conflict. Each has contrary interests and a different lived experience in the context of a shared history. Change in these relations is never simply quantitative or qualitative. Quantitative changes can lead to qualitative change, and qualitative change necessarily implies a quantitative change. Conflicts that result from relational contradictions may result in quantitative changes in those relations that build to a qualitative change. Rebellion by slaves may lead the masters to enforce stricter and stricter discipline, thereby heightening slave resistance until the relation of slavery is overthrown. The social relations that result from such a qualitative change are a mix of the old and the new; the old social form is remade not replaced.

Marxism is first and foremost a theory of *capitalism*, or more properly a theory of the inherent contradictions of capitalism (J. Jameson 1997: 175). Marx (1906) defined capitalism as a set of social relationships (a mode of production) in which workers must sell their labour power to the owners of the tools, resources, and raw materials necessary for production (the means of production) in order to survive. In the capitalist wage labour relationship the owners gain profit (surplus value) by paying workers less than the value that they add to the product. The capitalist class process is one of many different ways in human history that élites have appropriated labour and the products of labour from primary producers. Capitalism as an economic system developed in the modern era. Since the 1970s, Marxist scholars have debated exactly when within this era the transition to capitalism occurred (Sweezy 1976). Exchange theorists link the origins of capitalism to the establishment of production for profit in a global market that began in the sixteenth century (Wallerstein 1974). Production theorists argue that the Industrial Revolution at the end of the eighteenth century established wage labour as the dominant social relationship of the economy and marked the beginnings of capitalism (Wolf 1982: 296–298). Several British medieval archaeologists have contributed to this debate (T. Saunders 1991; Williamson and Bellamy 1987). More recently these discussions have shifted to more global perspectives and to theories that find capitalism's origin in European agrarian relationships (Blaut 2000; McAuley 2001; E. Wood 2002).

Marx found it necessary first to address fundamental questions concerning the nature of the human condition and human society before he could formulate his theory of capitalism. Marx argued that the ultimate determining factor in human history is the production and reproduction of real life (Marx and Engels 1977: 75). He also argued that the development of the productive forces in society over time would lead to both quantitative and qualitative changes in real life. Marx, however, did not seek to create a grand theory of human history but rather to explicate, critique, and revolutionise capitalism.

Marxism ultimately relies on a radical concept of history. For Marx, history created the context for social action but history was also created. The creation of history involves culture, identity and interpretation and thus affords the possibility for people to come to a critical consciousness of their own social actions. Marxists take a holistic and anti-reductionist approach to the study of human history. They reject the idea that scholars should reduce real life to its parts (culture, economy, politics, society, or history) and elaborate different theories to account for these parts. The logic of the dialectic guides scholars to study society as an interconnected whole. People experience and participate in society as a whole, not part by part. There can thus be no Marxist approach to archaeology that is separated from Marxism as a whole. Marxist archaeologists therefore reject the idea that archaeology needs to construct its own autonomous theory.

Marx reasoned that the labour process is a necessary condition for human existence (Marx 1906: 197–207). Human work entails the use of energy to transform and manipulate nature and to produce the products that humans need to live. *Labour*, however, implies more than just work because human labour presupposes a web of social relations and meanings that structure energy expenditure. Labour is conscious action. People must first imagine what they will make before they produce it (Marx 1906: 198). As did many of his contemporaries, Marx embraced a labour theory of value – seeing the labour necessary to transform nature into commodities as the basic measure of value. Since labour is socially determined, value is a social relationship between people that expresses the particular historical form of labour. In communal relations producers receive the full value of their labour. Exploitation exists when others have the ability to extract *surplus value* from the primary producers without an exchange or return of equivalent values. Marx saw the social form of surplus value (such as capitalist profit) as the main defining characteristic of a society. *Primitive accumulation* exists when élite individuals extract surplus value through direct or coercive means such as tribute or enslavement. In capitalism the relations of wage labour obscure the extraction of surplus value.

Marx labelled the objects that people use to transform nature as *instruments of production*. Thus the labour process always entails three factors: social, conscious human beings, nature (raw materials), and the instruments of production. The products of the labour process embody the social relations and consciousness that are the conditions of their production. Through the labour process, social relations, culture, ideas and meaning, indeed the whole of the human condition, are objectified; that is, it takes a material (objective) role in the process of the production and reproduction of real life (Roseberry 1989: 26). The labour process is objectified (becomes material) in all things that humans can perceive via their senses: sound, sight, taste, touch and smell. The material objects include many things such as speech, music, text, art, manners, customs, food, drink, artefacts, buildings and ritual. The things that archaeologists call material culture are prominent among these objects. Thus, a Marxist archaeology regards material culture as a product of social, conscious labour, and as part of the material conditions of the world that structure that labour. Or in other words, people produce material culture through social labour, but once produced, material culture both enables and limits the production and reproduction of real life that forms social labour. It is both the symbolism of the material and its physical reality that engages in a dialectic with social actors.

Marx and Engels (1970) characterised the development of the productive forces in society in terms of *modes of production*. In their various works they defined many different modes of production that had existed in human history. They examined non-capitalist modes of production primarily to lay bare the historical development of capitalism (Bloch 1983: 1–20). The mode of production is made up of the *forces* of production and the *relations* of production. Forces of production include the *means* of production (instruments of production, the raw materials, technical knowledge, the technical organisation of labour and skills necessary for labour) and labour power (people). Relations of production are those social relationships that people enter into to produce and reproduce real life. Traditionally, Marxists have stressed those relations such as property relations that connect most directly to the production of commodities. Contemporary Marxists have used the concept more broadly to include all social relations including gender, kinship, and race.

Marx and Engels (1970) employed a building-like metaphor of *base* (foundation) and *superstructure* to illustrate the idea that the mode of production of a society (the base) conditions the political forms, social consciousness, belief structure, and ideology of a society (the superstructure). *Ideology* refers to a distortion of thought (a false consciousness) that conceals social contradictions both within and between the base and superstructure (cf. De Cunzo and Ernstein this volume). Those who subscribe to materialist strains of Marxism recognise a dialectical relationship between base and superstructure but argue that the base will take primacy over the super-structure in the last instance (Engels 1954). These materialist perspectives tend to see contradictions between the forces and relations of production as the primary basis for revolutionary changes in the mode of production. A revolution produces contradictions between the base and superstructure that transform the ideology of the society. Humanistic Marxists argue that the base cannot be primary or determinate of the superstructure because both require and bring about the existence of the other. Neither the base nor the superstructure may exist prior to, or in the absence of, the other. Thus, the origin of change lies in the dialectic between base and superstructure and not in one or the other (Ollman 1971, 1993; Sayer 1987).

The concept of *class* is central to Marxism. The term refers to historically constituted groups of people, a driving force in history (class conflict) and to the starting point for the Marxist method of class analysis. Marx and Engels formulated their concept of class from the class structure of early capitalism and the class struggles of this society. In the abstract, class refers to social groups that stand in different relationships to the means of production that allow one class to exploit other classes by extracting surplus production. Classes, however, never exist in the abstract, but only in concrete historical circumstances. In such concrete cases Marxists study class relations as a process that is inherently conflictual. Dominant classes will seek to maximise the rate of exploitation of subordinate classes and these classes will resist such exploitation. This class conflict or class struggle drives the dynamics of history. To study class struggle Marxists first identify the class structure of a historical case and the interests of different classes and class fractions. They then analyse how that struggle plays out in specific historical circumstances (see Marx 1978).

Marxism is ultimately a theory of praxis (Crehan 2002). Praxis refers to theoretically informed practice (or agency). Praxis is the human activity through which people transform the world and themselves. The decisive goal of Marxism is a praxis that transforms both people and society. As a dialectical concept praxis implies that our agency both as scholars and more broadly as social beings must lie in the interconnections between human free-creative agency, and the material (that is concrete) conditions of human existence.

THE ARCHAEOLOGY OF CAPITALISM

Explicitly Marxist approaches to the archaeological study of capitalism began in the 1970s and came to fruition in the 1990s (McGuire 1992; Patterson 2003). At the end of the 1970s, the first cohort of Marxist historical archaeologists that included scholars such as Mark Leone (1981b), Russell Handsman (1983), and Michael Parker Pearson (1982) followed a theoretical path already laid out in the anglophone social sciences. They drew on French structural Marxism and the Marxist critical theory of the Frankfurt School to define a *critical archaeology*. At about the same time an approach often called *anthropological political economy* coalesced in the work of North American cultural anthropologists (Diamond 1974; Leacock 1981; J. Nash 1979; Wolf 1982). The next cohort of archaeologists found their Marxism in this anthropological theory (McGuire 1988; Paynter 1985). Since the 1990s anglophone archaeologists have dropped certain premises of the critical archaeology, and the two approaches have melded into the archaeology of capitalism (Leone and Potter 1999). This archaeology rejects a totalising theory of Marxism, and uses class as an entry point to study relations of power that also include gender, race, ethnicity and sexuality (Delle et al. 2000). Archaeological studies of capitalism use a relational concept of class to address themes of ideology, cultural production and struggle. Even historical archaeologists who have not explicitly embraced Marxism now find it necessary to discuss labour in terms of social relations rather than as simple economics (Dalglish 2003; M. Johnson 1996; Silliman 2004). The ultimate goal of the archaeology of capitalism is a praxis that challenges capitalism.

STRUCTURAL MARXISM AND CRITICAL ARCHAEOLOGY

French structural Marxism, especially the work of Althusser (1969; 1971a), Godelier (1977) and Meillassoux (1981) influenced British archaeology in the 1970s and 1980s (Friedman and Rowlands 1978; D. Miller et al. 1989). French structural Marxists sought to make Marxism more scientific by replacing a Hegelian dialectic with structuralism (McGuire 1992: 41–43). These theorists emphasised the contradictions that existed between different structural levels of society, especially those between the base and superstructure. As part of this approach they elaborated a Marxist notion of ideology and its importance in these contradictions. The British archaeologists who embraced this theory were by and large prehistorians. Their influence, however, brought considerations of ideology to the fore throughout British archaeology. This Marxist-derived concept of ideology became an important aspect of the 'postprocessual' archaeology of the 1980s and 1990s (M. Johnson 1999a: 94–115; D. Miller and Tilley 1984), and some British archaeologists used this notion of ideology in the interpretation of modern Western cases (D. Miller 1987; Parker Pearson 1982; Tilley 1990).

One product of these studies was an emphasis on oppositions between domination and resistance, and ideology and power. Daniel Miller (1987,

1998c) built on these oppositions to move into a realm of Hegelian material culture studies that shifted from the traditional Marxist emphasis on production to an examination of consumption. Miller stressed the everyday experience of consuming material culture and the practice of shopping that so dominates the modern experience. Many Marxists, however, remain sceptical of approaches that emphasise consumption and potentially obscure relations of production (Wurst and McGuire 1999).

In the United States 'critical archaeology' began with the research of historical archaeologist Mark Leone (1973, 1977, 1981b, 1982) and his colleagues (Handsman 1983; Handsman and Leone 1989; Leone and Potter 1988; Leone et al. 1987). They built critical archaeology from the structural Marxism of Louis Althusser (1969; 1971a) and the work of the Frankfurt School of critical theory (Hammond 1993; Macey 2001). Both of these approaches emphasise meaning as expressed in ideology. Althusser defined ideology as the taken-for-granted beliefs and assumptions that people have about society. He argued that an ideology serves to mystify the true nature of social relations and thus maintains relations of exploitation by resolving contradictions that exist within society. Members of the Frankfurt School contended that scholars engage in praxis through critiques that expose how ideologies were created and maintained. They argued that the revelation of such relations would move people to transform relations of exploitation. Critical archaeologists analysed how material culture served to maintain ideology in the Washington DC Mormon temple (Leone 1977), in museum displays (Handsman and Leone 1989; Leone 1981b), in formal gardens (Leone 1982) and in the mundane objects of everyday life (Little 1988). A 'dominant ideology thesis' underlies both of these approaches. In this thesis, ideology is dominant both because it is the beliefs of the dominant class and because it will dominate subordinate classes. Critical archaeologists assumed that ideology prevents subordinates from seeing the realities of their exploitation.

Leone and his students attempted a critical praxis in the Archaeology in Annapolis project (Leone and Potter 1996 [1984]; Leone et al. 1987). The project asked how during the colonial period the plan, architecture, landscape and material culture of the city established and reinforced an Enlightenment ideology or 'Georgian Order' of individualism, rationalism, equality and social contract. The project sought to reveal to visitors how the historic district of the city had been manipulated to reinforce an ideology of modern capitalism. The project questioned the ideological construction of Annapolis' past, on paper, in reconstructed and restored buildings, and in the ground. The project sought to expose the contradictions and social inequalities that the hegemonic history of Annapolis obscured (Leone 1995; Leone et al. 1987).

Leone's (1996 [1984]) study of the garden at the William Paca house in Annapolis is one of the most eloquent examples of this approach. William Paca was a signatory of the Declaration of Independence and a wealthy landowner, judge and governor. In the eighteenth century he built a palatial house in Annapolis with a formal, terraced garden behind it. For Leone, this garden embodied the key characteristics of ideology, illusion and contradiction. The garden was built using the rules of perspective to create optical illusions. These illusions suggested that distances were greater or lesser depending on the desire of the designer. The garden had three sections: the two closest to the house were orderly, laid out with great symmetry, while a third was a 'wilderness' lacking in symmetry. The optical illusions of the garden made the wilderness appear further from the house than it actually was. Leone concluded that the illusions were designed to hide the contradictions inherent in William Paca, the owner of enslaved Africans, signing a declaration that 'All men were created equal' and in the larger American society that could ignore such contradictions.

The organisers of Archaeology in Annapolis set up a participatory experience that would engage the tourists in a critical reflection on the colonial history of the United States. In the end this challenge to the standard ideological history of Annapolis failed. It could not overcome the official history and the cultural and social relations that produce that history (Leone 1995; Potter 1994). The tourists did not accept the alternative vision that the project offered but rather reinterpreted this vision in capitalist terms. The participatory experience did not lead them to abandon the preconceptions they derived directly from the ideology being critiqued. Their responses expressed the basic tenets of a capitalist ideology, such as a preoccupation with the value of objects, the time necessary to produce goods, and their availability in the market.

Marxist archaeologists have by-and-large rejected the dominant ideology thesis that underlies the early critical archaeology (H. Burke 1999; M. Johnson 1992; McGuire 1988; Orser 1996). They doubt that élite constructions such as formal gardens 'duped' waged and enslaved workers into a false consciousness that hid from them the reality of their oppression. They instead emphasise the negotiation of ideology in class conflict. Specifically they examine how dominant classes use dominant ideologies to create class-consciousness for those classes, and how subordinate classes manipulate these ideologies in struggles against domination. In this light, the reason for the failure of Archaeology in Annapolis to emancipate the tourists is clear. Annapolis is a high-end tourist destination that attracts primarily members of the privileged classes. These individuals interpreted the message of the programme with the dominant ideology of their class.

The results of Archaeology in Annapolis led Leone (1995) to adopt Habermas' (1984) notion of communicative action. He recognised that those people who would be the most open to alternative histories were those who have been subordinated by the contradictions, inequalities and exploitation of society. For this reason historical archaeology in Annapolis has moved away from the study of élite architecture and ideology to the study of the African-American working-class community of the city (Leone 1995; Mullins 1999; Shackel et al. 1998).

ANTHROPOLOGICAL POLITICAL ECONOMY

In the 1980s, the second Marxist cohort in historical archaeology formed around notions of 'anthropological political economy' (McGuire 1992; McGuire and Paynter 1991; Moore and Keene 1983; Paynter 1985, 1988). This approach grew out of the work of North American cultural anthropologists including June Nash (1979) Eleanor Leacock (1972, 1981), Stanley Diamond (1974) and Eric Wolf (1982; 2001). These Marxist archaeologists adopted Ollman's (1971; 1993; Sayer 1987) relational, Hegelian concept of the dialectic. They emphasised understanding the lived experience of people (everyday life). Following critical archaeology, they also adopted a reflexive awareness of archaeology's place in the modern world. One of the key relational aspects of this theory is the premise that class exploitation entails relationships to other forms of exploitation based in other social dimensions such as gender and race (Paynter 1989). This approach found the motor for cultural change in the conflicts that resulted from the ambiguities, tensions, or contradictions that exist within social relations. Social relations can only exist in historical contexts and between living human beings; they do not exist in the abstract. Therefore, while history is the product of human action, such action is always socially constituted.

The dialectic of these archaeologists defines the social world in terms of relations and not in terms of things. They reject the traditional definition of the key concepts of Marx, including mode of production, and superstructure, as discrete levels of society. Rather, they argue that these things are always different facets of the same social totality. As aspects of a whole, it is absurd to speak of one determining the other because the existence of one necessarily requires and entails the existence of the other. It is the relationship between mode of production (base) and superstructure that shapes society.

In one of the crucial archaeological works of anthropological political economy, Robert Paynter (1988) defined historical archaeology as the archaeology of capitalism. He began his analysis by asking why during the last three centuries the quantity and variety of materials that make up the archaeological record increased so dramatically. He advocated a class model that focuses upon changes in the means and relations of production to answer this question. Historical archaeologists have conventionally studied mould seams on bottles, a blue tint in a ceramic glaze or the replacement of hand-forged nails by machine-cut nails in order to date particular archaeological contexts. In Paynter's analysis, these things become the archaeological signatures for shifts in relations between capitalists and workers. In this way the study of artefacts becomes more than a sterile exercise in technology. Instead, it becomes the study of changes in social relations that keeps people in the analysis and puts them before technology.

STUDYING CAPITALISM

At the turn of the twenty-first century, discussions of capitalism permeate historical archaeology well beyond the reach of Marxist scholars. Archaeologists have used a variety of other theoretical perspectives in these studies. All of these discussions, however, share with Marxist historical archaeologists emphases on everyday life and social relations as the keys to understanding capitalism.

In the United Kingdom medieval and post-medieval archaeologists have continued to research the transition from feudalism to capitalism. Matthew Johnson's 1996 *An Archaeology of Capitalism* is the seminal work in this vein. Johnson argues that the roots of capitalism are to be found in the transformation of the English countryside in late medieval times. He specifically finds the transition in the movement from openness to closure in this landscape. More recently Chris Dalglish (2003) has looked to rural southern Scotland. Like Johnson he compares changes within the domestic space of the house with larger transformations of the landscape that were labelled 'improvements'. Both of these works emphasise the contradictions and conflicts between the domestic and the broader world and in the social relations that exist in each of these contexts. In *An Archaeology of Socialism* Victor Buchli (1999) used a similar approach of contrasting the domestic with the larger world in his study of the Narkomfin Communal House in Moscow, Russia. Buchli examines the dramatic transformation of the domestic in an environment of totalising Marxism.

Many archaeologists have looked at capitalism in terms of the processes of resistance that it engenders. A set of papers published in the *International Journal of Historical Archaeology* (Frazer 1999a) take up the topic of resistance in the British Isles. A number of these papers focus on resistance to enclosure (Frazer 1999b; Symonds 1999) and, like Marx and Johnson before them, see the move from openness to closure as key to the origins of capitalism. Sarah Tarlow (2002) points out the importance of archaeologists studying the radical alternatives to capitalism that were put forth by nineteenth-century utopian communities. She sees such studies as a way to understand the contradictions and complexities of Western society.

North American archaeologists have found new insights into the rural and native-American experience by examining them as aspects of capitalism. Mark Groover (2003) studied a rural farmstead in eastern Tennessee occupied by people who might be dismissed facilely as marginal hillbillies. He shows how the household was economically part of the larger experience of American capitalism, and how they were buffeted by and participated in the economic cycles of that experience. Stephen Silliman's work considers how in the history of California, native Americans are often invisible after the missions closed in 1840. They of course did not disappear, but instead became an ethnically distinct part of the Californian working class. In his archaeology of indigenous workers, field hands, cowboys, artisans, cooks and servants, Silliman reconstructs the everyday life of these people and the social relationships of labour that shaped that experience. His study shows how native Americans were a key component in the multiethnic labour force of mid-nineteenth-century California. Such studies bring rural folk and Native America in from the margins of the American experience to show how they participate in and recreate capitalism.

MARXIST HISTORICAL ARCHAEOLOGY TODAY

A mix of critical archaeology and anthropological political economy forms the most common approach among English-speaking Marxist historical archaeologists today. These scholars often view archaeology as a 'craft', that is, as a unified practice of hand, heart and mind (Shanks and McGuire 1996). They follow the Arts and Crafts movement of the turn of the twentieth century by defining craft in a Marxist critique of alienated labour (Marx 1906). From this perspective archaeology is a mode of cultural production embedded in the material, social, political and ideological relationships between different communities. They have applied their craft to a series of overlapping topics that include class, ideology, cultural production, struggle and praxis.

Marxists have proposed a relational theory of class to replace more estab-lished notions of status (Wurst and Fitts 1999). Historical archaeologists in the United States have traditionally discussed economic differentiation in terms of status. Status defines a graduated scale whereby people's position is determined by the sum of their wealth, income and/or prestige. In contrast a relational theory defines a class in terms of the social relations that link social groups one to the other. The basis of these relations is found in relations of production. LouAnn Wurst (1999; 2002) emphasises the importance of studying class in real historical contexts and applies the concept to both rural and urban contexts in nineteenth-century upstate New York. Brian Thomas (1998) looks at the relationship of class and race in his study of plan-tation slavery. Margaret Wood (2002) examines the relationship of class and gender in the creation of class consciousness during the 1913–1914 Colorado Coal Field Strike. Randall McGuire and Mark Walker (1999) use a relational concept of class to critique the class structure of contemporary archaeology.

Much contemporary archaeological research work builds on the Marxist concept of ideology. These studies go beyond the theory that Mark Leone and his students developed in their critical archaeology (H. Burke 1999; Leone 1995; Matthews 2002; Potter 1994; Shackel 2000a). Heather Burke (1999) uses a study of the nineteenth-century Australian town of Armidale to explain variation in architectural style through relationships of ideol-ogy, capitalism and identity. James A. Delle (1998) examines a nineteenth-century Jamaican coffee plantation as a cultural, ideological landscape that structured relations of race, gender and the division of labour.

Concerns with ideology have also expanded into broader Marxist studies of cultural production (Matthews et al. 2002). Stephen Mrozowski (2000) finds the cultural production of class in Lowell, Massachusetts to be fluid and cultural distinctions between managers' and working-class households ambiguous. Christopher Matthews (2002) takes a long view in his study of modernity and tradition in eighteenth- to twentieth-century Annapo-lis, Maryland. His focus is on how material objects, including the city of Annapolis, became meaningful through a dialectic of tradition and moder-nity. Also working in Annapolis, Paul Mullins (1999) examines how African-Americans used consumption to negotiate class and racial identities. Mark Leone's (2005) study of African hoodoo practices in the southern United States attempts to write an alternative history that challenges capitalism by revealing lifeways that existed at the edge of, or beyond, capitalism.

Challenge and struggle are themes that run through Marxist scholar-ship. Marxist historical archaeologists have argued that a focus on struggle provides a means to escape 'identity politics' and to focus on the real lived struggles of people (McGuire and Wurst 2002). Memory is a locus of struggles as social groups tussle over what will be remembered and what will be forgotten in order to define themselves and advance their interests (Van Dyke and Alcock 2003). Paul Shackel (2000a) examines ideology, memory and struggle in the historical creation and recreation of Harper's Ferry, Virginia as a historical place and a National Park. Pedro Funari (2003) demonstrates how the memory of the seventeenth-century maroon kingdom of Palmares in north-eastern Brazil links the historical conflicts with modern confrontations over social identity.

Marxism is foremost a theory of praxis that makes archaeology an explicit form of political action (Shanks 2004a). To take effective political action, archaeology needs to transcend the traditional middle-class community that the discipline usually serves. A Marxist archaeology should integrate archaeological research with communities of working people by asking questions that are important to them, about events that are meaningful to them, with the goal of working with them in the struggle for rights and dignity for all people. The Archaeology of the 1913–1914 Colorado Coal Field War Project has attempted to do this.

PRAXIS: THE ARCHAEOLOGY OF THE 1913–1914 COLORADO
COAL FIELD WAR

The Colorado Coal Field War of 1913–1914 was one of the most significant events in US labour history (McGovern and Guttridge 1972). On the morning of 20 April 1914, Colorado National Guard troops engaged in a pitched gun battle with armed strikers at a tent colony of 1,200 striking families near Ludlow, Colorado. For most of the day 200 Guardsmen with two machine guns fired on the camp. Several hundred strikers answered them with rifle fire. The battle continued until dusk, and then the troops swept through the camp looting it and setting the approximately 200 tents in it aflame. When the smoke cleared twenty of the camp's inhabitants were dead including two women and twelve children. The mothers and their children had taken refuge from the hail of bullets in a cellar under a tent. There they had suffocated to death when the tent above them burned. Enraged by these events the strikers launched a class war, burning company towns and mines, and killing company employees. The war continued for ten days until Federal troops arrived to keep the peace.

The Ludlow Massacre is the most violent and best-known incident of the Colorado Coal Field War, but its significance goes far beyond this struggle. The killing of innocents at Ludlow outraged the American public. Popular opinion soon turned against violent confrontations with strikers. The massacre marks a pivotal point in US history when labour relations began to

move from class warfare to corporate and government policies of negotiation, co-option, and regulated strikes. Today the United Mine Workers of
America maintain the site of the massacre as a shrine and descendants of
the strikers and union members make regular pilgrimages to the site.

The Colorado Coal Field War Archaeology Project consists of faculty
and students from the University of Denver in Colorado, and Binghamton
University in New York (Duke and Saitta 1998; Ludlow Collective 2001;
McGuire and Reckner 2003). The Colorado Historical Society has funded
the work. The project has excavated in the Ludlow strike camp and in the
coal-mining town of Berwind where many of the Ludlow strikers originated
(Figures 8.1 and 8.2). The project began with the assumption that archaeology should serve multiple communities (Shanks and McGuire 1996). These
communities include the scholarly community of archaeologists and historians, as well as the traditional, middle-class, public audience for archaeology.
But the primary community that the project addresses is unionised labour
in the United States. The project is building an archaeology of the American
working class that speaks to a working-class audience about working-class
history and experience (Figure 8.3).

The documentary record of primary texts, photographs, and oral histories for the Colorado Coal Field War is incredibly robust but it leaves a
major issue unexamined. Working families created the class consciousness
and solidarity necessary for the strike from their shared experience of day-
to-day life. These experiences shaped the lives of miners and their families,
but the documents' focus on large-scale, high-profile political responses
to the conflict obscure these mundane aspects of life. Historical archaeologists bring to the table a craft that reveals the material conditions of
day-to-day lives in the coal camps and tent colonies of southern Colorado.
The project has shown that the material conditions of home life cut across
ethnic divisions, before, during and after the strike. It has also demonstrated that women and children were active agents, with male miners,
in formulating a social consciousness to unify for the strike (M. Wood
2002).

The highly charged nature of the historical events surrounding the Coal
War clashes with most accepted narratives of class relations in the United
States, and particularly the American West (McGuire and Reckner 2002).
The powerful ideology of a classless US society, and the systemic silencing of
the history of class struggle in popular narratives of American history make
education an extraordinarily important part of the Coal War Archaeol-
ogy Project (Walker and Saitta 2002). The project has conducted *Colorado
Endowment for the Humanities*-sponsored institutes at the site for public

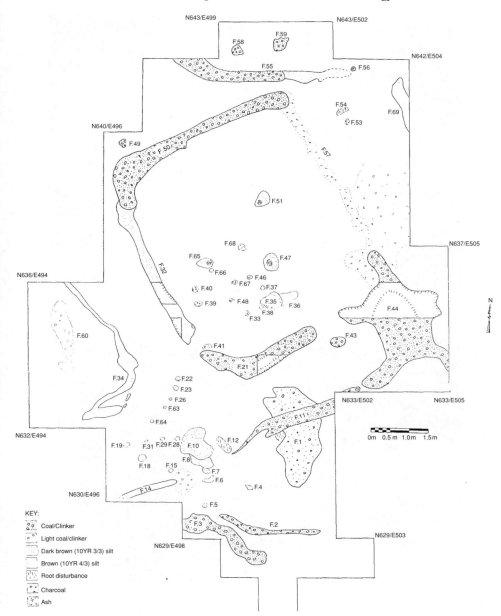

Figure 8.1   Plan of excavated tent platform at the Ludlow Massacre Site, Ludlow, Colorado.

Figure 8.2   Photograph of excavated tent platform at Ludlow Massacre Site, Ludlow, Colorado.

Figure 8.3   Cecil Roberts, President of the United Mine Workers, discussing the Ludlow Archaeology exhibit with miners and their wives.

teachers, prepared a 'teaching trunk' of materials relating to the strike for the Denver public schools, and developed curricula to teach labour history in Colorado. The project has also installed interpretation signs at the site to educate tourists who visit it.

The descendants of the strikers and the modern descendant community of unionised labour remember the history of Ludlow. Archaeology becomes part of this memory. The descendants' memorialisation is familial and personal. Their concerns are to establish a connection to this familial past and/or to see to it that their family's role in this past is properly honoured. The project has aided descendants in locating graves so that stones could be raised to family members who died in the massacre and by correcting errors in documentation or labels on photos in historical archives. The descendant community of the 1913–1914 Coal Strike is composed of the unionised working people of southern Colorado. This community has made the Ludlow Massacre a powerful symbol of their struggle. Archaeologists participate in this struggle by speaking at the annual memorial service for the massacre and in the union halls. The project has developed several portable exhibits that are set up at the memorial service and sent to union halls around the country. The project's message is simple. Labour's rights to a safe workplace, benefits, reasonable wages, a forty-hour week and dignity were won with blood. They were not freely given by capitalists but bought with the lives of working people like those who died at Ludlow.

WHAT MARXISM OFFERS HISTORICAL ARCHAEOLOGY

The application of Marxist theory to archaeology should stand or fall based on how well it allows archaeologists to comprehend the realities of human history (Trigger 1995: 325). Marxism addresses these goals through the logic of the dialectic, a theory of social development and praxis.

The dialectic helps archaeologists to escape many of the oppositions that frequent debates about archaeological theory; it also provides a method for archaeologists to study change. The oppositions include science versus humanism, objectivity versus subjectivity, the material versus the mental, and evolution versus history. The dialectic leads us to examine how these poles are interconnected rather than seeing them as irresolvable opposites. Scholars are connected to the social world that they study and thus must critically examine their role in that world. The dialectic as a method for studying change also emphasises the interconnectedness of human society, and it examines this interconnectedness for the contradictions that shape society. These contradictions provide a source for the cultural change that is internal to the society and that springs from the social relations of real life.

Marxism is a rich conceptual source of models and theories for the study of cultural change. Marx's basic – and often somewhat ambiguous –

observations have been interpreted anew by many others in light of the conditions of economic development of their own times. This fruitful tradition of scholarship has produced a copious body of theories, concepts, ideas and insights on human history. Marx's focus on the role of socially constituted labour in the production and reproduction of real life – and his realisation that these social relations are objectified in various ways, including through material culture – is compatible with the craft of archaeology (Shanks and McGuire 1996). Thus the archaeologist V. Gordon Childe (1944: 1) noted that material culture reflects and participates in the social relations that produce it and that we can therefore study these social relations using material culture.

Marxism is ultimately a theory of praxis (Crehan 2002). Praxis is human activity by which people transform the world and themselves. The ultimate goal of Marxism is a praxis that transforms both people and society. In this way archaeology becomes an instrument of political action (Shanks 2004a).

The unique contribution that Marxism can make to archaeology comes from the integration of social theory and praxis to gain knowledge of the world, to critique the world, and to take action in the world. If we accept a dialectical approach to Marxism, then this integration is an ongoing, dynamic and never-ending process.

CHAPTER 9

Historical archaeology and industrialisation

James Symonds and Eleanor C. Casella

INTRODUCTION

Britain was the first industrial nation. The impact of this early phase of industrialisation was far reaching and laid the foundations for the emergence of modern consumer society. Although recent scholarship has suggested that the origins of many modern industrial processes may lie in the medieval or early post-medieval period, the clustering of technological innovations that occurred in Britain between the mid-eighteenth and mid-nineteenth centuries is still widely upheld as evidence of a remarkable 'Industrial Revolution' (Symonds 2003).

Industrialisation transformed the towns and countryside of Britain and has left wide-ranging material legacies in the form of workshops, factories, warehouses, canals, railways, roads, mines, quarries, dockyards, and purpose-built workers' houses, to name but a few of the more visible classes of industrial sites. It has been estimated that 70 per cent of the built environment of modern Britain dates from the period of the Industrial Revolution (Cossons 1987: 12) and Britain's role as the birthplace of the Industrial Revolution has recently been recognised by the UK Government as its sole unique contribution to World Heritage. For this reason no fewer than 10 of the 25 sites presented to UNESCO as tentative world-heritage sites in 1999 were industrial (DCMS 1999). These ranged from mining and iron-working industrial landscapes at Blaenavon in Wales, to the cotton mills of the Derwent Valley in Derbyshire, to elements of the 'world's first industrial city' – Manchester – and the waterfront area of Liverpool, a leading nineteenth-century mercantile city (Cooper 2005: 156).

Given the wealth and significance of material remains that exist from this period in Britain, it is perhaps not surprising that it was here that the phrase *industrial archaeology* was first coined. Although it is unclear when the term first appeared in print (R. Buchanan 2000: 20) it gained widespread usage following the publication of a seminal article in the *Amateur Historian* by

Michael Rix, a lecturer in English Literature in the Department of Extramural Studies at the University of Birmingham (Rix 1955). The first use of the term in the title of a full-length monograph did not appear until the 1960s, in *The Industrial Archaeology of County Down* (E. Green 1963). This government-sponsored regional archaeological survey was followed in the same year by the first overview of the subject in Britain, *Industrial Archaeology: An Introduction* (Hudson 1963).

The origins of industrial archaeology can be firmly traced to the university extramural departments, and to Workers' Education Council evening classes. In the 1950s and 1960s industrial archaeology was conducted as a volunteer pastime. It combined the opportunity to engage with economic and social history with the ability to participate in the practical hands-on conservation of industrial monuments. The 'history with gumboots' approach was pioneered by Michael Rix who arranged a series of residential field schools in industrial archaeology at Preston Montford, in Shropshire (R. Buchanan 2000: 20). At about the same time, in 1964, R. Angus Buchanan, a lecturer in history at the Bristol College of Science and Technology, and Neil Cossons, curator in technology at Bristol City Museum, began their first winter adult-education classes on industrial archaeology at the Bristol Folk House (R. Buchanan 2000: 24).

The traditional scope of British industrial archaeology was described by R. Angus Buchanan in 1978:

> There is no agreed definition of industrial archaeology. My own preference is that it is a field of study concerned with investigating, surveying, recording, and in some cases, with preserving industrial monuments . . . in practice it is useful to confine attention to the monuments of the last 200 years. (R. Buchanan 1978: 53)

While undoubtedly stimulated by extra-mural classes and amateur special-interest groups, industrial archaeology was generally ignored by British universities. For many participants industrial archaeology was little more than a stimulating weekend pursuit (R. Buchanan 2000: 21). Research – if it took place at all – was generally limited in scope, and was pursued at local or regional level. This did not hinder the publication of a series of popular handbooks and guides to industrial archaeology, aimed directly at the enthusiastic amateur, in the later 1960s and 1970s (R. Buchanan 1972; Cossons 1975; Cossons and Hudson 1969; Hudson 1967; Raistrick 1972).

The growth of local societies such as the Bristol Industrial Archaeological Society (BIAS) encouraged the west country publishers David and Charles to commission a series of regional industrial archaeologies. The classic *Industrial Archaeology of the British Isles* series, edited by E. R. R. Green, ran to 20 volumes, and included several seminal works (Ashmore 1969; Rees 1975; Sherlock 1976; D. M. Smith 1965). The *Journal of Industrial Archaeology*, established by Kenneth Hudson in 1964, was also taken over in its second year by David and Charles, subsequently appearing as *Industrial Archaeology*.

Other publishers were keen to gain a share of this special-interest market. From 1969, the Longman *Industrial Archaeology Series* took a thematic approach to industries (e.g. English 1969; Gale 1969; Rolt 1969). Batsford *Guides to Industrial Archaeology* first appeared in 1976 and set out to examine industrial archaeology region by region (e.g. Hume 1976).

Recording of industrial archaeology in Britain in the 1960s benefited from the involvement of the Council for British Archaeology (CBA), which organised the first national conference on industrial archaeology in 1959, and lobbied the British government to establish a national survey of industrial monuments. The resulting card index record system entitled the National Record of Industrial Monuments (NRIM) was held at the Centre for the History of Technology at the University of Bath from 1965 and numbered 8,000 entries when it was transferred to English Heritage in 1980.

The CBA established an advisory panel on industrial monuments in 1967 to lobby for the recording and preservation of industrial sites. The Association for Industrial Archaeology (AIA) was founded in 1973. This national society, which was largely created by the initiative of R. Angus Buchanan at the University of Bath, successfully internationalised the study of industrial archaeology and was instrumental in setting up The International Committee for the Conservation of the Industrial Heritage (TICCIH), hosting the first meeting of this group at Ironbridge, in Shropshire, in 1973 (R. Buchanan 2000: 28). The subsequent growth of industrial archaeology in Britain has been fully explored in a number of recent publications (Casella and Symonds 2005; Cossons 2000; Palmer and Neaverson 1998).

Significant progress has been made in the range and scope of recording techniques employed by industrial archaeologists since the 1950s and the discipline has escaped its early fixation with individual monuments to embrace a far more holistic approach to the preservation and management of rural and urban industrial landscapes (Ayris and Gould 1994; Barnatt and Penny 2004; N. Jones et al. 2004).

The last twenty years have witnessed a concomitant growth in the resources that have been placed into the recording and conservation of industrial sites and landscapes by the statutory heritage agencies of England, Wales, Scotland and Northern Ireland. The English Royal Commission's move towards thematic surveys of threatened industrial buildings in the early 1980s has enhanced our understanding of a wide range of urban industries. Valuable studies have been made of workers' housing (Caffyn 1983; Leech 1981), textile mills (Callandine and Fricker 1993; Giles and Goodhall 1992), historic ports and naval dockyards (Coad 1989; Ritchie-Noakes 1984), railway stations and railway engineering works (Cattell and Falconer 1995; Fitzgerald 1980), potteries (Baker 1991) and commercial warehouses (Taylor et al. 2002). Local authority and commercial archaeologists now routinely undertake the excavation and survey of industrial archaeological sites as part of the process of regulating planning applications for development.

Only the university sector has failed to keep pace with developments in industrial archaeology and industrial heritage since the 1980s. This may be because British industrial archaeologists were content simply to describe the physical remains of the former industries that they studied. While this empirical approach undoubtedly succeeded in creating many worthy accounts of technological processes (W. Campbell 1971; McNeil 1972) and detailed chronologies for the growth of local and regional industries, it failed to inspire the general interest of academics as it usually stopped short of exploring the wider social relations of industrial production (Palmer and Neaverson 1998: 3). The continued absence of what may be regarded as a sustainable academic research base in industrial archaeology in British universities has led Shane Gould (2001: 67) to comment that the 'absence of an evolving intellectual tradition is arguably the Achilles heel of industrial archaeology and unless this weakness is addressed its academic future remains uncertain'.

EXPANDING THE FRAMEWORK OF INFERENCE

The recent history of British industrial archaeology has been characterised by increasingly global perspectives and influences. By the 1990s, the advent of 'interpretive' or 'postprocessual' approaches in British archaeology generated a fresh research concern with questions of power and inequality, labour relations and class formation, and social aspects of resource exchange – exactly, in other words, the topics that provided central research themes for industrial archaeology. As practitioners realised the degree to which they could join these emerging scholarly debates, their expanding interest in social theory began to strengthen an intersection with the existing subdiscipline of historical archaeology as practised in North America and Australasia.

Studies of specific transatlantic industries provided an initial comparative source, with the extensive work by Mary Beaudry and Stephen Mrozowski on the Boott Cotton Mills of Lowell, Massachusetts offering new perspectives on the everyday nature of workers' lives and residential habits within industrial sites (Beaudry and Mrozowski 1987a, 1987b, 1989). Through their close analysis of the nineteenth-century company-owned tenements and boardinghouses, Beaudry and Mrozowski explored the active material responses of skilled and unskilled workers to the economic and cultural forces of industrial capitalism. Additionally, this seminal project helped to broaden the focus of industrial archaeology from strictly defined workplaces (such as factories, mines and warehouses) to workers' settlements. In Britain and Ireland, a similar subdisciplinary expansion has been particularly evident in the comprehensive regional studies of industrial towns (e.g. Hughes 2000; Nevell and Walker 1999; Rynne 1999).

Work by Donald Hardesty (1988) provided another formative source for transatlantic comparative research, through comprehensive studies of nineteenth-century 'frontier' mining industries in the American West. Extensively demonstrating the processes by which one dominant extraction industry literally shaped the cultural landscapes of Nevada, California and Idaho, Hardesty's seminal work has most recently influenced similar work on nineteenth-century non-ferrous mining landscapes within Australia and New Zealand (P. Bell 1998; Gaughwin 1995; Lawrence 2000; Moore and Ritchie 1998).

Other sources from historical archaeology introduced an explicit focus on the exploitative relationships between capital and labour to the wider subdiscipline. In his various studies of mid-Atlantic industrial townscapes and workplaces, Paul Shackel demonstrated the need for an intersite scale of research to explore the impact of capitalism on workers' experiences of time and space. His publications illuminated wider social consequences of industrialisation by exploring the material role of capitalist ideologies, the subtle effects of work discipline on the production process, and the domestic responses that transformed workers' households (Shackel 1993, 1996). The complex operations of 'inequality' that formed and maintained North American settlements, factories and towns over the industrial era were also explored by others (e.g. McGuire and Paynter 1991). Through historical archaeology, these scholars aimed not only to read the built environment of industrial landscapes as expressions of hierarchical power relations, but also to consider the many ways in which workers refuted, subverted and alleviated the grinding poverty of industrial capitalism.

As the scope of industrial archaeology has diversified, so have its theoretical and professional encounters. Engagement with archaeological traditions from other international regions particularly invigorated concerns over the heritage management of complex industrial sites. For example, following her groundbreaking survey of industrial archaeology within Ironbridge Gorge (Alfrey and Clark 1993), Kate Clark drew explicitly on the Burra Charter – an Australian guidance document developed to outline national procedures for conservation planning of heritage sites – to reconsider British approaches to historic places (Heritage Lottery Fund 1998; Kerr 2000; cf. Hicks 2003). By adapting this Australian method of evaluating and documenting 'heritage values' to a British site, Clark was able to identify strategies for conserving industrial landscapes as intrinsic networks, rather than as groups of isolated and alienated workplaces (Clark 1987, 1999, 2005). Similarly, recent efforts by English Heritage to prevent the demolition of nineteenth-century mill-workers' terraced houses in Nelson, Lancashire (Cooper 2005) drew upon critiques of 'the slum' originally developed from comparative urban histories of nineteenth-century San Francisco, Birmingham, and Sydney (Mayne 1993).

A SHARED CRAFT: CURRENT RESEARCH DIRECTIONS

One primary result of these global scholarly encounters has been the emergence of a debate over the identity of the field. What exactly is industrial archaeology, as practised today? While traditional approaches would argue for a distinct research focus on 'the processes of invention, innovation and development' (Cranstone 2001: 183), this classic definition immediately begets a deeper identity crisis (Palmer 1990). Is industrial archaeology defined by period (an archaeology of the recent industrial past)? Or is it a study of industry regardless of period? What about single sites that have been used for industrial-style production through millennia? Particularly when we turn to examine the major industries that shape our world of 'late' or 'post' industrial capitalism, issues of consumption and distribution (as opposed to classic production) gain primary significance within our subdiscipline (Cook et al. 1996; M. Hall 2005; D. Miller 2001b; Mullins 1999; Spencer-Wood 1987). Others have questioned the very separation of these categories of activity. Quoting the archetypal industrial populist Henry Ford, Randall McGuire emphasised the intrinsic mutual dependency of production and consumption under late industrial capitalism:

They [workers] have time to see more, do more and incidentally buy more. This stimulates business and increases prosperity, and in the general economic circle the money passes through industry again and back into the workman's pocket. (H. Ford 1929: 17, quoted in McGuire 1991: 106)

Thus, the field of industrial archaeology can be seen to engage with explicitly social questions of conspicuous consumption and commodity fetishism, in addition to traditional descriptive accounts of technological innovation, mass-production systems, and distribution networks.

If we pause this consideration of a subdisciplinary identity crisis, a few central themes can be traced through the diverse practices of industrial archaeology. While debates continue to refine the theoretical and temporal scope of the field, at least three interrelated topics appear central to current research directions.

The globalisation of industry

Most would agree that industrial archaeology explicitly focuses on the production, distribution and consumption of commodities. This scholarship ranges widely from the traditional topics of extractive mining works, steel mills, forges, textile mills and potteries (Birmingham et al. 1983; Cossons 1987; Cranstone 2001; Palmer and Neaverson 1998) to intriguingly diverse examples of modern productive industries. Although gardens, for example, have traditionally fallen under sub-fields such as landscape archaeology or archaeobotany, research has also examined broad transformations of industrial productive economies through the analysis of plant remains from post-medieval urban deposits (Giorgi 1999), record books from colonial agricultural plantations (Landers 2000), agricultural 'relics' associated with the mechanical processing of plant crops such as grapes, hops, olives and cereals (Birmingham et al. 1979), and intensified transport systems for fertiliser distribution (Wade Martins 1991). Similarly, the analysis of electronics, leisure, fashion, and even information technology 'industries' suggest possible new frontiers for industrial archaeology (Falk and Campbell 1997; Lally 2002; Reilly and Rahtz 1992; Stratton and Trinder 2000).

Similarly, while we examine 'distribution' as traditional types of canal, rail, road and shipping networks, recent scholarship has also emphasised the very transnational nature of industrialisation by considering the distribution of technologies themselves. A variety of Australasian studies have recorded the local improvisation of industrial technologies imported from England, Scotland and the American West (Clough 1991; Gojak and Allen 2000; Jack 1995; Pearson 1996). Distributions have also been charted in archaeological studies of early modern workshops for gunflint production in northern Italy (Woodall et al. 1997). Supplying the Habsburg and Prussian militaries during the eighteenth and early nineteenth centuries, these small-scale workshops in Monti Lessini eventually bowed to competitive pressures from the

British gunflint industry, and shared specific artisan techniques developed for the crafting of locally available stone.

A similar transnational approach underlay Marilyn Palmer's comparison of the English textile village of Cromford, established by Richard Arkwright during the 1770s, with the German industrial village of the same name constructed in 1783–1784 by Joseph Brugelmann (Palmer 2005: 65–66). Interpreting patterns of paternalism, workplace discipline, and socioeconomic aspiration through the architecture and layout of these industrial settlements, Palmer traced further examples of these design elements within the vast Belgian colliery complex of Le Grand Hornu, established by the French capitalist Henri du Gorge during the 1820s.

Finally, industrial archaeology offers a unique temporal perspective on the transformations of capital that continue to shape our modern world. Particularly over the last fifty years, as labour-intensive and environmentally destructive industries relocate to the developing world, western nations have experienced an increasing proliferation of 'service' industries to replace traditional primary and secondary forms of production. Industrial archaeology offers not only an essential historical context for the current experience of 'globalisation', but also a critique of irresistible media, recreational, and 'lifestyle'-related commodities that result from these new forms of consumption.

Simultaneously, a restructuring of labour relations has transformed the nature of workers' unions across the world, with traditional powers of collective bargaining actively curtailed and circumscribed in the name of 'workplace reform'. By retaining an intrinsic focus on social questions of 'labour', industrial archaeology can provide a powerful commemoration of the 'long, arduous struggle of workers to secure a 40-hour workweek, and other concessions from capital that many take for granted today' (Shackel 2004: 44). In revealing the material conditions of labour itself, our research sustains profound debates over working conditions, health and safety regulations, provisions for housing and family support, and employment patterns related to age, gender, ethnicity and race.

INDUSTRIAL HERITAGE AS COMMUNITY HERITAGE

Many scholars have returned to their disciplinary origins by embracing a more practice-oriented scholarship. Such approaches emphasise the systematic recording and preservation required to expand our understandings of the industrial past (Clark 2005; Cranstone 2001; Palmer and Neaverson 1998; Rogic 2004). Within Britain, a hierarchical four-tiered recording system has been developed for standing structures by the Royal Commission on the Historical Monuments of England (RCHME 1996), with similar systems developed by Scottish and Welsh regulatory bodies. A method of tiered recording has also been created in the United States under the Historic American Engineering Record (HAER) through the National Park Service (Burns 1989). Others have focused their methodological attention upon the detailed recording of workplace activities at industrial sites, arguing that such social geographies provide 'an understanding of the skill base, which may now be lost, and an idea of what it meant to work there' (Badcock and Malaws 2004: 270). The important benefits of such systematic approaches to industrial landscapes include the comparative value of recorded data, and a more strategic investment of limited archaeological resources.

Nonetheless, an acknowledgement of relative scales of 'value' has immediately raised questions over different (and frequently competing) dimensions of global, national, regional and local significance for industrial sites. These concerns over the socioeconomic aspects of industrial heritage management have led to an acknowledgement of underlying responsibilities to a wide range of community-based interest groups. Affiliated communities can consist of amateur enthusiasts, former employees, local residents, and descendants of site occupants. They have also included broader affiliates, such as members of the United Mine Workers of America, who have adopted the Ludlow Massacre national landmark, the site of the most infamous and violent altercation of the 1913–1914 Colorado Coal Field War, as a symbolic emblem of the enduring struggles that face American labour activists (Ludlow Collective 2001).

By recasting community relations as a central component of industrial heritage (see Van Bueren 2002a), recent scholarship has deepened our understanding of the modern sociopolitical dynamics that surround industrial sites. In his recent study of conservation debates over the nineteenth- and early twentieth-century gas and grain distribution networks of colonial South Africa, David Worth critiqued politically motivated assessments of 'use', 'reuse' and 'disuse' of industrial sites within post-apartheid governmental regeneration and sustainable development schemes (Worth 2005). From the perspective of urban planning, Margo Huxley similarly questioned 'who has lost and who has gained' from recent urban gentrification projects in central Melbourne, Australia (Huxley 1997: 51). In contrast, Erik Nijhof demonstrated a positive role for the inter-war twentieth-century mining industry in the formation of multiethnic communities within the German Ruhr and adjacent Dutch and Belgian Limburg regions of Europe. Through a combination of workplace solidarity and shared leisure activities, the Polish, Czech, Slovak, Slovenian, Croatian, Hungarian, Dutch, and German mine workers developed both a unique pidgin language known as 'cité-German', and a distinct multiethnic 'industrial culture' acknowledged today by heritage initiatives within Belgium and the Netherlands (Nijhof 2004).

This new appreciation of community heritage has caused an important expansion in the range of sources traditionally collected, analysed and interpreted. To illuminate the social dynamics of their study sites, scholars have turned to oral histories, vernacular photographs, and amateur collections of local memorabilia as sources rich with the flavours of everyday community life. While the use of these materials has been criticised for presenting nostalgic, idiosyncratic, and sometimes inaccurate representations of the past, the stories they convey provide important personal and emotive links to industrial heritage. When approached as unique data sources, ones with their own 'difficulties, constraints and grammars' (Purser 1992: 28), these snapshots, souvenirs and stories offer a powerful narrative experience of the recent past. They bring the material record back to life.

Ultimately, the relative value of these sources 'depends upon the questions one is seeking to answer', as observed by American historian Ronald Grele (1985). That compelling emotive link can itself produce a valid critique of the entire premise of conservation and commemoration (Shackel 2004: 44). For many who laboured in industrial workplaces, the

dirt, noise, bad smell, hard labor and other forms of exploitation associated with these kinds of places make preservation [of industrial sites] ludicrous. 'Preserve a steel mill?' people say. 'It killed my father. Who wants to preserve that?' (Lowenthal 1985: 403)

For others, oral histories and family snapshots provide a means for celebrating craft traditions and local community networks disrupted by the postindustrial economic transitions of the last fifty years. When juxtaposed against excavated and archival sources of data, these narrative sources have yielded new perspectives on, for example, the skilled work practices that shaped the industrial structure (Badcock and Malaws 2004; Belford 2003), the embodied experiences of environmental stress, pollution, and diet that accompany everyday life in industrial settlements (Davis 2002; Maniery 2002; Rogge et al. 1995), and the intersecting class and racial inequalities that complicate heritage-development schemes (e.g. McDavid 1997; Worth 2005).

Like artefactual assemblages, photographs, oral histories and memorabilia collections offer uniquely democratic modes of insight into the broader cultural visions, work experiences, and cognitive structures of everyday life. From this interpretive perspective, that which is missing – the silences and shadows – becomes as significant as that which is present.

> Snapshots litter the contested ground between candour and concealment, between what's public and what's private in families. Imagine everyone gathered around the family photo album. The snapshot in view, depending on who's doing the looking, is horrifying, hilarious, pointless, or suffused with yearning. What a snapshot wants to have leak out of its neat rectangle is the messy network of human relationships for which the snapshot was made. (Waldie 2004: 16)

It is, in other words, not only the 'complicated relationship between the narrator and the events described' which creates social meanings, but also 'the stances he or she takes towards other participants in the events' (Schrager 1983: 77). These spoken, pictorial, and material images act as memorials, as partial and malleable depictions coded with social meanings about work, age, gender, family, community, class and national ideology (Sturken 1999). Even the brief relationship forged between the informant and scholar during the ethnographic process of sharing a memory and loaning a snapshot can provide social meanings (McDavid 1997). It is through this collaborative process of 'remembering and recounting', that project participants offer relevant 'historical *facts* articulated through the more immediate personal and political *truths*' (Purser 1992: 27), and thereby provide fresh understandings of the social life of industrial sites.

IDENTITY, AFFILIATIONS AND SOCIAL BELONGING

Industrial archaeology examines the ways people worked and lived during a period of revolutionary socioeconomic transformation. By exploring the formation of unique industrial cultures, the field illuminates powerful dynamics of social class that happen 'when some men, as a result of common experiences (inherited or shared), feel and articulate the identity of their interests as between themselves, and as against other men whose interests are different from (and usually opposed to) theirs' (Thompson 1966: 9). To this classic definition, industrial archaeology contributes an essential *material* perspective. By comparing, for example, the prevalence of alcohol and tobacco related artefacts within the residential neighborhoods of an early twentieth-century aqueduct construction camp in Los Angeles, California, Thad Van Bueren interpreted a set of shared values that destabilised employers' attempts at 'scientific management' of their transient workforce (Van Bueren 2002b). Similarly, in his study of the 'marginal neighborhood' of Steptoe City, located in the Robinson mining district of eastern Nevada, Richard Goddard found that long-term residents actively chose to occupy this peripheral work settlement despite its lack of running water, poor amenities and generally shady reputation. As an 'unconventional' community, Steptoe City provided residents with not only the ability to avoid the paternalistic intrusions imposed by the company upon residents of the nearby 'model town', but also a space for the cultivation of new business enterprises – primarily opportunistic 'service industries' such as brothels, gambling halls and illegal saloons (Goddard 2002: 85).

Industrial archaeology interrogates not only the formation of class identities, but the simultaneous and everyday experiences of gender, ethnicity, age and religious affiliations that equally shaped workers' lives. In their study of a primarily African-American coal-mining town in Buxton, Iowa, archaeologists demonstrated that racial dynamics of segregation and power, spatially represented in the site layout, were cross-cut against simultaneous participation in regional, national and international markets, as evidenced by the excavated material assemblages (Gradwohl and Osborn 1984). Similarly, studies of overseas Chinese workers have demonstrated the role of ethnic intergenerational obligations of religion, ritual and responsibility in the material remains of communal feasting sites (Gaughwin 1995), and in cemeteries associated with non-ferrous mining regions of Australia, New Zealand and the American West (Abraham and Wegars 2003). Other studies (Douglass 1998; Gillespie and Farrell 2002; Hardesty 1988; McGowan 2003; Ritchie 2003; Stankowski 2004) have explored the impact of chain migration in the clustering of ethnic communities around specific industries and working settlements. Forensic analysis of skeletal collections has revealed the profound impact of industrial labour on children's health and growth patterns (M. Lewis 2002). Still other scholars have explored the operation of gender roles through the distribution of tasks within the industrial workplace (Brashler 1991; Palmer 2005), the maintenance of working families and households (E. Wood 2002), and the material creation of workers' own identities (Hardesty 1994; Psota 2002).

The impact of these new research directions becomes immediately apparent when one examines current case studies within industrial archaeology. By interpreting the assemblages and built environments of industrial sites as 'artefacts and active voices' (Beaudry et al. 1991), the field has begun to contribute to wider understandings of power negotiations within the workplace, of modern-era class relations, of domestic relations and residential patterns, of family ties and the diaspora of ethnic working communities. To consider the social dimensions of the industrial past, industrial archaeology has

Figure 9.1   Hagg Cottages, Alderley Edge, c. 1930.

begun to explore the paradoxically commonplace yet revolutionary transformations of how working people both laboured and lived. We turn to
two recent British case studies, in order to contrast the diverse results made
possible through the adoption of an explicitly social research agenda in
contemporary industrial archaeology.

THE ALDERLEY SANDHILLS PROJECT

The Alderley Sandhills project was designed to illuminate the transformative
roles of industrialisation and subsequent deindustrialisation on working-
class domestic life in rural northern England. Funded by English Heritage through the Aggregates Levy Sustainability Fund, the project explicitly
questioned the dynamic relationship between industry and households by
studying the material impact of changing regional economies on everyday
residential practices at a domestic site located in Alderley Edge, northern
Cheshire. Containing the remains of two brick and sandstone dwellings
leased as accommodation for the families of local copper miners (Figure 9.1),
the 'Hagg Cottages' site was occupied from the mid-seventeenth century

Figure 9.2   Main image: (left to right) Mr Roy Barber, Mrs Edna Younger, and Mrs
Molly Pitcher visiting the excavated site of their childhood homes, September 2003.
Inset: (left to right) Edna Barrow, Roy Barber, and Molly Barber with the Hagg Cottages
in the background, c. 1930.

through the post-war period of the twentieth century. Excavations revealed
house foundations as well as associated yard buildings and garbage middens. Results included the retrieval of domestic and personal goods, tools
and equipment, building materials, and family heirlooms, as well as the
recording of architectural features related to the process of keeping house
and keeping family within these working households.

In addition to excavation and archival research, the project greatly
benefited from the generous involvement of the local community of
Alderley Edge. During excavations, former residents Mrs Edna Younger
(née Barrow), Mr Roy Barber and Mrs Molly Pitcher (née Barber) visited to
see their childhood homes emerge from the soil (Figure 9.2). Their memories, stories and family photographs of living in the Hagg Cottages provided
a unique personal perspective, as well as valuable ethnographic and historical data. In actively seeking and recording these oral histories as a central

Figure 9.3   Detail of Area A, Alderley Sandhills Project, September 2003.

source of primary data, the Alderley Sandhills Project offered a new source and method of research for English Heritage funded work on industrial period sites.

To survive long-term, inhabitants of this rural hamlet flexibly adapted to the rapid socioeconomic transformations that shaped their changing world. However, in stark contrast to the transient and portable material culture characteristic of single-occupation colonial and New World mining settlements (Gillespie and Farrell 2002; Goddard 2002; Hardesty 1988; Lawrence 2000), the socioeconomic adjustments required of this English mining community occurred within the context of continuous and long-term site occupation. As the social historian John Rule observed, the working populations of English rural districts 'occupied the old homes built-up by their ancestors and repaired and extended over generations by the labourers themselves' (J. Rule 1986: 76). Thus, in this Old World context, socioeconomic flexibility became materially expressed through sequential vernacular adaptations and creative improvisations of the durable built environment.

Excavations revealed a brick lean-to addition on the southern side of the mid-eighteenth-century eastern cottage (Figure 9.3). This extension was floored with a checkerboard of black and red stoneware 'quarry' tiles, a ubiquitous type of Victorian era flooring associated with kitchens and sculleries of domestic structures. Oral histories provided by project participants suggested that female occupants used these kitchen extensions for a range

of food-preserving activities. These women subsidised their limited household incomes by making jarred fruits, vegetables, jams and chutneys for both
family consumption, and for sale to village residents. Thus, the extension
appeared to represent an architectural elaboration of domestic workspace
undertaken to support the income-generating activities performed by the
women of this community. The durable fabric of this structure may also
have indicated both the relative importance of this income source to the
overall economy of these working households – as a certain cost would have
been required for the purchase and delivery of the necessary bricks and tiles –
and the expectation of continued site occupation.

Work-related modifications of this multi-purpose structure continued
into the twentieth century. A section of floor on the eastern side of the
extension was replaced with Portland cement, indicating a late nineteenth-
century repair of the structure. Although this type of mortar had been
granted a British patent in 1824, it became a mass-produced and affordable building material during the latter half of that century, eclipsing lime
in the English building trades by 1900 (Stratton and Trinder 2000: 133).
Additionally, two parallel lines of cement-bonded recycled bricks lay atop
the decorative flooring on the western side of the extension. They appeared
to have once supported something of great weight, as the original tile flooring had buckled in patches below. Oral histories collected from Mr Roy
Barber suggested that by the 1930s, the extension had evolved into a workshop and storage area primarily used by his father for agricultural contract
jobs undertaken to supplement his primary salary as a shop assistant in the town of Alderley Edge. Thus, the kitchen extension represented multiple periods of distinct household activities within the eastern
cottage. When approached from a social standpoint, this structural feature provided an important archaeological perspective on the flexible
continuity of gendered domestic industries over a two-hundred-year
period.

Oral histories related to the southern cottage demonstrated similar patterns of architectural recycling and reuse into the twentieth century. Exterior spaces immediately around this cottage were particularly adapted
for income-generating activities. When questioned about the location of
the front door of the southern cottage during a site tour, Mrs Edna
Younger instead related her mother's use of the area for laundry processing.
Contributing to the family income by taking in laundry from local elite
households, her mother had positioned a washtub and mangle next to the
exterior drain – establishing, in other words, an improvised domestic workplace within the paved courtyard at the front of her house.

For industrial-era households, daily life involved a fluid overlap between domestic and work-related spaces. The architectural adaptations and improvisations recorded within industrial-era settlements ultimately provide archaeological signatures of socioeconomic continuity. A tendency to convert (rather than replace) existing structures diversified the nature, form and function of workers' housing across industrial-era Britain. Residential sites were always places of production as much as places of consumption. By avoiding strict classifications of sites into settlement versus industry-related categories, industrial archaeology can illuminate a wide range of traditional productive practices that helped economically to sustain the lives of working families.

FROM WORKSHOPS TO MANUFACTORIES: JOHN WATTS: A SHEFFIELD CUTLERY FIRM

The following case study will explore the archaeology of the Sheffield metals trade. Two broad types of metalworking activity took place within post-medieval Sheffield (S. Pollard 1959). The *light* trades specialised in the manufacture of cutlery and edge tools. These had a highly localised distribution and were generally undertaken in small workshops by skilled workmen with little capital, using traditional working methods. In contrast, the *heavy* work of steel making and armaments manufacturing was usually carried out by large firms, using specialist machinery. These firms, which were often situated on the wide floodplain of the River Don to the East of Sheffield, were more forward looking, and tended to be influenced by technological developments in other industries (S. Pollard 1959: 7).

The derelict premises of the John Watts Cutlery Firm stand in Lambert Street, a little-used Sheffield backstreet (Figure 9.4). The façade of the building displays in raised plaster lettering the following advertisement:

JOHN WATTS, ESTABLISHED 1765, MANUFACTURERS OF CUTLERY AND OTHER SPECIALITIES, STAMPERS, PIERCERS, AND METALWORKERS. SAFETY RAZORS, SCISSORS, SKATES ETC.

At first glance this would seem to be the faded premises of a typical Sheffield cutlery firm. Buildings such as the John Watts works are taken to epitomise a golden age of local know-how and skill. Sheffield's reputation as 'one great workshop' (Wray et al. 2001) that supplied the world with metals goods is still cherished, and the putting-out system that made use of independent cutlers, or 'Little Mesters', is taken to represent the rugged

Figure 9.4   John Watts & Co., Sheffield.

individualism, fierce independence and home-grown ingenuity of the city's inhabitants. A strong sense of anti-modernism is also apparent in this vision, which upholds the value of traditional craft skills in opposition to the age of industrial mass production.

How accurate are these perceptions of Sheffield's former metals trades? Recent archaeological work at the John Watts works ahead of proposed redevelopment has offered some interesting insight into the origins and operation of the firm. The findings presented below, based upon unpublished reports by the archaeological contractor ARCUS, are intended to offer some general thoughts on the problems and potential of the industrial archaeology of urban workshops.

Lambert Croft (latterly Lambert Street) was laid out in 1728 on agricultural land beyond the West Bar (or medieval gate) of Sheffield. The Croft was named after the landowner, Edward Lambert, a linen draper from Manchester. Within fifty years a substantial number of small businesses had established themselves on the Croft, including six cutlers, a file maker, a razor maker, a scissor maker, and three button makers (Machan 1999: 88).

Census returns from 1841 indicate that Lambert Street, as it was by then known, lay at the heart of one of the poorest districts of the town, and was inhabited by a large number of unskilled labourers and their families

(Machan 1999: 89). Almost half of the residents listed in the census had been born outside Sheffield, and half of these came from Ireland. It is possible that many of these unskilled labourers had been employed in the previous decade as railway navvies working on the construction of the Woodhead Tunnel between Sheffield and Manchester. A sanitary report written in 1848 highlighted the Irish presence in the area in strongly disapproving terms:

the back lanes, and many of the smaller streets, [are] densely inhabited by the lower orders generally, including a great number of Irish, whose quarters are commonly filthy above the average. The narrow lanes and courts are of the worst possible description, being exceedingly close, tenanted by profligates of all descriptions, the houses are often dilapidated and badly supplied with air and light. Many of these serve as lodging houses in which congregate vagrants of every kind. The yards present the usual appearance, being unpaved, the soil often saturated with drainage and very filthy from accumulations of night soil and rubbish. (Haywood and Lee 1848: 28)

In 1872 John Watts & Co. purchased Court Six, which lay behind numbers 41–43 Lambert Street, and began installing a clog clasp-manufacturing workshop that it had taken over in premises on neighbouring West Bar Green in the 1860s. Court Six is shown on the First Edition Ordnance Survey Map of 1852 as one of a series of buildings ranged around five central courtyards. To the rear of the courtyards were two-roomed cottages; larger three-storey buildings occupied the frontages on Lambert Street. The 1871 Census recorded no fewer than 160 residents in the twenty small cottages that lined the five courtyards.

Over the next forty years John Watts & Co. gradually acquired all five courtyards and all of the surrounding cottages and related buildings. By c. 1910 an amalgamated works had been created. This sprawled over several properties, but appeared from the grand façade on Lambert Street to be one unified factory. Behind the façade, however, several of the original cottages and yards had been incorporated into workshop structures, and had in some cases been covered over beneath an over-arching roof.

John Watts & Co. showed remarkable flexibility and opportunism in the range of products that it manufactured. In the 1870s and 1880s the company was famed for the production of clog clasps, but as the company grew and absorbed new premises new products were also marketed. Thus in 1884, steel ice skates and graining combs were added to the customary output of clog clasps. In 1895 pens, pocket knives and safety razors were produced, and the company advertised its ability to manufacture stamped and pierced goods (Machan 1999: 91).

In the closing decades of the nineteenth century and the early twentieth century Watts' son, John R. Watts, acquired a number of local steel and cutlery-manufacturing firms and succeeded in bolstering the firm's trade in metal goods. He also pioneered a programme of diversification that led to the company producing new products, such as furniture, as well as exploiting the early twentieth-century passion for pleasure cruising by supplying wardrobe fittings for P&O luxury cruise liners. The importance placed upon personal appearance and smart dress shaped products in other ways. Throughout the 1930s the sale of tie and trouser presses accounted for almost half the annual turnover of the company (Machan 1999: 96).

During the two World Wars the factory was requisitioned by the British government and machinery was adapted for the manufacture of radar components and armaments, including parts for Sten-guns, and Bren-guns. In the years following World War II the prosperity of the company entered into a spiral of decline. The company struggled through several decades until its eventual closure in 2001. During this lengthy period of decline the firm had fewer employees, dramatically reduced its range of products and limited manufacturing activity to a small number of rooms within the former factory complex.

Archaeological survey of the abandoned building complex by Oliver Jessop and Tegwen Roberts (Roberts 2004) revealed a labyrinth of 89 rooms over 5 floors, linked by corridors and covered courtyards, that had developed during the company's 130-year occupancy of the site. The most striking feature of the premises was the way in which the firm had grown in an organic way to quite literally absorb and incorporate early domestic dwellings into the fabric of the factory (Figure 9.5). This can be taken as a metaphor for the way in which nineteenth-century Sheffield appropriated rural metalworking traditions and put them to use in an industrial context.

At another level it may be taken to illustrate the lack of a corporate ethos within the city. The majority of Sheffield cutlery firms were owned and operated by local families, and until the mid-nineteenth century there was a reluctance (possibly on the grounds of expense) to embrace the idea of purpose-built cutlery factories and mechanised production. Even when large integrated tenement factories became more common in Sheffield, after 1850, factories tended to be erected by speculators, who sub-let rooms, and even individual workbenches within rooms, to self-employed cutlers and grinders (Symonds 2002: 105).

Evidence of the various activities that had been carried out within John Watts' works survived, in varying degrees of completeness. Unlike the evidence from excavated cutlery-manufacturing sites in Sheffield

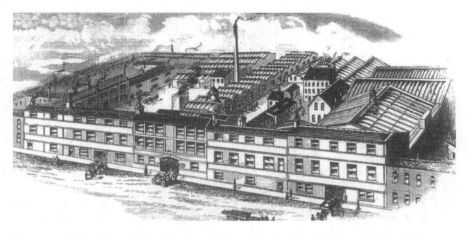

Figure 9.5   John Watts & Co. Works as depicted in a catalogue illustration from the 1930s.

(Symonds 2002: 3) the premises did not yield a large number of discarded or part-finished items of cutlery or other goods. Whereas archaeological excavation can locate artefact 'catchments', such as the wheel-pits beneath water wheels, where broken or otherwise intentionally discarded items have been tossed into the water and forgotten about, valuable materials that can be sold, recycled, or for that matter pilfered, are less likely to remain in situ in an operational workshop.

The position of abandoned machinery and room fittings did allow some rudimentary spatial analysis to be undertaken. It was possible to demonstrate that some rooms had been used for furniture manufacturing or storage, some for cutlery grinding and polishing, and others as packaging or show room areas. The layout of the factory as abandoned, in 2001, retained many elements that had been devised between 1910 and 1916. Some significant documented episodes of activity were nevertheless completely missing. The firm had initially been known for the production of clog clasps, but virtually no evidence of clog-clasp manufacturing could be found (Figure 9.6). It transpires that the machines and finished examples of this trade had been physically removed from the buildings when the company was still in operation and had been deposited with a museum of clog making in West Yorkshire (Ken Hawley, pers. com.).

The sheer range of manufacturing activities that had been undertaken by the firm tended to be masked by the passage of time. Equipment within the building complex was not stratified in a conventional archaeological sense, with a neat succession of discrete phases, but was jumbled and constantly reworked rather like a beach deposit; the ebb and flow of activity had left an

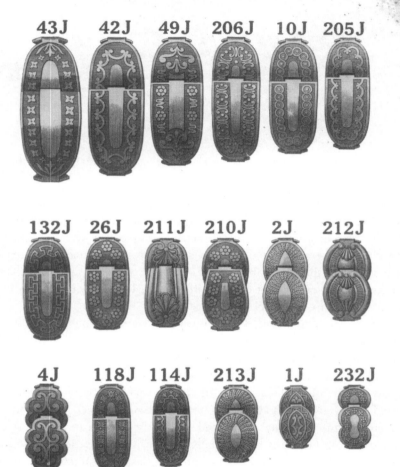

Figure 9.6 John Watts & Co. Watts' celebrated clog clasps.

accumulation of residues that occasionally adhered to the dark recesses of rooms, but at other times were entirely swept away. Often all that remained in a room was evidence of the final phase of activity, with hints of earlier phases of use. These were corroborated with reference to fire-insurance plans, old photographs, and other archival material.

A large amount of heavy machinery dating from the early twentieth century was still in use when the firm closed in 2001. Most of these machines had been used for turning, drilling and piercing metal. A detailed survey by Tegwen Roberts recorded a total of seventy-three machines, comprising presses, saws, rotary table presses, lathes and guillotines, milling machines, rumblers, shaping machines, drills, furnaces, drop stamps and a friction press.

The sheer practicality and durability of this equipment may explain its longevity in the workplace. A more cynical interpretation might be that this reflects the inherent conservatism of the metals trades, and the wider British failure to reinvest in modern manufacturing equipment. Nevertheless, this should not be taken to suggest a lack of industrial ingenuity. The machinery that remained within workshops displayed clear evidence of constant reuse and adaptation. All of the machines were powered by electric motors. In the main machine room electricity had been harnessed to power a system of overhead line shafting and drive belts, but in its original form the line shafting is likely to have been steam powered.

Where possible the place of manufacture of the machines was noted, although disappointingly, 23 of the machines had no identifiable maker's mark. Of the remainder, the majority had been made in Yorkshire, either in Sheffield (12) or Wakefield (12), approximately 25 miles away. Birmingham, another city known for its metalworking trades in the English midlands, had supplied 7 machines.

An unexpected discovery, made possible only by the close inspection of individual machines, was the presence of a number of American-made machine tools (8) in the main machine room. The origin of these machines varied, but included drills made by Prentice Bro's, Worcester, Mass., shaping machines by R. A. Kelly & Co., Xenia, O[hio], and Pratt and Whitney Co., Hartford, Conn., and a press by F. W. Bliss Co., Brooklyn, New York.

The date of manufacture of these machines suggests that they had been acquired as part of a 'lease or lend' scheme to facilitate the production of armaments in the early years of World War II. After VE Day in May 1945, the machines were modified and retained, and remained in use in the machine shop for more than fifty years.

The evidence contained within the factory illustrates several overlapping scales of manufacturing activity. There is evidence of local craft skills, the efforts that the company made to engage with national markets, and even the contribution that it made to global conflicts. But was John Watts & Co. a typical Sheffield cutlery firm?

The first clue to this question lies in the location of the firm's premises, outside the main area of the town. It has been noted that West Bar was an area that was populated by Irish immigrants in the 1830s and 1840s. In the 1851 Census more than half of the residents of this area were recorded as originating in Nottinghamshire. John Watts had been born in Retford, in Nottinghamshire, and had moved to Sheffield with his parents in the 1820s (Machan 1999: 86).

Second, did the firm specialise in cutlery? From its beginnings in 1765, the firm made clog clasps, and studded dog collars, at nearby West Bar Green. These were the main products of the firm for more than a hundred years (Machan 1999: 80). The process of diversification that commenced in the 1890s was a response to the growing pressure that Sheffield cutlery firms were being placed under from mass-produced goods made in the United States and Germany at that time (Symonds 2002: 6). Another explanation could be that the diverse range of trades that Watts engaged in was evidence of a small-workshop mentality; individual skill and connoisseurship was clearly valued, and was put to use wherever possible. Unlike larger corporate firms, the company was flexible enough to make use of new opportunities.

CONCLUSIONS

In the second half of the twentieth century, industrial archaeology developed from a purely amateur pastime, motivated by a desire to preserve the material remains of Britain's industrial past, into a more mature scholarly discipline. From the mid-1990s, the empirical focus of the field has been complemented by new studies that contribute to broader themes within historical archaeology – including global contexts, community heritage and the archaeology of identity. The work of a number of pre-eminent American historical archaeologists has been singled out as an instrumental influence in the development of social approaches to the archaeology of industrialisation (Beaudry and Mrozowski 1987a, 1987b, 1989; Hardesty 1988; McGuire and Paynter 1991; Rogge et al. 1995; Shackel 1993, 1996). Similar explorations of industrial landscapes as physical manifestations of hierarchical power relations have been undertaken by several industrial archaeologists in Britain, Ireland, Australia, New Zealand and continental

Europe (Lawrence 2000; Palmer and Neaverson 1987; Ritchie 2003; Rynne 1999).

Meanwhile, industrial archaeologists have also contributed to our historical understanding of the processes of industrialisation. The revolutionary impact of this period profoundly transformed the nature of everyday life within both households and workplaces. Archaeological perspectives offer a new material knowledge of the industrial past – incorporating aspects of social power and inequality, labour relations and class formation, in addition to details of production, trade and consumption. By examining changes in the everyday dimensions of life and work, industrial archaeology has the capacity to move beyond fixed or otherwise bounded accounts of the history of technology or of class identity to explore how people and things were intimately enmeshed within the wrenching transformations of industrialisation.

CHAPTER 10

Historical maritime archaeology

Joe Flatman and Mark Staniforth

Maritime archaeology studies human interactions with oceans, rivers and lakes in the past. In the historical period, maritime archaeology focuses upon the underwater remains of ships, boats or other watercraft or vessels and aircraft. It includes the study of objects and human remains that survive within such vessels as well as cultural material that was accidentally dropped, lost overboard or deliberately deposited into the water body. It also includes the remains of structures that were originally built wholly or partly underwater (such as bridges, piers, jetties and wharves) as well as the physical remains of human activity that originally took place on dry or marshy land but that has subsequently been inundated, either by rising water levels or by marine (or fluvial) erosion. Historical maritime archaeologists also increasingly examine terrestrial sites, structures and landscapes: places that are not underwater but that are related to maritime activities such as lighthouses, port constructions, shore-based whaling stations or wider coastal, lakeside or riverside maritime landscapes.

Maritime archaeology includes the overlapping fields of underwater archaeology, marine archaeology and nautical archaeology. *Underwater archaeology* is limited to material that survives in submerged environments: such evidence may exist beneath fresh (inland) waters or salt (marine) waters. It may be visible on the bed of the water body (i.e. seabed) or buried beneath sediment. The term 'underwater archaeology' simply refers to the environment in which the practice of archaeology is undertaken: an environment that often brings significant technical difficulties and high costs of research. *Marine archaeology* examines material remains that survive in marine (saltwater) environments, while *nautical archaeology* studies ships and shipbuilding, using not only underwater remains but also other material evidence such as ship burials, shipwreck remains in the terrestrial landscapes or shipyards. By drawing together these materials with other sources of terrestrial and documentary evidence, historical maritime archaeology has made many contributions to historical archaeology, playing an important part in the development of the discipline and increasingly providing distinctive interpretive frameworks that emphasise interregional and international connectedness and interactions in the past.

Maritime archaeology is a large, diverse and international field, and this chapter introduces just some aspects of historical maritime archaeology in the anglophone world. It outlines the development of maritime archaeology since the 1950s, and sketches the emergence of historical maritime archaeology in three regions: North America, Australia and the United Kingdom. It briefly surveys the range of sites at which historical maritime archaeology is conducted, and the analytical themes that have characterised its development, before presenting a case study drawn from recent research into the East India trade. In a concluding section, the chapter indicates a number of areas in which the field is developing, and in which it is beginning to make substantive contributions to the broader fields of maritime archaeology and historical archaeology.

THE DEVELOPMENT OF MARITIME ARCHAEOLOGY

The development of historical maritime archaeology dates from the mid-twentieth century, particularly the emergence of scuba after World War II and the subsequent growth of underwater projects. By the 1950s, scholars such as Diole (1952) had begun to recognise the potential offered by scuba to reach a range of submerged sites and to develop archaeological methodologies for underwater archaeology. In the United States and parts of southern Europe, particularly the Mediterranean, the roots of maritime archaeology lie in classical archaeology. George Bass' seminal work *Archaeology Under Water* (1966) outlined theoretical approaches and methodological principles still in use to this day, and Bass' early excavations were innovative. Cape Gelidonya, the excavation of a shipwreck dating from the twelfth century BC in 1960, was the first-ever fully recorded excavation underwater, and set high standards by using new methods designed to maximise the amount of information retrieved, many of which remain in use today. Bass' team went on to refine these techniques at a series of impressive excavations of ancient shipwrecks in the eastern Mediterranean during the 1960s and 1970s, at sites such as Yassiada (Bass 1982), Ulu Burun (Bass and Pulak 1989) and Serçe Limani (Bass 1979; Van Doorninck et al. 1988). At such locations, Bass experimented with methods of producing highly detailed, three-dimensional site maps. Bass provided maritime archaeology with sophisticated methodologies that could be compared with terrestrial archaeology, and were essential for the acceptance of maritime archaeology within the academic mainstream. However, despite Bass' interests in historical archaeology, his methods simply produced new data that could be fitted into existing explanatory frameworks in classical archaeology.

In contrast, in the United States, institutional contexts led to a much stronger influence upon maritime archaeology from cultural anthropology, rather than from classical studies. American maritime archaeologist Richard Gould proposed conducting 'shipwreck archaeology as anthropology' grounded in 'cultural relativism' (studying cultures on their own terms), 'cultural presentism' (problematising the projection of present-day experience and observation into the past) and 'cross-cultural comparison' (1983: 3ff. cf. Gould 1997). Gould's proposals led to an increased focus upon maritime social life – whether on board ship or in ports and harbours – and archaeological studies of the social history of maritime technologies (R. Gould 2000). Shipwreck anthropology also led some to examine international contexts, through 'world-systems' perspectives or by studying the colonial archaeology of the Portuguese, Spanish, British or Dutch. In contrast with such purely global contexts, alternative traditions of North American maritime archaeology were influenced by more contextual studies of James Deetz's historical archaeology (Deetz 1977). Such apparent 'historical particularism', considering the small-scale details of particular artefact assemblages (Bass 1983: 91ff.), has often produced excellent fine-grained investigations of historical shipwrecks, where favourable site conditions can lead to the survival of organic materials to an extent usually unseen on land (Curtis 1985), and which complement more general studies of items of historical material culture in maritime archaeology (Redknap 1997).

In Europe and Australasia, the scientific perspectives of 'processual' archaeology have played a very important role in methodological and theoretical developments in maritime archaeology since the 1970s. In the United Kingdom, maritime archaeologist Keith Muckelroy was a key proponent of such approaches, developing models of wreck formation processes and their spatial patterning, which he combined with the promotion of the integration of documentary and archaeological evidence (Muckelroy 1976). In successive seasons of work between 1973 and 1978 on the remains of the *Kennemerland*, a Dutch East Indiaman in the Shetland Islands, Muckelroy's statistical methods for examining distribution patterns, directly influenced by similar models already used on terrestrial sites, were developed (e.g. Muckelroy and Price 1979). Muckelroy aimed to work the wrecking process backwards to the moment of initial shipwreck, so as to model the relationship between the location of objects recorded archaeologically on the seabed and their location within the original ship, the process of wrecking, salvage operations afterwards, the disintegration of perishables, seabed movement, and characteristics of excavation. Like Michael Schiffer's (1987) studies of terrestrial 'site formation processes', Muckelroy represented the process of shipwreck site formation using flow diagrams (Muckelroy 1978). Muckelroy's wreck-site formation models and site distribution patterns continue to influence maritime archaeologies across the world (e.g. Ward et al. 1999), especially through his textbook *Maritime Archaeology* (Muckelroy 1978). For example, Colin Martin has built upon Muckelroy's techniques on sites across northern Europe, most notably on sixteenth- and seventeenth-century shipwrecks such as the *Dartmouth* (Holman et al. 1977) and *La Trinidad Valencera* (C. Martin 2001), arguing that ships represent complex artefacts in their own right (C. Martin 1997, 2001: 393–397).

The influence of processual archaeology upon British maritime archaeology was also visible in Seán McGrail's development of statistical models and studies of changing shipbuilding traditions (McGrail 1977, 1978). However, McGrail's 1970s work also drew on what became another important theoretical strain of British-based maritime archaeology, that of ethnoarchaeology (the use of ethnographic data in the interpretation of archaeological remains). With colleagues such as Basil Greenhill, McGrail aimed to integrate archaeological, documentary and ethnographic evidence for shipbuilding traditions around the world (Greenhill 1995; Greenhill and Manning 1988; McGrail 1984a, 1984b; cf. McGrail 2001). While the use of documentary and iconographic sources was developed further by others (e.g. Friel 1995; J. McKee 1983), integrating diverse types of evidence in a similar manner to that developed in documentary archaeology, such work generally remained limited to functionalist and evolutionary studies of ship technology in isolation from social life in the past.

Since the 1980s, maritime archaeology has witnessed a continued hegemony of scientific and processual approaches, and the influence of Gould's 'shipwreck anthropology' has gradually faded. In some regions the field has witnessed increasing diversity, sometimes in surprising directions. In particular, interest in archaeologies of 'maritime cultures' – studying relations between coastal societies and material culture and the social environments of shipping – has grown rapidly in continental Europe (Jasinski 1993; Westerdahl 1992, 1994). In a similar vein, scholars such as Timm Weski, Thijs Maarleveld and Fred Hocker have returned to the study of the technologies and 'cultural traditions' of shipbuilding (Hocker and Ward 2004; Maarleveld 1995). Studies of maritime art have also multiplied (Crumlin-Pedersen and Munch-Thye 1995; Kobylinski 1988). But since the 1990s it has been from outside conventional maritime archaeology that most promising shifts in the discipline have originated. Works by European prehistorians such as Andrew and Susan Sherratt (1991), Richard Bradley (1997) and Barry

Cunliffe (2001) have not only actively included maritime material along-side terrestrial archaeology, but also importantly have made use of maritime contexts in their interpretive frameworks. Such attention has led to a new confidence among some maritime archaeologists, who have argued that the field enjoys a clear methodological basis, growing intellectual profile and popular interest, and the ability to contribute to theoretical discussions (J. Adams 2001; Gibbins and Adams 2001). Others, however, have expressed concerns over the continuing and conservative descriptive and empirical focus of most maritime archaeology, driven by reactions to chance discoveries of vessels rather than by coherent research strategies, and the limited consideration of potential interdisciplinary contributions (Flatman 2003). In historical archaeology in particular, such limitations are beginning to be overcome: especially through wider definitions of maritime sites and landscapes, to which we now turn.

MARITIME SITES IN HISTORICAL ARCHAEOLOGY

Most historical maritime archaeology is carried out on the sites of shipwrecks. This focus upon watercraft is the result of the historical development of maritime archaeology, as well as a reflection simply of the numerical predominance of shipwrecks around the world in comparison to other types of site. The best analyses of shipwrecks can be excellent examples of historical archaeology, combining detailed, historically specific studies of particular archaeological remains within a broader appreciation of life on board ship and the sociocultural significance of a vessel. The range of historical maritime archaeological sites includes many notable vessel sites, but rather like the development of historical archaeology of buildings, where studies of the houses of particular celebrated individuals have given way to broader analyses of historical structures (Hicks and Horning this volume), so in maritime archaeology the range of sites is far richer and more complex than the evidence provided by the remains of particular named ships alone. This section therefore outlines the range of historical maritime sites and landscapes available for archaeological study, before describing watercraft and aircraft sites.

Maritime landscapes

Maritime archaeological remains survive in all environments, including dry land, the coastal and inter-tidal zones, shallow and deep water. Increasingly, maritime archaeologists of all periods are focusing upon notions of 'landscape' and 'seascape' (Cooney 2003; A. Parker 2001). Maritime landscapes – ports, harbours, industrial sites and other waterfront sites – represent a significant resource for historical maritime archaeology, each of which is complex. Harbour constructions, for instance, include wharves, quays, jetties, piers, canals and artificial docks that remain above water or have become submerged by rising sea level, caused by catastrophic events such as earthquakes or simply as a result of natural site formation and deterioration processes. The remains of the port of London have been excavated since the 1950s, in work that has highlighted the richness of the material remains of wharves, jetties and associated features – including the broken up and reused remains of numerous vessels, and a diverse array of material culture associated with daily life in the port (Ayre and Wroe-Brown 2003; Divers 2002; Douglas 1999; Marsden 1981; Milne 2003; cf. Milne 1987).

The remains of urban maritime infrastructure have also been excavated in the United States, most notably at the excavation of Hoff's Store, a nineteenth-century ship chandler's on the quayside of old San Francisco that burned down and collapsed into shallow water in 1851 and was subsequently buried by landfill, which provided an distinctive insight into the material culture of the Californian Gold Rush (Delgado 1991). A contemporary ship-breaking yard (Pastron and Hattori 1990; Pastron and Delgado 1991), and the remains of the merchant vessel *Niantic* (1851), the lower hull of which revealed a well-preserved cargo and goods stored aboard the ship during the Californian Gold Rush, have also been examined in San Francisco. The goods that survived on board demonstrated the tremendous buying power of Californian gold, and the global supply of goods to that inflated market (J. Parker 1980).

The most striking example of an archaeological study of a historical maritime landscape is Port Royal, Jamaica, where the remains of a seventeenth-century town that sank into Kingston harbour during an earthquake in 1692 survive underwater. Major excavations began in the 1950s and have continued virtually without break since the 1980s, producing a wealth of materials and an insight not only into the town, but into the entire early colony of Jamaica and its place in the colonial structure (Marx 1973; Pawson and Buisseret 2000; G. L. Fox 1999, 2002; D. L. Hamilton 1991). The benefits of long-term archaeological investigations of maritime landscapes are clearly demonstrated by the sustained investigations of the nineteenth-century dockyard and floating dock at Bermuda, coordinated by the Bermuda Maritime Museum, which includes remains of the British Royal Navy dockyard together with the hull of *HMS Vixen*, an early ironclad ram. Surveys of the dockyards during the 1980s and 1990s (R. Gould 1990; Gould and Souza

1995; Harris 1989) have been built upon by ongoing and sustained underwater and terrestrial archaeological fieldwork across Bermuda promoted by both the Bermuda Maritime Museum and the Bermuda National Trust, and published in the first-class annual journal *Bermuda Journal of Archaeology and Maritime History* – providing increasingly significant perspectives upon the material culture of the Atlantic world during the past four hundred years.

Watercraft

Archaeologists, aided by chance or deliberate discoveries by fishermen, divers, the military, dredging, construction, or salvage, have inventoried and studied thousands of shipwrecks dating from the sixteenth to twentieth centuries. For instance, numerous finds have been recorded in the polders of Holland (Oosting 1991; Oosting and Van Holk 1994; Reinders 1979), an area of low-lying land in the Netherlands reclaimed from the sea between 1930 and 1968. Within this former seabed the remains of an extensive collection of medieval and post-medieval vessels, often in excellent states of preservation and buried within deep, wet, anaerobic sediments, have been recorded. The excavation of these vessels began as early as 1940, and has provided a wealth of information on localised shipbuilding, life on board ship and late-medieval material culture (Oosting 1991; Oosting and Van Holk 1994; Reinders 1979). Ships have been discovered in landfill, for example in Quebec City, New York, and San Francisco (Delgado 1991; Lepine 1983; J. Parker 1980; Riess 1991), and at the sites of former river courses, such as the *Bertrand* and *Arabia*, two mid-nineteenth-century river steamers discovered in the central United States (Hawley 1995; Petsche 1974). Shipwrecks on beaches or in the littoral zone have also yielded significant archaeological results, including *Amsterdam* (1749) at Hastings in Britain, and *La Belle* (1686) at Matagorda Bay, Texas in the United States (J. B. Arnold 1993; Bruseth and Turner 2005).

Historical archaeologies of watercraft range from the analysis of submerged evidence for particular vessels, such as the mid-nineteenth-century *H. L. Hunley*, a Confederate submarine that was the first submersible to sink another vessel in combat, recovered near Charleston, South Carolina (Hicks and Kropf 2003; Figure 10.1) to studies of particular groups of vessel remains from distinct geographic areas. For example, the remains of a series of nineteenth- and twentieth-century vessels survive within Isle Royale National Park on Lake Superior in Michigan, and form a representative cross-section of wooden- and steel-hulled Great Lakes merchant

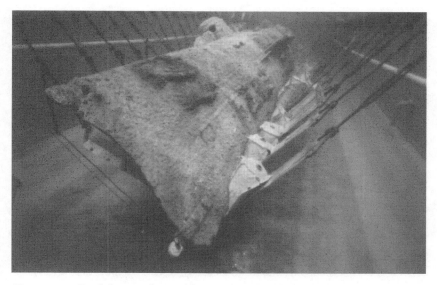

Figure 10.1   Confederate submersible H. L. Hunley in its storage tank shortly after recovery in August 2000.

steamships from between 1870 and 1947 with a communal significance far greater than any one of these vessels would enjoy on its own (Murphy and Lenihan 1994). In some cases, individual ship excavations come to hold tremendous contemporary cultural significance: most notably the exceptionally well-preserved *Mary Rose* (built in 1545, see Figures 10.2 and 10.3) in Britain and the *Vasa* (built in 1628) in Sweden. At both sites, major hull remains survive together with hundreds of thousands of artefacts providing a unique insight into life on board these ships and the relationship of this lifestyle to parent cultures (Landström 1980; M. Rule 1983; Soop 1992). In other cases, the significance of an excavation derives from the connection of the vessel to a particular global event: such as the *Titanic* (Ballard 1985) or the fragments of the lower hull of the *Sea Venture* (built in 1609), which was lost off Bermuda while en route to the colony of Jamestown, Virginia, inspiring Shakespeare's *The Tempest* (J. Adams 1985; Wingood 1982, 1986).

The development of submersibles, remotely operated vehicles and remote-sensing technologies (especially side-scan sonar, magnetometers, metal detectors, sub-bottom profilers or high-resolution sonar systems), which offer increasing opportunities for maritime archaeology to work at depths where diving is impossible with current technologies, will open up more deep-ocean wreck sites for potential investigation (Manley and Foley 2004). The highly publicised late twentieth-century discovery of modern

Figure 10.2   Domestic items recovered from the wreck of the *Mary Rose*.

Figure 10.3   Personal items recovered from the wreck of the *Mary Rose*.

wrecks such as *RMS Titanic* (1912), *KMS Bismarck* (1941), *USS Yorktown* (1942) and Japanese, US and Australian ships lost at Guadalcanal (1942) by teams led by Robert Ballard underscore the archaeological potential of deep-water vessels, and of the technologies used to reach such craft (Ballard 1985, 1990). Indeed, opportunities extended by Ballard have been taken up by archaeologists such as Anna Marguerite McCann and Brendan Foley (Ballard et al. 2000; McCann and Oleson 2004).

In several cases, the excavated remains of both military and civilian watercraft have come to function as national icons. Archaeological finds such as the *Mary Rose* and *Vasa*, as well as historical vessels such as *HMS Victory* and the *USS Arizona* have at times been seen physically to embody cultural values of national pride and historical legitimacy. In this process, such vessels attain significance well beyond their immediate intellectual or historical value. While often positive, sometimes the use of maritime heritage has been pernicious: as with the use of the recovery of the *Mary Rose* (1545) in 1982 by the British Conservative government to help legitimate the Anglo-Argentine conflict in the Falklands/Malvinas through images of British maritime military excellence (Hewison 1987; Wright 1985). Replica vessels have also sometimes been used to this end, as witnessed in the furore surrounding different replicas' voyages during the 1988 bicentennial in Australia (Macintyre and Clark 2003: 102–107). The discovery of a fifteenth-century cargo ship in Newport, South Wales, recently highlighted another manifestation of this tendency, the vessel being used as a weapon in an unseemly struggle for power and money between the newly devolved Welsh National Assembly based in Cardiff and the London-based central government of Britain, in which the vessel became emblematic of a wider 'conflict' between the English and the Welsh with roots deep in the historical origins of the 'United' Kingdom. Such contemporary matters are central to the distinctive nature of archaeological studies of maritime history.

Aircraft

One newly emerging field of maritime historical archaeology is the study of the underwater remains of aircraft, especially military aircraft. While aircraft crash sites are also excavated by terrestrial archaeologists (e.g. Holyoak 2002; Legendre 2001; Webster 1998), the investigation of underwater crash sites emerged in the United States in the 1990s as part of the underwater archaeology programme of the Naval Historical Center in Washington DC, and was initiated in response to threats to submerged remains of such craft from souvenir hunters (Neyland and Grant 1999). The field is now growing in significance in historical archaeology, especially in World War II archaeology, and the sites investigated stretch across North America, the Pacific, Australia and Europe. Research has also been undertaken into sites such as the group of flying boats attacked by the Japanese off Broome, Western Australia (Souter 2003), and training-flight crash sites off Victoria in

Australia (J. Ford 2004). Specific aircraft have also been identified, such as the remains of the *USS Macon*, a US navy dirigible that crashed off the coast of California in 1935 (Vaeth 1992).

REGIONAL TRADITIONS IN HISTORICAL
MARITIME ARCHAEOLOGY

While new thinking in historical maritime archaeology increasingly extends the notion of 'sites' to wider landscapes, the consequences for maritime archaeology of calls for the acknowledgement of the global complexities of the 'multi-sited' contexts of historical maritime worlds (Lucas this volume) are increasingly felt. Maritime archaeologists are particularly aware of the materiality of global interconnections during the past five hundred years – perspectives which, as archaeologist Chris Gosden has suggested, are just as significant for studies of Europe as for the wider world:

> what we are looking at is the incorporation of Europe into a new colonial order, rather than the imposition of European habits and power on the colonies . . . much of British culture (and that of the rest of Europe) from at least the 17th century onwards had a colonial origin or influence. (Gosden 2004: 127)

In this postcolonial global context (cf. Lawrence and Shepherd this volume), almost all historical archaeology might be said to be maritime historical archaeology, in that the existence of virtually all historical–archaeological remains is contingent upon global maritime movements of people and things. Archaeologists increasingly see 'modern colonialism [as] a process of gradual incorporation of the whole world into colonial structures . . . [creating] new networks of social interaction on a global scale' (Gosden 2004: 114–115). From the sixteenth and seventeenth centuries, the enforced, large-scale appropriation of lands by Europeans, the emergence of industrial slavery, and the development of a global market of consumer goods all involved new material geographies. Archaeologists such as Martin Hall (2000) and Mark Staniforth (2003) have explored the global nature of colonial material culture, where societies located at vast distances apart shared a demand for and use of the same objects.

One consequence of such observations is an increasing need to acknowledge particular regional traditions in archaeology – the wider 'landscapes' of the discipline (Hicks 2003: 324). In this section, therefore, we aim to sketch three of the most influential regional traditions in historical maritime archaeology – an endeavour that must always be partial and broad brushed. While maritime archaeology has been conducted in virtually every corner of the globe, and in depths of water ranging from a few centimetres to many thousands of metres, the development of strong traditions of historical maritime archaeology has been limited to North America, the United Kingdom and Australia. While important studies have been carried out elsewhere in the world, and an appreciation of global interconnectedness is at the heart of contemporary historical maritime archaeology, the material studied in the development of these regional traditions forms an important context for global maritime archaeology, and is therefore sketched below.

North America

The diversity of historical maritime archaeology in North America can be illustrated by a short chronological sketch of the range of material that has been investigated in recent years. The seventeenth-century terrestrial sites of European settlement in North America that have been investigated by historical archaeology, such as those at Roanoke in North Carolina or Ferryland, Newfoundland (Noël Hume 1997; Tuck 1996; Tuck et al. 1999) were dependent upon support and supply across the ocean for their survival. Similarly, later colonial settlements in the Chesapeake, such as Williamsburg, Virginia or Annapolis, Maryland, while less dependent upon resupply by sea than the initial colonies, were still closely bound up with maritime contexts, both in the long-distance provision of consumer goods and in more localised activities such as fishing (Brown and Samford 1994; cf. Hicks 2005: 379). At rural sites in this region the exploitation of maritime- and land-based resources were frequently enmeshed, particularly in geographically distinct areas such as Chesapeake Bay where activities along and off the coast remained as important to daily life as work inland (Greeley 2005; Yentsch 1992: 21, 33).

The American revolutionary war left its own archaeological legacy across many maritime landscapes, such as the Yorktown River where a range of vessels were lost or scuttled in the 1780s and harbour and shipbuilding remains also survive (Broadwater 1985, 1992). Similarly, archaeological remains have been investigated at a number of maritime sites associated with the Anglo-American war of 1812, including Lake Ontario (Cain 1983). Archaeological evidence for eighteenth- and nineteenth-century commercial shipbuilding is particularly rich along the Mississippi River and Great Lakes (see contributions to S. Smith 1993; Erwin 1994). The archaeological remains of specific events in the maritime history of nineteenth-century North America have also been investigated: especially the Civil War of 1861–1865. The historical archaeology of the port city of Charleston in South

Carolina, for instance, comprises a unified assemblage of historic town and harbour, the rivers and surrounding coastline and islands (particularly specific sites like Fort Sumter), and the submerged remains of different vessels (Wilbanks and Hall 1996): a diversity that is mirrored in the historical maritime archaeology of the Civil War elsewhere (Arnold et al. 2001). For the twentieth century, similarly distinctive material has been explored, including 'single event' sites such as materials associated with the Japanese attack on Pearl Harbour in 1941, including the battleship *USS Arizona* (Lenihan 1989).

Australia

Archaeological evidence of the earliest European interaction with Australia and its peoples is fragmentary, mainly comprising various Dutch and British East India company vessels (Kist 1990), and more occasionally associated shipwreck-survivor camps (M. Nash 2001, 2004). Indeed, as Geoff Egan (1990) has observed, in this early period it is sometimes small items of material culture such as leaden seals that hold evidence for the East India Company's trade in textiles that hold the most research potential.

The maritime archaeology of formalised colonisation from 1788 is significantly more defined, partly because 'European' Australia remains an extremely maritime culture (Broeze 1998; Henderson 1986). At major settlements such as Sydney, Melbourne and Adelaide, maritime-related materials survive both on land and under water (Connah 1988; Lydon 1999b). At Adelaide, for example, archaeologists have investigated the traces of a sequence of ports, quays and wharfs alongside related infrastructure such as a quarantine station, naval installation and dumping ground for 'hulks' – old, unseaworthy or economically unviable vessels (Richards 1998). Around the port, the distinctive suburban settlement that sprang up nearby to provide housing, shopping and entertainment facilities for dock workers also forms part of the maritime landscape (Couper-Smartt 2003). Studies of artefacts recovered from such sites, both consumer goods such as ceramics as well as larger items like the remains of steamship technology, have provided insights into the nature of colonial material culture, and how such communities fitted into the global consumer society of the European colonies (Staniforth 2003; see McCarthy 2001, Veth and McCarthy 1999).

Marine sites elsewhere in Australia reflect other aspects of the country's maritime history. The penal settlement of Port Arthur in Tasmania was begun as a timber station in 1830, and by the 1840s had a population of over one thousand convicts, troops, civilians and their families (Figure 10.4).

Figure 10.4 Remains of a slipway at the nineteenth-century convict shipyard at Port Arthur, Tasmania (courtesy of the Department of Archaeology, Flinders University).

Archaeological investigations have traced how the settlement became the hub of a complex maritime network, with vessels large and small moving supplies and people around the entire Tasman Peninsula to coastal outstations, each provided with its own jetty and infrastructure. Shore-based whaling and sealing stations have also proved a significant focus for Australian historical archaeology. The global nature of the whaling industry has been emphasised in studies of common processing facilities and technologies at such sites. Susan Lawrence and Mark Staniforth (1998) have pointed to studies of social life through material culture recovered from these sites which demonstrate the presence of women and children, as well as interaction with local indigenous communities – a picture that is at odds with the commonly perceived view of whaling stations as solely male preserves (Staniforth et al. 2001; cf. Nash 2003). Such Australian work builds upon pioneering studies of whaling at Red Bay in Labrador, Canada, where excavations revealed not only the submerged remains of the Basque whaling galleon *San Juan* and several of its whaleboats, but also the land-based remains of the whaler's settlement on the nearby shore. The excavation produced a wealth of details about early whaling and life in this remote outpost (Grenier and Tuck 1981; Tuck and Grenier 1989; Waddell 1986).

Britain

Historical maritime archaeology in Britain has been dominated by studies of industry and trade: especially the diverse material remains of imports of luxury materials and foodstuffs and exports primarily of cloth, machinery and weaponry. This is clear at a number of scales: both in archaeological studies of 'small finds' such as ceramics and tobacco pipes, and also in the surviving maritime infrastructure of ports such as London, Glasgow, Bristol or Liverpool, and at many other smaller maritime settlements. The major underwater developments were sketched above, but in this section we want to consider the terrestrial maritime archaeology conducted in Britain.

In the post-war period, urban-rescue archaeology has allowed the terrestrial remains of maritime activities of all periods, and especially the post-medieval, to be explored (Ottaway 1992; C. Thomas 2003; c.f. Hicks and Jeffries 2004; Knight 2002). Harbour or riverside sites, often with significant waterlogged remains, have yielded evidence for the long-term development of harbour infrastructure, and associated housing, manufacturing and industrial areas, alongside the material remains of personal items, foodstuffs and exotic imports preserved within middens and rubbish dumps.

As well as such urban contexts, British maritime archaeologists have also studied the standing-building remains of shipyards and coastal defences. The shipyard at Buckler's Hard in Hampshire, England, for example, which was created in the early eighteenth century by the second Duke of Montagu, has been the subject of historical and archaeological study (Holland 1985). The duke planned to build a free port on the banks of the Beaulieu River for the import and export of sugar from the West Indies, but the idea failed to get off the ground. As a result, this initial plan was scrapped, and from the 1740s Buckler's Hard was used for shipbuilding. Excavations at the site in the late 1990s revealed sophisticated timber-lined slipways at Buckler's Hard, together with contemporaneous industrial developments along the banks of the Beaulieu River (Jon Adams pers. com.). The widespread remains of successive coastal defences in Britain have also been extensively investigated, particularly along the south coast of England. Begun in the Middle Ages via initiatives such as the 'Cinque Ports' of Sandwich, Dover, Hythe, Romney and Hastings (Madox Ford 2000), many of these defences were formalised during the reign of Henry VIII (Biddle et al. 2001; Morley 1977), and developed by successive governments until the later twentieth century. Particular bursts of activity have been identified during the Georgian and Victorian periods in response to the threat from France, and again in the twentieth century in response to the threat from Germany. The ultimate refinement of such sites came during the Cold War, in response to the threat presented by the Soviet-led Eastern Bloc and the anticipated third world war (Cocroft and Thomas 2003, Lowry 1995, Osborne 2004).

While after 1700, British material culture was characterised by a new diversity, derived from its maritime empire, historical archaeology of this period and place can also be more localised. Fishing and farming communities, particularly in more isolated and less developed regions such as the Scottish western islands and the Northern Irish coast, also provide rich archaeological evidence: including both evidence of wider maritime connections and also of distinctive, localised material culture (Martin 1998; McErlean 2004). Similarly, the dense communications network provided by the canals of Britain had obvious links with global trade and exchange, while still encouraging a distinctive community and material culture in the canal boats and families who operated these, together with the supporting infrastructure of locks and quays, shops, pubs, maintenance and repair facilities (Burton and Pratt 2002; J. Stone 2002). The integrated study of this range of terrestrial with underwater archaeological remains is an important and emerging field for British historical maritime archaeology.

CASE STUDY: MARITIME ARCHAEOLOGY AND THE EAST INDIA TRADE

A brief excursion into the contributions that historical archaeology can make to our understanding of the Honourable East India Company (EIC) and Dutch East India Company (Verenigde Oostindische Compagnie, or VOC) provides a useful illustration of the potential of historical maritime archaeology. Archaeological sites associated with the East India trade are spread across the globe, and include both shipwrecks and maritime landscapes (Bound 1995; Egan 1990; Fenwick and Redknap 1990; Kist 1990). Sites associated with the EIC and VOC have been studied by both professional and avocational groups since the mid-twentieth century, and the sheer number of investigations of material remains relating to the EIC and VOC now provides a significant resource for the study of these companies' structures, organisation and interests, particularly when the archaeological data are combined with other sources like documentary evidence.

While the documentary evidence for EIC and VOC cargoes is plentiful, and while the headquarters and land-based infrastructure of these companies often survives to this day (particularly in the Netherlands), without the material evidence from shipwrecks little would be known of the types of cargoes carried by the EIC and VOC. This is particularly true for perishable organic remains, which frequently made up a small but highly profitable element of any cargo: they never survive on land, but can sometimes be found within well-preserved shipwrecks. Furthermore, time and again maritime archaeology demonstrates that while the official records of these ships tell one story of their inventories, archaeology paints a very different, more complex picture, with all sorts of additions, as individual captains made decisions about additional cargoes en route, and crewmen engaged in private enterprise. Similarly, documentary records of the design and structure of these vessels often varies from the reality presented by archaeological data, with numerous modifications. The careful survey and excavation of these wreck sites also gives a unique insight into everyday life on board EIC and VOC ships, their organisation, layout and command structure, with constant reminders of the lifestyle of ordinary sailors.

The combined social, economic, political and military influence of the EIC and VOC stretched around the world. Their influence on the physical environment was also profound, and their material cultural remains distinctive: EIC and VOC sites are highly similar wherever they are found in the world, and the remains of these vessels and their bases give an insight into the global spread of European material culture and settlement – especially in India, modern-day Indonesia, and Australia. Recently, the remains of shipwreck survivor camps of VOC ships have also provided a unique insight into the changes in structure and organisation that take place when the rigid hierarchy of shipboard life breaks down (Gibbs 2003; M. Nash 2001, 2004). The 'archaeology of crisis' demonstrates that supposedly ephemeral survivors' camps in fact include a diverse array of artefacts, including much secondary reuse of materials. Such sites also provide evidence for early interaction between Europeans and indigenous communities, often before formalised contact was made.

The *Amsterdam* (built in 1749) is probably the best-known example of the excavation of a VOC vessel in Britain. Here, the hull remains and contents of the vessel were identified in the surf zone off Hastings. In the 1980s the interior of the stern of the vessel was carefully excavated by an Anglo-Dutch team, producing a variety of artefacts and demonstrating the excellent survival of the hull (Gawronski 1997; Gawronski and Van Rooiji 1989). In comparison, the *Witte Leeuw* (built in 1613), a VOC vessel lost off the British-controlled island of St Helena in the South Atlantic, is an example of the range of materials that often survive at such sites. The excavation recovered bronze cannons bearing the monogram of the company's Amsterdam *kamer* (branch), with an inscription indicating they were made by a Henricus Muers in 1604, as well as Chinese porcelain and Rhenish stoneware, spices, Indo-Chinese ceramics and Indo-Chinese 'curiosities', reflecting the types of mixed cargoes that the early VOC carried (Van der Pijl-Ketel 1982). The best-known VOC wreck off Australia is that of the *Batavia* (built in 1629), the remains of which included well-preserved hull fragments from the vessel's stern and a rich assemblage of artefacts being shipped to the settlement of Batavia (modern-day Jakarta), including an entire portico façade being shipped in pieces (Dash 2002; J. Green 1989; Stanbury 1975). Of equal significance are less well-known Australian VOC wrecks such as that of the *Zeewijk* (built in 1727), rediscovered by a team from the Western Australian Maritime Museum (WAMM) in the 1970s after extensive archival research. A three-year excavation encompassed not only the wreck site but also the associated survivors' camp, producing a wealth of materials (Henderson 1986; Ingelman-Sundberg 1977).

Beyond the evidence from shipwrecks, a number of historical archaeologists have demonstrated the rich archaeological evidence for the East India trade. For instance, archaeological analyses of surviving material culture of VOC bases such as Batavia and modern-day Cape Town have begun to explore the particular, distinctive nature of everyday life in such colonies. Such studies provide insight not only into the material culture of the VOC, but also into how this organisation and the people whose lives it came to dominate fitted into an expanding pattern of global enterprise and material culture, in which communities divided by thousands of miles of ocean have tangible links through their demand for, and use of, specific material culture (Curtis 1985; M. Hall 2000). As Jordan and Schrire (2002: 266) comment, these materials

provide a window into the global and local movements that contributed to the creation of a colonial material culture. A variety of economic, social and geographic factors created the situation.

The maritime archaeology of the East Indies trade, then, can include both detailed artefactual analyses and also broader regional and global models of shipwreck anthropology, placing the minutiae of daily life on board East Indiamen within a global context. Indeed the contextual nature of studying an international network such as that of the EIC and VOC over time provides an important perspective upon calls for the construction of 'global historical archaeology' (e.g. Orser 1996). As maritime archaeologists increasingly strive to develop the field outside Europe, North America and Australia – especially in Central and South America, and in the Indian Ocean (e.g. Flemming 2004; Manders et al. 2004; Sundaresh et al. 2004; Tripati et al. 2003, 2004) and as partnerships are built between local archaeologists and those based in western institutions, the manner in which 'global' contexts are imagined becomes increasingly important. The maritime archaeological potential of other regions of the globe, notably Africa and parts of Southeast Asia, remains virtually unexplored. The case study presented here, however, demonstrates the potential of connecting and comparing material between places that were connected in the past, in what Hicks has termed 'situational' studies, rather than constructing overly simplistic models of 'world archaeology' (Hicks 2005: 375).

DISCUSSION

The potential of such approaches in maritime archaeology could be fruitfully developed in the archaeology of the African diaspora. As Fred McGhee has suggested,

nautical archaeology has not sufficiently problematised the concept of empire; it has not critically engaged European colonialism, its own colonial legacy, nor situated itself, in terms of power, in relation to the human subjects it studies. (McGhee 1997: 1)

At present, despite the fast-developing studies of African diaspora among African-American archaeologists – most visible in the recent formation of the African Diaspora Archaeology Network (Fennell 2005) – McGhee is virtually the sole voice in this respect within maritime archaeology. It is striking that the limited research agendas within historical maritime archaeology have meant that practically no vessels associated with slavery have been studied beyond the poorly excavated *Henrietta Marie* (built in 1699) in the United States (Cottman 1999; Sullivan 1994), the better-excavated but ambiguous evidence of the *James Matthews* (built in 1841) in Australia (Baker and Henderson 1979; Henderson 1976), and various vessels elsewhere that may possibly be slave ships, such as the *Gem* in Rhode Island, USA (Zarzynski and Abbass 1998). The *James Matthews* is undoubtedly the best-excavated example of a slave vessel, a nineteenth-century former Portuguese (illegal) slave ship captured by the British and subsequently lost on a trading voyage to Australia (Baker and Henderson 1979; Henderson 1976). Its late date and secondary reuse in trade means that it is not necessarily indicative of the slave ships used during the 'peak' period of international slavery. However, plantation historical archaeology both in the eastern United States and especially in the island Caribbean, increasingly fills out this story, providing an insight not only into the layout, organisation and control systems of plantations, but also of everyday life at such sites (Armstrong 2003; Hicks 2000; Honychurch 1997, Meniketti 1998).

Historical maritime archaeology has contributed a great deal to the study of several fields. Most prominent, perhaps, are its investigations of the material remains of military activities: whether through the study of warships, or through naval dockyards, aircraft or coastal defences. Sunken military vessels such as the series of World War I and World War II vessels in Scapa Floe, Orkney, and the remains of World War II vessels at Truk Lagoon and Bikini Atoll in the Pacific (Jeffrey 2004) have often been focused upon. The field has recently witnessed increasing interest in the archaeology of recent military sites, particularly those of World War II and the Cold War, where the opportunity exists for archaeology to be combined with oral and documentary history (Schofield and Johnson this volume). The ethics of exploring such recent vessels, many of which are war graves, remain complex, and legislation has not kept pace with our technological ability to find and access such vessels in ever more inaccessible parts of the globe.

The analysis of trade and exchange has also dominated many maritime archaeologies, ranging from the analysis of trade routes throughout history, of different types of cargo and cargo vessel, or of infrastructure like lighthouses, beacons and seamarks. One aspect of this type of study that regularly captures the public imagination is that of piracy, although as is demonstrated by the debate over the identity of the Beaufort Island Shipwreck in the United States – said by some to be the remains of the pirate vessel *Queen Anne's Revenge* – it can be extremely hard to securely identify such single-use vessels or specific remains within the archaeological record (Rodgers et al. 2005).

Many studies have used maritime perspectives to present detailed analyses of fishing, whaling and mining communities (Lawrence and Staniforth 1998; McErlean 2004; O'Sullivan 2001; Pfaffenberger 1998). Such studies, and especially fine-grained studies of particular fishing communities (Bowen 1992; H. Fox 2001; F. Harrington 1992; Yentsch 1992) or of particular extractive industries such as kelp production (McErlean 2004), hold the potential to contribute to broader historical accounts, such as those of the salt or cod trades (Kurlansky 2002; Pope 2004). Historical archaeology and oral history can demonstrate how these were frequently socially and/or culturally exclusive communities, sometimes living within environmentally unforgiving conditions, and their material remains under these conditions reflect this balance (Mauk 1997; Staniforth, Briggs and Lewczak 2001).

But these traditional themes, and the limited engagement with the maritime archaeology of the African diaspora, indicate not only the untapped potential of contextual, or situational, studies in 'global' maritime archaeology, but also the strong conservatism of the field's research agendas. Maritime archaeology has also begun to contribute to studies of European colonialism and interactions of the past five hundred years (compare Finamore 2004). Maritime archaeologists have explored the material remains of undocumented Polynesian or medieval Chinese societies (Phillips 2004), but maritime dimensions of indigenous and contact archaeologies remain relatively unexplored in maritime archaeology which has not yet developed studies as sophisticated as historical ethnographies of the 'entangled' roles of material culture in the processes of colonial contact (e.g. N. Saunders 1999; N. Thomas 1991).

Nevertheless, historical maritime archaeology has come a long way since its emergence in the 1950s, and is uniquely positioned to contribute further fine-grained studies alongside more ambitious, and yet contextual, studies in maritime archaeology. In realising its enormous potential, however, the field must integrate further within historical archaeology.

PART III

Historical archaeology and material culture

CHAPTER II

Material culture studies and historical archaeology

Matthew D. Cochran and Mary C. Beaudry

INTRODUCTION

Material culture is ubiquitous in our everyday lives; we are surrounded by it and arguably can do little without it. The proliferation of new material forms is troubling to some, often forming the basis of debates over globalisation, modernity and the contemporary production of locality. But while it is true that people are regularly confronted with new objects and technologies, without question many understand and embrace them and consciously use them in the creation of multiple and often intersecting identities.

As historical archaeology has emerged as a field of study, understanding and interpreting material culture has become more important than simply identifying and classifying excavated objects (cf. Barker and Majewski this volume). In the United Kingdom, historical archaeologists have followed conventions established by archaeologists of earlier periods, typically grouping and describing their finds according to material (e.g. pottery, iron, bone). In North America, where historical archaeology emerged at approximately the same time as archaeologists' redefinition of their field through the introduction of the scientific method and the search for laws of cultural behaviour, the overwhelming emphasis has been upon classification of finds according to functional categories (e.g. 'personal', 'military', 'architectural': see South 1977a). Until the 1990s, many American historical archaeologists were anxious to develop universal, standardised schemes for artefact classification so that artefacts and assemblages could be readily compared among historical sites. As a result, historical archaeologists were slow to accept alternative approaches to studying artefacts, approaches arising from the field of material culture studies (for a review, see Yentsch and Beaudry 2001). Our goal in this chapter is not to review typological and generalising approaches to artefact analysis; rather, we explore recent developments in transdisciplinary, interpretive material culture studies, and the opportunities they offer for material culture analysis in contemporary historical archaeology.

Archaeologists and anthropologists have long recognised the significance of material culture as a means of studying people, and anthropology and archaeology as disciplines both have long traditions of material-culture study. Archaeology has always used material remains to interpret human behaviour, but the interests of sociocultural anthropology during the latter half of the twentieth century shifted away from the focus on material culture that characterised its formative years. From the 1980s, however, sociocultural anthropologists, especially historical anthropologists, have turned their attention to how people express themselves and interact through material culture (e.g. Comaroff and Comaroff 1992; N. Thomas 1991). Material culture studies as a distinctive interdisciplinary field of study has emerged in North America, with strong links to architectural history, decorative arts, and folklore, as well as to archaeology and anthropology (Lubar and Kingery 1993; Martin and Garrison 1997; cf. Rathje 1981). Concurrently, anthropologists and archaeologists in the United Kingdom have begun to bridge the gap between archaeology and sociocultural anthropology by incorporating within ethnography the political sensitivities and material focus from post-processual and Marxist archaeologies, to develop a broadly defined anthropological material culture studies aimed for the most part at studying the role of objects in contemporary contexts (e.g. Gosden 1999; D. Miller and Tilley 1996). A British school of 'material culture studies', arising largely out of work conducted by Daniel Miller and the material-culture group at University College London (Buchli 2002a; D. Miller 1998b, 2001b), remains distinct from archaeological material culture studies, but has nevertheless influenced many historical archaeologists.

Other archaeologists studying material culture have been influenced by alternative traditions of 'interpretive' interdisciplinary material culture studies that focus upon the body, especially through phenomenological or feminist perspectives (e.g. Meskell 1999, 2004; J. S. Thomas 1996; Tilley 1994, 1999, 2004). Such approaches have been concerned with embodiment – about how humans experience and enact the material world through the medium of the body – considering not so much the biographies of objects but how people create their own biographies through objects and in the ways they care for, present, and make use of their bodies throughout the course of their lives (cf. Gilchrist 2000; J. Hoskins 1998).

In this chapter we consider the range of subjects examined in material culture studies, and the distinctive contribution that historical archaeology can make to the interdisciplinary study of materiality. We explore how excavated 'small finds', such as objects of personal adornment, from historical sites provide intimate portraits of individual lives and of the construction of personal and social identity. We then present a case study drawn from Cochran's application of perspectives derived from anthropological material culture studies to the contemporary historical landscape of Annapolis, Maryland – a much-studied landscape in historical archaeology – in order better to understand the materialities of contemporary heritage.

MATERIAL CULTURE AND HISTORICAL ARCHAEOLOGY

Historical archaeologists have long depended upon research by 'material culture specialists' who produce identification guides to artefact types of all sorts; for present purposes it is perhaps best to think of such work as 'artefact studies' because it stresses identification, chronology, and typology over interpretation (e.g. Brauner 2000; Deagan 1987, 2002; Karklins 2000; Noël Hume 1969). Barker and Majewski (this volume) rightly stress the importance of such 'foundational' studies for ceramics researchers, and it is clear that historical archaeologists require accurate information about, and descriptions of, the artefacts that they excavate before they can move on to interpretations of them. Prior to the 1990s, however, interpretative analyses of ceramics and other artefacts were largely absent from historical archaeology in the United Kingdom and in the Americas tended to focus on a narrow range of research issues, namely consumer choice, status, and, to a lesser extent, ethnicity (see Barker and Majewski, this volume). This has changed as over the last three decades material culture studies in historical archaeology have increasingly combined theories and methods from across the humanities and social sciences and as more and more historical archaeologists have approached their research with perspectives drawn from postprocessual archaeology (e.g. Lawrence 2000; M. Praetzellis and A. Praetzellis 2004; Tarlow and West 1999; Wilkie 2000, 2003). However, the fragmented nature of the practice of much archaeological fieldwork and post-excavation analysis – in which things from particular contexts are studied in isolation from each other by specialists in clay pipes, textiles or ceramics – remains a major challenge for the development of interpretive archaeologies of excavated material culture.

The study of material culture has a long intellectual history in the social sciences from the late nineteenth and early twentieth centuries (see the reviews by Buchli 2002a; Buchli and Lucas 2001c: 3–8). A new phase in material culture studies developed in the 1970s, which in its early stages began with the 'insistence that things matter and that to focus on material worlds does not fetishise them since they are not some separate superstructure to social worlds' (D. Miller 1998d: 3). Studies of 'small things' in historical archaeology (Deetz 1977) emerged at the same time as anthropological consumption studies (e.g. Douglas and Isherwood 1979). Such researchers used material culture as specific data sets but each studied material culture from within the confines of particular disciplines. In contrast, during the 1980s a number of scholars began to focus on material culture as a specific problematic in approaches that drew from both archaeology and sociocultural anthropology. Two foundational works stand out in this regard: Arjun Appadurai's edited volume *The Social Life of Things* (1986), and Daniel Miller's monograph *Material Culture and Mass Consumption* (1987). In many of the contributions to Appadurai's volume, and especially in Miller's monograph, the use and consumption of material culture was depicted as central to everyday social life. This turn was significant in that it constituted material culture studies as a people-centred, relational field of study, using material culture to comprehend aspects of everyday social life that often go unmentioned, or are obscured for varying ideological reasons.

These new approaches to material culture were distinct from traditional object-oriented studies in the decorative arts and in architectural history, which paid little attention to social and cultural context. However, such conservative studies persisted, and strands of such work can still be seen, for example in 'connoisseurship' models influenced by E. M. Fleming (1974). Such connoisseurship models in decorative arts studies and some strains of American studies, emphasise the typological classification and comparative analysis of objects based on their physical characteristics. For example, an eighteenth-century teapot would be assessed according to the materials of which it is made, judged by its style and design and evaluated within a field of similar objects. Such analyses did not extend to the uses of these objects, nor to people's diverse experiences of objects within social contexts or relationships between people and objects. Connoisseurship divorced material objects from their social contexts and promoted an élitist fetishising of subjective qualities of the object by the analyst in the present.

In response to post-structuralist critiques such as that of Igor Kopytoff (1986), from the mid-1980s the archaeological and anthropological study of material culture began to shift focus towards addressing the formation of relationships between peoples and things within specific social contexts. Particularly relevant to historical archaeology are contextual approaches to material culture that developed within American studies and folklore research within the United States, emphasising the details of the production of material culture by individuals in contemporary contexts. Such work included Grey Gundaker's study of cosmological references within contemporary African-American yard art (Gundaker 1998, 1996), Michael Owen

Jones' study of the poetics of chair making in the mountains of eastern Kentucky (M. Jones 1993, 1989) and Henry Glassie's work on the production of diverse folk objects ranging from woven carpets to pottery (Glassie 1999). These researchers developed methods that involved the detailed study of material culture forms and their placement within historically situated folk practices, alongside interviews with the producers of those forms in the present. By integrating these sources of evidence, these scholars produced nuanced, multi-tiered analyses centred on the production of particular objects by particular people, examining the production of form and style, how the processes of production play an active role in shaping individual producers' identities, and the broader contexts of producers' social and cultural identities. Such behavioural approaches to material culture understood objects as to some extent manifestations of their producers, carrying with them human cultural sensibilities bound to their materiality.

Meanwhile, in anthropological material culture studies in the United Kingdom, scholars consciously sought to bring archaeology's material focus to bear upon sociocultural anthropology by combining ethnographically based research methods with political sensitivities towards the study of material culture derived in part from postprocessual and Marxist archaeologies (Buchli 2002a; D. Miller 1998b, 2001b). In this work, material culture was seen as a means of providing 'insights into cultural processes that a more literal "anthropology" has tended to neglect' (D. Miller 1998d: 3). In such a view, material culture, and especially the study of consumption, provided a distinctive set of data, the study of which could penetrate many taken-for-granted aspects of the everyday. Miller argued that consumption studies held the potential to 'transform' social anthropology (D. Miller 1995). By trying to focus less on what informants say they do than on their everyday material engagements, these new studies aimed to uncover anthropological 'matter' within field research; and insisted that material culture should not be viewed as a passive subject or object, but as a potentially active agent in social life.

The precise methodologies of fieldwork in such material culture studies remained undefined and open. Uncovering anthropological 'matter' within fieldwork contexts involved developing an 'emic' and contextual perspective, seeking out 'a more diffused, almost sentimental association that is more likely to lead us to the concerns of those being studied than those doing the studying. It put the burden of mattering clearly on evidence of concern to those being discussed' (D. Miller 1998d: 10). The methodological openness of this work was fruitfully combined with a concern with the production of socially and politically relevant anthropological research. Examples include Barbara Bender's work with the contemporary travellers' communities and their relationship to the prehistoric monument at Stonehenge (B. Bender 1998), and Daniel Miller's work on contemporary shopping practices in north London (D. Miller 2001a, 1998c; D. Miller et al. 1998). By focusing on material culture as actively involved in the construction of social identities and community values, Bender and Miller allowed their research to be guided in part by the groups that they were studying.

The notion of the 'active' role of objects in social life has been extended in recent archaeological and anthropological literature through the notion of material agency. Influenced especially by the work of Alfred Gell (1996, 1998), anthropological material culture studies have considered material culture has the potential to act as a 'quasi-agent' in everyday social life (cf. Knappett 2002; Latour 2000b). In such a view, material culture has the potential to shape our experiences of the world – not only in terms of physicality or materiality as we move through and negotiate material forms in everyday life, but as metaphor. Christopher Tilley's reading of West African Batammaliba houses and Victor Buchli's reading of the Narkomfin apartment building in Moscow (Buchli 1999; Tilley 1999) are both fine examples of the active role of material culture in social life. Both scholars explore how material forms such as the home come to manifest particular social ideologies and worldviews centred on the body's relation to the material. The curvilinear architecture of Batammaliba houses is read by Tilley as metaphors of the body that shape and reinforce ontological structures of the family; while the shifting conceptualisations of Soviet interior design within the Narkomfin apartment building are interpreted by Buchli as physical manifestations of ideological conflict centred on the dialectic of modernity and tradition. Material culture as material *and* metaphor can hence be seen as reinforcing ideologies, shaping family structures, and acting in a very real sense on the body. The home in this sense becomes a model by which the body is construed.

INTERPRETING MATERIAL CULTURE IN SOCIAL ANTHROPOLOGY

The new anthropological material culture studies, especially as practised by Daniel Miller and the material culture group at University College London from the early 1990s, has been characterised by engagements with a very wide range of materials. Miller and Tilley argue that the study of material culture may be most broadly defined as the investigation of the relationship between people and things irrespective of time and space. The perspective adopted may be global or local, concerned with the past or the present, or the mediation between the two. Defined in this manner, the potential range of contemporary disciplines involved in some way or other in studying material culture is effectively as wide as the human and cultural sciences themselves. (1996: 5)

Contemporary material culture studies aim to create transdisciplinary scholarship, to disable conservative boundary-maintaining devices within the academy and to avoid rigid and totalising social theory. Its protagonists argue that in many ways 'material culture [studies] is better identified as a means rather than an end' (D. Miller 1998d: 5). In this section we want to underline five areas in which anthropological material cultures studies have especially focused: consumption, landscape, architecture and the home, heritage, and art and visual culture.

As described above, consumption studies represented a key element in the emergence of anthropological material culture studies (Appadurai 1986; Douglas and Isherwood 1979; D. Miller 1987). Challenging views of consumption as based in a chronic, inward-looking 'imaginative hedonism' (C. Campbell 1986: 77), such work presented consumption as meaningful and creative social action. Thus, Daniel Miller's work on shopping practices in a north London neighbourhood (D. Miller 1998c, 2001a; D. Miller et al. 1998) explored how shopping strategies comprise patterns of value, thrift and sacrifice within specific social contexts. Such work demonstrates how the consumption of material things can be very important in constructing highly personal social relationships, as people 'make love in supermarkets' through shopping (D. Miller 1998c: 15–72), or conceptualise the 'local' through consumption of globally itinerant goods (D. Miller 1998a).

Landscapes – both contemporary rural and urban cityscapes and the remains of past landscapes that survive – have also been studied by anthropological material culture studies. In such work, landscapes have been conceived as 'open-ended, polysemic, untidy, contestational and almost infinitely variable' (B. Bender 2002: 137) and are read as malleable. Researchers often intentionally strip them of naturalistic connotations to examine landscapes in terms of cultural and social interactions. Landscapes have often been studied as sites of conflicting views of local and national heritage, of memory and forgetting, of tourism and of negotiation of identity politics (Basu 2001; B. Bender 1993, 2001, 2002). As noted by De Cunzo and Ernstein (this volume), many recent studies address the phenomenology of landscapes, stressing embodied perspectives based on multisensory experience (B. Bender 1998; Tilley 1994, 1999, 2004).

The study of the materiality of architecture, households and the home has been common in anthropological material culture studies, as in historical archaeology (Hicks and Horning this volume). The negotiation of architectural spaces as part of daily social practices has proved a fertile field (Froud 2004; Tacchi 1998), while relationships between architecture, conceptualisations of the body, and social ideologies (Low 2003), and experiences of 'home' and memories based on personal relationships with material culture (Daniels 2001; Young 2004) have also been studied. These studies take nuanced approaches to the materiality of architectural spaces and social negotiations of those spaces. One development of this work on architecture and the home was the founding in 2004 of a new interdisciplinary journal *Home Cultures* (Buchli et al. 2004), which is an increasingly influential force in the open-minded exploration of alternative approaches to the materialities of homes.

Heritage studies within anthropological material culture studies transcend neat categorisation. Conceptually the focus on the materiality of heritage can be read in diverse areas such as the Neolithic landscape of Stonehenge (Bender 1998), the architectural space of the Acropolis (Yalouri 2001) and the production of banners used during Orange Order parades in Northern Ireland (Jarman 1997; McCormack and Jarman 2005). What has set this area of study apart, however, is not only its focus on the materiality of heritage, but also an emphasis on how 'we live in an era of unprecedented concern with preserving and restoring the past' (Rowlands 2002: 105). These perspectives have led to studies of the role of objects and monuments in cultural memory and loss (Forty and Küchler 2001); the construction of local and national identities via relationships with monumental architecture (B. Butler 2001; Rowlands 2001; Van der Hoorn 2003) and the exploitation of a 'sense' of heritage to create new attractions and destinations for 'heritage tourism' (Basu 2001).

Lastly, the anthropological study of art and visual culture has developed, especially through the influence of Alfred Gell's *Art and Agency* (1998), which examined 'distributed agency' in material art objects (cf. Gell 1996). In this tradition, Nicholas Saunders has studied the 'trench art' made by soldiers in World War I from recycled shell casings (N. Saunders 2003a). Suzanne Küchler has studied the ephemeral 'Malanggan' figures from the Pacific (Küchler 2002) and Christopher Pinney has examined contemporary portrait photographs from India (Pinney 2002). By examining how art and visual culture can 'act' as a quasi-agent – expressing senses of intentionality within prescribed social contexts in a view akin to Walter Benjamin's notion of the *auratic* (Benjamin 1969) – these studies have focused the study of art upon materiality, in relational, rather than aesthetic, studies of art objects and people.

INTERPRETING MATERIAL CULTURE IN HISTORICAL ARCHAEOLOGY

In this section, we want to explore how historical archaeologists are starting to work with this body of anthropological work on materiality. First, we consider how the 'social archaeology' of historical artefacts is increasingly examining issues of identity, gender, sexuality, age, and other aspects of social difference in relation to materiality and the body (Meskell et al. 2001: 5). This is followed by a discussion of Cochran's new study of Annapolis, Maryland. These examples bring different epistemological perspectives to bear, but share much in terms of approach and interpretive sensibilities (compare Buchli 2004: 182).

'Small finds'

Historical archaeologists have become increasingly aware of the interpretive potential of all manner of small, excavated finds for comprehending the construction of personal identity (White and Beaudry n.d.). Their research into artefacts related to dress and personal adornment have proved especially fruitful despite the obvious challenges in interpreting dress and personal appearance in the present, which are multiplied by the lens of time and the inevitable scrappiness of the archaeological record of apparel and the presentation of the self.

Historical archaeologists have been successful in interpreting 'small finds' such as buttons, buckles, beads, and jewellery because they are able to link such items to a broader literature on clothing, embodiment and cultural biographies not just of *objects* but of *individuals* through the objects they own and use (e.g. Burman and Turbin 2003; J. Hoskins 1998; Küchler and Miller 2005; Küchler and Were 2005). For instance, Diana DiPaolo Loren's research has explored how groups interacting on colonial frontiers employed items of dress as a means of personal expression as well as of contesting colonial hegemony by adopting 'social skins' in defiance of orthodoxies around appropriate dress (Loren 2001; Loren and Beaudry 2006). Carolyn White has analysed artefacts of personal adornment to explore how colonial New Englanders constructed visual appearance in ways that 'communicated a host of information about class and status as well as ideas about gender' and age (White 2004: 63). In her work, Laurie Wilkie has deftly linked the interior furnishings of a late nineteenth-/early twentieth-century fraternity house to changing notions of masculinity (see Wilkie this volume). Beaudry's research into the artefacts of needlework and sewing has led her to examine ways in which close readings of archaeologically recovered sewing implements provide insights not just on the task of sewing but also upon women's presentation of themselves as embodied beings as well as upon how sewing and its accoutrements were used by reformers to promulgate notions of industry, cleanliness, and spirituality (Beaudry 2006; Loren and Beaudry 2006).

This kind of research on 'small things' has led historical archaeologists to realise that despite several decades of artefact studies, we still lack critical information for making useful statements about many categories of material culture. This is because 'small finds' have simply been dismissed as having little value for addressing issues such as status and consumer choice that long dominated research in historical archaeology, and as not amenable to statistical analysis. The new trends in interdisciplinary material culture studies have encouraged some historical archaeologists to abandon quantification and generalisation in favour of close, critical analyses of artefacts that, while not recovered in abundance comparable to ceramics, glass, and architectural fragments, are nevertheless interpretively potent once the contexts or social fields in which they once operated are understood. The result has been a move towards the production of a new genre of artefact guides that stress interpretation as well as identification (Beaudry 2006; C. White 2005) and has spurred the inauguration of a new series of such guides to be published by Left Coast Press. The development of specialist methods in material culture studies in historical archaeology holds enormous potential if combined in this way with the interpretive approaches of anthropological material studies.

Annapolis

In Annapolis, Maryland, Cochran has employed an anthropological material culture studies approach to the changing object worlds of the Annapolis Historic District since the eighteenth century, and the ways in which those changes have been conceptualised as part of the historic environment and are enacted in the contemporary world. The Annapolis Historic District forms a one-square-mile core of the city of Annapolis, with its late seventeenth-century Baroque town plan (Leone 1995; Leone and Hurry

1998). Located near major interstate highway systems, and in close proximity to the Chesapeake Bay, the Historic District's picturesque Main Street, lined with stores and restaurants and bordered by side streets containing many restored eighteenth- and nineteenth-century historic buildings, is a popular tourist destination for day trippers and boaters within the Washington DC–Baltimore metropolitan region (Anderson 1984; Miller and Ridout 1998; Moose 2001). Tourists and new residents alike often cite the Historic District's quaintness and apparent sense of historical integrity as a reason for coming to Annapolis.

The Historic District was the focus of the Archaeology in Annapolis project (see McGuire this volume) from the early 1980s. The project researchers emphasised the importance of ethnographic enquiry as part of historical archaeological research, and have called for its application within a broader scheme of public archaeology (Leone et al. 1987; Potter 1992, 1994). Cochran's research at Annapolis aims to respond to such calls. Ethnography within the Archaeology in Annapolis project was initially conceived as a means of uncovering 'ideologies' in the present, and as a guide from which to undertake archaeological excavation and the public dissemination of archaeological interpretations (De Cunzo and Ernstein this volume). This strategy has been applied on a range of sites over the project's history (e.g. Matthews 2002; Mullins 1999; Potter 1994).

In contrast, Cochran's fieldwork aims explicitly to focus upon the materiality of the Historic District in the present, and the ways in which diverse experiences of that materiality construct overlapping and divergent senses of place and the past. Through written phenomenological descriptions of the Historic District, participant observation, structured and semi-structured interview techniques, and analyses of local history and tourist-related material culture (including architecture and the built environment, local magazines and postcards), Cochran seeks to explore the materiality of how the past is enacted in the present. Represented in the fieldwork are residents of the Historic District, tourists, and administrative groups including local preservation organisations and city officials.

One focus of the study has been the use of different kinds of brick paving within the Historic District's many streets and sidewalks by the Public Works Department (Figure 11.1). The Annapolis Public Works Department is part of the city's managerial administration responsible for constructing and maintaining many of the Historic District's physical elements and public 'viewsheds'. During an interview and walking tour, the director of Public Works described to Cochran the varying types of brick pavers, commenting on their colour and texture, and the bond patterns in which they

Figure 11.1   Laying brick pavings in the Historic District of Annapolis, Maryland.

were laid. The director commented on what constituted acceptable types of brick pavers within the Historic District: comparing multi-coloured clay-brick pavers with uniform coloured concrete pavers, and discussing what constituted an acceptable bond pattern (herringbone versus a running bond pattern).

At issue here were management practices within the Historic District that aimed to achieve bricks arranged in self-consciously random ways. Acknowledging the mandate to make the Historic District into a recognisably coherent whole – texturally distinct from areas outside of it – the director repeatedly emphasised that in creating the brick-paved pathways through the District there was a need to avoid regular patterns. Large swathes of single coloured brick and areas made up of regularly patterned running bond pavers would result in 'predictable' spaces, a practice deemed appropriate for shopping mall-style architecture and wholly inappropriate for the Annapolis Historic District. The director described the artistry required in managing the Historic District: creating visually random patterns balanced by texturally coherent surfaces. This had nothing to do with recreating the way Annapolis looked in the past: 'No. None of this looks the way it used to. If people wanted I could open up the sewers. It looks better now than it ever did.'

Tourist guidebooks often refer to the Historic District's scale, and its 'walkability': and material culture studies, by combining anthropological and archaeological methods, can highlight the essential role of objects (in this case, bricks) in the creation of 'walkability', from the practice of which in turn particular pasts emerge. By focusing upon the materiality and material practices of Historic Annapolis, we expose how important objects are in the creation of the past in the present. The focus upon bricks is revealing: these are objects that guide the walking tourist around the sites through sidewalks, engaging with the walker in enacting the past. Thus, for the director, 'getting it right' did not mean restoring the Historic District with historical authenticity, as ostensibly advocated by the city's Historic Preservation Commission, but rather bringing people and things together for the past to be enacted, through the varied textures and layouts of pavers and bricks, and through the soles of shoes (compare P. C. Adams 2001; Tilley 2004).

CONCLUSION

The increasing interdisciplinary interests in material culture, and in particular the analytical perspectives that have emerged in anthropological material culture studies, hold great potential for historical archaeology. In the work sketched here, the transformative relationships between individuals, groups, and material forms in the practice of everyday life have been exposed, in the past and the present. By acknowledging the active role of objects in everyday life, historical archaeologists avoid the limitations of rigid classificatory schema that segregate objects from people. By studying things, we reveal situations that do not fit patterns, and in which we can come closer to understanding what people really hoped to accomplish through the production, consumption, collection, display or use of material goods. This can be achieved by integrating our highly developed empirical methods with interpretive approaches, integrating these 'two cultures' in a manner similar to that proposed by Andrew Jones (2002: 1–22). Historical archaeologists studying material culture are beginning to achieve such creative integrations.

For instance, in their highly detailed technical study of goods and food remains excavated from sites occupied by working-class households in West Oakland, California, Mary and Adrian Praetzellis also combine material and documentary sources to write the material histories of individual households. They note that 'there was no neat correspondence between a family's wealth and the purchase of high-quality cuts of meat in nineteenth-century Oakland'. The frequency of these people purchasing commodities above their conventionally assigned status leads the Praetzellises to conclude that residents of Oakland were 'seeking to advance goals that had less to do with nutrition or class emulation than with pride and identity' (M. Praetzellis and A. Praetzellis 2004: 83). Just as the historical archaeology of household material culture is rich and complex (2004: 116), so too the potential for analysis of the material culture of place and space, of private life and public personhood, is great. Historical archaeologists have only just begun to realise the full potential of integrated archaeological and anthropological material culture studies for illuminating and interpreting the relationships between people and their material worlds.

CHAPTER 12

Ceramic studies in historical archaeology

David Barker and Teresita Majewski

WHY CERAMICS?

Ceramic studies have played a central role in the development of archaeology – a fact that is equally true for historical archaeology as for studies of earlier periods. Ceramics represent by far the largest class of artefacts recovered during excavations of historical sites. As in other periods, ceramic materials survive in the ground when objects made from other materials do not, and their archaeological value is very high even though they generally only survive in a fragmentary state. As ubiquitous products prone to stylistic change in response to new fashions and consumer preference, ceramics are readily datable, and often prove the most important diagnostic materials recovered when an archaeologically excavated sequence is being interpreted. In addition to their value as sensitive temporal markers, ceramics have the potential to provide insights into a wide range of other topics: cultural change and colonisation; the identities of groups and individuals; the social and economic status of consumers; the emergence of changing practices relating to the consumption of food and drink; patterns of trade and of local and regional variations in trade; and technological change and industrialisation.

The past five hundred years have witnessed massive increases in the production, exchange and consumption of ceramics in Asia, Europe, North America and around the world. In Europe, an intensification of international trade in commodities was a central part of nascent colonialism and the transition from medieval to modern societies, as the Old World was opened up to new commodities from the East and as new markets for new commodities developed in the New World and beyond. A chapter on ceramics could be written from many geographical perspectives. The main focus of the present chapter is European-made ceramics, but discussion of non-European ceramics is interwoven throughout.

The development of historical ceramic studies has been primarily a British and North American phenomenon, and the parallel and separate trajectories on either side of the Atlantic are traced in the first section of this paper. The second section provides an overview of ceramic production and technology, primarily told from an archaeological vantage point. Subsequent sections provide case studies that illustrate how the analysis of ceramic assemblages has informed the study of trade, exchange and consumption. In the concluding section, we sketch some of the new and innovative ceramic studies that are currently emerging.

THE DEVELOPMENT OF CERAMIC STUDIES IN HISTORICAL ARCHAEOLOGY

Until the mid-twentieth century, collectors, decorative artists and art historians dominated ceramic studies. Their work provided sound empirical research and classification schemes, resulting in reference works of continuing usefulness: such as Godden's (1964) encyclopaedia of manufacturers' marks on British pottery and porcelain and Lehner's (1988) similar work for the United States. Such studies were not concerned with the production of ceramics or the social and economic contexts in which they existed, and consideration of the consumption of ceramics was limited to the finest wares possessed by the highest levels of society. Ceramic objects were most commonly viewed as *objets d'art*, demonstrating the perceived skill of their makers and illustrating the design influences contemporary with their creation. A preoccupation with attribution – the need to know who made what – and the elevation of a small number of factories to an undeserved prominence resulted, giving a distorted view of the development of the ceramic industry. The early literature is therefore of limited use for archaeologists who want to move beyond artefact descriptions.

In the United Kingdom, as 'post-medieval' archaeology developed in the post-war period and the number of large-scale urban excavations increased, it soon was evident that the most recent material culture was in many ways the least understood. In 1963, the Post-Medieval Ceramic Research Group was founded, and in 1966 broadened its interests to become the Society for Post-Medieval Archaeology (Barton 1967). The chronological focus of this work (AD 1500 to 1750) led to many studies of the medieval–post-medieval ceramic 'transition', examining sixteenth- and seventeenth-century coarseware industries and their products (e.g. Coleman-Smith and Pearson 1988; Gaimster and Stamper 1997; Moorhouse and Roberts 1992; Pearce 1992).

Archaeological knowledge of European post-medieval ceramics has developed rapidly in recent years, drawing together evidence from excavated ceramic production sites and from 'pit groups' – excavated assemblages from sealed archaeological contexts. In the 1980s, British urban archaeology generated several impressive, city-wide studies, notably in Norwich (Jennings 1981) and Exeter (Allan 1984). In continental Europe, the strong tradition of urban archaeology, especially in Belgium, Germany and the Netherlands, has yielded vast quantities of artefacts from urban contexts. For instance, in the Netherlands an impressive study of the contents of 176 excavated pits in the Dutch towns of Deventer, Dordrecht, Nijmegen and Tiel has resulted from the 'Rubbish Pits and Cess Pits Project' (Bartels 1999). The ceramics from such deposits represent the full range of wares available within north-western Europe and illustrate the chronological development of ceramic types, ceramic use, and the impact of regional and international trade. Notable English language works on European ceramics, drawing on evidence from pit groups, from production sites and from the extensive study of European wares in colonial and trading contexts, have been produced by Hurst et al. (1986) for the full range of later medieval and early post-medieval wares, and by David Gaimster (1997) for German stoneware.

In North America until the 1970s most ceramic studies focused on sites in the eastern seaboard – the region of English colonisation and initial spread of settlement. Ceramics from nineteenth- and twentieth-century sites, and even for earlier Spanish- and French-occupied sites away from the east coast, were rarely studied. The neglect of home-produced ceramics and ceramics produced elsewhere in the Old World was sustained. This emphasis on early sites was particularly visible in Noël Hume's 1969 classic *A Guide to Artifacts of Colonial America*, and in the papers in Quimby's (1973) conference volume, *Ceramics in America*. During the 1970s, however, the advent of US government-funded cultural resource management projects led to new studies – whether of rural farmsteads or inner-city dwellings. Archaeologists were poorly prepared to analyse the nineteenth- or twentieth-century assemblages that were produced, especially because ceramic analysis had previously relied heavily on collector literature, which usually dealt with earlier time periods.

In two influential articles, George L. Miller (1980, 1991) pioneered a systematic approach to the classification of nineteenth-century refined earthenwares based on decoration rather than ware. He argued that this system paralleled the terms used by potters, merchants, and consumers in that period, avoiding the problems caused by historical archaeologists adopting terms coined by collectors (e.g. 'china glaze' versus the collector term 'pearlware'). Miller used documentary materials to establish price index values for various ceramic forms, to inform the comparative analysis of archaeological assemblages to determine expenditure patterns.

In 1987, Majewski and O'Brien recommended categorising ceramics based on body type and degree of vitrification. Their scheme, equally applicable to all ceramics produced during the historical period, from colonoware to tin-glazed earthenware to porcelain, allows the researcher to better understand the interconnectedness of global technological advances and stylistic movements. While Miller focused primarily on ceramics dating to the nineteenth century, Majewski and O'Brien extended the discussion into the twentieth century (see also Majewski and Schiffer 2001), integrated information on ceramics produced outside of the United Kingdom, and discussed the importance of understanding style when categorising ceramics.

Most American ceramic studies in historical archaeology have focused on refined earthenwares. Some notable exceptions include studies on coarse redwares by Beaudry et al. (1983) and Turnbaugh (1985), or on stonewares by Greer (1981), on 'Rockingham' ware by Claney (2004), and on Asian-manufactured ceramics (particularly porcelains) by Costello and Maniery (1988). Significant work has also been carried out on 'colonowares' – the coarse, low-fired, unglazed earthenwares made in European forms found throughout the eastern United States and in the Caribbean, which appear to have been made and used by native Americans and enslaved African-Americans (Ferguson 1992).

Colonoware was first noted in the Chesapeake Bay area of the eastern United States in the 1930s, but was not formally recognised until 1962 when Noël Hume published a brief article on the topic (Noël Hume 1962). Believing that the pottery was made by native Americans during the colonial period, he coined the term 'Colono-Indian ware'. Within the next decade, researchers were leaning towards an African-American rather than a native-American origin for the ware (Deetz 1977: 236–245), which is now generally referred to as 'colonoware'. More recently, scholars (e.g. Ferguson 1992) have suggested that the ware was made by both groups. Based on the accumulated evidence for its distribution, it is clear that 'colonoware' was by no means a homogeneous ware type made by a single cultural group; rather, the manufacture of unglazed earthenwares that combined non-European technologies with European shapes was a diverse and 'creolised' material dimension of new colonial situations.

The study of historical ceramics has developed as an interdisciplinary field. The launch of an annual publication, *Ceramics in America*, in 2001 marked an important moment in the development of 'a new level of interdisciplinary dialogue in the study of historic ceramics' (Hunter 2001: xiv). Meanwhile, archaeological guides to historical ceramics have been published in Canada and Australia (Collard 1984; Brooks 2005). In Britain, later industrially made ceramics have been increasingly studied, synthetic accounts of the post-medieval delftware (e.g. Bloice 1971) and stoneware industries (C. Green 1999; Pryor and Blockley 1978) have been written, and the study of later eighteenth- and nineteenth-century ceramics has been pioneered in north Staffordshire (Barker 1991). The increase in developer-funded archaeology in Britain since the early 1990s has brought a marked increase in the number of excavations undertaken on later ceramic-manufacturing sites (e.g. Francis 2001; Haggarty and McIntyre 1996; STAS 2003), and the first of many important publications resulting from these are beginning to appear (e.g. Gregory 2004; Killock et al. 2003). Ceramic studies in Britain are increasingly driven by archaeology, in contrast with the previous influences of ceramic enthusiasts or collectors.

EUROPEAN CERAMIC PRODUCTION AND TECHNOLOGY

These developments have made possible much clearer accounts of the development of European ceramic production from the sixteenth century. These new accounts are underpinned by archaeological studies of production sites, which range from the recovery of factory products on manufacturing sites or in deposits of ceramic 'wasters', to the excavation of kilns, workshops and the range of material associated with production. In this section, we consider the historical processes through which masses of new ceramic products were distributed across the world.

Between the sixteenth and the eighteenth centuries, Europe witnessed the gradual but widespread and radical appearance of new ceramic types and vessel forms. This 'ceramic revolution' (Gaimster 1999a) witnessed an increase in the scale of the manufacture and consumption of ceramics, while the appearance of ceramics at the table 'represent[ed] the transformation of the medium from an exclusively utilitarian to a social commodity' (Gaimster n.d.). The main new ceramic ware types to emerge during this period were salt-glazed stonewares, tin-glazed earthenwares, and new types of fine earthenwares with an all-over lead glaze.

The first of these ceramic types is primarily associated with the Rhineland (Gaimster 1997). The production of vitrified stonewares fired to temperatures of 1200°C was well established there before the sixteenth century at, for example, Siegburg, Langerwehe and Raeren. From the sixteenth century, production developed on an industrial scale in and around the centres of

Cologne, Raeren and Frechen and in the south-west Westerwald to meet the demands of an expanding market. Wheel-thrown vessels, frequently decorated with applied reliefs, were fired in kilns fuelled by wood. From the early sixteenth century stoneware production benefited from the widespread adoption of salt glazing. A distinctive type of horizontal stoneware kiln has been revealed by excavations in Frechen, with antecedents in Siegburg and Langerwehe (Gaimster 1997: 42–45), while a kiln of very similar form was excavated at Woolwich in London (Pryor and Blockley 1978), where it had almost certainly been built and operated by German potters in the mid-seventeenth century.

From 1672, John Dwight secured a monopoly to produce stonewares in London; his wares closely copied Rhenish types, but German influence did not extend to the type of kiln used. Excavations at Dwight's Fulham factory have shown that he adopted the rectangular kilns then favoured by London tin-glaze potters for firing his stonewares (C. Green 1999: 21–28); an outlier of this 'London-type' of stoneware kiln has been located at Yorktown, Virginia, where William Rogers produced English-style stonewares during the 1720s–1740s (Barka 2004).

Tin-glazed wares were an equally widespread phenomenon in medieval and post-medieval Europe. Introduced into Europe from the Near East, the production of elaborate lustre-decorated tin-glazed wares was established in Moorish Spain by the thirteenth century. During the fifteenth century, lustreware production flourished in Valencia, and the industry's products were still being traded within western and north-western Europe during the sixteenth century. Following the discovery of the Americas, however, it was Seville that developed as Spain's leading producer of earthenware, with a virtual monopoly on overseas trade. Its products are known from the New World, rather than from excavations in Seville, and the main tin-glazed types – such as the decorated Isabella Polychrome and Yayal Blue, and the undecorated Columbia Plain – are named after find spots across the Atlantic (Hurst et al. 1986). Deagan (1987) and Marken (1994) review tin-glazed types found in the Americas.

By the sixteenth century, white tin-glazed ware, *maiolica*, was being produced in northern Italy at centres such as Montelupo, Liguria and Faenza (Hurst et al. 1986: 12–30). The painted decoration of these fine earthenwares ensured them a market throughout Europe, while wares from Montelupo are found in the Americas (Hurst et al. 1986: 12, 21). Maiolica kilns have been excavated at Cafaggiolo, and waster dumps are widespread at Montelupo and elsewhere in the region (Blake 1987: 15).

The expansion of tin-glazed earthenwares into north-west Europe during the sixteenth century has been charted in papers published in an impressive British Museum volume (Gaimster 1999b), which draws upon scientific analysis to distinguish between the products of different centres. By the early sixteenth century, Italian-style tin-glazed wares were being produced in Antwerp (Veeckman 1999), and during this century production was established in France, the Netherlands and in England.

By the seventeenth century, the impact of Dutch tin-glazed wares, with blue-painted decoration influenced by imports of Chinese porcelain, was felt throughout Europe and the colonial world (Figures 12.1a and 12.1b). Identical wares were produced in London, at pothouses established in Southwark and Lambeth; the industry expanded throughout the seventeenth and into the eighteenth century, with abundant archaeological evidence in the form of kilns and waster deposits (e.g. Bloice 1971; Tyler 1999). Tin-glaze production spread to other British ports – Brislington, Liverpool and Glasgow (Crossley 1990: 265), but ultimately competition from superior Staffordshire wares brought about the tin-glaze industry's demise.

During the sixteenth century, earthenware manufacturers in western Europe developed products to accommodate contemporary fashions in food preparation and, for the first time, dining and drinking. Distinctive fine lead-glazed drinking vessels became common, with the products of the different manufacturing centres being identified either by their clay bodies or by variations in style or form. Earthenwares were decorated with coloured slips throughout western Europe during the sixteenth century, but it was during the seventeenth and early eighteenth centuries that 'slipware' became ubiquitous.

The slipwares which had the greatest impact upon ceramic consumption, and which are therefore most useful to archaeologists, are those manufactured in the Netherlands, Germany, and England. Slipwares with *sgraffito* decoration – that is with a design being scratched through a slip-coat to reveal the body beneath – had been made in the Low Countries until the mid-sixteenth century, but it was the slip-trailed North Holland wares of the later sixteenth and seventeenth centuries which had dominated European and overseas markets (Hurst et al. 1986: 154–175). German slipwares which combined trailed and *sgraffito* decoration were also widely marketed throughout Europe at this time, reaching North America by the mid-seventeenth century (Hurst et al. 1986: 242–250). These wares were produced at centres along the Werra River, such as Wanfried, Witzenhausen and Hannoversch-Munden, at all of which waster deposits have been found.

Figure 12.1 Post-medieval ceramics I. Top left (12.1a), tin-glazed earthenware jar with polychrome painted decoration, Dutch, early to mid-seventeenth century. Wares such as this are found across western Europe and those areas of European economic and colonial interest. In England, such wares prompted the development of the English tin-glazed industry, whose products initially were indistinguishable from those of the Netherlands.

Top right (12.1b), porcelain saucer with blue-painted decoration, from a domestic rubbish pit in St Mary's Grove, Stafford, Chinese, 1760–1770. This is typical of the millions of pieces of tea- and tableware exported from China during the mid-eighteenth century, before English creamwares and pearlwares took over the market. (12.1a and 12.1b, Courtesy of the Potteries Museum and Art Gallery, Stoke-on-Trent).

Bottom left (12.1c), US importer's mark (Chauncey Filley) with 18 December 1856 registry mark for 'Berlin Swirl' pattern by Mayer & Elliot, Longport, and impressed workmen's marks.

Bottom right (12.1d) 'London'-shape bone-china cup and saucer with blue-printed chinoiserie temple-and-bridge pattern, probably Staffordshire, 1810s–1820s. Similar bone-china teawares with oriental temple patterns inspired by the 'willow pattern' were made by many British potteries; bone china rapidly became the most successful of British-made porcellaneous bodies. Figure composed by C. Elsner Hayward.

During the seventeenth century, slipware became one of the defining post-medieval ceramic types in England. The *sgraffito*-decorated slipwares of north Devon which had separate biscuit and glaze firings (Grant 1983: 49), not hitherto a feature of English earthenware production, suggest European influence. The main manufacturing centres were the seaports of Bideford and Barnstaple which developed a substantial coastal and overseas trade, supplying Ireland and the Caribbean and North American colonies (Grant 1983: 85–130; Outlaw 2002; Watkins 1960). Coarse gravel-tempered wares, from the same pottery-making workshops, also formed part of this trade. *Sgraffito*-decorated slipwares were also made at Donyatt in Somerset (Coleman-Smith and Pearson 1988), an industry serving a large regional market. However, small quantities of Donyatt wares have also been recognised in seventeenth-century contexts in Virginia (Kiser 2001) and Newfoundland, and in eighteenth-century contexts in mainland Canada (Allan and Pope 1990: 51).

Elsewhere in England it was North Holland slipwares which influenced manufacture. During the early seventeenth century 'Metropolitan' slipwares, produced predominantly in Harlow in Essex (Barker 1993: 11; Crossley 1990: 251), dominated the market for decorated wares in London and southeast England. Metropolitan slipwares with trailed slip motifs of the kind used on the North Holland wares were a catalyst for slipware manufacture throughout much of England. This influence can be seen in major developing industries at, for example, Wrenthorpe in West Yorkshire (Brears 1967; Moorhouse and Roberts 1992) and in north Staffordshire (Barker 1993).

During the second half of the seventeenth century, north Staffordshire became England's main slipware-producing centre. The excavations of production groups and kilns have provided evidence for the range of wares produced and for manufacturing processes (e.g. Celoria and Kelly 1973). Staffordshire's output was predominantly of decorated wares and these, combined with the migration of potters, had a marked influence on slipware production elsewhere in the country. By the early eighteenth century, Staffordshire-type slipwares were being made in places such as Bristol, Clifton in Cumbria, and Jackfield in Shropshire (Barker 1993: 19–20, 2001: 77).

Throughout Europe the production of coarse utilitarian earthenwares continued alongside that of decorated wares. While these were often for local consumption, the products of some industries were more widely marketed. Dutch redwares, English and Welsh black-glazed redwares, and olive jars from Seville, for example, had a major impact upon European and colonial markets, but the products of smaller industries may also occur in overseas contexts, given the right circumstances. For example, coarse earthenwares from workshops in and around the port of Totnes, in south Devon, occur in seventeenth-century contexts in Newfoundland, which suggests the activity of Devon fishermen (Allan and Pope 1990).

As Rhenish stonewares had dominated the European and overseas trade in ceramics in the sixteenth and seventeenth centuries, so Staffordshire wares came to define ceramic trade and consumption from the mid-eighteenth century. From the mid-seventeenth century, the north Staffordshire industry was expanding and producing good quality earthenwares and salt-glazed stonewares which are found in many parts of Britain. There is evidence for a limited overseas trade from the 1610s, but by the 1690s Staffordshire ceramics are common finds on Caribbean and North American sites.

The greater accessibility of tea and the growing popularity of tea drinking in the early eighteenth century stimulated a demand for home-produced teawares as affordable alternatives to imported Chinese porcelains which had hitherto been the only teawares available. Around 1720, Staffordshire potters responded to this market opportunity with fine white salt-glazed stonewares and red earthenwares. By the 1740s, tablewares of white salt-glazed stoneware competed in price and quality with pewter and fragile tin-glazed earthenware, while at the higher end of the market creamwares challenged the role of porcelain at the tables of the well to do from the 1760s. The Staffordshire ceramics industry was transformed during the 1720s–1740s (Barker 1999), with changes in scale, organisation and manufacturing methods which ultimately set the tone for pottery production elsewhere in Britain and beyond (Barker 2004).

New types of ware required more efficient preparation of clays and new processes, such as lathe-turning, moulding, and separate biscuit and glost firings for earthenwares. A growing market demand for white-bodied wares led to the development, during the 1740s, of 'creamware'. White wares required white-firing clays which were imported from Devon and Dorset, while the flint used in clay bodies and lead glazes was brought in from the south and east coasts of England. A national supply network operated by dealers and carriers brought these raw materials into the area by sea, river and road, while also facilitating the movement out and export via the seaports of the industry's finished products.

Several eighteenth-century production sites have been excavated in north Staffordshire, but the excavation of the factory waster dump of the potter William Greatbatch offers the clearest archaeological evidence for developments within the pottery industry in the later eighteenth century (Barker 1991). Greatbatch's manufacturing career spanned the years

1762 to 1782, during which time his factory's wasters were dumped in an adjacent clay pit along with tools, moulds, kiln furniture and saggars. Documentary evidence provides a limited perspective on this factory, but the excavated ceramics demonstrate without ambiguity the development of this factory's products and manufacturing processes during a critical twenty-year period in the industry. Wares were recovered in proportions that reflect both a rapidly changing market and the difficulties of manufacture.

Greatbatch was primarily a manufacturer of creamware, although he produced most of the wares typical of this period. His creamwares underwent stylistic changes during the life of the factory. Elaborately moulded and coloured rococo-style wares made in the form of cauliflowers and pineapples in the 1760s were replaced, in the 1770s, by more restrained vessel forms, often with neo-Classical details. Coloured glazes and under-glaze colours gave way to over-glaze painted decoration which was better suited to the lighter glazes of the later wares. Creamware wasters indicate the establishment of a decorating shop at the factory by the 1770s, but decorated creamwares were always a minority product. The pearlwares, by contrast, are all decorated; numerous finds of practice pieces show decorators' attempts to copy, in under-glaze blue, the Chinese-style landscape patterns which were typical of this new type of ware. The quantities of pearlware, or 'China glaze', present here support the argument for a mid-1770s introduction of this new ware (G. Miller 1987). Pearlware's visual appearance, with a blue-tinted glaze over a white body, and its initial reliance upon Chinese-style decoration, suggest the deliberate copying of Chinese porcelain, which was still widespread, but expensive.

The success of Staffordshire ceramics during the later eighteenth century led to the establishment of factories making Staffordshire-type wares in many parts of Britain, in Europe (Kybalová 1989), and in North America (South 1993). Standardised production developed in part because of the movement of potters, but more significantly because an expanding Staffordshire-based infrastructure supplied everything from moulds to colours and, by the early nineteenth century, engraved copper plates used in transfer printing (Barker 2001: 77–78); by the mid-nineteenth century machinery, brushes, tissue paper and even kiln furniture were being supplied to factories elsewhere in Britain and beyond.

While creamware was produced into the nineteenth century, it was pearlware which was to become the earthenware body of the early nineteenth century, and almost without exception it was decorated in some form. Under-glaze painted decoration in blue or polychrome was common on teawares, while moulded and painted 'shell edge' defined the less expensive tablewares. By c. 1800, more expensive tea- and tablewares carried transfer-printed decoration. Introduced to earthenware manufacture in the 1780s, transfer-printing allowed the mass production of identically decorated wares with images lifted from an engraved copper plate, increasing standardisation of production even further. Printed decoration, at first mainly in blue, but in a range of colours from the late 1820s (G. Miller 1991: 9), underwent stylistic changes throughout the nineteenth and twentieth centuries which can be identified and dated with some accuracy from the collector literature (e.g. Coysh and Henrywood 1982, 1989); this accuracy is likely to be the greater when a maker's mark is used. Makers' marks can include a range of useful information (Henrywood 2002: 36–46; Majewski 2002), not least of which is the identity of the manufacturer and occasionally the importer (Figure 12.1c); in the case of printed marks, patterns are often named; a registration mark or number indicates the date of a pattern's or shape's registration and is a useful *terminus post quem* for vessels so marked.

Printed decoration dominated nineteenth-century pottery production, being used on all earthenware bodies introduced from the 1820s. It was the most expensive type of decoration on earthenware on account of the processes involved in its manufacture (G. Miller 1980: 28; 1991).

While archaeologists define white-bodied earthenwares as creamware, pearlware or, from c. 1830, 'whiteware', nineteenth-century manufacturers defined their products by their decoration – printed, painted, dipped and edged. A growing preference for decoration during the nineteenth century significantly changed the composition of excavated ceramic assemblages and has rendered them more open to interpretative analysis using the relative cost of wares to determine spend-profiles (G. Miller 1980; 1991). However, not all wares were decorated, and from the 1850s the popularity of transfer-printed wares declined in the Americas. At this time the North American market came to favour moulded 'ironstone china' or 'white granite', a type which owes little to the patent ironstone wares of the earlier nineteenth century, and which is simply a heavy-duty earthenware. White granite wares were durable and weathered shipment to the country's frontier regions; they were also stylish, emulating the more expensive white French porcelains that were then in vogue. White granite is widespread in archaeological deposits in North America and, more recently, its production and consumption in the United Kingdom have been highlighted (Barker 2001: 85–86). By later in the nineteenth century, American potteries in the Ohio Valley and the north-east were producing large quantities of 'white granite' (Majewski and O'Brien 1987) which laid the foundation for the flourishing hotel ware industry that took off in the early twentieth century, with manufacturers as far afield as California.

The production of many British factories also included ceramic building materials (Atterbury 2003; D. Hamilton 1978). In the late eighteenth century, painted and transfer-printed tin-glazed earthenware tiles were in high demand for use in fireplace surrounds. Later, Victorian tiles were generally white-bodied earthenwares with transfer-printed or slip-glazed decoration and were used in fireplaces, as furniture insets, and to cover wall surfaces. Other Victorian era products included encaustic tiles, architectural terracotta and brickwork. Architectural ceramics opened up the design possibilities and technology available to architects in Great Britain and its sphere of influence. Buildings were constructed out of refined and virtually impenetrable terracotta, using custom- and ready-made components, frequently with intricate moulded designs. From the 1870s, terracotta became the most important building material for public and commercial buildings in urban Great Britain and in many parts of the world. A variety of architectural components – chimney pots, door and window frames, trusses, finials and other details, drain pipes, roofing tiles, and garden ornaments – were mass produced in terracotta, marketed in catalogues, and used to decorate houses of all market levels (Atterbury 2003).

Porcelains made in Europe from the early eighteenth century have not yet been mentioned. The amount of collector literature devoted to British and European porcelains exaggerates their contemporary significance, for these were expensive wares which would have been beyond the reach of all but the wealthy. Of the English porcelains, those which are likely to have a wider distribution are blue-printed wares from factories such as Worcester and Caughley. Excavations on a number of eighteenth-century porcelain factories, such as Longton Hall in Staffordshire (Cherry and Tait 1980; Tait and Cherry 1978) and Limehouse, London (Tyler and Stephenson 2000), have shed light upon the operations of individual factories and the processes employed there, but have added little to an understanding of the wider contemporary role of porcelain. A large corpus of work by J. V. Owen and colleagues (e.g. Owen and Sandon 2003) focuses on the compositional characteristics of different porcelains in an attempt to correctly attribute them and understand their technological development.

In one area of porcelain production, Britain was to have a significant impact upon the international market. Bone china, introduced in the 1790s, was rapidly adopted by Staffordshire factories and was soon established as *the* British porcelain. A 'soft paste' porcelain, with a body made from a mixture of China clay, China stone and calcined animal bone, it was easily worked,

Figure 12.2 Post-medieval ceramics II. Top left (12.2a), small, white bodied earthenware plate with 'cabbage rose' lithos and relief-moulded 'trellis' rim decoration, US manufacturer Homer Laughlin, c. 1920s.

Top right (12.2b), small Nippon porcelain plate with painted floral decoration, c. 1910s, typical of large quantities of Japanese porcelains exported to the West during the first quarter of the twentieth century.

Middle (12.2c), small Bavarian porcelain plate with Art Nouveau decoration painted by an amateur, whose signature appears on the base, c. 1910s. (12.2a–12.2c, photos L. Kain, private collection.)

Bottom left (12.2d), stoneware *bartmann* bottle from moat fill at West Bromwich Manor House, West Midlands; Rhenish, probably Frechen, mid-seventeenth century. This type of vessel was one of the most widely traded seventeenth-century European ceramic wares and is commonly found in British, Caribbean, and North American archaeological assemblages of the period. (Photo D. Barker, courtesy of the Wednesbury Museum and Art Gallery.)

Bottom right (12.2e), white-bodied earthenware plate sherds with brown printed decoration in Aesthetic style, probably English, c. 1870s–1880s. (Photo L. Kain, private collection.) Figure composed by C. Elsner Hayward.

extremely white and very translucent. As such it could be adapted to both the higher and lower ends of the market, and is commonly found as teaware (Figure 12.1d) in nineteenth- and twentieth-century contexts with a limited range of simple decoration, or with no decoration whatsoever. Bone china is known archaeologically from deposits dating to the early nineteenth century onwards in North America though it is frequently misidentified (Majewski and O'Brien 1987).

British and European fondness for transfer-printed decoration did not decline during the later nineteenth century. Printed patterns were frequently embellished with additional painted decoration to create multi-coloured designs. Wares decorated in this manner with Aesthetic and later Aesthetic-derived motifs were popular from the 1870s to c. 1900 when the over-glaze lithographic transfer, or 'decal', effectively replaced under-glaze transfer printing as the major method of decorating ceramics (Majewski and Schiffer 2001) (Figure 12.2a).

The litho transfer process allows for the decoration of ceramics with intricate polychrome designs that mirror fine hand-painting, at prices within the means of the average consumer. Specialist manufacturers produced the lithographic designs which were sold in sheets. At first these were backed with paper and covered with varnish. The designs were soaked in water to soften and remove the backing paper; a sticky size was painted on the ware and the designs applied and rubbed down. The varnish was burned away during firing in an enamel kiln, leaving the completed design. This 'stick-down' lithography was replaced from the 1950s by 'slide' or 'water slide lithography, in which prints were printed onto plastic film and soaked in water to loosen the paper backing. The plastic film carrying the design is slid onto the pot and rubbed down, then burned away through firing.

Lithographic decoration remained the most common decorative technique used on dinnerware into the 1950s, even though coloured slip-glazed wares such as 'Fiesta' produced by the American pottery company Homer Laughlin (and related spin-offs made by other companies) were popular between the late 1920s and the early 1940s.

Traditional European ceramics lost ground to British industrially made wares during the eighteenth and nineteenth centuries, but manufacturers continued to supply local and regional markets with a range of familiar utilitarian products and ornamental wares for which there was no outside competition. British production had increased in scale during the nineteenth century; the industry's success was based upon decorated white-bodied wares of a reasonable quality, which were affordable by the majority of consumers. Their success resulted in emulation at a number of European factories, such as that of Petrus Regout of Maastricht in the Netherlands which produced British-type whitewares for European and overseas markets for much of the nineteenth and twentieth centuries (Bartels 1999: 883–928).

Britain retained its firm grip on the American ceramic market until the last decades of the nineteenth century, when Japanese, German, French, and other European hard-paste porcelains were vying for a share (Majewski and O'Brien 1987: 129). Restrictive tariffs were partly to blame, but consumers were influenced by a combination of factors when making their choices. These porcelains, which are widely found in archaeological deposits from the late 1800s onwards, offered porcelain elegance along with enamelling and gilding (later frequently with lithos), all at a lower cost (Figure 12.2b). Also popular were porcelain 'blanks' which were sold to amateur china painters who decorated them in various styles (Figure 12.2c; Majewski and Schiffer 2001: 39).

In Britain, manufacturing processes changed little between the mid-nineteenth century and the mid-twentieth century, although a degree of mechanisation was gradually introduced as legislation restricted the use of child labour from the 1860s. The manufacture of wares by slip casting became more widespread after 1900; there was a gradual move towards lead-free glazes; and gas and electric 'tunnel kilns' gradually replaced coal-fired ovens. Ceramic literature focuses upon the new stylish 'art-deco' wares which appeared during the 1930s, and upon the designers and artists responsible for them. In reality, however, British manufacturers remained very conservative in the wares that they produced, relying for the most part upon what had been popular with customers for fifty or a hundred years.

TRADE AND EXCHANGE

Archaeological ceramics are of special significance as evidence for trade at a range of geographical scales. They can usually be traced to a particular manufacturing source, and their post-production lives can be charted by combining documentary research with the study of excavated distribution patterns. Such work requires a broad understanding of the economic contexts in which such trade took place, knowledge of the wares produced by manufacturing centres, preferably supported by archaeological evidence from production sites, and the willingness to study ceramic assemblages from a range of domestic sites across a wide geographical area. Studies of ceramics recovered from shipwreck excavations have proved particularly useful in understanding the nature of international trade (Flatman and Staniforth this volume; Staniforth 2003).

The most successful post-medieval ceramics industries were those that supplied wider regional or international markets. The stoneware industry of the lower Rhineland in particular characterises the new contexts of trade in the early post-medieval world. Trade in Rhenish stonewares in north-western and northern Europe was well established during the medieval period, but expanded considerably during the sixteenth and seventeenth centuries. Gaimster's (1997) detailed study of the trade in stonewares in Europe and colonial contexts draws on documentary sources such as customs accounts and port books alongside archaeological evidence from both terrestrial and shipwreck sites (Gaimster 1997: 51). The remarkable scale of the production and trade of Rhenish stoneware vessels was due to a range of factors, including their durable and easily cleaned fine vitrified bodies, and their range of forms for drinking and serving liquids which made a range of uses possible, in wealthier and poorer households alike, and their low cost. These stonewares appear to have been traded as vessels in their own right, rather than as containers for other commodities (Gaimster 1997).

While stonewares from Langerwehe, Cologne and especially Raeren are found throughout Europe in fifteenth- and sixteenth-century contexts, from the mid-sixteenth century overseas markets were served on a vastly increased scale by the expanding Frechen industry (Figure 12.2d). This industry was almost completely geared for foreign trade, shipping the majority of its output down the Rhine to the coastal ports of the Netherlands, whence they were sent across the English Channel to London and other English ports (Gaimster 1997: 55). Documentary sources indicate the increased regularity and size of shipments during the early sixteenth century, and the regular involvement of continental ports such as Antwerp, Dordrecht and Rozendaal (page 79).

John Allan has studied the importation of Rhenish stoneware to Exeter, which increased considerably during the second half of the sixteenth century, although 75 per cent of this trade came through London (Allan 1984: 118). London was the centre for the stoneware trade to England during the reign of Elizabeth I, a position strengthened by the granting of a series of stoneware import monopolies (Gaimster 1997: 80). This pre-eminent position was maintained until the mid-seventeenth century, and Gaimster has calculated that around ten million stoneware vessels were shipped to London during the period 1600–1640 (1997: 82), many being redistributed to other English ports. Thereafter Exeter (Allan 1984: 123) and other English ports were more likely to trade directly with the continent than with London (Gaimster 1997: 82). For more than two centuries, Rhenish stonewares were the largest single category of imported ceramics traded to Britain, but the importation to London of stoneware bottles from Frechen virtually ceased once John Dwight commenced stoneware manufacture there in the 1670s (1997: 83).

Rhenish stonewares have been found at some early European colonial sites in mainland North America and the Caribbean (Gaimster 1997: 98–100). The strength of Dutch trade in the seventeenth-century Atlantic world appears to have influenced the volume of stonewares recovered through archaeology, but Rhenish stonewares were transhipped to the colonies from London and other English ports (Allan 1999). Just as Frechen brown stonewares dominated the ceramics trade during the later sixteenth and seventeenth centuries, so grey stonewares with moulded decoration and cobalt blue colouring from the Westerwald became the main German export ware from the late seventeenth century. Westerwald stonewares are well represented on sites on the British mainland and in the colonies; their reduced occurrence from the 1770s appears to have been a result of competition from the growing exports of the developing British refined-ceramics industry.

During the early colonial period, wares from colonial industrial metropoles dominated each country's territory. Spanish ceramics predominated in South America, Florida, Mexico, and the Spanish borderlands encompassing northern Sonora and what is now the US Southwest. French ceramics dominated in Nova Scotia and New France prior to their acquisition by the British in the late eighteenth century. British ceramics, such as tin-glazed wares and North Devon slipwares, were common in Virginia, New England and Newfoundland, while Dutch tin-glazed wares are known from the seventeenth century in what is now New York state. The appearance of other wares corresponds with later immigrants, often maintaining a dominant local position within newly settled areas which had a distinct cultural or ethnic identity. From the mid-eighteenth century, this picture changed, as ceramic assemblages came more to reflect the global complexities of trade (Lawrence 2003).

Growing trade with the east from the sixteenth century brought increasing quantities of Chinese porcelain to the west. Fine, lightweight and translucent, porcelain was a perfect medium for decoration and ideal for the consumption of tea, which was also brought to Europe along with cargoes of spices, silk, cotton, lacquer and exotic woods. From the beginning of the seventeenth century, the key players in this eastern trade were the Vereenigde Ostindische Companie (VOC), the Dutch East India Company, and the English East India Company (EIC) (cf. Flatman and Staniforth, this volume). Together they were responsible for the importation of millions of pieces of porcelain into Europe through Amsterdam and London, from which ports they were redistributed throughout Europe and the European colonies (see Figure 12.2). Initially expensive items, they were highly prized by the wealthy, but as the scale of importation increased they became more affordable and more widely available (e.g. Allan 1984: 105). Chinese porcelains had a major impact upon European material culture, and upon the products of the developing European ceramics industries that reproduced porcelain forms and decoration and attempted to produce the porcelain body. The massive trade in porcelain, and the popularity of porcelain tea- and tablewares were threatened and ultimately supplanted by the products of Staffordshire's developing ceramics industry.

Staffordshire wares have been found in seventeenth-century contexts in the Caribbean and North American colonies, but from the 1720s Staffordshire refined earthenwares and stonewares began to constitute an increasingly important item of trade. The attention given to Staffordshire ceramics in North America, both by archaeologists and by scholars from a decorative arts background, has highlighted the importance of this market but has at the same time exaggerated its early significance. Despite the large quantities of Staffordshire ceramics excavated on eighteenth-century North American sites, and their frequent mention in newspaper advertisements, Europe rather than North America was the main market for British wares until 1835 (Ewins 1997: 6).

Little synthesis of the archaeological evidence for the eighteenth- and nineteenth-century British ceramics trade with Europe has been undertaken, despite its clear significance. Between 1760 and 1780 Josiah Wedgwood, for example, was selling to Russia, Spain, Portugal, the Netherlands, France, Italy, Germany, Sweden and Turkey (J. Thomas 1971: 116), and he was not alone. Documentary and archaeological evidence for this trade is abundant, and substantial assemblages with British ceramics have been published (e.g. Bartels 1999: 883–936; Thijssen 1991: 29, 112–123). Besides the Staffordshire potteries, other significant participants in the trade with Europe were the potteries of Yorkshire, Newcastle-upon-Tyne, Stockton-on-Tees and Sunderland.

Excavated assemblages of unrefined wares of the seventeenth and early eighteenth centuries can be traced to their sources of manufacture by the characteristics of their ceramic bodies, form and decoration. For tin-glazed wares, a considerable literature on British and European production sites (e.g. Gaimster 1999b; Hurst et al. 1986) exists, and the manufacture of refined 'Staffordshire-type' wares of the mid-eighteenth century was limited to a clearly defined group of centres. In nineteenth-century contexts, the increase in marked wares allows excavated ceramics to be sourced with more certainty, emphasising the growing importance of Staffordshire, north-east English and Scottish manufacturing. More difficult is the archaeological study of those between production and consumption – 'middlemen', dealers, merchants, carriers and retailers. Ewins (1997), however, has charted the development of Staffordshire manufacturers' trade with North America, demonstrating how Staffordshire manufacturers gained access to the American market and the means by which they were able to respond rapidly to changing American tastes.

As the North American markets for British ceramics expanded during the nineteenth century, other new markets developed. A snapshot of destinations for ceramics exported from Liverpool in April and May 1827 (Customs Office 1827) highlights New York, Boston, and New Orleans as the main recipients of British ceramics, while in Canada, St. John's, Halifax, Restigouche, Miramichi, Montreal, New Brunswick, Prince Edward Island and Québec were regular destinations. South American receiving ports included Bahia, La Guaira, Pernambuco, Rio de Janeiro, Valparaiso and Lima, as well as Veracruz in Mexico, and Bermuda. Barbados, Antigua, Havana, Kingston, St Thomas, St Vincent and Trinidad are amongst the islands of the western Atlantic listed. European ports receiving ceramics including St Petersburg, Lisbon, Gibraltar, Barcelona, Livorno, Naples, Messina, Palermo and Malta, and Tunis are also mentioned. The growing importance of the eastward trade is evident by the inclusion of 'Africa', Bombay, Calcutta, Demerara and Singapore. The list is by no means exhaustive. Late nineteenth-century manufacturers' advertisements represent a significant source here: in 1861, for example, the Staffordshire firm William and James Butterfield advertised 'All kinds of printed and fancy printed common bodies suitable for the East and West Indies, Australian, Russian, North and South American Markets' (Harrison, Harrod and Co. 1861).

Historical archaeology contributes much to our understanding of the role of British ceramics in the development of global trade. Ceramics excavated from domestic sites or from the wrecks of trading ships provide a unique record of trade and consumption, while work undertaken on production sites can recover wares destined for export. Foreign-language inscriptions, overseas retailers' details and importers' marks are commonly found on a range of nineteenth-century wares, while customers such as hotels and steamship companies can be identified from printed emblems. Archaeological work underlines, for instance, the popularity of flow-blue and flow-mulberry printed wares, together with undecorated 'white granite' among North American consumers in the 1840s–1860s, and their use within Britain is confirmed by finds in domestic assemblages.

CONSUMPTION AND CONSUMERISM

While we have described the potential of archaeological studies of ceramic production, trade and exchange, historical archaeologists most commonly engage with ceramics in contexts related to their consumption. A. Martin (1993: 142–143) has usefully distinguished the study of consumption from that of *consumerism*, which extends beyond simple acquisition to denote the complex cultural relationships between humans and consumer goods. The historical archaeology of ceramics has much to contribute to interdisciplinary 'consumerist studies' (Majewski and Schiffer 2001). Such work can explore how material goods mark or confer social identity or status, the role of fashion and demand in spurring changes in manufacture, and the ways in which people construct their own meanings for objects produced by themselves or others.

As noted above, George Miller (1980) pioneered the use of documentary materials such as potters' price-fixing lists, bills of lading and account books to establish price-index values for plates, cups and bowls with various types of decoration for the period 1787–1880. The prices of undecorated cream-coloured (CC) vessels were used as the scale against which to measure changes in the value of the other decorative types. Miller then used the values as the basis for comparing expenditure patterns from various archaeological assemblages after a minimum vessel count had been completed and the forms were grouped by decoration. In his later paper (G. Miller 1991), Miller corrected some misconceptions about the stability of CC vessel prices throughout the nineteenth century and provided more in-depth information on English ceramics exported from the 1780s to the 1880s.

George Miller's work inspired many studies of ceramics using the CC index, especially in North American historical archaeology. These studies often went beyond simply establishing expenditure patterns to make statements about socioeconomic status and consumer preference (e.g. Spencer-Wood 1987). Researchers generally found no simple correlation between the value of ceramic assemblages and the social and economic situation of the individuals or households that used the assemblages. Klein (1991: 83) notes that multiple factors influence the value of a given ceramic assemblage, including household organisation, size and life cycle; income strategies and external economic conditions. He advises that ceramics should not be used as the sole measure of socioeconomic position, and that other goods, such as foods and textiles, would be more accurate indicators. Klein (1991: 88) and others (e.g. Beaudry 1987) recommend that the household is perhaps the most appropriate scale for most historical–archaeological research and stress that the artefacts recovered from such excavations should be studied within the social and economic contexts of the people who lived in particular households (King this volume).

Ceramic style is also an important focus of consumerist studies. In ceramics, as in many other areas of material culture, 'traditional' and 'popular' (or 'high') styles coexist (Majewski and Schiffer 2001: 34). In 1930s contexts, for instance, abstract Art Deco table- and teaware forms are often recovered alongside traditional shapes decorated with conventional floral patterns. Historical archaeology is well placed to examine how ceramic styles are juxtaposed in consumption, or repeated or recycled through time in production (Samford 1997).

Combining documentary research and archaeological data from particular middle-class households, Majewski and Schiffer (2001) explore the archaeological evidence for the use of ceramics decorated in the Aesthetic style by residents of late-nineteenth-century downtown San Bernardino, California. The Aesthetic movement, a British art movement which influenced the emergence of Art Nouveau, stressed Japanese influences, in the production of furniture, metalwork, ceramics, glass, textiles, wallpapers and books. By the 1870s, Japanese-like motifs – cherry blossoms, bamboo, birds, fan shapes, reserves with scenes within a scene, and stylised clouds (Figure 12.2e) – were applied asymmetrically on goods of all kinds (Majewski and Schiffer 2001: 36–37). Transfer printing and less frequently enamelling were used to express Aesthetic motifs on ceramic tableware, teaware, toilet sets, tiles, and decorative ware. By the 1890s, the Japanese style had faded in popularity.

Majewski and Schiffer suggest that 'data from the archaeological record, while challenging to collect, may provide some of the best information on the actual use of these materials by members of different social classes' (2001: 43). Since such study requires the combination of documentary with material sources of evidence in order to uncover the identity, social class, family composition and ethnicity of a site's occupants, the most successful work in this field focuses upon household contexts.

For example, during excavations in downtown San Bernardino (Doolittle and Majewski 1997), one of the fifty features excavated was a privy. Documentary sources indicated that this feature lay on the site of the household of the middle-class Whaley family, who had lived in that location from around 1860. Almost 800 ceramic sherds representing 150 vessels were recovered from this feature, and most dated to the 1870s–1880s. Two examples of English-made earthenware vessels decorated in different Aesthetic-style patterns were represented – a toothbrush holder from a toilet set and an earthenware saucer. Such construction of profiles of ceramic use by particular households, recording the percentage of popular versus traditional wares, or the ranges of forms used, hold the potential for broader comparative studies of the impact of the Aesthetic movement on the consumption of material culture. A household-based approach allows us, for instance, to consider the role of women as the primary purchasers of goods in late nineteenth-century America, a role they increasingly assumed as personal incomes rose and urban retail stores and mail-order catalogues offered increased purchasing options after the American Civil War. The approach also makes the study of the use of material culture by children possible, since numerous complete or partial children's tea sets decorated with Aesthetic motifs were produced (Formanek-Brunell 1993).

The interpretation of ceramics in consumption contexts by historical archaeologists has been diverse. Historical archaeologists have emphasised the ideological properties of artefacts since being introduced to Binford's (1962: 219) concept of 'ideotechnic function' in Deetz's (1977) classic *In Small Things Forgotten*. More commonly in the interpretation of ceramics, however, have been studies of identity, especially ethnicity, through consumer choice or distinctive foodways – for example Griggs' (1999) study of Irish immigrants in New York City, Fitts' (2002) study of Italian immigrants in Jamaica, Queens County, New York, or by Adrian and Mary Praetzellis' (1998) examination of overseas Chinese communities in Sacramento, California.

Studying social status and occupation through ceramics, Dyson's (1982: 361) analysis of eight ceramic assemblages from sites in Middleton, Connecticut dating from 1780 to 1830 identified 'many basic similarities related to common behavior patterns', but aimed to explore changing tastes of the individual households in relation to their worldviews. Examining the changing consumption from painted, blue-on-white chinoiserie motifs to later transfer prints of the Blue-Willow tradition, Dyson suggested that

the classic order based on upper-class British values had given way to the twin movements of local patriotism and European Romanticism. The latter reflected considerable nostalgia for the British world, from which the colonists had so recently separated. (1982: 376).

Brooks (1999) has considered how the emergence of British identity in the eighteenth and nineteenth centuries influenced the designs of transfer-printed wares. Brooks argues that the negotiation of English, Welsh, Scottish and Irish ethnicities in relation to the emergence of Britishness was worked out through material culture, including ceramics – especially transfer-printed patterns that presented themes of 'rural prosperity', 'war' and 'nationality'. He suggests that cultural affiliation of a particular site's inhabitants might be assigned through comparative analysis between geographical areas, and corroborated by using other material culture evidence such as gravestone inscriptions.

In an innovative report on the results of the Cyprus Freeway Replacement Project in West Oakland, California, Mary and Adrian Praetzellis (2004) characterise the material culture from segments of the populations of known demographic and ethnic character who had lived in this urban area in the nineteenth and twentieth centuries: white Euroamericans, overseas Chinese, and African-Americans. The Pratezellises characterise the material culture from the assemblages using a system of categories derived from South's (1977a) function-based system. They contend that the material culture associated with particular households is an expression of the values of the families who occupied them.

Studies of historical-period ceramics used by native peoples in North America also show that various groups appropriated British-made wares and used them for their own purposes. Louise Jackson (1991) documents how the Eskimo in south-western Alaska incorporated British transfer-printed, painted, and sponge-decorated teawares into their late nineteenth-century mortuary rituals. Burley's (1989) work on the Metis of the northern plains of North America indicates that Metis women used British teawares to create social relationships with white traders. In a study of the material culture of the Inuit of Labrador and of Alaska, Cabak and Loring (2000) have demonstrated their participation in the global system, but by selectively adopting European goods – in this case ceramics, and especially sponge-decorated ceramics – and adapting them for use in Inuit foodways.

Another important theme in the studies of ceramic consumption has been the study of the impact of European industrially made goods upon non-European societies, or those geographically remote from industrial activity. For example, archaeological work in the Western Isles of Scotland has examined nineteenth-century crofting communities which were physically remote and culturally distinct from mainland Britain, and which were poor in the extreme (Barker 2005: 112, 118; Symonds 2000). Excavations of nineteenth-century 'blackhouses' on Barra, South Uist and the Shiant Islands have revealed material culture which has much in common with that of other marginal or remote groups. These islanders had no real tradition of ceramic use in the preparation and consumption of food or drink, and yet excavated assemblages show that from c. 1800 they were participating fully in trade with mainland Britain, acquiring and using industrially made white-bodied ceramics to an extent hitherto unknown. The new ceramic wares were adapted to island foodways, which comprised a limited diet of barley meal or oat gruel prepared in a single iron cooking pot, supplemented with potatoes and occasionally fish or cockles (Barker 2005: 112–113). The high proportion of bowls in the blackhouse assemblages is consistent with a diet of this kind, and the choice of bowls reflects their suitability for established habits of food consumption (Symonds 2000: 207). Similarly, in the southern United States, excavations at slave cabin sites consistently produce higher percentages of ceramic bowls than are recovered from assemblages associated with overseers, while they are much less well-represented in groups from the houses of the plantation owners (Otto 1977). Otto (1984: 167) suggests that bowls are a vessel form associated both with poverty and with a diet based upon slow-simmer foods cooked in a single pot.

Bowls excavated in Hebridean blackhouses are mostly of the cheapest decorated types (G. Miller 1991: 6) – slip-decorated and, from the 1830s, sponged. Poverty, a limited diet and an absence of furniture for dining and display might suggest that the Western Isles represented a limited market for industrially made ceramics, and yet the archaeological evidence indicates a more general acceptance of these, and a willingness to participate in mainland British domestic customs and practices. Plates, present in all of the blackhouse assemblages, indicate that a wider range of ceramics was used in the consumption of food, although the documented absence of tables, forks and knives suggests that meals were taken in a more traditional manner. Analysis of use-wear marks on plates holds the potential to determine what, if any, cutlery was used. Contemporary documentary sources indicate the late introduction of tea to the islands, and yet teawares are present at all of the sites; at Balnabodach on Barra, for example, teawares comprise between 20 and 22 per cent of the vessels present in three pre-1850 assemblages (Barker 2005: 113–114).

Whatever the economic circumstances of the crofters, consumer choices were being made in which cost was not the only determining factor. The blackhouse ceramics consistently indicate a preference for decorated wares, including vessels with printed decoration (e.g. Barker 2005: 115), which was the most expensive type of decoration available on earthenware at the time (G. Miller et al. 1994: 234). However, while the presence of more expensive decorated wares argues for a closer examination of the means and motives of the consumer, the high incidence of ceramics with evidence of repair, with holes drilled through the vessels' bodies so that sherds could be joined by metal 'staples', might suggest an owner's inability to afford a replacement. Repaired ceramics are commonly found in assemblages from remote locations, such as the seasonal fishing stations of Red Bay, Labrador (C. Burke 2000), or in the Inuit camps of Labrador (Cabak and Loring 2000: 24), and their presence on Hebridean sites suggests that the irregularity of supply of goods to these islands might be the main cause for repairs to broken vessels. Such studies aim to integrate knowledge of the history of ceramic studies (technology, trade, and consumerism) with interpretive and comparative analysis.

FUTURE DIRECTIONS

The admittedly Eurocentric perspective upon ceramic studies in historical archaeology adopted here has aimed to provide a broad introduction to the range of specialist work carried out by practitioners in the field. Many of the methods used are applicable to the study of other ceramic traditions from the historical period. Considering the wares that influenced, or were influenced by, European ceramics allows for a better understanding of the nexus of colonial connections forged from the fifteenth century onwards, but this approach would also apply to other geographic areas and time periods. Fundamental to these studies is an empirical knowledge of the history of ceramic production and technology, grounded in an integration of archaeological and documentary evidence. Although research has been carried out on these topics in Europe and the Americas, the archaeology of the technology and development of Asian ceramics and their use and influence around the globe remains little explored. Nineteenth- and twentieth-century wares from the continent also demand further study. The research highlighted here has primarily focused on tablewares, to the exclusion of the wide range of products that were produced industrially and on smaller scales for use in contexts other than food consumption (e.g. food preparation and storage, dairying, institutional uses). Scholars shy away from the study of these wares because they are often difficult to identify and categorise, which may be linked to their production and use in less industrial settings.

Given the findings of researchers working in the area of trade and exchange, one cannot but be impressed by the global scope and influence of the European ceramic tradition. The consumption of ceramics, however, is intricately bound up with themes such as consumer choice, identity, aesthetics and meaning. To reach their full potential, studies in these areas must be contextualised within larger societal and historical frameworks.

Several recent provocative studies forge new territory in this direction. Alasdair Brooks (1997, 1999) moves beyond cost-based analysis of transfer-printed wares and links specific patterns with themes in the history of Great Britain and the creation of a British identity. Transfer-printed wares with literary themes are the focus of Gavin Lucas' study of 'reading pottery' (2003), in which he explores the social and individual choices underlying the purchase and use of tablewares depicting scenes from popular early nineteenth-century novels, such as those written by Sir Walter Scott. His argument that manufacture and consumption of 'literary ceramics' is connected to the emerging acceptance of fiction as appropriate reading material in early nineteenth-century Britain is grounded in the context he builds for literature and society 1780–1850. The work of Lucas and Brooks illustrates that interpretive approaches in historical archaeology are leading scholars in new directions, yet their work builds upon the understandings that have been achieved through more traditional approaches to the study of ceramics. This juxtaposition of approaches bodes well for future innovations in ceramic studies in historical archaeology.

PART IV

Historical archaeology and landscapes

CHAPTER 13

Landscapes and memories

Cornelius Holtorf and Howard Williams

INTRODUCTION

All landscapes are 'historical', provided that they are now – or were once – altered, inhabited, visited, or interpreted by people. Indeed, the problematic and theoretically flawed use of the terms 'historical landscapes' and 'historical archaeology' presume that only societies with written sources have 'history' embedded in, and mediated through, their landscapes. In fact, it can be argued that very few parts of the world do not fulfil the criterion of being 'historical landscapes'; landscapes in which the past accumulates or is created through human action. Since landscapes can embody memories, and therefore be 'historical' in many different ways, this historical dimension of practically all landscapes can be actualised through material remains or knowledgeable understanding, evoking the past in the mind of the beholder (Schama 1995) and through social practice and inhabitation (Ingold 2000a). Moreover, we cannot even restrict historical landscapes to the study of human action and transformation since the 'natural' landscape is often itself 'read' by people as the result of the actions of past generations, ancestors, ancient peoples or supernatural forces (Bradley 2000). In as much as they can thus evoke, or indeed hide, the past, landscapes are linked to socially or culturally mediated remembrance and memory. By memory, we refer to the increasingly common conceptualisation of 'social memory' as collective representations of the past and associated social practices rather than personal recollection (see Connerton 1989; Samuel 1994). By landscape we refer to the inhabited or perceived environments of human communities in the past and present incorporating both natural and artificial elements (see Ingold 2000a [1993]; Lynch 1972).

Acknowledgements: The authors would like to thank David Harvey, Brynmor Morris, Harold Mytum, Martin Rundkvist, Adam Wainwright and Elizabeth Williams for discussing topics covered in this paper, as well as Dan Hicks and Mary Beaudry for encouragement and additional advice.

235

In this essay, through a series of case studies we shall explore examples of how archaeologists, particularly those studying the last 500 years of human history, have considered the relationships between memory and landscape. This topic has in recent years attracted great interest among archaeologists dealing with this period (e.g. Lahiri 2003; Reckner 2002; N. Saunders 2003b; Shackel 2001; Tarlow 2000b) and lies now at the heart of the discipline. We intend to argue that any division between 'prehistoric' and 'historical' periods is false, and has tended to obscure broader themes in the way in which landscapes are implicated in social remembering and forgetting. We will start by considering 'accumulative landscapes' – landscapes composed of the traces of human action and natural features that form the focus of retrospective memories. We then move on to discuss created landscapes and the prospective memories they contain. These distinctive types of landscapes, although often interacting and overlapping, provide a valuable theoretical starting point for understanding the ways in which both past and future memories are produced and reproduced through spatial action. Many of the case studies are taken from European contexts, although it is hoped that they illustrate broader themes relevant to the archaeological study of landscape and memory throughout the world.

MEMORY IN ACCUMULATIVE LANDSCAPES

Archaeologists have previously studied a wide range of accumulative landscapes, and have increasingly addressed important themes in the landscape change of the last half millennium, such as the process of rural settlement and land enclosure, the development of townscapes and industrial landscapes. Some studies have even specifically addressed commemoration in the landscapes of recent centuries through the study of battlefields, war memorials, burial grounds and cemeteries (Mytum 2004a, 2004b; Tarlow 1999c; 2000b). However, most of these studies lack an explicit consideration of the landscape context of death, burial, commemoration and ancestors (but see Mytum nd.). Many archaeological studies regard the landscape as the 'richest historical record that we possess' (W. G. Hoskins 1955: 14) from which the character and evolution of the landscape can be 'detected', 'deciphered' and then 'interpreted' by 'those who know how to read it' (W. G. Hoskins 1955: 14; see also Muir 2000). Yet the landscapes in question are most often landscapes of living people and their contemporary environments; they hardly ever encapsulate the dead and the past. Ironically, studies intended to chart objective 'landscape history' risk denying the importance of history for people inhabiting past landscapes. These studies rarely consider how memories (including mythologies, genealogies as well as cultural, community, and personal histories) were inherited, inhabited, invented and imagined through the landscape. Equally ironic is the fact that those archaeological studies that have begun to address the relationship between memory and landscape have tended to focus on prehistoric and ancient societies (e.g. Bradley 2002; Chapman 1997), rather than those of the last half millennium. This is despite the fact that recent centuries offer considerably greater potential for rich, contextual and interdisciplinary analyses of memory and landscape incorporating archaeological evidence.

Viewing the landscape will often involve seeing the remains of very many different periods of the past from a single vantage point (Lynch 1972). By providing information on how to observe and how to interpret what is seen, onlookers can 'remember' both recent 'familiar' pasts and earlier pasts from the existing remains. The landscape of Hanabergsmarka at Jærmuseet near Nærbø in southern Norway is a good example (Figure 13.1). Viewing and studying it reveals a temporal collage, the elements of which are each explained to the visitor:

— a burial mound from the Bronze Age
— a stone wall from the Iron Age
— a track, probably from the Middle Ages
— the site of a haystack, probably from the Middle Ages
— ruins of German fortifications from World War II
— a clearance cairn from the Iron Age
— house foundations from the Iron Age
— a shooting range from the early twentieth century
— a medieval cultivated field
— a split stone, c. 1920
— a medieval stone wall
— a burial mound from the Iron Age
— a stone wall, pre-1870, repaired c. 1925
— a stone wall, c. 1939
— house foundations from the early twentieth century
— farm buildings from the 1700s
— plantation forestry, c. 1945

A landscape historian would conventionally, and profitably, consider this a 'palimpsest', a sequence of traces of the past that have been built up, written over and rewritten over decades, centuries and millennia (Muir 2000). Such a landscape can also be described as one of 'retrospective memory'; a landscape through which the past appears to impact upon the present through physical and material traces as people look back at what has happened in the

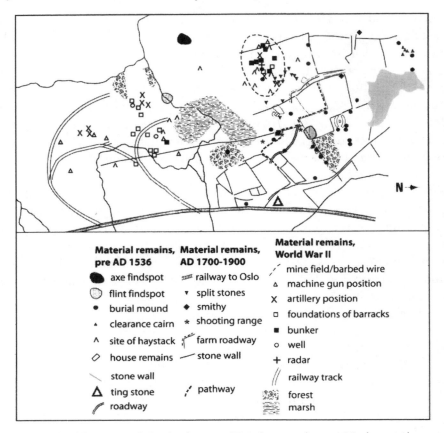

Figure 13.1 The accumulative landscape at Hanabergsmarka near Nærbø, southern Norway. A historical palimpsest created in the present (based on a map by Hanne Thomsen and Hilmar I. Løland in *Fossil Landscapes* (1995, Hanabergsmarka, Hå kommune, Rogaland)).

same landscape before their own time. Retrospective memories create the past at particular places and through certain social practices (Holtorf 2000–2005: 2.0). For past societies without the convenient heritage signboard of Hanabergsmarka, memories may be created through social practices as well as oral and literary transmission; in combination these different strategies might serve to create memories from the surrounding topography. For example, memories can be evoked through the enactment of both everyday practices and rituals at certain locations across the landscape and along the pathways connecting them. This kind of 'looking-back' is not necessarily about accurately recalling past events as truthfully as possible: it is rather about making meaningful statements about the past in the given cultural context of a present as well as evoking aspirations for the future.

REMEMBERING AND FORGETTING IN LANDSCAPES

By the same token landscapes can serve to hide the past, or make people forget it. For example, industrial landscapes can be very much about 'forgetting'. David Gwyn's recent study of nineteenth-century slate-mining communities in North Wales highlights how chapels and their burial grounds provided an invaluable commemorative focus of class and religious identities for the workers. These were particularly important in landscapes dominated by the planned settlements and slate quarries where other layers of meaning were in danger of being 'forgotten' within the spatial structures of the quarry owners (Gwyn 2004: 50). Forgetting can also encapsulate deliberate acts of destruction. For example, in District Six of Cape Town the Apartheid regime sought from 1966 onwards to establish white ownership and occupation in new townhouses and high-rise flats. Its mostly 'coloured' inhabitants were forcibly removed and their buildings demolished in an effort to render the past forgotten. However, the dispossessed and displaced former inhabitants did not forget, and neither did the urban landscape. From 1997, after the regime change, many of the former inhabitants reclaimed the remains of their familiar urban landscape and proudly displayed their 'treasures' and memories in the new District Six Museum (Hall 2000: 156–176). The past, then, is always present in landscapes, but when certain elements are made visible, this can be at the expense of others that are suppressed, distributed and dispersed. The British commemoration of the 1857 revolt in Delhi, for instance, involved raising monuments and the performance of rituals to remember the British dead, combined with the wholesale demolition of buildings and districts connected to the Indian uprising. This 'forgetting' of those that fought the British in the decades after the revolt was a situation only reversed following Indian independence, a century later, in which a nationalist commemorative agenda turned the tables and emphasised a glorious revolt and suppressed the places and monuments of imperial commemoration (Lahiri 2003).

While forgetting can be deliberate and involve violent suppression, such as in District Six during the Apartheid period or with the despoiling of statues of toppled dictators, forgetting is often more subtle, and tied closely to remembering. Rather than separate strategies of commemoration, they are part of the same process. In landscapes where people experienced war, migration or death, all of which are largely invisible and easily 'forgotten', selected memories can distil in other media. Whether invested in portable artefacts, the home, or rendered in songs, stories, folk beliefs and ritual performances, memories can be present in landscapes of the imagination rather than invested in monuments and traces within the physical landscape commemorated.

In fact, many episodes of the past that people remember, whether individually or as members of communities, have a spatial dimension and are linked to certain places in the landscape. In Palestine, for example, numerous locations of events described in the Bible became sacred places of the collective memory of religious groups even though the exact places were often later inventions rather than accurately remembered. In particular, it is likely that the early Christians, including the writers of the gospels, were trying to fortify their memories of events in the life of Jesus by connecting them with locations that were already meaningful in the Jewish religious tradition of the Old Testament. Halbwachs argues that this 'legendary topography' was drawn upon by subsequent generations in order to construct a meaningful past of the Holy Land (Halbwachs 1992).

Archaeologists working in England have similarly explored the relationships between landscapes and remembering. From the late Middle Ages, cathedrals, churches, chapels and their graveyards developed as complex and evolving 'landscapes' of memory (see Williams 2003). Increasingly filled with tombs, vaults and crypts, both before and after the reformation, church architecture was a medium for commemoration (Finch 2003; Tarlow 1999c, 2000b). Churchyards were also complex, evolving, sometimes competitive, commemorative topographies. As well as gravestones and tombs, churchyards might include exclusive family burial plots, crypts, mausolea or chapels, through which the history of families and communities were mapped out and materialised (Mytum 2004a, 2004b). Harold Mytum's (2004a) graveyard survey at Kellington church in North Yorkshire and Sarah Tarlow's (1999c) study of burial grounds in Orkney have suggested that during the late eighteenth and early nineteenth centuries churchyards took on an enhanced role as spaces of commemoration, through the proliferation of enduring memorials to the dead.

The commemorative significance of churches and their graveyards is further illustrated in instances where churches served dispersed rural communities and in cases where villages became deserted. For example, in the parish of Witton, Norfolk, archaeological research has demonstrated that the church stood in relative isolation in a landscape of dispersed farmsteads for much of the last millennium (Lawson 1983).[1] Therefore, for innumerable generations, living worshippers and the corpses of the dead had to traverse

---

[1] We would like to thank Brynmor Morris for suggesting the relevance of this evidence to the argument.

roads and tracks for long distances to reach their church. Both the place of worship and the paths connecting the church to fields and farms served to create the memories and identities of the parish community (Lawson 1983). Andrew Fleming has made a similar point with regard to the parish church of Grinton located in Swaledale, North Yorkshire. While chapels were available for regular worship serving the farms and mining communities in the dale and on surrounding moors, until the chapel at Muker was granted a licence for burial in 1580, the church at Grinton ('the cathedral of the dales') remained the only burial site and focus for commemoration. Indeed, corpses had to be carried to Grinton from townships up to sixteen miles away for burial (A. Fleming 1998: 10).

The significance of the church as a place of memory is also shown in the famous case of the deserted medieval village of Wharram Percy in East Yorkshire. Archaeological research by Maurice Beresford and John Hurst has demonstrated that while the village was abandoned by the early sixteenth century, St Martin's church remained in use for worship, burial and commemoration until 1949 (Beresford and Hurst 1990: 52). Churches, like prehistoric monuments, last for many human generations. They do not only function as landmarks but even act as time-marks connecting the living with ancestors and the past, even in instances where communities have moved elsewhere (Chapman 1997).

CHANGING MEMORIES OVER TIME

Individuals learn many of their collective memories through socialisation, although they can also modify existing views of the past according to what they themselves consider right or appropriate (Holtorf 2000–2005: 2.7). Although certain dominant narratives about the past are astonishingly resistant to change (Reckner 2002) they often vary at any one time as much as they change over time. Landscapes have largely been interpreted anew by each community of interpreters studying them in the light of their own particular values and worldviews.

Stonehenge in England, for example, has been a mysterious ruin inhabiting successive historical landscapes for far longer than it was ever a prehistoric ritual site. By the same token, other stone monuments originally erected during the Neolithic or Bronze Age across many parts of Europe have remained visible landscape features that have attracted many different types of reuse and reappropriation. In historical times, the stones of megaliths were occasionally reused for purposes such as building houses, roads, or churches, but in recent centuries they also attracted folktales about giants, treasures, and fairies (Holtorf 2000–2005: 5.2.5, 5.2.7; cf. Chippendale 2004). Attracted by such folklore and influenced by an emerging interest in history and a fascination with ancient ruins, Romantic poets, painters, and travellers visited megaliths increasingly during the late eighteenth and early nineteenth centuries. These pursuits were complemented by antiquarian studies of ancient monuments and succeeded by archaeological investigations. Today, many ancient monuments are local tourist attractions and have been comprehensively restored. After studying the twentieth-century restorations at the prehistoric sites of Avebury and Stonehenge in Britain, Brian Edwards (2000: 76) concludes that 'our ancient past is a ruination plundered by early antiquarians and despoiled by the heritage industry.' This condemning description can, however, be relativised somewhat by placing the modern changes to ancient sites into a broader historical context. In fact, every age has appropriated prehistoric monuments in its own way as part of distinct uses and interpretations of the landscape; our own time is simply no exception.

Prehistoric artefacts and monuments, and even their seemingly natural and unaltered components, might have lengthy 'biographies' (Holtorf 2005: 78–91), and yet the same is true of buildings, monuments and landscapes from historical periods. The archaeology of changing memories is also visible in the reuses of former religious houses in England and Wales after their Dissolution by Henry VIII in the sixteenth century (cf. Crossley 1990: 53–56). Dissolved abbeys, priories and nunneries had many different 'afterlives'. In many cases, religious houses and their estates were appropriated and reused as readily available quarries and the value of their estates as rich economic resources. Yet frequently these acts of reuse appear to have been bound up with the appropriation and transformation of social memories. This argument explains the careful manipulation of monastic architecture and landscapes in the post-reformation era in which elements of the material past were selectively remembered and forgotten. For example, this applies to the transformation of the Cistercian abbey at Neath (South Wales) into a luxurious Tudor great house by building over the abbot's house; the prestige and power evoked by its new use was likely to have been enhanced by its former history (Robinson 2002). Similarly, the evocation of the monastic past was achieved by the integration and 'improvement' of the ruins of another Cistercian house at Fountains (North Yorkshire) as a centrepiece of the eighteenth-century picturesque landscape gardens of Studley Royal (Coppack 2003: 133–139).

The wealthy medieval Benedictine monastery at Glastonbury, Somerset was the centrepiece of a medieval mythical landscape that endured and evolved around the site's ruins and topography from the Dissolution and into the present day. In the medieval period, the abbey combined the cults of numerous Irish and Anglo-Saxon saints, the legend of Joseph of Arimathea, the Holy Thorn and the Holy Grail as well as Arthurian myth. For example, in 1191 during the rebuilding of the abbey following a fire, the monks of the abbey claimed to 'discover' the graves of King Arthur and Queen Guinevere: an early example of 'archaeological' activity serving to enhance origin myths (Rahtz and Watts 2003: 53–66). Following the Dissolution, the natural topography of the Tor and the Chalice Well, together with the built environment of the town, its churches, the monastic precinct and the abbey ruins, combined to create a landscape of memory and myth that has attracted diverse and competing interpretations to the present day. Like Stonehenge, in recent decades, tourists, Christian pilgrims, Arthurian, New Age and pagan enthusiasts, Glastonbury Festival-goers, archaeologists (and even the local people of this small market town themselves!) have ensured that the Glastonbury landscape continues to materialise many different stories and identities (Rahtz and Watts 2003: 159–166).

And yet memories do not simply reside in impressive monuments and buildings. One particularly interesting approach to how the past is remembered in the modern world has been promoted in a series of volumes edited between 1984 and 1992 by the French scholar Pierre Nora (1984–1992). His ambitious study of realms of memory (*les lieux de mémoire*) in contemporary France includes not only places such as museums, cathedrals, cemeteries and memorials, but also concepts and practices (e.g. generations, mottos and commemorative ceremonies) and objects (e.g. inherited property monuments, symbols, classic texts and even Nora's own books). It might be worthwhile in the future to consider extending the notion of historical landscapes from places and spaces to include, as Nora proposes, all realms of memory that together create the historical surroundings within which we live, including those that exist only in our imagination (cf. Hall and Bombardella 2005; Schama 1995). These realms signify a wide range of different histories, and these significations again have pasts that we should seek to understand better in order to put both historical landscapes and historical archaeology into broader perspectives built around the concept of memory. Intriguingly, many realms of memory do not only contain interpretations of the past but also aspirations for the future and what will be remembered then.

MEMORY IN CREATED LANDSCAPES

'Prospective' memory is what those creating realms of memory intend for the future (Holtorf 2000–2005: 6.6). For example, war memorials of the nineteenth and twentieth centuries were built with distinctive prospective memories in mind, namely to remember why they had been erected. Many of them played their part in the national cult of fallen soldiers glorifying death on behalf of the nation. War memorials are effectively attempts at creating elements in the landscape that will evoke a particular version of a (future) past. Yet as already indicated in the previous section, the specific variety of changing (retrospective) memories about a given historical realm could neither have been intended nor foreseen.

As time moved on, the meanings of memorials and their landscape settings have been changing. Grieving relatives, even of the most recent war in Western Europe, World War II, have become rare, and the nationalist spirit in which most memorials were once erected is now suspect, or downright embarrassing, to many. By the same token, many landscape parks containing references to a desired past (see below) are now being frequented increasingly by people who are merely seeking a pleasant destination for a walk on a Sunday afternoon. References to specific events in Classical mythology, the medieval past, or Christian metaphors of religious sacrifice may be lost to those walking past memorials at a railway station, or taking a short cut through a park on their way to work (Marshall 2004). Nevertheless, many memorials have retained some meaning in local communities and become revitalised during times of commemoration through the year and threats to their survival and accessibility can quickly acquire political significance.

Situated in a park outside of Demmin in Vorpommern (Germany) is a huge memorial, commemorating the dead of the *2. Pommersches Ulanen-Regiment Nr. 9*, which had been based in Demmin from 1860 until 1920 and fought in the wars of 1864–1866, 1870–1871 and 1914–1918 (Holtorf 2000–2005: 8.9). This so-called *Ulanendenkmal* was built under the direction of the artist Fritz Richter-Elsner and opened on 3 August 1924, exactly 10 years after the *Ulanen* rode off into World War I. A chain was put at the entrance to the site and an inscription reminded everyone of Germany's situation after the treaty of Versailles: 'As you step over these chains, remember that the fatherland's honour and freedom must be reinstated.' The history of this memorial reflects only too obviously the difference between prospective and retrospective memories, and illustrates once again the dramatic changes which retrospective memory can be subjected to. In the 1920s, it was built as a huge memorial for the war heroes, with many symbolic references to the prehistoric past, Teutonic ancestors and Germanic mythology, thus strengthening German nationalism at the time. After Hitler had reintroduced military service in Germany in 1935, the chain was broken in a symbolic act and its ends fixed on either side of the entrance stones. The site had thus become a political symbol for the Third Reich's new power. In 1946, after the war was lost, the memorial had become an embarrassing document. It was shut down, the Germanic symbols were removed, and this site of former pride gradually dilapidated and became a huge rubbish pile. Yet after the collapse of the socialist GDR in 1989 the entire memorial was restored and reappreciated as a historical monument of the unified Germany. It was reopened in 1995.

Archaeologists have begun to contribute to the interdisciplinary study of battlefields, war cemeteries and war memorials (e.g. Tarlow 1999c), but the detailed analysis of how the locations and landscape contexts of these places influenced their roles in remembering and forgetting remains to be studied (see also Mytum nd.). Rare exceptions include Michael Dietler's study of how resistance by the Gallic tribes to Julius Caesar's armies led by Vercingetorix was portrayed in French national monuments in the nineteenth and twentieth centuries. The monuments were intended to embody contemporary national identity, and were linked to sustained campaigns of archaeological research. The 'oppida' (late Iron Age fortified settlements) of Alésia, Gergovia and Bibracte became associated with particular battles and events recorded in Julius Caesar's *Gallic Wars*, associations that were built upon through archaeological excavations, most notably those commissioned by the Emperor Napoleon III during the 1860s. These sites were subsequently to become landscapes of national commemoration, monumentalised by statues, monuments and/or museums during the later nineteenth and twentieth centuries (Dietler 1998). Napoleon III paid most attention to the site of Vercingetorix's defeat; a site where sacrifice and martyrdom rather than triumphal victory provided the most powerful ingredient to facilitate the commemoration of national unity (Dietler 1998: 76).

SACRIFICIAL LANDSCAPES

Moving beyond the biography of sites and monuments to consider the commemorative significance of their broader landscape context, Nicholas Saunders has discussed the Western Front of World War I as a sacrificial landscape, in which Calvary crosses became symbols of sacrifice and memory. Saunders argues that the Calvary crosses were important because they had been such a widespread element of the pre-war rural landscape. Crosses embodied Christ's sacrifice and were often believed to 'miraculously' survive enemy action as the only visible and recognisable monuments in the decimated countryside. The cross subsequently became employed in the memorials and cemeteries that became prominent features of the commemorative battlefield landscapes after the war. For example, Saunders shows how the cross at 'Butte de Warlencourt', the site of a Gallo-Roman burial mound and focus for successive military offensives, was memorialised during the war by British and then German crosses. After the war the cross was re-erected in commemoration of the Allied dead, but once more was replaced by a German cross in 1944 during the German occupation of France. Saunders suggests that the constant replacements and removals of the crosses were examples of the symbolic conflict of commemoration in sacrificial landscapes created by war (N. Saunders 2003b: 12).

Similar themes can be ascribed to the commemoration of those who did not die at the front. Marcia Pointon has discussed the complex funerary and sexual topography created by the funeral of Diana, Princess of Wales, in 1997. In this case, commemoration ranged from her place of death in a car crash in a Paris underpass, through the national monuments integrated into her funeral (including St. James' Palace and Westminster Abbey in London), to the transportation of her cadaver to its final resting place on an island within the grounds of her family's ancestral home at Althorp, near Northampton (Pointon 1999). Across the United Kingdom, war memorials were among the locations selected for the commemoration of her memory; the monuments served as foci for public expressions of commemoration but reconfigured with new memories and associations contradictory to their original intended significance (Pointon 1999; see also Marshall 2004). The case of Diana also serves to remind us that landscapes of remembrance can incorporate 'ephemeral' monuments, even in recent western society when the temptation is to regard all monuments as necessarily public and enduring (see also Küchler 2002). What are the more memorable 'monuments' to Diana in the public imagination and disseminated worldwide by the media? It might be argued that the short-lived carpets of flowers that surrounded her London residence at St James' Palace and her grave at Althorp were powerful 'ephemeral monuments' created by many separate commemorative acts. In many ways they have served as more effective commemoration monuments than the officially sanctioned 'memorial fountains' and other statues that have been subsequently erected across the United Kingdom.

CREATING LANDSCAPES OF DEATH AND COMMEMORATION

War memorials are only one of many evolving contexts of landscape commemoration. In Europe, for instance, the dead were present in post-medieval landscapes in many other ways. While we have discussed churches and churchyards as places of memory, during recent centuries we see increasingly complex topographies of commemoration, from memorials and statues, parks and gardens, the growth of Nonconformist chapels and their adjacent burial grounds, and the rise of garden cemeteries.

Landscape parks contain carefully created references to a desired past. They could incorporate churches and contain the tombs of aristocratic families close to their country houses (R. Morris 1989: 377–384). Further aspects of these élite commemorative landscapes are specifically designed family mausolea situated as prominent features within parks. Mausolea were 'objects in space, set immutably in the landscape, silent and grand' (Curl 1980: 168). They were designed to evoke the designs of antiquity, and the rotunda at Castle Howard in North Yorkshire has been described as 'one of the greatest of all examples of buildings in this genre, and probably the first monumental free-standing tomb built in Western Europe since Antiquity' (Curl 1980: 179–180). These were mortuary monuments explicitly intended to dominate the designed, idealised and timeless landscapes of the eighteenth-century country home. As antique monuments situated in Arcadian landscapes, they served to freeze mortality in the distant past (R. Morris 1989: 385; Mytum nd.; Schama 1995: 517–578).

Richard Bradley has recently discussed the relationship between memory and the landscape gardens at Stourhead made by Henry Hoare, grandfather of the famous antiquary Sir Richard Colt Hoare. Hoare created an English Palladian landscape filled with water features, trees, temples, a grotto and statues. The landscape materialised Virgil's *Aeneid* in the English countryside, perhaps an attempt to connect the classical past to Hoare's personal biography and family history (Bradley 2002: 150–151). In turn, such overt appropriations and creations of mythical past through the manipulation of landscape may have provided the motivation for Sir Richard Colt Hoare's subsequent passion for investigating ancient burial mounds. Indeed, the antiquarianism and archaeology of the late eighteenth and early nineteenth centuries might be seen, in part, as an extension of a burgeoning consideration of landscape as a vehicle for social commemoration.

The ambition to create specific sceneries in the landscape that support particular memories has also influenced cemetery location and design. Created as mnemonics for the dead, they were also built with a particular form of future commemoration in mind, starting with the process of the funeral itself. Dying, death and the dead have a special place in our discussion of landscape and memory (Williams 2003) although interpretations have tended to ignore the landscape dimension of mortuary practices which has instead been subsumed within 'church archaeology' and a focus on skeletons, coffins and gravestones, detached from their spatial and landscape settings (cf. Mytum 2004a, 2004b).

The planning and arrangement of garden cemeteries provides an example of the link between death, landscape and memory. These cemeteries were a response to the hygiene problems of urban churchyards and were driven by the Nonconformist desire for interment away from Anglican influence. Yet their design suggests an arcadian theme with close similarities to eighteenth-century landscape gardens including lawns, winding paths and tree plantings (Tarlow 2000b: 223–224). The strength of antiquity, and the timelessness that these landscapes of death evoked, was central to their evolving mnemonic roles. In a detailed analysis of a York cemetery, Sue Buckham (2003) has discussed how these cemeteries became landscapes of memory that incorporated the competitive display of elites, but also the selective expression and suppression of class, religious affiliation, age and gender identities in the location and form of grave monuments (see also Mytum 2004b: 137–155). Similarly, the growth of Nonconformist burial grounds in the eighteenth and nineteenth centuries provided an alternative commemorative topography to those provided by Anglican churchyards in which religious identity, language and class were negotiated (Mytum 2003).

The procession of the corpse through the landscape was as important a means of commemoration as the places where the dead were finally interred. These themes of place and movement are incorporated in Tony Pollard's discussion of the repeated close geographical relationship between medieval and post-medieval burial grounds and the sea in Highland Scotland (T. Pollard 1999: 34–36). For many in these fishing communities, the sea was a grave and beaches perceived as liminal places where those drowned at sea were washed up and buried. Burial grounds also tend to be situated on promontories, cliff tops and knolls within sight of the sea or on islands within lochs. Such locations, away from the dispersed settlements they served, required long 'coffin tracks' winding along the coast from settlements, their routes punctuated by cairns where the coffin would be rested. Therefore both burial ground and the procession to the burial ground were related ways in which death and commemoration were mediated by landscape.

The commemoration of the dead has not been limited to churches, churchyards and cemeteries in recent centuries. Boundaries, crossroads and old mounds were often perceived as liminal places, locations distant both physically and spiritually from the church at the centre of the community. They were therefore places seen as appropriate for the execution and burial of criminals from the late Saxon period onwards but they were also intended to be places of memory situated to enhance commemoration of the 'bad death'. In this context, Nicola Whyte (2003) has recently explored the location of gallows in the Norfolk landscape of the seventeenth and eighteenth centuries. Executions were public and memorable events in themselves, but subsequently travelling through the landscape of Norfolk would necessitate encountering the decomposing bodies of criminals hanging from gibbets beside roads in prominent locations away from settlements. These served to remind the living of mortality and the authority of the élite that could assert such power over criminals. Gallows were therefore mortuary monuments to bad deaths, the antithesis to the 'good deaths' provided by the tombs of the wealthy in and around the church.

A further category of 'bad deaths' provided with a distinctive landscape location are the *cillin* (infant cemeteries), found in Ireland and used from medieval times into the twentieth century. The sites selected are usually abandoned burial sites or ancient monuments, perceived as suitably 'liminal' places for the interment of unbaptised babies and suicides distant from the churchyard burial (Finlay 1999). Therefore, landscapes in recent centuries can constitute complex mortuary and commemorative topographies that incorporate a range of different locales associated with the commemoration of the dead and the past in diverse ways.

'THEATRES OF MEMORY'

In the contemporary world, all sorts of newly created shopping malls and heritage sites have transformed landscapes and surroundings into what Raphael Samuel (1994) has described as 'theatres of memory'. Among them are open-air museums, performed events such as historical re-enactments, or large visitor destinations like Stonehenge, as well as theme parks and other themed environments like the hotel–casino–shopping malls of Las Vegas and similar destination resorts elsewhere (Hall and Bombardella 2005; Holtorf 2005: 130–149). Insofar as it makes people remember episodes of a collective past, the cityscape of Las Vegas can be seen as a complex historical landscape.

For example, Caesars Palace opened in 1966 as the first Las Vegas resort to embody consistently an archaeological or historical theme. It signifies the popular myth of a decadent and opulent Rome associated with excess and indulgence as it is depicted in movies like *Ben Hur, Cleopatra*, or (more recently) *Gladiator*. Arguably, Caesars Palace creates a museum for the mass audience, a museum free of admission fees, velvet ropes, and Plexiglass panels and (falsely) appearing to be free even of security guards. Its architecture and design bear the signs of historicity but lack the tedious labels. Almost the same might be said about the Luxor, a more recent Las Vegas resort. Here, too, an atmosphere of exotic luxury is created to stimulate spending. Completed in 1993 in the shape of the world's largest pyramid, and with a gigantic sphinx in front of it, the Luxor embraces the clichés of ancient Egypt, incorporating the pyramids, pharaohs, mummies, occult mysteries, fabulous wealth, and archaeological excavations. The main lobbies of the building are filled with full-scale Egyptian architecture, and in each room walls, wardrobes, and bed linen are adorned with Egyptian-style murals and hieroglyphics.

Further interesting examples of contemporary theatres of memory are zoological gardens, which since the beginning of the nineteenth century have been built in many parts of the world. Although some zoos contain historical remains from various periods, they are also historical landscapes in the sense that they deliberately create representations of the past, which are best appreciated by moving through the zoo (Holtorf nd.). Firstly, zoos often commemorate individuals: usually people who have acted as benefactors to the zoo. To sponsor a bench or contribute financially in some other way earns you the right to have your name, and occasionally a personal message, displayed to later generations for as long as the bench or the plaque will last. A more lasting memorial in the form of a portrait bust is only given to former zoo directors like Carl Hagenbeck in his *Tierpark* in Hamburg or to particularly generous benefactors like Lord Swaraj Paul in the case of London Zoo. London Zoo also features a memorial commemorating five employees who died during World War II. Virtually the only animal individuals for which one occasionally finds memorials in zoos are primates and especially gorillas. In Bristol Zoo, for example, lowland gorilla Alfred remains unforgotten as a local icon and celebrity of the 1930s and 1940s and is honoured with a bust in the zoo.

Secondly, zoos commemorate collective pasts in order to appeal to visitor preconceptions. Until well into the twentieth century, exotic animals and 'exotic' people were exhibited in zoos, side by side, as strange curiosities. In Hagenbeck's *Völkerschauen*, this practice was pioneered through demonstrations of the appearances and customs of 'primitive' cultures seemingly living in a timeless, natural state of primordial humanness. Even today, many contemporary zoos continue to contrive crude connections between

Figure 13.2 The farmstead of the Meyer family. A created landscape at Hannover Zoo.
Photograph: Cornelius Holtorf 2002.

the animals displayed and the native people living in the same area, sustaining an idealisation of 'primitive' cultures in the 'wild' in antithesis to 'modern' civilisations. The new Tropical Zoo within Copenhagen Zoo, for example, features a display about people of the rainforest, from where visitors access directly the living quarters of the chimpanzees. Similar displays are now also being created about farmsteads in the Western world. Hannover Zoo, for example, features *Meyers Hof*, complete with happy cows, cute ponies, dirty pigs, and cheeky geese, signifying a nostalgic idealisation of assumed former farming realities (Figure 13.2). In this way, zoo architecture serves to commemorate the image of a timeless preindustrial past that forms such a widespread element of European nationalism. Whereas many old zoo buildings resemble the architectural styles of the animals' countries of origin, in some cases styles of the past were chosen, much in the way English landscape parks featured romantic follies such as artificial ruins (as in Stourhead discussed earlier). That is not coincidental, as modern zoological gardens emerged when these landscape parks were popular too. The ostrich house in Berlin, for example, was opened in 1901 in the style of an Egyptian temple including painted murals and hieroglyphics as decorations.

This was done with so much attention to detail that the building was later used as a teaching aid for the local university students of Egyptology.

Thirdly, zoos commemorate animal species that are extinct in the wild as well as other episodes of 'natural history' such as human origins. Some zoos, for example, display life-size models of long-extinct species like dinosaurs. Also, many zoos are particularly proud to keep animal species that are either endangered or already extinct in the wild, and this is increasingly considered to be their main justification. Sometimes living specimens of preserved animal species are being reintroduced into the wild, as in the case of the Przewalski horse which, thanks to successful zoo breeding, roams freely again through Mongolia after thirty years of extinction. By making up for historical extinctions, zoos are thus even undoing the past for a better future.

With this complex conflation of past, present and future, the landscapes of zoos are but one instance of the invention in the present of pasts for the future. Many shopping malls and heritage destinations too take aspects of popular conceptions of the past and mould them as a space for the future (Hall and Bombardella 2005). It is therefore increasingly difficult for archaeologists to consider heritage parks and archaeological sites as exclusively contributing to the relationship of landscape and memory.

CONCLUSIONS

Although prospective and retrospective memories are theoretically distinct, they are often combined with each other in specific landscapes. Churches and their environs can be regarded as landscapes of commemoration that incorporate both prospective and retrospective memories; evocations of the past and aspirations for the afterlife. Meanwhile, particularly dense cityscapes like that of Exeter, a city that provided the home for the famous landscape historian W. G. Hoskins (Hoskins 2004), are both rich historical palimpsests of subsequent occupations and places for 'remembering' certain futures. Like many European cities, Exeter is a tapestry of the ancient, medieval and recent past with early remains including the preserved Roman city walls with subsequent Saxon, medieval and Tudor additions. The city retains its medieval cathedral, churches and chapels, townhouses, guildhall, underground passages that brought water to the city, and the bridge that once conveyed traffic across the river Exe. Also preserved are elements of the early modern, Georgian and Victorian expansion of the city as well as the substantial redevelopments of the modern era. Equally significant however are the many losses through fire, war and city planning (Hoskins 2004 [1960]) that has seen large parts of the city transformed over the centuries. The cityscape is constantly 'on the move', and a new redevelopment at Princesshay is likely to bring more of the city's past back 'into memory' through archaeological excavation. The contrasting periods and selective retention that has become embodied within Exeter's cityscape is no better emphasised than in the location of the medieval church of St Pancras, the only structure to be retained during the development of the Guildhall Shopping Centre. Perhaps this serves as an example of selective remembrance incorporating retrospective and prospective elements. The church is now stranded and detached from the cityscape it inhabited in former times; marooned by the concrete paving slabs of a modern plaza surrounded by shops. However, the church is not only a lonely leftover of a historical palimpsest that was once far richer. It has also become an element of the new 'theatre of memory' that is the shopping centre in contemporary civic life. Through renovation and restoration, old buildings such as this are effectively employed to construct new pasts and aspired futures out of selected elements of the old.

Likewise, the presence of the dead in the landscape implied both prospective aspirations for the future and later a retrospective evocation of the past. As we have seen, the landscapes of the period from c. AD 1500 contained dramatic changes in the way the dead were perceived, engaged with, and the way the dead and the past were remembered. Rather than confined within specific locales, memories saturated the landscape. In this way, memories of the past, and aspirations of future pasts, were both a consequence of, and something that had a profound impact on, the identities of those inhabiting and experiencing town and country.

However we view the dead and the past though and whatever we do with its remains and evocations has to be understood within a particular present context. In other words, how people relate to the past and its remains is not subject to some unchanging principles but is always governed by the specific agendas and interests of the people involved. As some of the examples discussed in this chapter illustrate, memories in landscapes, whether accumulated or created, are therefore often contested (cf. Bender and Winer 2001; Shackel 2001). Key questions to be raised in relation to remembering the past in any landscape have to include the following: Who benefits in each case? Who is disadvantaged? Are anyone's interests affected other than those of people directly involved? Which power relations are at work, and have all living people represented or evoked been adequately consulted and listened to?

At the beginning of this chapter, we argued that studies of the landscape of the last five hundred years have focused on 'reading' its character and evolution, whether the focus is on industry, towns, rural settlements or the enclosure of fields. While these are valid and profitable approaches to the study of the landscape of recent centuries, archaeology is in a strong position to address the importance of the past, the dead and memory. From this perspective, archaeologists cannot fully consider the complex significance and meanings of landscape to past people without considering the memories that were deemed to have inhabited them.

CHAPTER 14

Landscapes, ideology and experience in historical archaeology

Lu Ann De Cunzo and Julie H. Ernstein

Historical archaeologists have studied landscapes at a number of scales and from diverse theoretical stances (e.g. Casella 2002; Delle 1998; Ireland 2003; Kelso and Most 1990; Leone 1996; Orser 1988; Williamson 1995; Yamin and Metheny 1996). This chapter examines some of the ways in which historical archaeologists have sought to understand the complexities of landscapes past and present (see also Holtorf and Williams this volume, O'Keeffe and Yamin this volume). It traces historical archaeologists' initial studies of ideology and power in landscape through 'critical archaeology', and underlines the diversity and utility of such approaches. It considers the emphasis in later studies on the diverse meanings of designed landscapes, especially the critiques of critical archaeologies that presented landscapes as 'duping' subaltern populations and that assumed easy distinctions between ideological truths and falsehoods in landscape. Sketching how such contextual critiques have encouraged new interpretive archaeological studies that eschew grand narratives of 'domination and resistance' and produce more nuanced understandings, we review more recent approaches to the materialities and experiences of enacted landscapes. Discussing a range of work drawn from around the world, we emphasise the diversity of approaches to historical landscape archaeology, and underline the value of theoretical plurality as archaeologists confront the fluidity, expressive power, and importance of historical landscapes in shaping human social life.

'CRITICAL' ARCHAEOLOGIES OF LANDSCAPES AND IDEOLOGY

As Matthew Johnson (1999a: 192) has observed, archaeologists understand ideology to be 'a set of overt or implicit beliefs or views of the world'. In historical archaeology, the relationship between worldview and the built environment has been a central object of study since James Deetz sought

Acknowledgements: We thank the editors for initiating and facilitating this 'landscape work'.

to explore the Georgian Order in the eastern United States (Deetz 1977; see review by Hicks and Horning this volume). Deetz described historical archaeology's ability to draw on multiple lines of evidence to understand 'the world view that underlay the organisation of [past people's] physical universe, and the way ideology shaped their lives' (Deetz 1977: 23, 40).

During the early 1980s, critical archaeologists joined the Deetzian critique of processualism's understanding of material culture as merely reflecting social relationships, rather than actively involved in creating them (Leone 1996). These historical archaeologists used the notion of ideology to describe symbolic systems deployed through material culture, especially landscapes, to negotiate power relations. Designed landscapes were presented as serving 'to legitimate or mask the "real" state of social relations' in western capitalism (M. Johnson 1999b: 192), and archaeologists set out to examine how these material ideologies mediated contradictions between the material forces and social relations of production (cf. M. Johnson 1996). Critical archaeologists emphasised designed landscapes' role in the creation of 'false consciousness' by a dominant class.

Critical archaeologists' interest in ideology stemmed from the influence of the Frankfurt School. Althusser's (1971b) reading of Marx and Engels' *The German Ideology* (1970) was particularly influential because it understood ideology as reified through the manipulation of the material and symbolic world. Althusser argued that ideologies subtly express and legitimise power, or lack of power, in the interests of the ruling class. In such a 'top-down' view, ideology 'signifies the way men live out their roles in class–society, the values, ideas and images which tie them to their social functions and so prevent them from a true knowledge of society as a whole' (Eagleton 1976: 16–17). Alongside Althusser, Habermas' (1984) conceptions of 'emancipatory knowledge' and its revelation in individual 'lifeworlds' influenced critical archaeologies of landscape both implicitly (Leone 1996; Leone et al. 1987) and explicitly (A. Wylie 2002). Habermas saw the potentially liberating value of knowledge as resulting from self-reflection and a conscious awareness of the presence and workings of ideology as a social construct. Thus, critical archaeologists aimed to study how ideology is made manifest through communicative action in the material world – whether at outdoor living-history museums, towns, or gardens (Handsman and Leone 1989; A. Wylie 1985). These archaeologists sought to perceive and pierce the ideology in landscapes, thereby revealing their status as illusions and the structural inequalities at their base.

More recently, Henri Lefebvre's (1991) extensions of analytical Marxism to urbanism and the realm of everyday life, and geographer Edward Soja's (1989) development of Lefebvrian notions of the relationships between space and time, have influenced archaeologists working in the critical tradition. Soja formulated concepts of 'spatiality' and 'spatial trialectics' to explore the social production of space, viewing 'human spatiality [a]s the product of both human agency and environmental or contextual structuring' (Soja 2000: 6). Historical archaeologists such as James Delle (1998: 40–43) and Barbara Little (1988: 228) have cited Lefebvre and Soja in their studies of landscape and the ideologies of modernity in global capitalism. The influence of the Frankfurt School, read through the perspectives of critical archaeologists, continues to resonate throughout historical archaeologies of landscape (but see review by Wilkie and Bartoy 2000).

North American critical historical archaeologies of landscape responded to processualism's focus on cultural ecology and nomothetic reasoning (e.g. South 1977a, 1977b). In his influential study of 'spatial inequality', Robert Paynter (1982) sought to determine the geographical scale at which historical archaeologists might most profitably examine relations of inequality. His study of regional patterning in early nineteenth-century western Massachusetts stressed that settlement patterning both reflects and reinforces the maintenance of social stratification. Ideology, he argued, served to 'legitimize leaders, establish law for dispute resolution . . . and suggest "natural" justifications for inequality' (Paynter 1982: 22). His study aimed to use empirically grounded spatial data to reveal how Massachusetts leaders built inequalities directly onto the landscape.

In the same year, a group of archaeologists based at the University of Maryland, College Park, launched the Archaeology in Annapolis programme (see also McGuire this volume, O'Keeffe and Yamin this volume). Strongly influenced by Cambridge-based archaeologists who were studying power and domination through ideology (Miller and Tilley 1984; Shanks and Tilley 1982), they aimed to demonstrate the range of means by which 'material culture can be used to express interests and ideas which may very well be contradictory' (Miller and Tilley 1984: vii). From the 1980s, Archaeology in Annapolis examined landscapes at a range of scales: from individual houselots and the gardens surrounding those houses, to urban neighbourhoods and the Baroque town plan of Annapolis, Maryland (Leone 2005; Leone and Shackel 1990; Leone et al. 1989). They have mapped, analysed, and interpreted several Annapolis gardens, viewing them as symbolic statements that employed elaborate geometrical principles to address and redress social relations (Leone 1988b, 1996; Leone and Shackel 1990; Kryder-Reid 1994).

Leone's (1996 [1984]) early work focused on the 1760s terraced garden of patriot and later governor William Paca. He aimed to provide an alternative to garden historians' studies of single sites, which emphasised the historical evolution of garden and landscape styles rather than their wider social and material histories (Leone 2005: 66–67). Moving beyond the study of aesthetics and the details of planting, Leone sought the garden's meaning or purpose as it related to the social history of eighteenth-century Annapolis. For Leone, the Paca garden was part of a strategy in élite social and political negotiations that worked to demonstrate a mastery of the natural world. Through illusions built into the garden, Leone argued, Paca deployed a naturalising ideology that masked the unequal social relations that lay behind his wealth, presenting them as timeless and rooted in the natural world (Leone 1988b: 33). Where James Deetz had emphasised the increasing importance of the individual within an evolving Georgian worldview, Leone has described his approach as one that studies the emergence of a 'possessive individualism' (Leone 2005: 34) – a distinctive set of new attitudes to material culture and individuals that involved a mastery of skills and abilities meant for public display – that accompanied the shift from merchant to industrial capitalism. It was 'a function of capitalism and historically of the production process of early industrialization, where people constantly had to remake themselves' (Leone 2005: 154). For Leone, possessive individualism's deliberate manipulation of the material world was visible through historical archaeology in designed landscapes such as the Paca garden landscapes.

Many archaeologists have criticised Leone's use of Althusserian notions of ideology in his study of the Paca garden (Hodder 1986; Beaudry et al. 1991; see review in Hicks 2005). Alternative studies have understood ideology in historical landscapes as subject to individuals' and groups' diverse conceptions, and therefore as situated and contested (cf. J. S. Thomas 2000b: 11). Since these debates several archaeologists working in the critical tradition have responded to such critiques in their studies of landscape and ideology. Most prominent here is the work of Barbara Little, Christopher Matthews and Mark Leone in Annapolis, and that of Charles Orser, James Delle and Terrence Epperson conducted at other sites.

In her work in Annapolis, Barbara Little challenged earlier applications of the dominant ideology hypothesis while simultaneously employing 'multilocal' approaches (Rodman 1992). She engendered the landscape of craft in colonial Annapolis by studying the home and workplace of Anne Catherine Green, the widow of Jonas Green and his successor as printer to the colony. Drawing inspiration from Soja's (1989) understanding of spatiality, Little (1998: 228) formulated the concept of *printscape*. This unique approach not only integrated time and space on the Green's property at 124 Charles Street, but also detailed diachronic change on and within the pages of the *Maryland Gazette*. Little documented and contextualised Anne Catherine Green's reconnection of home and printshop – a significant reorganisation of the spatial relationships between domesticity and craft which her husband and many contemporaries had worked hard to separate – and interpreted Green's actions as a rejection of the emerging dominant ideology. Little's study focused upon ideology in landscape, but strove to highlight the agency of women such as Green, who represented those who had been muted, rather than depicting powerlessness. Through her analysis, Little argued for a multi-sited, integrated analysis of the dynamic relations between home and work, between products and the spaces of production, between householder and business owner, and between public and private spheres.

Christopher Matthews' work similarly exemplifies the new directions and multi-scalar approaches of more recent developments in the Archaeology in Annapolis project. At the Bordley-Randall property, Matthews critiqued the notion of Annapolis' 'Golden Age', extending Little's approach to probe the opposition between modernity and tradition over the long term. His work explored how multiple generations selectively inscribed *their* version of past events on the land in order to achieve social aspirations (Matthews 2002: 31–50, 84–88, 92–97, 113–129). As with Little's study of the Green family's printshop and houselot, Matthews studied a private property just off State Circle (originally known as Public Circle) on which the Maryland State House was constructed in the 1770s. While acknowledging his intellectual debt to Althusserian Marxism, Matthews highlighted the agency of ordinary Annapolitans, visible in the archaeological record as they reworked the landscape.

Alongside such innovative responses to the interpretive critiques of Hodder, Beaudry and others, the influence of critical approaches to the archaeology of landscape and ideology has also persisted in 'archaeologies of capitalism' inspired by the work of Matthew Johnson (1996), Mark Leone (1995) and Robert Paynter (1988). Such work has emphasised the contested nature of epistemological ideologies in designed landscapes, most commonly through the study of the plantations and escaped-slave communities of North America, the Caribbean, and South America. Thus, Charles Orser's (e.g. 1988) studies of plantation landscapes have emphasised the role of spatial arrangements in unequal power relations, and have been extended into places 'dedicated to resistance and rebellion' such as maroon settlements (Orser and Funari 2001: 63). Similarly, James Delle's work on nineteenth-century Jamaican coffee plantations has sought to unravel both the racist ideology that maintained the inequalities of slavery, and the acts of resistance that sought to fracture this system (Delle 1998, 2000b). Delle has envisaged the manipulation of designed spaces as a 'set of active forces' during capitalist crises, emphasising surveillance, confinement and restriction of movement as forms of Foucauldian 'spatial discipline'.

While such studies have aimed to locate resistance as well as oppression, their models of power bound up in contests of spatial ideologies have moved away from contextual accounts of archaeological sites to an approach that makes more scholastic uses of historical landscapes and historical maps. Through maps and plans, Delle analysed coffee planters' *conceptions* of space, but his discussions of plantation landscapes remain purely descriptive. Studies such as Delle's seek to illustrate wider social and historical processes, but provide little sense of how archaeology can explore the particular materialities that these processes constituted in specific situations.

More promising is Terrence Epperson's (2000) application of a more nuanced Foucauldian perspective in his consideration of the 'panoptic' in landscapes (after Foucault 1979). Epperson's microanalyses of George Mason's and Thomas Jefferson's use of point-perspective landscape manipulation at Gunston Hall and Monticello plantations reveals their purpose as observation posts. Building upon postprocessual studies of dominance and resistance (e.g. D. Miller et al. 1989) by studying surveillance in the plantation landscape, in his study of Gunston Hall Epperson inverts John Rajchman's (2000: 64) notion of 'spaces of constructed visibility' by considering 'spaces of constructed invisibility'. Epperson's reformulation of the materiality of surveillance represents a conscious effort to resituate critical theory within discussions of art and design philosophy as applied to the built environment, and produces a less deterministic interpretation. Epperson identified this shift, or redirection, when explaining that while others have focused on the assertion of social or political legitimacy or the imposition of spatial discipline, 'I . . . focus our gaze upon the subjectivity of the eye/I that constructs and controls these landscapes' (2000: 60). This notion of subjectivity on the part of the constructor of such landscapes, and by implication quite probably also the visitors to such spaces, represents a break with previous models of domination and resistance and a movement toward reinserting aesthetics into archaeologists' considerations of the social implications of landscape and the built environment.

Critiques of critical archaeology's conceptions of landscape (since Hodder 1986) have led to attempts by historical archaeologists to find alternatives to 'top-down', totalising models of social change, and quite profitably through more relational approaches that incorporate multiple perspectives and dimensions (Hicks 2005: 383–388; Wilkie and Bartoy 2000: 749). Some responses have used documentary and material sources to explore landscape imagined as text or image deployed in 'negotiated' social relations. Often, however, these approaches serve to smooth out the inherent ambiguities, contradictions, and incoherences in created landscapes, emphasising only purpose and 'power' (De Cunzo 2006; Hicks 2005: 386; Spencer-Wood 2001: 102; Tarlow 2000a). In contrast, a distinctive body of work in 'interpretive' archaeologies of landscape has emerged within historical archaeology.

INTERPRETIVE ARCHAEOLOGIES OF HISTORICAL LANDSCAPES

Critical and interpretive historical archaeologies share a dissatisfaction with the functionalist, evolutionary ecology born of the new archaeology or processualism of the 1960s and 1970s. Influenced by Deetz's (1977) structuralism and Hodder's (1986) contextual archaeology, interpretive archaeologists have emphasised the ethnographic dimensions of historical archaeology. Some interpretive work on landscape, best exemplified by Tracey Ireland and Martin Hall, has continued to work within the frameworks set by critical archaeologies.

Critical theory informed Tracey Ireland's (2003) study of the archaeology of discourses of 'land' in Australia, but she also underscored the need for a reflexive awareness of the situations in which modern understandings of land have emerged. For Euro-Australians, landscape acted 'as a determinant of not only the course of colonial history but also of the distinctive characteristics of national identity' (Ireland 2003: 56). The ideology of colonialism in Australia, Ireland argued, constructed the 'land as the prime object of desire' (Ireland 2003: 59), portraying it as a hostile environment that the 'bushman' – the masculine ideal – battled to tame. The bushman represented the nation conquering the 'other', the land – the desired, possessed, tamed feminine body – of Australia (Ireland 2003: 60–61). Archaeologists have helped to 'historicize and perpetuate this colonial act of possession', Ireland concluded, through the stories they tell and the landscapes they choose to research and preserve as the material locations of the nation's heritage. In contrast with critical archaeologies, Ireland aimed to reveal multilocal, multidimensional landscapes crossed by a network of paths 'leading in all directions, towards untold stories' (Ireland 2003: 68).

Similarly, Martin Hall's studies of the consequences of European trading companies' global interests in South Africa and the Chesapeake engaged with many key themes of critical archaeology, but aimed to avoid obscuring the contexts of daily interactions. Hall studied landscapes, buildings and objects as public 'transcripts' involved with the exercise of power, alongside 'hidden transcripts' of resistance viewed through Homi Bhabha's notion of a 'third space' – 'a zone of uncertainty and ambiguity' (M. Hall 2000: 21). He sought to 'capture a particular quality of being' (M. Hall 2000: 15) through the analysis of material culture and landscape. Focusing especially upon town plans, houses and gardens, he described material metaphors inscribed with clear and substantial, but also deniable, meanings contested in performances staged within them (M. Hall 2000: 70, 85, 96–97, cf. M. Hall 1992). Gardens could embody sexual ambiguity through their functions as places in which to grow food, marking the success of men's labour but dependent on female fecundity. In colonial contexts rife with indigenous and enslaved women, the dangers of female sexuality became heightened, and some landscapes were idealised as an untamed woman to be controlled by man (M. Hall 2000: 46). Hall suggested that these interpenetrating ideologies of gender, race, and sexuality continued to influence the late twentieth-century South African landscape of apartheid. In his insightful examination of Cape Town's District Six as an appropriated and contested 'heritage' landscape of memory, Hall demonstrated the difficulties of segmenting ideology and memory in current landscape theory (M. Hall 2000: 151–176).

While the interpretive work of Ireland and Hall continued to operate within the frameworks set out by critical archaeologies of landscape, the work of Beaudry (1989b) and Mrozowski et al. (1989) in mid-nineteenth-century Lowell, Massachusetts has drawn upon broader interpretive approaches in sociocultural anthropology. Their work examined the intersections between industrial capitalism and the ideology of corporate paternalism in the town's landscape, exemplified by their assessment of health and sanitary conditions in the company-owned workers' and managers' houses. Detailed analysis of documentary sources alongside the archaeological evidence led them to conclude that

the corporations evolved from a public 'benevolent' paternalism, to a begrudging acceptance of limited responsibility and maintenance of workers' housing to a time when the corporations divested their interests in housing the workforce. (Mrozowski et al. 1989: 308)

Rather than simply presenting this 'top-down' interpretation of an all-powerful corporation and victimised workers, these scholars described highly personal landscapes: workers' personal hygiene practices, their self-presentation in the public landscapes of the city, their efforts to shape the boardinghouse landscapes, and their appropriation of 'out-of-sight' spaces in the yard for drinking and disposing of alcohol bottles.

Anne Yentsch's historical ethnography of eighteenth-century Annapolis, *A Chesapeake Family and their Slaves* (1994), adopted a similar approach to landscape. A former co-director of the Archaeology in Annapolis project, Yentsch combined Deetz's structural frameworks (Deetz 1977) with the 'thick description' of Geertzian ethnography (Geertz 1973) in her study of Maryland's proprietary family, the Calverts (Yentsch 1994). Yentsch examined continuity and change in the worldviews of the eighteenth-century Anglo-colonial world through multiple material sources. She described the material dimensions of trends toward privacy, individualism, separation, segregation, order and symmetry that have been associated with the emergence of the Georgian worldview (Deetz 1977; Leone et al. 1987; see also Hicks and Horning this volume). Yentsch (1994: 82) considered how colonial Annapolitans transformed their urban landscapes from 'space' into 'place'. Landscapes were tools with which people created and maintained the 'visual images of authority' and social order on which power was based, by sculpting and nurturing possessed land into formal gardens ornamenting monumental architecture. For Yentsch, the vocabulary of elements that élite Annapolitans deployed in the landscape communicated cultural mastery through the symbolic control of nature to create vistas and boundaries and reference the values of the exotic, antiquity, and classicism. By also emphasising how women, enslaved Africans, and working people acted and interacted in the urban landscape, Yentsch evoked the diversities and materialities of the performance of landscapes.

Diana Wall (1994) examined the historical archaeology of postcolonial transformations in American urban culture. Focusing on middle-class women, the restructuring of gender roles, and the construction of the ideology of 'domesticity', Wall described how in early nineteenth-century New York, population growth intensified the movement to separate home and work, concentrating work in a central business district, and segregating residence based on class. Wall described how structuralist perspectives suggest that new ideologies of gender were visible in distinctions between the home (female/private/traditional/reciprocal labour) and workplace (male/public/commercial/modern/commodified labour), but emphasised how middle-class women participated actively in constructing this new world. Like Yentsch, Wall rejected 'top-down' analyses in which powerful men imposed an ideology that imprisoned women in the private, sanctified landscape of the moral home. Importantly, she argued that changes in gender practices *preceded* their spatial representation in the separated landscapes of work and home.

Meanwhile, in Sydney, Australia, Grace Karskens began her archaeological work also expecting the ideology of 'domesticity' to have informed architecture, landscapes, and material life in the nineteenth-century working-class neighbourhood, 'the Rocks'. The complexities of her findings in the field, however, led her to reconsider Deetzian structuralist perspectives. She came to understand the worldview of the Rocks' inhabitants 'as a complex palimpsest of . . . new and old, compatible and contradictory' (Karskens 2003: 51). She problematised the middle-class, Victorian portrayal of this working-class landscape as a 'slum'. Observers, she concluded, did not so much misrepresent the neighbourhood's poorly maintained physical landscape as imbue it with the moral ideology that tainted the mostly Irish Catholic and Chinese residents with the corruption of filth and disease. Inside the tenements, she documented a contradictory landscape of consumption, domestic comfort and cleanliness. To make sense of these interior landscapes, Karskens (2002: 77) turned away from notions of dominant ideology, 'in which cultural identity was *exclusively* a site for struggle and inevitable domination'. She explained the shared and the distinctive personal elements of genteel culture as products of an ideology of 'aspiration'.

Also with a focus on the Victorian era, the feminist work of Suzanne Spencer-Wood (1996, 2003) has examined the materialities of women's 'domestic' landscape work. She has drawn archaeologists' attention to nineteenth- and early twentieth-century reform movements and their vision of women's rights and economic independence. In the 1980s, Spencer-Wood began research in Boston and Cambridge, Massachusetts with the understanding that urban reform landscapes worked as 'active social agents' (Spencer-Wood 1996: 407). She documented the ways in which women reasserted their moral reach beyond the home to domesticate the public landscapes of the nation's cities through their 'clean and green' efforts. In so doing, she argued, they manipulated dominant ideologies to reclaim physical, economic, and symbolic spaces for themselves even as they worked to beautify America's urban landscapes.

In California Adrian and Mary Praetzellis (A. Praetzellis and M. Praetzellis 1992; M. Praetzellis 2001; M. Praetzellis and A. Praetzellis 2004) have examined 'modernising' Victorian ideologies in the urban landscapes of the

American West. Their work has exposed the range of options for action and reaction in West Oakland, the structure capitalism imposed, and the ways corporate capitalists and diverse middle- and working-class producers and consumers negotiated the world as *they* understood it. Their interpretations have challenged the hegemony of modernisation, globalisation, materialist aspirations, and the seeming inevitability with which these replaced other ways of being, knowing, and relating in the world. By studying landscapes, objects, and the people dwelling on and with them together, this kind of historical archaeology aims to demonstrate how everyone's history 'matters'.

EXPERIENCED AND ENACTED LANDSCAPES

From the mid-1970s, Clifford Geertz's (1973: 5) semiotic view of cultures as 'webs of significance' promoted a new emphasis upon meaning in sociocultural anthropology (Stahl 2002: 829) and provided crucial inspiration for the interpretive archaeologies of landscape described above. Critics of these interpretive historical archaeologies have argued that a neoliberal individualism underlies some of the searches for human agency in these 'human the meaning-maker' approaches (Mullins 2000: 767; Orser 2000: 768; J. S. Thomas 2000a: 770). Archaeologist Ann Stahl (2002: 829) has observed how such approaches remain deeply rooted in a Cartesian mind–body duality, privileging linguistic signification in the search for meaning. Such logocentrism certainly characterised the structuralist 'worldviews' of Deetzian historical archaeologists to which many interpretive landscape studies continue to owe a great debt: distinguishing male from female, wild from tame, public from private, and so on. In the past two decades, alternative perspectives in the historical archaeology of landscape have challenged the primacy of language, meaning and material culture as text, seeking to reunify mind and body in an archaeology of embodied experience.

In 1978, before critical historical archaeologies linked material landscapes with dominant ideologies, British social historian E. P. Thompson challenged Althusserian Marxism and called for a return to the study of individual human 'experience' (Thompson 1978: 167, cited in Wilkie and Bartoy 2000: 749). Similar concerns with experience have gained increasing attention within historical archaeology. As Dell Upton has reminded historical archaeologists,

Our experience of the material world is complex and multisensory; it is a reverberating, constantly permutating tangle of I–it/it–me relationships, and it must be studied on all these levels. (1992: 52–53)

Since the 1980s, some historical archaeologies of landscape have explored
enactment, dwelling, taskscapes, inscription and other concepts in order to
achieve a better understanding of how ideology works as embodied practice.
Such work has been strongly influenced by British studies in European
prehistory, especially since Christopher Tilley's (1994) *A Phenomenology of
Landscape* and British prehistorian Julian Thomas' (1996) use of Martin
Heidegger's (1962) concept 'being-in-the-world'. For Thomas (1996: 19),
human knowledge, of landscapes for instance, is constituted only through
'our bodily engagement with' or 'immersion in' our world. Fundamental
spatial ordering centres on the human body. In this 'experiential space'
(J. S. Thomas 1996: 86), humans build intimate relationships with the
spaces they 'inhabit' in everyday life, transforming these spaces into places,
experiencing these spaces sequentially, and ordering them into narrative
sequences or pathways. Individuals' paths cross, but different experiential
sequences produce different understandings and meanings of place.

Anthropologist Tim Ingold has also influenced this new phenomenology
of landscape in historical archaeology. In a classic essay, Ingold emphasised the temporality of landscape as the key to moving beyond the 'sterile opposition' of the natural landscapes as 'neutral, external' backdrops to
human activities, and cultural landscapes as particular 'cognitive or symbolic
orderings of space' (Ingold 2000a [1993]: 510). Ingold describes embodied
'taskscapes' – heard, seen, enacted and interacted (Ingold 2000a [1993]: 511,
519–520). This view captures the evanescence and lack of fixity of 'temporality' as performed and experienced through the life-course of the self, other
people, plants, animals and 'inanimate' things such as buildings (Ingold
2000a [1993]: 526–528).

In historical archaeology, Carmel Schrire (1995: 1) has wedded critical,
interpretive and these experiential approaches in her provocative and radical
study of 'the history and consequences of colonialism and racism', *Digging
Through Darkness* (Schrire 1995: 1). Examining the archaeology of European
colonial endeavours in South Africa and Australia, Schrire (1995: 1) employs
acts of imagination to express the long-term impacts of European global
expansion on the landscape and the 'lives of those people who endured
it' (cf. Joyce this volume). European colonial ideologies of ownership and
racism were often used to justify acts of violence against people and land. The
emotional power of imagined experience leads Schrire to try to reanimate
the local material worlds of filth, pain, and disorder, of both colonised and
coloniser, in the past and in the present. She evokes inhabited landscape, in
which meanings emerge through sensory enactments of home, exotic places
and bodies, and violated spaces.

Other feminist archaeologists, such as Marie Louise Stig Sørensen (2000) and Lynn Meskell (1996) have also turned to embodiment, often informed by the work of Heidegger (cf. J. S. Thomas 1996) and Maurice Merleau-Ponty (1969). The influence of such work is particularly visible in historical archaeologies of institutions in colonial situations, which have addressed the culture and economy of capitalism, and relationships of power in the modern world, through embodied practice.

De Cunzo's (1995, 2001) interest in the historical archaeology of institutional landscapes began with a study of the Magdalen Society Asylum in Philadelphia, Pennsylvania, established in 1800 for 'fallen' women. Like its contemporaries, the asylum not only offered a temporary home to 'fallen' women, but also aimed to reform the soul and to retrain the body's work, and the asylum's landscape participated in each. The society located the asylum to isolate it from the environmental and social defilement and temptation of the Magdalen's former neighbourhoods. High fences and later a wall enclosed the asylum grounds, ensuring former associates could not seek out the inmates. Its rural setting and the garden maintained within the asylum's enclosure surrounded the Magdalens with nature's purity. The rites of passage performed at the asylum effected a change in a young woman's moral state, her social position, and her cultural milieu. The process of ritual separation from her previous life and identity began with a woman's removal to the asylum. Within the asylum walls, a strict daily routine inscribed the practices and identities of new life as women differentially enacted the landscape's 'social hierarchy' – kitchen, laundry, dining room, bedroom, exercise yard, garden. Women contested these ideologies of class and moral motherhood by refusing to enter the asylum landscape, escaping from it, and appropriating goods and spaces within it for their own purposes.

Eleanor Conlin Casella (2001a, 2001b) has expanded this emphasis on the experiential dynamic of the encounters between reformer and to-be-reformed in her studies of Tasmania's female factories (i.e. workhouses). She has masterfully evoked the ideological topography of female convicts negotiating nineteenth-century Victorian gender ideals on the Anglo-Australian colonial frontier. Readers follow the women up and down the landscape, encountering walls that constrained movement and grated windows that framed views, and feeling the textures of wool garments and cold water. Casella (2001a: 105–106, 110–111) revealed the strictly ordered, regulated procession through the factory that 'meticulously choreographed' women's reformation. She also uncovered a coexisting, alternative geography that transgressed the procession of reform and the isolation of semi-subterranean, cramped, dark, silent cells (Casella 2001b: 57–58, 62–63). Like Julian Thomas

(1996: 19), Casella views power as embedded, but not fixed, in the landscape, and recoverable through detailed attention to materiality and context.

These studies by Casella and De Cunzo borrow a Foucauldian understanding of institutions' social-control functions. These arguments are convincing, and yet are not quite enough. Meskell's (1996: 9) work on 'somatisation' highlights the essentialism and reductionism that such models risk: selling short individuals' life experiences and produce self-fulfilling, over-simplified understandings of society. Concepts of ritual had served such work well in studies of institutions as landscapes of reform and transformation, but the privileging of the larger social body in discussions of ritualised negotiations of gender are problematic. The performance of ritual acts on the *individual* body embodies meanings that thought alone cannot frame. The materiality of ritual spaces shapes both the actions and perceptions that become 'sedimented' via routine (Sørensen 2000: 145–149). Such embodied perspectives describe people and things in action, refusing the choice between societal or individual approaches (Meskell 1996: 5, 14; Sørensen 2000: 152). They aim to avoid reducing the body to a 'product of representations' and neglecting the individual 'deviant' within the institution, as Foucault did. Archaeology is well situated to study these individual, embodied histories, which extend beyond the time spent in the institution, to people's lifetimes of practice and performances (Meskell 1996: 8; see also Casella 2002: 77–78). In the historical archaeology of landscapes, the individual must become more than a narrative trope or an illustration: he or she must be human subject and analytical object.

Individual life-worlds and their complex physicalities constitute human reality. Each of us makes our own: appropriating, acting on, and transforming the 'world-out-there' into a lived reality that is not reducible to single meanings. Beyond the boundaries of the institution, De Cunzo has examined the landscapes created by farming people in Delaware, which lie at the heart of their 'cultures of agriculture' (De Cunzo 2004). This work examines how through their everyday practices, the routine and the non-routine, farming people worked out global processes. Farming people dwell in the land as they come together, act upon it, and move through it in the process of completing the tasks of cultivation. With their rhythmic actions and interactions, people create taskscapes in which communities form, work, and disperse. Historical archaeology does not merely follow people from task to task, or place to place: it seeks to understand how past experiences, social engagements, expectations, and outcomes continually recreate each taskscape. Dwelling is more than a hierarchically arranged, logocentric set of dichotomies, and more than visual metaphors of surveillance or masking can capture: it is at once situational, cumulative and material (see also Casey 1996; Stahl 2002).

These experiential perspectives present historical archaeologists with new challenges. Critical archaeologist Paul Mullins (2000: 767) has argued that a

phenomenological vision of self-empowered individuals . . . elevate[s] the 'individual' – itself an ideological abstraction – to a position that is, at best, loosely related to power relations, . . . and shifts deterministic power from the economy to the constructed notion of 'experience'.

Julian Thomas (2000a: 770) shares Mullins' concern with approaches that accept the 'individual' as a universal, transhistorical category. These critiques, however, serve to conflate agency with the individual, denying that agency emerged from situated social relations – from contexts. They encourage us to find empathy, or identification, with the historical subjects that we study. But 'we are not them', and archaeologists are unable to understand landscapes as people experienced them in the past (Barrett 2000: 762).

These critiques underscore the contemporary nature of the archaeological study of historical landscapes such as the eighteenth-century gardens in Prince George's County, Maryland, examined by Ernstein (2004). Ernstein worked outward from the specifics of five landscapes constructed between 1740 and 1790 to demonstrate that eighteenth-century landscaping was a field of social action in which the landed, the landless, and the many in between engaged in an ongoing process of self-fashioning and place-making (Ernstein 2004: 35–87). In adopting a 'layered' approach to enacted landscapes, Ernstein argues that the professional necessity of diachronic analysis and a commitment to advocacy for recent past resources emerges (Ernstein 1998, 2000; Ernstein et al. 2005; see also Schofield and Johnson this volume).

These increasingly sophisticated and nuanced interpretive and ethnographic studies of embodied landscapes in historical archaeology have much in common with recent developments in cultural anthropology and cultural geography, especially in the study of walking in landscapes (Lorimer and Lund 2003; J. Wylie 2002; see also Cochran and Beaudry this volume). Cultural anthropologist Wendy Darby (2000) has examined the politics of access to the countryside in England's Peak and Lake Districts, likening her approach to that of a Foucauldian archaeology of landscape because it 'shows how people literally in the same place can inhabit figuratively quite different places' (Darby 2000: 9). By incorporating detailed historical research alongside participant observation among hiking groups, Darby carefully contextualised these landscapes in terms of changing notions of British nationalism, the popularisation of the picturesque, and the changing politics of enclosure and access. By examining the material and social relations of hiking, Darby (2000: 250) connected individual lives with broader social contexts in a similar manner to that proposed in recent historical archaeologies of embodied landscape.

CONCLUDING THOUGHTS

Since the 1970s, historical archaeologists of landscape have developed a diverse range of approaches to ideology and individual and group experience. Such genuine pluralism (Funari 2000: 765) and avoidance of what might be construed as an 'ideology of orthodoxy' (Williamson 1993, 1995, 2005; Williamson and Bellamy 1987) is a strength of the field, despite the calls by some for unity and homogeneity in theory and practice (e.g. Cleland 2001; Orser 1988). Historical archaeologies are increasingly contributing to transnational and transdisciplinary debates over ideology, power, resistance, meaning and experience in landscapes. Critical archaeologies of landscape have cast into relief issues of control over access to places, resources, people and goods. Archaeologies of class, race, gender, ethnic, and other inequalities in colonial and postcolonial societies have highlighted the role of landscapes and material culture in such processes, linking people in complex social and economic networks infused with acts of resistance and rejection. By studying the materiality of how landscapes are enacted, historical archaeologists increasingly bring distinctive perspectives to bear upon the landscapes investigated by colleagues in cultural geography, sociocultural anthropology and other disciplines. Taking seriously the partiality of historical landscapes, and how they are enacted in the past and in the present, historical archaeologists will continue to build upon the intensive work on landscapes since the 1970s, and to make increasingly significant interdisciplinary contributions.

PART V

Historical archaeology and buildings

CHAPTER 15

Historical archaeology and buildings

Dan Hicks and Audrey Horning

The emphasis upon buildings in the present volume – which includes chapters on the archaeology of cities and households as well as this chapter on buildings archaeology – will surprise some historical archaeologists. For many, studying the historical built environment is the field of architectural and art historians, historical geographers or local historians, and the buried remains of structures encountered by archaeologists are often seen as of less significance than the artefacts recovered from buried deposits associated with them. Thus, the study of buildings is virtually invisible in some overviews of historical archaeology (e.g. Orser and Fagan 1995), the field instead being explored in surveys of vernacular architecture studies (e.g. Glassie 2000; Lanier and Herman 1997). For others, aware of the importance of a more integrated archaeology of buildings, whether in interpretations of Neolithic Europe (Hodder 1990) or descriptions of medieval Britain (Platt 1990; Grenville 1997), such perspectives appear strangely limited. Moreover, despite the relative silence on the study of buildings in mainstream literature on historical archaeology, building remains – whether surviving above ground or below ground as wall foundations, floor surfaces or post holes – have been a major focus in research and cultural-resource management by historical archaeologists around the world, employing a diversity of perspectives and with a range of methods, over the past forty years.

This chapter takes stock of some of this material. We argue that built structures represent a highly significant part of the material remains of the past five hundred years, the study of which deserves to be integrated with the analysis of sites, artefacts and landscapes. We view the field's potential for transdisciplinary contributions to studies of relationships of humans with the built environment as a significant opportunity. Considering the diversity of work in historical archaeology, the chapter provides a brief sketch of the emergence of the study of buildings by historical archaeologists working in two regions: the eastern United States and the United Kingdom. Some of the distinctive interpretive approaches through which historical archaeologists

have built upon such studies are then discussed. In a final section archaeological alternatives to the 'bounded' study of buildings, especially through
biographical and relational approaches that explore distributions across time
and space, are explored.

THE EMERGENCE OF THE ARCHAEOLOGY OF HISTORICAL BUILDINGS IN THE UNITED STATES AND BRITAIN

In North America, especially at sites in New England and Virginia, developments in historical archaeology and the study of standing historic buildings
have been closely associated. The second half of the nineteenth century witnessed occasional studies of buried structural remains – such as James Hall's
exposing in 1853 of the cellar foundations of the home of Miles Standish in
Duxbury, Massachusetts (Beaudry et al. 2003: 155; Deetz 1971: 209). Much
more widespread than such excavations, however, was the development of
preservation efforts. Preservation organisations, such as the Mount Vernon
Ladies Association (founded 1853), the Association for the Preservation of
Virginia Antiquities (founded in the 1890s), and the Society for the Preservation of New England Antiquities (founded 1911) argued for the national
importance of their standing, or reconstructed, historic structures. While
these were most commonly the homes of notable settlers, they were also normally relatively ordinary houses that happened to survive rather than polite
houses of great distinction. These interests developed quickly with the 'colonial revival movement', which emerged in a period of significant shifts in
industry and immigration in New England and the South, and which was
characterised by the imagination of a 'colonial' period far removed from
such contemporary concerns. Between the 1930s and 1960s, at various sites
in Virginia and New England, dual interests in early colonial America and
the preservation of historic buildings came together in new projects in historical archaeology – most famously at Williamsburg and nearby Jamestown,
Virginia. Colonial Williamsburg opened to the public in 1932, and today
includes a 173-acre 'historic area' – 'the reconstructed capital of the colony of
Virginia at the dawn of the American Revolution', which has been recreated
according to archaeological and documentary evidence (Brown and Samford
1994; cf. Gable and Handler 2000: 237; Leone 1981b). Until the increase in
development-funded excavations from the 1980s, virtually all North American historical archaeology was carried out at well-defined sites with standing
buildings – especially forts and other sites pertaining to the American Revolution, contact-period European and native-American sites, and especially
the settlement sites of early French, Spanish and English exploration.

The developments at Colonial Williamsburg and the burgeoning historic preservation movement inspired the use of excavation to aid in the reconstruction of buildings associated with people who were perceived as historically significant – in practice, these were almost without fail white, male patriots. Landscape architect Morley Jeffers Williams' excavations at the home of George Washington at Mount Vernon, Virginia, during the 1930s are perhaps the most notable example of this approach (Singleton 1990: 70). With the 'New Deal' establishment of the Historic American Buildings Survey (HABS) in 1934, however, and the influence of individuals such as geographer Fred Kniffen (1936), alternative traditions in historic buildings preservation continued to highlight the significance of the vernacular buildings of ordinary people, while at Williamsburg the foundations of the Governor's Palace of 1722 were exposed to great fanfare between 1930 and 1932, and architects and workers funded by the philanthropic donations of John D. Rockefeller, laboured to make Reverend W. A. R. Goodwin's dream of a reborn colonial capital a reality. At nearby Jamestown, HABS architects crowded in to examine and record the brick buildings that were being unearthed at a feverish pace by crews of African-American Civilian Conservation Corps volunteers (Cotter 1958, cf. Cotter 1957). At Jamestown and Williamsburg, reconstruction, preservation and the exposure of brick buildings great and small through excavation created a new 'historic' landscape of buildings (D. Brown 1998; Horning 2000).

In Britain, the emergence of historical buildings archaeology was strongly influenced by the developments in local history in the post-war period of growth, which also led to the emergence of British industrial archaeology (Symonds and Casella this volume). It drew upon late nineteenth-century impulses towards the preservation of old houses, especially in rural areas: impulses which often drew upon the perspectives of William Morris and John Ruskin, and included the establishment of the Society for the Protection of Ancient Buildings in 1877 and the National Trust in 1895 (W. Morris 1877; Ruskin 1849; cf. Lowenthal 2005: 83–85). The classic study of fifteenth-, sixteenth- and seventeenth-century houses in Monmouthshire, Wales by Sir Cyril Fox and Lord Raglan (Fox and Raglan 1951–1954) was a seminal work for this field, radically combining fieldwork with documentary research, and attending to post-medieval houses other than those polite structures built by known architects. Indeed, these volumes set the tone for an intensive period of activity during the next twenty-five years in which, as Robert Machin put it, 'archaeological work . . . far outstripped historical investigation' of traditional houses, 'buil[ding] an imposing structure on the foundations of *Monmouthshire Houses*' (Machin 1977: 34). During the 1960s and 1970s, more and more local studies aimed to define and to refine typologies, in order to discern regional traditions (see especially Brunskill 1974; E. Mercer 1975; J. T. Smith 1965; Wood-Jones 1963). At the same time, similar concerns with typology characterised the study of American buildings: Abbott Lowell Cummings' (1979) careful studies of New England's seventeenth-century domestic structures inspired a generation of scholars, and regional and typological concerns continue to frame the vast majority of work in historical buildings archaeology.

In Britain, while the descriptive surveys were sometimes 'insipid' (Johnson 1990: 246), such work not only continues to be important in providing sound data sets for studies of vernacular architecture, but also was crucial to the emergence of a distinctive set of methods for researching and recording standing buildings. This methodology integrated historical map regression with photographic and measured drawn survey and written description, at times including specialist analysis such as architectural paint analysis or dendrochronology (Clark 2001: 72–89; see N. W. Alcock et al. 1996; Andrews et al. 1995; T. Buchanan 1983; Morriss 2000: 118–150; J. Wood 1994). The systematic recording of standing building types by the Royal Commission on Historical Monuments led to a series of highly detailed volumes, most notably the surveys of the industrial buildings of the Staffordshire potteries (Baker 1991) and the Birmingham jewellery quarter (Cattell et al. 2002). The use of dendrochronology in dating standing buildings is also employed in North America, most recently through the work of the Oxford Dendrochronology Laboratory (2005; see also Cummings 2004). From an early date, another important aspect of British practice was the exploration of the remains of buildings through survey of their earthwork remains – most famously in historian Maurice Beresford and archaeologist John Hurst's classic study of the remains of *Deserted Medieval Villages* (1971) – settlements abandoned, often during the early post-medieval period, through urbanisation or agricultural change. The development of church archaeology, from the work of figures such as Reverend John Willis during the last quarter of the nineteenth century, also influenced the development of the study of post-medieval buildings (see Gilchrist and Blair 1996).

In the Chesapeake, the development of large open-area excavations from the 1960s led to the archaeological recognition of seventeenth-century 'earthfast' timber structures and palisades, the evidence of which survives as post holes, giving rise to a new field of enquiry (e.g. Carson et al. 1981; Noël Hume 1983). The increasing activities of the Vernacular Architecture Group in the United Kingdom (formed in 1952), the establishment of the North American Vernacular Architecture Forum in 1980, and especially

transatlantic transmission of the knowledge of British archaeologists familiar with post-built structures from medieval and earlier periods, led to this
'discovery' of post-built architecture in excavated contexts. The work of
Norman Barka, William Kelso, Garry Wheeler Stone and, especially, Dell
Upton was highly influential here, particularly in the identification of these
structures in the field (cf. Upton 1986). Since the 1980s, re-examination of
the archaeological data unearthed during the 1930s and 1950s at Jamestown
has revealed the previously overlooked presence of many early modern post-
built structures (Horning 1995).

Similarly, in the United Kingdom, as post-war development affected
more and more urban landscapes from the 1960s, the rise of 'rescue archaeology' in towns and cities led to a dramatic increase in the excavation of the
buried remains of post-medieval structures – including not only structural
remains but also 'pit groups' (artefacts buried in backfilled domestic pits)
(Crossley 1990: 76–79; cf. Ottaway 1992). Studies of post-medieval building materials developed rapidly (e.g. Betts et al. 1991). The results of such
work often remain in descriptive 'grey literature' form, still awaiting fuller
interpretation, integration and publication.

W. G. Hoskins, whose influence upon the development of landscape
archaeology is widely recognised (Holtorf and Williams this volume;
M. Johnson 2005), played an important role in the post-war development
of studies not only of rural vernacular houses but also those in towns, seeing
the study of buildings as 'the classical example of a marriage between fieldwork and documents' (W. G. Hoskins 1967: 94). This close relationship
with local history led in particular to development of the use of probate
inventories and related documents in studies of domestic houses. Probate
inventories were published in large numbers in local history at this time
(W. G. Hoskins 1967: 95–97), and have continued to be significant resources
for social historians and historical archaeologists since, in the UK (Weatherill
1988; De Vries 1993) and North America (Main 1975; see e.g. M. Brown
1988, cf. Green Carr and Walsh 1988; Shammas 1990). In Hoskins' work,
the details of room names, layout and objects were revealed through such
documents with all the breathless anticipation of archaeological discovery:

[Sometimes] one may find inventories among the Special Commissions of Enquiry.
Thus I found in this series an inquisition into the possessions of one John Strobridge
of Hooperhayne in Colyton (east Devon) in 1576. This includes a full list of all his
household goods room by room, from which we discover that his large farmhouse
contained a hall, parlour, great chamber, little chamber, closet, kitchen, buttery,
chamber over the buttery, chamber over the kitchen, maids' chamber, and men's
chamber. We also get a list of the service-rooms and outbuildings, informing us of

what to look for in an Elizabethan farmhouse on this scale. They included the 'new house with chamber over', the 'brysshinge house' with a room over, malthouse, 'Wrynge house', brewhouse, out chamber, and the 'Cherse house' [sic] whatever that may have been. The contents do not help us here to decide: a pair of virginals, hangings, cushions, mustard mill, garden rake, etc. (W. G. Hoskins 1967: 97)

In one particularly influential early paper, Hoskins defined a process which determined the direction of many studies in post-medieval buildings archaeology in the United Kingdom – a 'Great Rebuilding' in England, taking place between 1570 and 1640 (W. G. Hoskins 1953). He described a 'revolution in the housing of a considerable part of the population', not unlike Fox and Raglan's account of a transition from medieval to Renaissance house forms in Monmouthshire (W. G. Hoskins 1953: 44ff.; Johnson 1993b: 118). Hoskins set out his thoughts on how such a significant process had gone unrecognised in conventional English histories:

This revolution in English housing had two aspects. There was, first, the physical rebuilding or substantial modernisation of the medieval houses that had come down from the past; and there was, almost simultaneously, a remarkable increase in household furnishings and equipment. The rebuilding movement has remained unnoticed because historians, unlike archaeologists, have yet to learn to look over hedges and to treat visual evidence as of equal value to documentary. Most of the evidence lies in the surviving buildings themselves, but once we recognise it for what it is the necessary documentary evidence is forthcoming. As for the evidence for the improvement in fittings and furnishings, it is derived in the main from the documents, chiefly the inventories of personal estate deposited in various probate registries all over the country. (W. G. Hoskins 1953: 44)

Such 'looking over hedges' characterised much of the emerging buildings archaeology. As historian Maurice Beresford observed, one immediate effect of Hoskins' paper was to 'establish the veteran houses of the Old English Village of the travel posters as emphatically post-medieval', rather than medieval (Beresford 1971: 171). Two more radical effects of Hoskins' paper, however, were to define buildings in the post-medieval and later periods as of a very different character from earlier structures, and to focus buildings archaeology upon vernacular domestic housing – away from other kinds of buildings (e.g. industrial buildings), or from the houses of the elite.

In North America, a similarly influential model of revolutionary change in domestic buildings emerged from Henry Glassie's influential structuralist study of *Folk Housing in Middle Virginia* (1975). Although Glassie's study was poorly executed, with little attention to the actual dates and sequence of the houses he discussed – the early eighteenth-century 'folk' buildings in Louisa County, Virginia, for example, have since been shown to postdate his attributions (A. Bell 2002; G. Stone 1988) – its general argument was developed by James Deetz (1977), extended by Mark Leone (1988b), and applied to English material by Matthew Johnson (1993a: xi-xii, 1996). This diverse body of work (Glassie, Deetz, Leone, Johnson) has come to be known as the 'Georgian Order' thesis. In this work, a transformation in traditional buildings to new forms fitting with a 'Georgian worldview' (ordered, rational and symmetrical) came to be seen as 'outlining a fundamental shift in the organization of space between the early and late 18th centuries' (Johnson 1992: 45–46), in which 'regional traditions of vernacular architecture became subsumed under the national style and form of the Georgian house' (Johnson 1996: 178).

The Georgian Order can be seen as a consistent set of rules applied to architecture, material culture, and ways of living. Georgian houses are symmetrical in plan and elevation; internally they are two rooms deep, divided between front and back, strictly segregated between master and servant and give a high stress to personal privacy in their layout. Rooms are assigned single functional uses; the hall is now an entrance vestibule rather than the bustling centre of a traditional house. The external façade is governed by rules of order. (M. Johnson 1996: 202)

Criticising the descriptive regional studies discussed above, Johnson studied historical process, 'with reference to . . . cultural principles' (1993b: 123), which brought new ceilings, chimneys, glass windows, new furnishings and more internal subdivisions into rooms with specialised functions, replacing medieval halls. He presented a shift from premodern 'openness' to 'closure' in domestic architecture, which paralleled the enclosure of fields (Johnson 1993a: 164–170), and was associated with the 'emergence of capitalism'. The model bore strong similarities to Ian Hodder's (1990) account of Neolithic 'domestication', which studied the relationships between local situations and 'cultural structures and their history' (Gibbon 1993: 712).

Johnson's account was strongly influenced by Hoskins' model of the 'great rebuilding', and the related notion of a 'vernacular threshold' (Johnson 1993b: 121): a field which raises the issues of the relationship between the rates of survival of vernacular buildings (E. Mercer 1975: 1–39) and genuine early modern shifts in architectural traditions (e.g. Carson et al. 1981: 159–160, 176). Johnson's account drew together architecture with other forms of material culture, and arranged and narrativised diverse architectural forms as evidence of revolutionary change – 'a deep-seated cultural shift' – during the seventeenth century (Johnson 1993b: 123). This model was mortgaged to notions of material culture as rationally and coherently involved in social life – in contrast with Hoskins' mute, and yet evocatively chaotic, 'virginals, hangings, cushions, mustard mill, garden rake' (1967: 97).

The notion of the great rebuilding has been widely critiqued as overly simplistic (e.g. Machin 1977). Alan Dyer (1981) and Colin Platt (1994) have suggested that changes in the late fifteenth and sixteenth centuries were distinct from a second rebuilding, in both town and country, during the late seventeenth century. So too, in its latest incarnations (e.g. Johnson 1996: 202–206) the 'Georgian Order' thesis was monolithic, serving to obscure not only regional complexities but also the intimate and powerful nature of buildings and things presented in James Deetz's groundbreaking study (1977), and the diverse agencies of new forms of material culture in social change within Mark Leone's (1988b) account. Johnson's (1993a) acknowledgement of historical change (see now Williamson 1998), regional variation and the contingency of post-medieval architecture upon medieval situations represented a crucial moment in vernacular architecture's 'loss of innocence' (Johnson 1997), especially through its proposal of a 'genealogical' perspective upon the archaeological study of historical buildings (Johnson 1996: 206– 212; Lucas this volume). But by recourse to a model of the 'emergence of capitalism' that failed to accommodate the situational diversity highlighted by others studying capitalism (McGuire this volume), by the mid-1990s the Georgian Order thesis had become another normative model of change in material culture and the built environment (Johnson 1996). It represents a cautionary tale for historical archaeologies of buildings, which underlines the importance for historical archaeology of eschewing totalising narratives, and acknowledging the complexities of its materials.

INTERPRETING BUILDINGS

While descriptive approaches continue to dominate many studies of standing and excavated building remains, the interpretive efforts that led to the formulation of the Georgian Order thesis have also led in alternative directions, as some archaeologists have aimed to view buildings and their associated material culture as 'not simply a reflection of social ideals or large-scale patterns but equally the response of individuals . . . to such trends' (Lucas and Roderick 2003: 198). As sketched above, the emergence of buildings archaeology often led to a focus upon domestic houses, but these new studies of buildings in historical archaeology during the past twenty years have extended studies of vernacular and industrial buildings to interpret the material remains not only of houses (Upton 1986) but also of agricultural structures (De Cunzo 2004; J. King 1997), the polite houses and gardens of the elite (Hicks 2005; Leone 1996), prisons (Garman 2005; McAtackney 2005; Watson 2004), asylums (Piddock 2001) and hospitals (S. Gould 1999: 144–147), civic buildings (Giles 1999), workhouses (Lucas 1999), military structures (Schofield 2002a; Starbuck 1999), theatres (Bowsher 1998), industrial buildings (Symonds and Casella this volume), churches (Blair and Pyrah 1996; Rodwell 1989) and other religious buildings (Leone 1977; M. Terrell 2004), and even fast food restaurants (Hess 1995).

The close, often intimate, relationships between people and buildings is a central aspect of interpretive studies of buildings. Dana Arnold has described how in the study of the country house by art historians, a 'biographical approach', focusing on the life of an architect or patron, has proved limiting – restricting interpretation to the period of construction, and 'mapping' architecture 'against the personal development of the designer . . . imply[ing] some kind of progress' (D. Arnold 1998: 1). Arnold has aimed to refocus architectural historians' attention upon the broader social history of the country house (1998: 16–19). In this section we want to examine how interpretive historical archaeologists have aimed to fold together individual biographies with the broader, material histories of buildings.

In the United States, from the late 1960s, one highly influential approach to associating people and buildings was to aim to distinguish definitive ethnic architectural types, disentangling 'cultural origins' from the strands of the diversity of contemporary American society. The pages of journals such as *Pennsylvania Folklife*, *Pioneer America*, *Winterthur Portfolio* rapidly filled with descriptions of Dutch barns, Scots-Irish dwellings, Rhenish houses in Virginia, French *pieux-en-terre* structures, and African-American shotgun shacks (e.g. Chappell 1986 [1980]; Vlach 1986 [1976]). For example, Henry Glassie's classic study of buildings in the southern mountains (1968) separated Scots-Irish, German, and English methods of horizontal log construction. Scots-Irish pioneers, according to Glassie, built rectangular houses with opposing front and rear doorways employing V-notches or half-dovetail notches to join the logs.

Unfortunately, such studies generally drew upon simplistic approaches to historical identities, similar to historian David Hackett Fischer's (1989) sweeping model of four static ethnic groups from the British Isles bringing complete 'cultural packages' to the New World, still recognisable in the cultural landscapes of New England, the Chesapeake, the Upland South, and the mid-Atlantic. Such reactionary studies of 'origins' and pristine ethnic identities gloss not only the influence of the diversity of native American or African populations but also the diversity of European identities, both 'at home' and in new colonial situations (cf. Lawrence 2003).

Such problems have been visible in some archaeological studies of African-American buildings. John Michael Vlach's classic study of the ubiquitous Southern shotgun house endeavoured to examine the house type in terms of its Yoruba origins, translation through the western Caribbean, and subsequent dispersal throughout the South (Vlach 1986 [1976]). He convincingly demonstrated that the house form was brought to the New Orleans region from Haiti in the massive movement of peoples from that island in the wake of the successful uprising of the enslaved population in the closing years of the eighteenth century. Vlach chose to emphasise the 'Africanness' of the architectural forms, based on comparison with similar Yoruba forms in Nigeria, rather than other influences in the Caribbean or American situations. As Dell Upton (1996: 3–4) has argued, approaches such as Vlach's are grounded in a static notion of identity, rather than emphasising the 'dynamic' and 'creolised' dimensions of ethnicity. Similarly, in colonial situations, historical archaeologists' use of the term 'creolisation' has sometimes served to mask the diversity of new identities (e.g. Delle 2000a). Similar models of pristine ethnic identity (cf. S. Jones 1997) informed Glassie's work, which failed to consider the active nineteenth-century American Protestant construction of Scots-Irish identity, formulated in intentional opposition to the famine-era Catholic Irish migration (Horning 2002). Similarly, his study of German log architecture supposedly adapted by these 'Scots-Irish pioneers' failed to acknowledge the long-running arguments (since H. Mercer 1976 [1926]) over whether it was the Swedes, the Germans, or the Finns who deserve credit for introducing what has been described as the quintessentially American pioneer architecture type (e.g. Jordan 1980; Jordan et al. 1986; Lay 1982).

An alternative to such 'culture historical' accounts is offered by more contextual, situated studies of the relationships between buildings, identities and ethnogenesis. For example, Vlach's West African shotgun prototype was only one building within a compound: a compound that structured and was structured by family and community life. To be of interest to an anthropological archaeology, the questions to be asked of any structure must involve the people who built, inhabited and abandoned or demolished it, and the wider situations in which it existed. Thus, Neiman (1993) has noted that as the number of enslaved African and African-American individuals increased in the Chesapeake, one material result was a sharp increase in the number of plantation outbuildings (cf. Vlach 1993). Epperson (2001) has explored such shifts further, considering the layout of plantation buildings in light of the development of ideas of whiteness and blackness – in essence, seeing buildings and material culture as involved in the construction of ideas of race in colonial America.

Such work indicates the importance, highlighted especially by Deetz (1977), of the integration within archaeological studies of buildings of studies of portable objects used in everyday life indoors. As Victor Buchli has observed, 'of all the categories in material culture, architecture stands out as an artefact of great complexity, but also as the context in which most other material culture is used, placed and understood' (Buchli 2002c: 207). Combined studies of buildings and objects have been explored especially in archaeological studies of households. The close, often intimate, relationships built up by people with things in their houses lie at the heart of the success of archaeological studies of probate inventories, and the combination of excavation and documentary research to provide histories not of people and things but what Mary Beaudry (nd.) terms 'studies of people and *their* things'.

One highly successful example of such work is Victor Buchli's examination of the materiality of everyday domestic life during a period of great social change. Buchli studied household life in the apartments of the 1930s Narkomfin Communal House in Moscow during the late 1980s. The building was constructed during the pre-Stalinist period in such a way as to encourage communal living, but over time the use of the building changed in many different ways. During the fieldwork conducted amid the radical shifts from socialist to post-socialist society, Buchli recorded how social change was negotiated through objects in domestic settings. The buffet cabinet of Elena Andreevna provided one vivid example. This was placed in the traditional Russian Orthodox red corner of her apartment, and contained an eclectic collection of radically juxtaposed items: the collected works of Lenin and Stalin alongside vials of holy water and religious icons. Buchli described how

Elena Andreevna in her declining years, while raging at Yeltsin's 'democratic-fascists' who had overturned what was left of her world, had managed improbably to contain adequately the superfluous and contradictory 'scraps' of her life in her buffet cabinet and realise a momentary accommodation that saw her into the next world. (1999, 182–183)

For Buchli, these personal 'scraps' are integral to the 'practice' of everyday life: a position inspired by the growing attention upon domestic settings in consumption studies (Buchli 1997; D. Miller 1984), and shared by household archaeologists such as Jane Lydon in her analysis of the domestic refuse from Mrs Lewis' boarding house in 'the Rocks' in Australia (Lydon 1999a). In this light, it is notable that Bourdieu's theory of social 'practice' based upon *habitus* emerged from his study of the Kabyle house (Bourdieu 1977, 1990). Buchli's study of the Narkomfin communal house attempted to relate the 'practice theories' of Bourdieu and Giddens, 'to a body of material culture' (Buchli 2002b: 132). His study examined the 'competing materialities and their social effects' that emerged from people's constitution of the material environments that are required by them at any particular point in time, and from their partial and ongoing replacement in changing circumstances (Buchli 2002b).

In household archaeology, historical archaeologists (King this volume; Barile and Brandon 2004) have focused upon the everyday material lives of people interacting with the built environment, contributing material perspective to ethnographic studies of the importance of 'houses' in social organisation (e.g. Carsten and Hugh-Jones 1995; Levi-Strauss 1987). Household archaeology has sometimes been perceived as a field concerned only with the archaeology of adult-female identity, but it holds the potential to reconstruct the experiences of each member of a household in terms of their day-to-day activities. It can study how those activities shape and are shaped by the home itself – its layout, materials, construction, alteration, and perception, and the immediate outside environment. In so doing, the presence of women and of male and female children, which is often written out of historical narratives, alongside adult men is considered, and the diversity of kinds of 'households' is recognised (see review by Beaudry 1989a). Thus, Joyce Clements (1997) has examined households at a nineteenth-century military garrison in Massachusetts, discussing the domestic materialities of women's social relations, especially through house cleaning and household dinner parties, in relation to the material performance of gendered roles. In their reformulation of Levi-Strauss' notion of 'house societies', Rosemary Joyce and Susan Gillespie have considered the broader implications for cultural anthropology of focusing upon everyday life in houses. They argue that a focus upon the 'social and material' dimensions of houses – land, dwelling, ritual and non-ritual objects – offers an alternative to structuralist and classificatory understandings of kin relations by emphasising materiality, time depth and historical change in the working out of social relationships over time (Gillespie 2000; Joyce 2000). The potential of such sophisticated studies of the archaeology of buildings, space and gender is demonstrated by Roberta Gilchrist's examination in *Gender and Material Culture: The Archaeology of Religious Women* (1994).

This focus upon everyday life in buildings has often revealed the remains of transitional and ephemeral settlements or inhabitations, which survive more commonly from the recent past than from earlier periods of archaeology. While the issue of 'impermanence' was central to early inter-pretations of post-built ('earthfast') seventeenth-century domestic buildings identified through excavation (see Carson et al. 1981), it is unclear whether such architectural practices in reality indicate temporary constructions. Fleeting situations of building and dwelling are more clearly demonstrated in Michael Morris' (1994) study of navvy settlements in Britain. Morris demonstrated how archaeology can identify the remains of temporary workers' housing on construction sites – whether eighteenth-century canals, nineteenth-century railways or twentieth- century motorways. Similar archaeologies of communities defined by work have been undertaken in the United States (Van Bueren 2002a, 2002b). Military sites archaeology has also expanded from traditional interpretations of battle strategy and fort design to studies that seek to disentangle and expose the often banal day-to-day existence of soldiers – through the ephemeral traces of camp tents (Orr 1992), of hospitals which were erected overnight (Whitehorne et al. 2000), or of temporarily commandeered civilian dwellings (Manning-Sterling 2000). In the United Kingdom, John Schofield and Mike Anderton (2000) have extended military archaeologies still further into ephemeral archae-ologies by studying the material remains of the protest camp at Greenham Common Airbase in Berkshire, which include not only the earthwork remains of campsites but also cut and repaired military perimeter fences – evocative reminders of the layered and messy nature of many archaeological remains of built structures (Figure 15.1). In household archaeology, Victor Buchli and Gavin Lucas' powerful study (2001b) similarly explored the material remains of ephemeral moments by studying a council house that had been abandoned suddenly by a single mother and her children – the personal objects left behind at the moment of departure. Such work throws into relief the materialities of everyday life in buildings, and the potential of archaeology to witness its remains. In such work, as for anthropologist Tim Ingold,

building . . . is a process that is continually going on, for as long as people dwell in an environment. It does not begin here, with a pre-formed plan, and end there, with a finished artefact. The 'final form' is but a fleeting moment in the life of any feature, when it is matched to a human purpose, likewise cut out from the flow of intentional activity. (Ingold 2000b: 188)

By focusing upon the intimate relations between buildings, things and people in everyday life, these interpretive archaeologies have contributed highly nuanced studies of the materiality of buildings.

Figure 15.1   Tattered fence at Greenham Common Airbase. Photograph by John Schofield, from Schofield and Anderton 2000, Figure 5. (Courtesy of *World Archaeology* and Taylor & Frances Ltd www.tandf.co.uk/journals/)

'DISTRIBUTED' BUILDINGS

Having introduced these interpretive and contextual archaeological studies of historical buildings and people, in this section we want to consider multiple scales of archaeological analysis of buildings – the field's potential to combine access to large geographical and temporal scales through particular detailed and nuanced material stories. Let us begin by returning to art historian Dana Arnold's discouragement of 'biographical approaches' to buildings. This represents an important critique of the limitations of conventional art historical descriptions of polite buildings arguing, like Matthew Johnson's work in buildings archaeology, for approaches that engage with broader social history. In this section, however, we wish to explore a different direction: the potential of examining the distributions of buildings across time and space, especially through 'archaeological biographies' and notions of material agency.

From the early 1980s, ethnographic and archaeological studies of buildings have examined material (as well as simply human) agency in a variety of ways. From the early 1980s, ethnoarchaeological studies of buildings underlined how they can in certain situations be 'powerful' (e.g. Donley 1982). Postprocessual archaeologists extended such understandings of the 'active' role of things in social life by making use of models such as Hillier and Hanson's account of built space *constraining* social action (Hillier and Hanson 1985; Locock 1994b: 9). In historical archaeology, these impulses have been clearest in the way in which Foucauldian or Lefebvrian perspectives have been cited by archaeologists wishing to underline the influence of the designed environment upon 'power relations' and discipline imposed by elite groups (e.g. Delle 1998; Shackel 1993; cf. Foucault 1986a; Lefebvre 1991). The critique of the dominant ideology thesis within archaeology (see Hicks 2005: 376ff.) has led to studies of the multiple 'readings' of built environments, rather than implying the particular intentionalities of designers, among interpretive and Marxist archaeologists (McGuire this volume; De Cunzo and Ernstein this volume); and yet it is remarkable that so many archaeological studies of buildings continue to focus exclusively upon buildings being 'read' as intended (but see Beaudry et al. 1991; M. Hall 1992).

Moreover, whether emphasising 'original' or multiple/contested meanings, the emphasis upon meaning and coherence – a theme particularly visible in the numerous studies of buildings in the early 1990s (Kent 1990; Locock 1994a; Parker Pearson and Richards 1994; Samson 1990), often borrowing from studies of buildings as 'communicative' (e.g. Rappoport 1982) – has in many ways served to obscure the complex and changing nature of the materialities of buildings. Unlike communicative approaches, more recent approaches to 'material agency' have encouraged studies of buildings as the 'indices' of human agents, or else in some respects actors in their own right. It is notable that in concluding his seminal essay on material agency (1998), anthropologist Alfred Gell chose to adduce Roger Neich's detailed survey of traditions of figurative painting in the meeting houses of the Maori of North Island. The example of these traditions of painted houses serves as a useful point of entry in our discussions of buildings' biographies. Examining the changing styles in these painted houses, Neich traced

the development of figurative painting from diverse directions in the 1870s, until the 1885 to 1905 period, when intensive cross-sharing and interchange of traditions accelerated this development immensely. Much of the innovation and experimental combination of traditions in this period was concentrated in the area from north-ern Hawke's Bay through the Poverty Bay district to the southern Ngati Porou territory . . . Then after 1905, this wide-ranging interchange of traditions abruptly ceased, breaking down into various separate combinations of certain traditions that tended to diverge and develop independently in areas of the island, usually somewhat marginal to the core region of the high period of figurative painting. (Neich 1994: 220)

Neich presented a table that summarised 'the transmission of selected figurative painting traditions' in houses distributed across time and space (Figure 15.2). The black circles represent particular meeting houses examined by Neich during his fieldwork, each of which is numbered. The letters refer to particular traditions of figurative painting identified on the houses.

Gell reproduced Neich's table in his discussion of how 'the structures of art history demonstrate an externalised and collectivised cognitive process'.

A person and a person's mind are not confined to particular spatio-temporal coor-dinates, but consist of a spread of biographical events and memories of events, and a dispersed category of material objects, traces, and leavings, which can be attributed to a person and which, in aggregate, testify to agency and patienthood during a biographical career which may, indeed, prolong itself long after biological death. (1998: 222)

For Gell, the Maori meeting houses studied by Neich were 'collective "indexes of agency"': complex assemblages of many material parts, and bringing together many people (1998: 252). Importantly, he suggested that one implication of this approach was that the temporality of house-painting traditions might be understood in non-linear terms, rather than as forward-looking artistic 'progress' or 'backwards-looking' traditional architectural retentions.

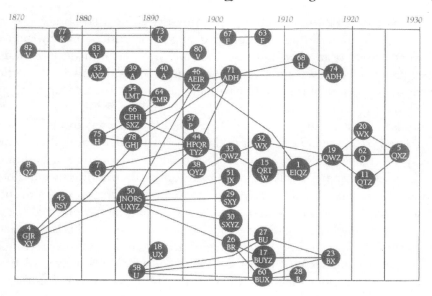

Figure 15.2 'Transmission of selected figurative painting traditions in the meeting houses of the Maori of North Island', from Neich 1994, Table 14.

The temporal object constituted by the totality of the meeting houses displayed on Neich's diagram consists . . . not of a network of temporal relations which can be totalised in a single synoptic mapping; but only as a 'file' consisting of a whole series of such mappings corresponding to different temporal (and spatial) points of vantage; each one of which generates a distinctive distribution of retentional and protentional relations between any given meeting house and its spatio-temporal neighbours. The logically mandatory nature of such a continuously shifting perspective on tradition and innovation in an historical assemblage of artefacts means that the process of understanding art history is essentially akin to the processes of consciousness itself, which is marked, likewise, by a continuous perspectival flux. (Gell 1998: 256)

By arguing that objects can act as the 'indices' of the 'distributed agency' of humans, Gell evokes an 'extended temporal field' (Gell 1998: 257) of houses and complex intentionalities. These perspectives bear similarities to Bruno Latour's more radical extension of agency to objects, which describes complex and intermingled 'collectives' of both human and nonhuman agents (e.g. Latour 1996).

The implications of this work for the historical archaeology of buildings are considerable. Archaeological notions of the human-like 'social lives' of nonhuman objects have since the mid-1980s been increasingly extended into 'biographical' approach to things (Gosden and Marshall 1999; Holtorf

2002; Kopytoff 1986) underlining not only the contextual observation of how objects' or buildings' meanings change from one situation, period or perspective to another, but also how an object's 'life history' includes assemblage, change, creation and destruction. As we have seen in earlier sections, historical buildings archaeology has usually focused upon stemming the processes of destruction and decay, and often limiting construction, use and elaboration, through conservation or preservation. This has distracted from the 'afterlives' of buildings – their persistence, change and decay. Acknowledging the biographies and distributed nature of buildings leads us away from an emphasis upon 'reading' the meaning of bounded objects to the messier and entropic processes of the 'transformation of substance' that lie at the heart of archaeology's contemporary, material focus: moments of 'the breaking down of objects and substances [that] frees them from the binding conventions of categorisation, and allows their recombination in new and hybrid forms' (J. Pollard 2004: 60). Roberta Gilchrist has pointed out how, especially through the influence of third-wave feminist studies, the acknowledgement of human biographies underlines the importance of humans changing – through stages of life within a lifespan (Gilchrist 2000: 325) – and of how 'the human lifecycle is connected closely with that of houses, settlements and monuments' (2000: 327). The potential for buildings archaeology, inspired by Gell's perspectives upon the 'distributed' nature of nonhuman agency (cf. Knappett 2002), is to extend such decentred approaches to buildings' spatial and temporal distributions, examining how human and buildings' biographies are bound up together.

The point can be made by returning to historical archaeologists' use of Hoskins' model of a 'Great Rebuilding'. In 1988, architectural historian Chris Currie published an influential paper examining 'attrition in old houses'. Currie argued that since small variations in the survival of houses in one area or another 'can mean dramatic differences in final survival . . . apparent waves of rebuilding may be illusory' (Currie 1988: 6, quoted by Johnson 1993b: 119). While Matthew Johnson has suggested that an important part of vernacular architecture's 'loss of innocence' was that *we cannot and do not interpret vernacular architecture independently of the present* (Johnson 1997: 16, original emphasis), this observation leads us beyond simply recovering past contexts of meaning, or being aware of the contemporary social contexts of our work, to the study of people and things in flux: changing physically through human action, or fragmenting over time and space. The attrition emphasised by Currie reminds us that one distinctive contribution of a historical archaeology of buildings lies in its working upon material remains that have outlasted any 'original' intentionalities or meanings: the fragmented remnants of human–material interactions.

While the study of the fragmented nature of the archaeological record, resulting both from deliberate breakages in the past and also from natural processes of decay, has emerged as an important field of enquiry in prehistoric archaeology (Chapman 2000), in buildings archaeology, as in mainstream material culture studies, the 'presumption of object durability' (Colloredo-Mansfeld 2003: 246) has prevented the full study of the temporality of buildings that survive.

Recent work in cultural geography has underlined the potential of acknowledging the interlinked nature of natural and cultural process of decay in the built environment. Paul Cloke and Owain Jones (2004) have examined how 'the nonhuman agency of trees' has affected both the fabric of listed buildings and the trajectories of conservation efforts at the Victorian Arnos Vale Cemetery in Bristol. Tim Edensor, in his studies of British abandoned industrial buildings, has argued that by acknowledging the 'disordering' effects of ruination, in which 'haunted' elements of buildings mingle together, we come closer to realising the potential of the contemporary nature of the study of built remains (2005a; 2005b). Most explicitly, in her study of residuality at a derelict homestead in Montana, Caitlin DeSilvey (2004) has proposed an 'entropic' heritage practice, which aims to observe and celebrate, rather than arrest, processes of decay and renewal in the built environment. Foregrounding ruin holds significant potential for historical archaeology, as is clearly demonstrated by the delicate study by Michael Shanks, David Platt and Bill Rathje of the ruins of the World Trade Center (2004), which reminds us that all archaeology works on the chaotic fragments outlasting the past, surviving in the present.

This interdisciplinary work reminds us of how often in studying buildings we discover the reused remains of earlier structures, or evidence of the robbing out of stone foundations. Individual buildings comprise, in Stuart Brand's (1997: 12–23) evocative phrase, 'shearing layers' that continually build up and break down buildings' fabric over time. Writing archaeological life histories of buildings reveals shifting assemblages, which are continually 'dispersed' over time and geographically through combined human and nonhuman agencies. Through the historical archaeology of buildings, we reveal moments at which things and people come together in buildings: the apparent 'boundedness' of structures is broken down: through the creation of social relations, and through ruin and loss. We are reminded that one of the major results of Bill Rathje's 'garbology' project was a realisation of how much human refuse is actually building rubble (Rathje and Murphy 1992;

cf. Shanks et al. 2004: 67). The challenge for historical buildings archaeologists is to use their acknowledgement of the contemporary nature of their
practices, and to bring to studies of the temporal and spatial distribution of
buildings the analysis of the powerful and intimate relationships between
human and nonhuman, material biographies – so successfully written in
the archaeology of households (Beaudry 1999) and interdisciplinary studies
of 'home cultures' (Buchli et al. 2004) – in the past and the present.

CHAPTER 16

Household archaeology, identities and biographies

Julia A. King

Sometime in the late 1670s, Charles Calvert, the third Lord Baltimore and proprietor of the Maryland colony in North America, made the decision to erect the colony's magazine adjacent to his family's plantation dwelling at Mattapany in Maryland. Clearly, Calvert was making a social and political statement about his power as proprietor, setting the magazine on the public approach to his large brick and timber house. But this decision also suggests Calvert's growing anxiety about the political state of affairs in his colony. Along with members of his council, Calvert worried about the pirates who, he was certain, plied the waters of the nearby Patuxent River, and in 1675 he was particularly shaken when a large number of Susquehannock leaders unexpectedly arrived at Mattapany. More mundane but no less a problem was Calvert's relationship with his colony's denizens, many of whom were growing to resent the proprietor's extraordinary legal and political power. Indeed, Calvert may have at this time erected a substantial log palisade around his dwelling in an effort to provide his family an additional measure of protection from these and other political uncertainties (Chaney 1999).

Across the river from Mattapany at a much smaller plantation known today as Patuxent Point, an unidentified English family and their servants were living in a modest 'earthfast' timber domestic structure. No palisade or paling fence enclosed the dwelling yard and, from all appearances, a visitor could just walk up to the dwelling's principal door. Archaeological evidence suggests that the site's occupants were perhaps not as concerned about pirates or unwelcome Indians as were Calvert and his council. Indeed, comparatively large numbers of Indian-made earthenware tobacco pipes from this site suggest interactions with local native people were frequent and perhaps

Acknowledgements: Analysis of the Patuxent Point materials was funded in part by grants from the Maryland Historical Trust and the National Endowment for the Humanities (RZ-20896–02). The work at Mattapany was funded by a grant from the Department of Defense's Legacy Resources Program. I am grateful to Catherine L. Alston, Edward E. Chaney, Sara Cofield-Rivers and Douglas H. Ubelaker for their assistance with both projects.

friendlier than those taking place at Mattapany. Still, two archaeological features suggest that the Patuxent Point site's occupants were also preoccupied with a need for protection. A small pit outside one of the dwelling's doorways contained four inverted case bottles which, although now broken, had been placed in the ground intact. Associated fragments of corroded nails suggest that these bottles were part of a ritual intended to counter a witch's spell. The second feature, a grave containing the remains of a woman approximately twenty-eight years old who had died in childbirth, lay apart from the other individuals in the nearby cemetery with her head positioned in the east end of the grave. In some parts of England, newly delivered women were believed vulnerable to the spells of witches and other malevolent forces, and a woman dying in childbirth could have been denied a Christian burial (K. Thomas 1971: 38–39). This may possibly explain the location and orientation of this grave at Patuxent Point (King and Ubelaker 1996: 43, 116–117).

The differences in household-protection strategies evident at these two domestic archaeological sites, both occupied at roughly the same time and located only a few miles apart, reveal the potential for exploring early colonial worldviews through household archaeology. The archaeological evidence from Mattapany and Patuxent Point suggests that the two households shared a desire to mark out plantation boundaries, but perceived and responded to external forces or threats in different ways. Such differences represent a localised example of much broader and more profound transformations visible in England in the second half of the seventeenth century, involving shifting assumptions about the nature of, and relationship between, the real and the supernatural worlds (Lloyd 1990; K. Thomas 1971). Archaeological and documentary evidence for the late seventeenth-century settlements at Mattapany and Patuxent Point, recovered as part of a long-term and ongoing research project documenting colonial occupation in Maryland's Patuxent River drainage, reveals how within the same plantation neighbourhood in a colonial situation, understandings of these worlds could vary from household to household.

Historical archaeologists have long devoted considerable attention to the excavation of domestic sites, focusing upon the households once occupying these sites. Such studies have traditionally examined 'lifestyles', or the details of how people lived, what they owned, and what they ate. Increasingly, these studies have been complemented by those which examine the social construction of domestic spaces and the ways in which the composition and forms of households created the circumstances out of which specific forms of domesticity and domestic life emerged. This chapter reviews these approaches and others regarding the study of the household, including key concepts, themes, and theoretical approaches that have proven especially useful in the field as well as some of the serious methodological challenges of studying domestic sites. Through a case study drawn from the colonial Chesapeake, the potential of archaeological evidence for interpreting historical households, including how they have changed during the modern period and how they reveal aspects of larger economic, social, and cultural realities, is explored.

The development of household archaeology

Interest in the *archaeology of houses* among international historical archaeologists can be traced to the rise of the historic preservation and architectural conservation movements of the twentieth century (Hicks and Horning this volume). In contrast, the development of *household archaeology* has been a more or less North American phenomenon influenced especially by theoretical perspectives developed in Mesoamerican archaeology, the emergence of the 'new social history', and an increasing interpretive desire to study domestic archaeological sites as locations in which household practices took place in the past. Elsewhere in the world, the archaeology of houses has not systematically explored domestic sites and assemblages as the remains of households (but see Dalglish 2003: 206–209; Johnson 1993a, 1996: 79–87, 160–162). This chapter, then, examines the North American tradition of household studies in historical archaeology, the development of which has been largely driven by a desire to acknowledge the actions of individuals in social and cultural change, and the social construction of domestic space.

In a recent survey of North American historical-household archaeology, Brandon and Barile (2004: 2–3) point to the continuing importance of the historic preservation movement for drawing attention to the archaeology of standing buildings. In the Chesapeake region in particular, household archaeology got its start during the 1930s as a result of New Deal programmes aimed at putting people to work during the Depression. While such programmes were important for stimulating the economy, at the same time the homes of American 'founding fathers' were increasingly understood as places where national values and ideals were formed and shaped on an everyday basis. Archaeology was used to collect information for reconstructing architectural space and the domestic furnishings of these households, often emphasising the 'good taste' of the forefathers (Wells 1993). Today, some of the nation's oldest archaeology programmes are found at many of these sites, themselves now functioning as museums and civic shrines (Heath nd.; Kelso 1997; Pogue 1996; Reeves nd.). Research at these and other 'great-man' places have generally followed theoretical and methodological trends in the discipline while continuing to focus on the households of these unique or exceptional individuals (cf. Duncan and Sanford 2005).

The rise of the 'new social history' in the 1960s also shaped historical archaeologists' thinking about the household. Reacting to what they viewed as an overwhelming emphasis on political and 'great-man' history, historical archaeologists were increasingly interested in social histories that emphasised the everyday lives of ordinary people. Understanding the past not only as a series of political events, but also as a series of demographic and social processes (Novick 1988), the goals of the new social history dovetailed well with the emerging new archaeology for historical archaeologists, who began to turn their attention to the reconstruction of past 'lifeways' (cf. Binford 1962). Archaeological evidence was defined as an important source of information about all sorts of poorly documented and previously understudied historical groups, such as poor and middling farmers, urban tenants, and enslaved Africans. Thus, Henry Glassie (1977: 29) described historical archaeology as promising 'an authentic history' by 'rescuing from anonymity the average people of the past', and since the 1970s social historians and historical archaeologists have collaborated in new ways to provide histories for people previously ignored by historical scholarship.

Household studies in historical archaeology have also been influenced by the extensive literature generated on pre-Columbian households and household archaeology in Mesoamerica. More than forty years ago, Mesoamericanists began focusing on Early Formative households and their variability to interpret the evolution of villages, 'subsistence, division of labor, craft activity, social status, and so on' (Flannery 1976: 16). Some of the first efforts to link definitions of households as social units with archaeological evidence came from this quarter, and a sophisticated discussion about households and household archaeology continues apace in the field (Alexander 1999; Brumfiel 1991; Hendon 1996; B. McKee 1999; Santley and Hirth 1993; Wilk and Ashmore 1988; Wilk and Rathje 1982). Indeed, Bill Rathje, who was trained in Mesoamerican archaeology, refocused his energies on the weekly garbage generated by contemporary households in Tucson, Arizona – research that has informed public policy as much as it has revealed the social life of late twentieth-century households (Rathje 2001). Mesoamerican studies have served in large part to shape the discussion of studying households in historical archaeology (Brandon and Barile 2004), and importantly have called into question the cross-cultural validity of notions such as domesticity, private/public space, and sacred/secular practice (Hendon 1996: 46–47).

Above all, however, North American household archaeology has emerged from the real-world situations in which historical archaeology has been practised. Domestic sites – defined as places of habitation, or where people lived – constitute a very significant portion of the sites investigated by historical archaeologists (Figure 16.1). Indeed, a historical archaeologist can (and many do) spend years excavating and researching a single domestic site. Domestic archaeological sites provide the surviving physical and material evidence of the setting in which household actions, events and practices took place. While 'domestic archaeological sites' are not the same thing as households, relationships exist between the two (cf. Hendon 1996: 47) and household archaeologists continue to develop sophisticated methods for establishing the nature of those relationships (Beaudry 2004).

DEFINING HOUSEHOLDS IN HISTORICAL ARCHAEOLOGY

Although most social scientists generally agree that the household forms a primary human social unit, definitions of the term vary and, more importantly, often fail to account for all ethnographically known households (Brandon and Barile 2004; Goody 1971; Hendon 1996; Laslett and Wall 1972; Yanagisako 1979). A particular problem stems from conflating the concepts of 'family' and 'household', two related but distinct social categories (G. Bender 1968; Yanagisako 1979). To some extent, archaeologists have resolved the problem by focusing on what a household *does* (or did), rather than on what a household *is* (Beaudry 1984; Deetz 1982; Hendon 1996). While early efforts emphasised the organisation of household economic and reproductive activities (cf. Hammel 1984; Netting 1993; Wilk and Rathje 1982), such approaches have generally given way to understandings of household activities as more complex social practices, and as processes through which social life is constituted and transformed. Rather than simply assuming that households do more or less the same thing – producing, consuming, reproducing – archaeologists now stress how categories of class, gender, and ethnicity operate to structure social action in the household (cf. Hendon 1996: 46). Such approaches view households as critical locations in broader social and cultural change (Franklin 2004: xiii; see also Hendon 1996: 46–47) and are inspired by anthropology's use of intensive, small-scale research to elucidate aspects of larger social and cultural phenomena, and by the 'micro-histories' of some social historians (Levi 2001).

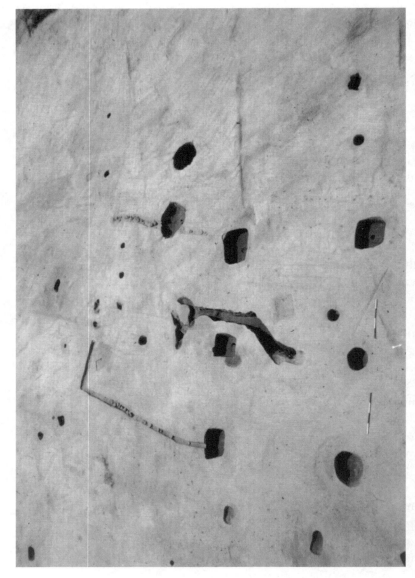

Figure 16.1 Overall shot of Carter's Grove 8, Williamsburg, Virginia: the remains of a c. 1625–1650 domestic site occupied by unidentified tenants of low economic status. Note the structural post holes. The linear trench represents the location of a paling fence.

Like micro-history, historical archaeologies are also concerned with scale, not for the purpose of simply developing manageable data sets or for finding 'microversions of larger social entities' (Meskell 2000), but for studying how social and cultural change begins with the choices, decisions, and actions of individuals. Many contemporary household archaeologies celebrate historical archaeology's access to individuals in both the documentary and archaeological records, and the opportunities for examining individuals in the world in which they lived. In addition, household archaeology is concerned with the life cycles of individuals and the developmental cycle of households (Gilchrist 2000). This scale of analysis recognises the dynamic nature of households and the ongoing daily, monthly and annual rhythms of life which comprise social experience. Although documenting life and developmental cycles through archaeology can be challenging, documents coupled with rigorously excavated and analysed evidence can provide powerful information about these cycles. Surviving probate inventories, for example, reveal an individual's material goods and debts at a single point in time, while meticulously recovered archaeological evidence can reveal other sorts of material goods, where these goods were used and discarded, and changes in household material culture through time (Carson 1990; King and Miller 1987; Main 1982).

ADAPTIVE, STRUCTURALIST AND CRITICAL APPROACHES TO HOUSEHOLDS

Historical archaeologists have experimented with a number of different theoretical frameworks in their interpretations of households, ranging from those that abstract patterns from sets of site assemblages to more recent approaches emphasising individual human agency and the contingencies of particular situations. Where some researchers have brought a functional or adaptive approach to the subject, explaining the changes observed in archaeological patterning with reference to external environmental or social pressures, others have approached households primarily as sites of conflict and struggle, emphasising class, ethnicity, race, or gender. Most recently, households have been explored as sites of practice, of ongoing negotiation and the construction of meaning, and as places where social and cultural relationships are produced and reproduced almost continuously. In these latter studies, conflict and struggle are just one of a diversity of interactions taking place within the household.

Studies viewing the household as a kind of adaptive mechanism were especially popular in the 1970s and 1980s, influenced largely by processual

archaeology. Historical archaeologists linked the variations they observed
in domestic archaeological assemblages to conditions in the physical or
natural environment. Faunal and, to a lesser extent, floral remains were
considered an important measurement of a household's interface with the
natural environment, and patterns of dietary consumption were linked to
environmental constraints and sometimes to larger economic and social processes (cf. H. Miller 1988a; Reitz and Scarry 1985). Similar arguments were
made to explain the development of colonial (or 'frontier') domestic Chesapeake architecture (Carson et al. 1981), variations in Indian and European
domestic ceramic patterning in Spanish St Augustine (Deagan 1983) and
status and class differences between households on antebellum plantations
(Otto 1980). Identifying adaptive responses to social and environmental
processes underpinned Stanley South's (1977a) influential effort to develop
a model of the relationship between artefact patterns and site function (see
Yentsch 1991). While adaptive approaches to archaeological evidence are
uncommon today, the best of this work contributed to our understanding
of how social groups, particularly those in colonial situations, responded to
changing environmental and social circumstances.

During the mid to late 1980s, functional or adaptive interpretations of
household behaviour in historical archaeology were being criticised for min-
imising the conflicts and struggles that surely existed in what was viewed as
a competition for limited natural and social resources. American 'interpretive' historical archaeologists such as James Deetz or Mark Leone argued that
social groups and their social behaviour were not just found reflected in artefact patterning, they *had become* those patterns. They criticised approaches
in which social interactions among and within various groups and the
relationships these interactions implied remained unexplored and, at best,
were represented as proportions of artefact types and little more (e.g. South
1977a).

To circumvent this problem, Deetz and folklorist Henry Glassie advocated a structuralist paradigm for interpreting domestic archaeological materials, focusing not on what social groups *did* but on what they *thought*. Deetz
and Glassie used material culture to plumb for the 'deep mental structures'
people used to comprehend the world around them. Thus, Deetz (1977)
argued that patterns observed in aggregated assemblages from New England
domestic sites revealed a profound transformation in worldview over the
course of two centuries, from a 'medieval' perspective emphasising an
'organic, corporate communality' to the 'Georgian mindset', one privileging
rationalism, individualism and privacy. Glassie (1975) used a similar model
to explain changes in the floor plans of vernacular buildings in the region

west of Richmond, Virginia, between 1700 and 1950. For Deetz, Glassie, and the many historical archaeologists who were influenced by their models, the rise of the modern world and the changes it brought about in worldview were clearly (and materially) evident in artefact patterning.

During the 1980s 'critical archaeologists' such as Mark Leone (e.g. Leone et al. 1987) built upon Deetz's historical structuralism by paying closer attention to ideology (De Cunzo and Ernstein this volume). In the houses and gardens of eighteenth-century Annapolis, Maryland, Leone and his colleagues argued that a new capitalist order was both reflected in and shaped by a growing segmentation and standardisation in material culture. Distributions of ceramics from household contexts suggested the increasing segmentation and standardisation of meal consumption – the influence, they concluded, of a 'new etiquette', one that 'served both as a training ground for the new [mercantilist] order and as reinforcement for it' (Leone et al. 1987: 287–289). The separation of work and home life as well as new perceptions about time and space were brought about through the new capitalist order, and this new order was evident in material culture at virtually every level of society, including within the household. Similar changes were observed in the organisation of domestic space in eighteenth-century Montblanc in Catalonia, Spain, especially in the conversion of formerly public defensive towers into private dwellings with their increasingly segmented, gendered, and commodified spaces (Mangan 2000).

An interest in social power in households, including its distribution and its use, was central to such critical or 'critical materialist' approaches to households (defining material culture as one form or symbol of social and political power, the analysis of which can reveal how some people assert power even as others resist) and also to structuralist studies of households (building upon Deetz's work by seeing material culture as a kind of text or discourse, in which artefacts serve to shape and structure meaning through the social messages with which they have been encoded). From the production of colonoware bowls and other vessel forms on eighteenth-century Carolina plantations (Ferguson 1992) to the contents of storage pits associated with slave workers in eighteenth-century Cape Town (M. Hall 1992), structuralist archaeologists have suggested how such unremarkable objects could be read as 'everyday forms of domination and resistance' in their contexts of use.

Critical archaeologists have taken a slightly different approach, drawing upon Marxist theory to argue that, in a capitalist society, ideology functions to misrepresent the conditions of everyday life, structuring relationships of power through a 'false consciousness' and representing social relationships as natural (McGuire this volume). Clocks, watches, and scientific and musical instruments, for example, began appearing in early eighteenth-century Annapolis, Maryland urban households at about the same time that household wealth in the colonial port town was becoming more unequally distributed (Leone 1988b; see also Leone et al. 1987). For critical archaeologists, the eighteenth-century interest in these particular new consumer goods signalled an interest in the workings of natural law and how that law also applied to social and cultural life, especially in terms of naturalising social inequality and hierarchy (Leone 1988b; see also Leone et al. 1989). In another, less sophisticated, example, the size and location of postbellum farm housing is used to show not just economic status, but the 'physical manifestation of plantation power, or domination' (Orser 1988).

HOUSEHOLDS AND INDIVIDUAL LIVES

These interpretive studies have suggested that people's worldviews might be recovered from archaeological evidence, and that material culture was central to power relationships and struggles in the recent past. Still, neither Deetzian-inspired structuralism nor critical archaeology fully transcended the criticisms levelled at the functional and adaptive approaches to household analysis. Material culture continued to be understood as reflective of social and cultural realities, albeit ideological rather than ecological or technological ones. An almost relentless emphasis on form, such as architectural layout or ceramic colour and shape, virtually eliminated discussions of how domestic spaces and other artefacts might have been used (or by whom). While critical archaeologists do acknowledge that material culture does play an active as well as a passive or reflective role in social life, critics argued that household conflicts were rarely worked out as class struggle, and that sometimes household materialities negotiated more than domination or resistance (cf. Beaudry 1996, 2004; Tarlow 2000a; Yentsch 1991).

Perhaps more importantly, adaptive, structural and critical archaeologies depend in large part on models of normative behaviour, or the fiction that the complexities of individual households can be reduced to statistical abstractions which are then in turn considered representative of broader cultural realities. As artefact assemblages are manipulated to fit or to reveal larger archaeological patterns, atypical or unusual observations tend to be dismissed as idiosyncratic behaviour or are otherwise ignored, usually because of problems of small sample size. Households become 'faceless blobs', that is, undifferentiated and unproblematised social units that, at best, might be identified in terms of the household head (Beaudry 1989a; Tringham 1991). While no one would deny the importance of studying the diversity of agency in households, few archaeological studies considered the social and cultural differences found *within* households and the impact of difference on decision-making at that level. In part, this is because identifying individuals and individual agency in the archaeological record can be challenging. Nonetheless, social interaction within households is rarely a simple 'microversion' of society, and the relationship between households and broader social contexts requires better definition (Hendon 1996), especially if social and cultural changes are to be linked to individual decision-making or innovation (cf. Shennan 1989, 1991).

The importance of identifying individuals in the archaeological record has been especially apparent for those historical archaeologists interested in exploring engendered behaviour and relationships at domestic sites. These archaeologists were concerned that gender and its materiality within the context of the household was more often than not assumed, with these assumptions grounded in twentieth-century notions of proper gender roles and behaviour. Even more disconcerting was a deafening silence when it came to archaeological discussions of women in the past, either as individuals or as a group. Some early work, then, set out to explicitly find women and their artefacts in the archaeological record, an approach now characterised as 'remedial scholarship' (McEwan 1991; Nelson 2004: 4–5; cf. Starbuck 1994).

Even in such 'remedial' work, many feminist archaeologists argued that basic assumptions about women's and men's work remained entrenched and unexamined (cf. Gero and Conkey 1991). These archaeologists began by disentangling the categories of sex (as a biological construct) and gender (as a social construct), and showing how biology is not necessarily always conflated with gender, particularly in single-sex households where domestic functions nonetheless remain to be done (cf. Kryder-Reid 1994; Norton 1996: 183–202). From this work emerged a sense that women's experiences were indeed different and that gender was an important structuring principle worthy of investigation (Seifert 1991a; Spencer-Wood 2004). Feminist historical archaeologists began exploring how material culture was used to mark both individual gender and engendered behaviour, from patterns of household purchasing to the use of tea-drinking and other food consumption rituals to shape notions of domesticity (Seifert 1991b; Spencer-Wood 1999; Wall 1991). Archaeological evidence could also be used to show how productive behaviour – such as cheese-making – became engendered depending on the context in which it took place (Yentsch 1991).

Ironically, third-wave feminist theory is now challenging some of this early scholarship as essentialist, particularly the idea that all women share roughly the same experiences and problems. Race, ethnicity, class, religion and age, for example, are social factors that influence and transform engendered experiences in radical ways, such that women's experiences can in no way be considered 'all the same.' Third-wave feminists are also wary of models that artificially separate sex and gender, given that social expectations are in fact often formed by the social significance attached to physical bodies and their 'biological' characteristics (Lamphere, Ragone, and Zavella 1997). For these feminists, the individual and all the social and cultural baggage bound up in that person must be the focus if we are to make any kind of broader social statements about gender in the past.

Julian Thomas (1992: 12) has argued that feminist theory ultimately 'does fundamental damage to the established traditions of working within archaeology'. But studies of households in historical archaeology suggest that the challenge of exploring gender in archaeology is, *pace* Thomas, the same challenge facing all archaeologies of social life. How do we move from static archaeological sites to the individuals who helped create the sites and then on to statements about broader social and cultural realities? This question has both theoretical and methodological implications. Method will be considered in the next section of this chapter. Theoretically, however, a number of archaeologists have made use of the notion of *practice* for interpreting household social life (Beaudry 2004; Brandon and Barile 2004). Influenced by 'practice theory' (Bourdieu 1977; Giddens 1979; cf. Hodder 1982), such studies examine not just what households do, but how social action becomes meaningful and how it reproduces or transforms social and material situations. Social relationships or interactions that are organised by gender, class, ethnicity, race, or any other socially meaningful category are no longer understood as fixed 'underlying structures' driving behaviour. Rather, these imagined categories are in a state of continuous change and negotiation, with ever-changing material outcomes of everyday household social practice. What economic status 'means' in one household may 'mean' something completely different in another, and these differences become crucial locations for observing how social order is reproduced, changed or even subverted.

For example, in a study of nineteenth-century West Oakland, California households, Mary and Adrian Praetzellis (2004) found that ethnic and class differences among households either were not apparent in material-culture patterning or were much more subtle than expected. Indeed, many of the families occupying these households were purchasing goods or consuming foods that might be considered socially or culturally 'out of bounds', such as the Jewish household that made regular use of pork in their diet or the African-American working-class family that acquired expensive ceramics. Such purchases or uses suggest efforts, in the one case, to transform identity and, in the other, to subvert mainstream-white expectations (M. Praetzellis and A. Praetzellis 2004).

The potential for household archaeology to examine individual lives, mediating local and wider scales of analysis, is especially evident when previously analysed and interpreted excavations are reopened for examination: as was done with the case study reported below. Before exploring that example, however, a note upon methodology is necessary.

METHODOLOGY IN HOUSEHOLD ARCHAEOLOGY

Moving from artefacts recovered from archaeological contexts to statements about the individuals once living at a domestic site and then on to interpretations about social and cultural processes and practices presents extraordinary methodological challenges. Archaeologists have struggled to make this leap more transparent through discussions of uniquely archaeological issues: analogy, ethnoarchaeology, site formation processes and 'middle range theory' (Binford 1967; Hodder 1992; Kent 1987; Schiffer 1987; A. Wylie 1982). Equally frustrating, different sets of data from a single site may yield very different interpretations or conclusions about the same problem or topic (Nelson 2004: 67). Historical archaeologists generally argue that a 'contextual archaeology' is critical for developing sophisticated, reasonable and responsible interpretations about the past – to identify those 'faces' in the households historical archaeologists study and to situate the individuals behind those faces socially and culturally.

Contextual archaeology is obviously about context, particularly contexts of use (practice), and it is an especially valuable approach for archaeologists seeking to identify the 'faces' in the households they study (De Cunzo 1996). Context, defined through material and documentary sources (cf. Wilkie this volume), provides a basis from which to investigate the household as an assemblage of social actors, capable of making decisions or choices that may be socially structured but that nonetheless are key to understanding the forms households take and how those forms change. Under this framework, material culture is not the sole source of information about what households 'do'. Legal documents, maps, newspaper accounts, novels, oral histories, paintings, environmental data and many more evidentiary sources are critical for building the context which serves to inform archaeological interpretation.

Although it is today *de rigueur* in historical archaeology to claim the value of a contextual archaeology, such an approach faces its own challenges in the real-world social and economic situations in which much of historical archaeology is undertaken today. The overwhelming majority of archaeology undertaken in the United States and around the world emerges from cultural resource management (CRM), funded in order to mitigate the archaeological impact of new development. Indeed, the Advisory Council on Historic Preservation, the agency responsible for the regulation of federally mandated CRM, estimates that as much as 90 per cent of the archaeology done in the United States is driven by legal compliance. While some of the best examples of 'contextual archaeology' have been generated by commercial historical archaeologists (e.g. Cheek 1998; M. Praetzellis and A. Pratezellis 2004; Yamin 1998b), such work is thoughtful and time-consuming, and is therefore a more expensive process than one which privileges the quantitative analysis of artefacts, sometimes without a detailed study of the relationships between artefacts and the strata or deposits from which they come.

A single household can be presented as a single, irreducible entity occupied for fifty years or more. What is more troubling is the discovery that excavation methods often foreclose the evaluation of microstratigraphy or sequences that permit the narrowing and refinement of site chronology and spatial structure (cf. Beaudry 2004). The artefacts may have been recovered, but their context may be too generalised. This is a larger, more serious issue, and one demanding broader disciplinary discussion.

The reality is, the internal structure of rigorously excavated domestic archaeological sites can be organised temporally and spatially, and often persuasively linked to the life histories of the individuals who lived at those sites. More than thirty years ago, for example, Deagan (1973) was able to define deposits that could be linked to native Florida women who married colonising Spanish men in an effort to enhance their (and their family's) status, a process described as *mestizaje*. Mrozowski, Zeising, and Beaudry (1996) examined household deposits associated with skilled and unskilled workers at a nineteenth-century textile mill in Lowell, Massachusetts, revealing both the poor and unsanitary conditions in which the workers lived and the ways by which the workers attempted to control and improve their domestic surroundings. Yentsch (1994) was able to sort out materials associated with enslaved members of the Calvert household in mid-eighteenth-century Annapolis and link these materials, including beads and food, to efforts to mark identity among the African community living at the site and elsewhere in the neighbourhood.

Numerous studies in and outside of North America have examined how nineteenth-century households, whether in urban areas or on European frontiers, used ceramic tablewares to mark domestic environments and help set them apart from spaces increasingly used for work (Lawrence 2000; cf. Wall 1991, 2000). King and Miller (1987) used ceramics to date ploughed midden deposits at a seventeenth- and eighteenth-century site in Maryland more precisely, using these middens and their contents to identify changing uses of architectural and yard space throughout the household's occupation. Even shovel test pits spaced at close intervals on a ploughed site can reveal changes in domestic 'yardscapes' (King 1994). Such studies identify material details of domestic life in a similar manner to Boivin's (2000) use of plaster layers found on walls at the Neolithic site of Çatalhöyük in Turkey to document what appears to have been an annual domestic ritual – a phenomenal example of microchronology represented in the archaeological record.

Identifying individuals, activities, events, and the ongoing rhythms of a household's history or development can be challenging but is not impossible. In the next section, I use a case study from the Chesapeake region in North America to show how ethnicity was given material reality at a late seventeenth-century domestic site, an interpretation that involved the identification of individuals and groups of individuals living in the household.

CASE STUDY: LIVING AND DYING IN A SEVENTEENTH-CENTURY MARYLAND HOUSEHOLD

At the beginning of this chapter, I described measures taken by two contemporary colonial households, located only a few miles apart on the Patuxent River in Maryland, to secure their households from circumstances each perceived as threatening. In this section, I focus more closely on one of those households – Patuxent Point – and the challenge of examining the material conditions of social difference among the individuals once living there. Patuxent Point was excavated over the course of two years prior to residential development, yielding an extraordinary assemblage of archaeological materials from the second half of the seventeenth century. Traces of at least one and probably two buildings were recovered, an associated cemetery containing nineteen individuals was excavated, and ploughed midden deposits at the site were extensively sampled (King and Ubelaker 1996).

The period during which Patuxent Point was occupied has been described by historians as a 'golden age', characterised by political stability and

considerable upward economic and social mobility, at least for the Chesapeake yeoman planter (Carr et al. 1991). This was also a period during which
people in the Chesapeake colonies, as elsewhere in the Atlantic world, continued to work out new understandings of social and cultural difference. In
Maryland and Virginia, English and other European colonists, local Indian
groups, and people from the west coast of Africa came into increasingly
close everyday contact with one another. By the late 1680s, this English
'golden age' was starting to come apart, thanks to a prolonged depression in
tobacco prices. Some scholars suggest that it was the collapse of the tobacco
economy that forced Chesapeake planters to switch to an enslaved labour
force, a switch made possible in part by understandings of ethnic difference
developed over the course of nearly half a century.

Although few documents survive specifically referring to the plantation
at Patuxent Point or its household, we know from the analysis of human
remains recovered from the cemetery that at least one individual of probable African ancestry was living at the site in the very late seventeenth
century. The remaining eighteen individuals in the cemetery are probably of European ancestry, some of whom were almost certainly indentured
labourers and all of whom exhibit work-related stress injuries. While we
may never know the names and personal histories of the individuals buried
at Patuxent Point, analysis of the organisation and use of household space
(including the cemetery) provides some insight regarding how understandings of difference were marked here in the material world. To be sure,
the Patuxent Point household cannot be considered representative, given
that a growing body of comparative work in the Chesapeake is revealing that there is no such thing as a 'representative' site. Nonetheless, the
archaeological evidence recovered from Patuxent Point provides powerful,
if sometimes ambiguous, evidence for colonial understandings of ethnic
difference.

Four major refuse middens formed simultaneously throughout the site's
occupation, one associated with the principal dwelling and two on the north
and south sides of a second smaller building (Figure 16.2). Although the
middens had been ploughed for at least a hundred years, they nonetheless yielded large numbers of ceramics, tobacco pipes, animal bone, bottle glass, nails, and other materials typically found at seventeenth-century
Chesapeake domestic sites. An analysis of the materials recovered from each
midden revealed little difference in their contents, suggesting that similar
activities took place in both buildings, including the processing, storage, and
consumption of food, drinking, and tobacco smoking. Nor did the middens reveal any difference in the quality or cost of the materials deposited

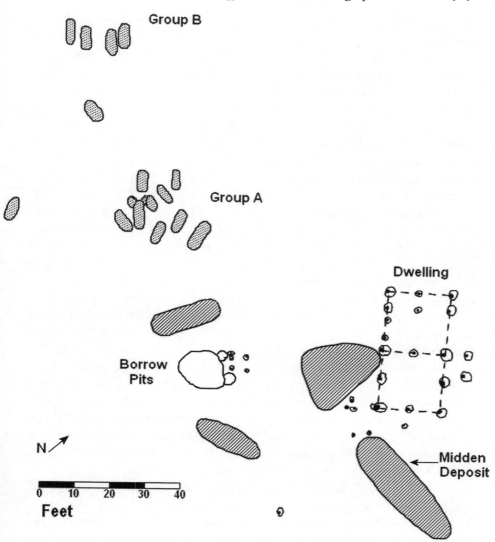

Figure 16.2 Plan view of architecture, middens, and cemetery, Patuxent Point.

in them. About the only difference between the three middens is revealed through their association with two separate but close residential structures.

While physical traces of the second building are ephemeral at best, consisting of a flat-bottomed storage pit and a few erratic posts, this building was probably a one-room structure, neither as large nor as well-built as the principal dwelling with its two or three rooms, wooden floors, and one or two glazed windows. The principal dwelling had a room (or hall) that served similar domestic purposes as the second building, but the principal dwelling also had additional (if unheated) space that could be used for storage, socialising, or sleeping in areas apart from the hall. Architecture, including its size and construction – and not the portable material goods and furnishings of everyday use, appears to have been the principal way by which an individual's social identity at Patuxent Point was materially marked. The people occupying the two structures took their meals from similar vessels and consumed their tobacco from similar pipes, but those living in the main dwelling enjoyed a better built, more comfortable and spacious structure. This observation echoes an earlier study which found that, while élite colonists in the Patuxent drainage (like Lord Baltimore) invested heavily in architecture, their domestic furnishings varied little from those found at sites occupied by middling planters (King and Chaney 2003).

In the nearby cemetery, which served the Patuxent Point residents for a period of thirty to thirty-five years, two burial clusters indicate that some effort was made to segregate individuals in death. Groups A and B may represent a distinction between free and bound or possibly just related and unrelated people living at Patuxent Point. Group A included twelve graves containing three adult females, three adult males, and six children ranging in age from nine months to thirteen years, all of European ancestry. All were buried in east–west Christian fashion, although four individuals (all children) were positioned with their head in the east end of the grave. The presence of young children in Group A suggests this portion of the cemetery was used for the planter's family. Given the number of adults, labourers could also conceivably be represented in Group A.

Group B included an adult female and adult male of European ancestry, an adolescent male of likely African ancestry, and a thirteen to fourteen year old of undetermined sex and ancestry. The skeletons of both males displayed evidence of heavy lifting, pushing, or pulling, a likely consequence of the hard work of tobacco cultivation. The thirteen to fourteen year old had suffered a broken femur in his or her life, an injury that had healed fully prior to the child's death. All four people found in Group B were buried in Christian fashion, wrapped in a shroud pinned about the head. A

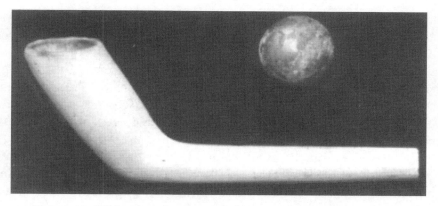

Figure 16.3 White clay tobacco pipe and button recovered from Burial 18.

silver- or tin-plated dome-style button was found in the area of the African male's pelvis, but does not appear to have been worn as a form of jewellery. In addition, this individual was buried cradling a white clay tobacco pipe in his hands, a practice documented among enslaved Africans at a plantation in Barbados and on at least one eighteenth-century Virginia plantation (Figure 16.3; Handler and Lange 1978: 255–256; Kelso 1984: 109).

The architecture and midden evidence at Patuxent Point mirrors the cemetery evidence: in life, as in death, the household's residents were organised into two groups, one likely defined by legal status and/or kinship relationships and the second by residents probably having no kinship relation with the planter's family and in bound service to that family. The family, which appears to be somewhat extended, probably occupied the well-built principal dwelling while the labourers occupied a flimsy, smaller second structure. The sixteen to seventeen year old individual of likely African ancestry, whose skeleton was already showing evidence of hard physical labour, was not separated out in death from other Europeans. As was the case for the woman mentioned at the beginning of this chapter who died in childbirth, the residents at Patuxent Point were clearly able to bury an individual apart when circumstances demanded it. Ancestry, however, does not seem to have demanded spatial segregation, at least not in this case.

Yet, while the African youth may share burial space with other Europeans, the treatment of his body in death suggests an acknowledgement of difference, perhaps based on religion as much as on ancestry. The young man was interred in traditional Christian fashion, wrapped in a shroud with his head placed in the west end of the grave. That this likely African individual may have been Christian is not especially surprising. In an examination of the relationships between Christianity and West African religions, John Thornton (1997: 235–271) found that not only did Africans in Africa know of Christianity through missionaries, for many Africans, conversion to Christianity was facilitated by similar understandings of the physical world and its relationship to the supernatural world. The white clay tobacco pipe carefully inserted in this adolescent individual's hands during burial may mark religious belief, ancestry, or both.

The evidence from Patuxent Point suggests that identity at this late seventeenth-century household may have been defined as much by kinship and religious belief as by ancestry. Indeed, for Englishmen and women during this period, difference based on skin colour or ancestry 'first and foremost . . . presented a series of theological problems' (Kidd 1999: 239). Ethnic classification became a question of 'confessional identity' tied into ideas about the peopling of the world and the popular belief that all human beings were descended from the sons and grandsons of Noah, who then spread throughout the world (Kidd 1999: 9). This is not to say that ancestry as inferred from skin colour was not an identifying factor at Patuxent Point or elsewhere in the Chesapeake. After all, the late seventeenth-century court records in Maryland are careful to describe individuals of darker skin colouring as 'Negroes'. Bound up in that description, however, is more than a simple descriptor referring to skin colour. Religion was also a powerful component of identity in the early modern era, one that in our more secular age might be easily overlooked. In our effort to link ethnic and racial identity in the present to past processes and transformations, we risk overlooking how the categories themselves and their meanings have changed (Hannaford 1996; S. Jones 1997: 1–14). In contrast, examining these archaeological materials in household contexts provides one powerful perspective from which the complexities and materialities of ethnicities in the past can be revealed.

CONCLUDING THOUGHTS

Interest in household archaeology has waxed and waned since the 1960s, but, as this chapter has traced, a sophisticated body of distinctive material has developed in North American historical archaeology. A particular strength of this field is its tradition of shifting between individual lives and wider social contexts, identifying the complexities of particular situations that are invisible in conventional normative models of everyday life. Through their material remains, archaeologists can generate far richer, nuanced interpretations of households: studies that Roberta Gilchrist (2000: 327) suggests might be approached in a 'biographical' manner. No longer simply sets of 'artefact patterns', household sites represent a rich resource for the multi-scalar study of individual and social lives in the past. As historical archaeologists continue to construct finely detailed biographies of households, replete with the details and textures of everyday life that are less visible in conventional historical studies, the methods developed in North American household archaeologies increasingly hold the potential to make distinctive contributions to the archaeological study of other material, periods and parts of the world.

CHAPTER 17

Afterword: historical archaeology in the wider discipline

Barry Cunliffe

No one who has read this far can be in any doubt that historical archaeology is alive and well. The individual contributions which make up this volume, as vigorous as they are varied, reflect a branch of the discipline of archaeology that is defining its scope, developing its theoretical constructs and honing its techniques. The purpose of this brief endpiece is not to review the individual contributions but to reflect on the position of historical archaeology, as it is here presented, in the broader field of archaeological studies. The viewpoint taken is unashamedly that of an archaeologist whose perspective is that history is a valuable way of studying some aspects of the most recent fragment of the archaeological record.

We need not spend too much time on definitions. Within 'historical archaeology' are nested various other kinds of archaeology: urban, colonial, industrial, maritime, each capable of subdivision; maritime, for example, embracing underwater and nautical archaeology. All are treated in the chapters above but we should not forget that there are other subsets of historical archaeology which have successfully demonstrated their value in recent years, the study of battlefields and of gardens, for example, both with their very distinctive methodologies.

In geographical scope historical archaeology covers the world but may, for convenience, be divided into three broad groupings – occidental Old World, oriental Old World and New World – each emphasising different aspects of the shared agenda. The present volume offers little on the oriental Old World, for the very good reason that the literature is inaccessible to the majority of the western audience, but it is well to remember that potentially this region, with its deep history, has an enormous amount to contribute to the general debate and must, in due course, be brought into the mainstream of the study.

In the western part of the Old World – essentially Europe, North Africa and the Near East – historical archaeology has, from the beginning, been an essential part of archaeological studies. One has only to browse through the early volumes of the British journal *Archaeologia*, the first volume of which was published in 1779, to appreciate the wide breadth of the study as it was, even then, practised. For those working in Britain it has long been recognised that we live amid the detritus of our past and that it is the responsibility of all excavating archaeologists to treat with equal diligence all phases represented in the archaeological record. This is nowhere more apparent than in urban archaeology which began to develop in London in the 1930s under the driving force of Mortimer Wheeler, then Director of the London Museum, and since World War II has become such a prominent aspect of the archaeological scene.

Many European cities have their origins in prehistory and only begin to enter the sphere of recorded history in the Roman period. Each act of construction places constraints on the 'landscape' within which subsequent generations have to navigate. To take the example of Winchester, which has been extensively studied (Biddle 1983; Qualman et al. 2004), here the construction of an Iron Age defence in the second century BC, sited so as to control a river crossing, influenced the early Roman settlement and its access points which in part determined the later development of the walled Roman town and its street grid. Later, in the late Saxon period, the Roman wall and gates were a controlling factor in the late Saxon land apportionment within. This in turn provided a structure of streets which dominated the medieval town and is still extant, today causing problems to modern traffic flow.

Clearly, given an archaeological record of such complexity, the only proper way to study it is in its entirety, beginning with prehistory and eliding gently into the historical present. Archaeologists brought up in this tradition naturally find being compartmentalised into 'prehistoric', 'Roman', 'medieval' or 'historical' archaeologists arbitrary and alien to the reality of their work. European urban archaeology has, then, been a forcing ground for the holistic approach which gives it a particular strength.

By definition, towns and cities perform much the same cluster of functions through time, and therefore respond to historical changes within certain constructed parameters. Other types of site provide different insights. Take, for example, the coastal fortress of Portchester Castle in Hampshire (Cunliffe 1975, 1976, 1977; Cunliffe and Garratt 1994; Cunliffe and Munby 1985). Here a Roman fort was established in the late third century as a fortified enclosure commanding a harbour, though the precise function of these sites is in debate. In the early Saxon period the old walls provided legitimacy and protection for a small monastic establishment and later for an élite residence. With the Norman conquest the defensive possibilities of the site determined its use as a castle which eventually became a royal residence for kings intent on hunting in the nearby Forest of Bere or preparing to embark for the continent (the troops *en route* for Agincourt stayed here). By the sixteenth century Portchester Castle was obsolete as a fortification but used from time to time as a military store and a prison, culminating in its development as a major prisoner-of-war camp during the Revolutionary and Napoleonic Wars. Thereafter it became a focus of antiquarian interest. During the Depression large numbers of out-of-work miners were employed by the state preparing it for presentation as a visitor attraction and now it takes its place in the service of England's heritage industry. Once fortified by the Romans the trajectory of development was set, each stage further circumscribing what followed. Portchester, then, reflects the changing military, political, social and economic needs of the larger community. It plays to many agendas: its value to archaeology (and to historical archaeology) lies in the deep-time perspective which it offers.

Much the same point can be made of landscape studies in the Old World. In Britain many of our parish boundaries originate in the late Saxon period and there is some evidence to suggest that even older land divisions may have had some impact on the late Saxon landscape. In parts of France ecclesiastical boundaries can be traced back to late Roman times.

Sufficient will have been said to stress the point that in the Old World in particular, what might be characterised as historical archaeology is part of a unified study which covers the full span of human activity. The research aims and the techniques used to study a nineteenth-century croft on the Outer Hebrides are exactly the same as those employed in the examination of an Iron Age wheelhouse on the same island. What the archaeologists of the historical period have, in addition, is a fragmentary and often anecdotal historical record which may help to explain or contextualise the archaeological data. That said, what has come out of many of the studies discussed in the chapters above is that the archaeological evidence may contradict, or at least qualify, the perceptions and generalisations derived from documentary sources. Herein lies its particular strength.

The chapters in this volume highlight some interesting differences between the ethos of historical archaeology in the Old and New Worlds (taking the New World to include the Americas, Africa and Australasia). In the Old World, as we have stressed, the emphasis is on the *longue durée* in an attempt to identify continuity and change, whereas in the New World a focus on the impact and process of colonialism has shaped the field. This has encouraged the examination of a number of extremely interesting themes, among them the 'adaptation' of immigrant communities to their new environments, the maintenance of ethnic identity by different national, racial and religious groups of immigrants, the impact of colonialism on indigenous communities and the degree of 'assimilation' of these communities by the colonisers. These themes run through many of the studies outlined in this volume. Since, as Chris Gosden has convincingly argued, colonialism is essentially a material phenomenon and power lies in the new sets of material culture and practices associated with a symbolic centre (Gosden 2004), the methods of the archaeologist are particularly powerful in exploring the nature of the processes of colonisation in far more detail than is possible from the documentary sources alone. The case studies referred to in this volume, and the many others of which they are representative, deserve to be studied by prehistorians. For far too long there has been a tendency among European prehistorians to avoid explanations involving large-scale folk movement. Whilst they may be right, there is much in the experience of historical archaeologists of the New World that could inform their thinking about, and modelling of, the cultural discontinuities they observe.

The same methodologies are directly applicable to other cultural interactions around the world. Most directly comparable would be the impact of Greek, Phoenician and Roman colonisation on indigenous communities. There is great scope here for introducing new ways of exploring these interactions. In Britain, for example, it is becoming clear that Roman material culture, and in particular domestic architecture, was being selectively adopted by the indigenous rural population, the patterns emerging reflecting the socioeconomic structures and political leanings of the different tribal groups. There is much here which deserves to be explored in more detail enlivened by an understanding of similar processes studied by historical archaeologists in the New World.

Nor should we overlook other 'colonial' interfaces such as the Indian subcontinent with its different styles of European interaction – Portuguese, French and British – over an extended period of time developing within changing economic and political scenarios. Or the maritime cultures of East Africa with their vibrant mix of indigenous, European and Arab cultures. The methodologies developed in America and Australasia are directly applicable to these very different historical contexts.

Another type of colonisation which falls within the ambit of historical archaeology is the settlement of remote marginal landscapes be they Siberian forests or desert fringes. One example, in which much highly innovative work is currently being done, is the Landscapes circum-*Landnám* project directed from Aberdeen University which is studying in meticulous detail the Norse settlement of the Faroe Islands, Iceland and Greenland using a battery of scientific technologies and methodologies, together with Saga texts and later documents, to characterise the progress of sustainable economic strategies in these extreme environments (Landscapes circum-*Landnám* Project 2005). It is tempting to coin yet another phrase for this kind of study – marginal archaeology.

It will be clear from what has been said that the umbrella of historical archaeology when fully extended would cover the world. Practitioners in the anglophone region should be encouraged to promote their expertise more widely, though perhaps it might be an advantage to shed some of the polemics of political correctness on the way. The subject deserves to be more than just a eurocentric archaeology of capitalism.

From the world scale, let us return to the basics of historical archaeology. Having read, with considerable excitement, all the contributions in this book, perhaps most remarkable is the way in which the historical archaeologist is able to address the household in exceptionally vivid detail, sometimes even treating the life histories of individual rooms or other single-purpose private spaces. These household archaeologies provide the raw material for entirely new social histories replacing the old, and often biased, generalisations based on historical sources alone. They are also the building blocks for new community archaeologies which are far more than just local histories. Most of this is, of necessity, land-based but community archaeology can also, though rarely, be written from shipwreck archaeology. Perhaps the most dramatic example of this is the *Mary Rose*, a Tudor warship of the time of Henry VIII which sank off Spithead in 1545 and was excavated and raised in the 1980s. As the result of the remarkable preservation of the wreck and the skilful excavation and conservation of its artefacts, it has been possible to build up an incomparable picture of seafaring life in Tudor England beginning with the seachests of individual sailors and contextualising the entire set of material culture against the background of the maritime and political history of Tudor England (Gardiner 2005; Figures 10.2 and 10.3). Maritime archaeology, like land-based historical archaeology, enables us to move across a range of scales from the individual to the global.

Finally, several writers have reminded us that historical archaeology often interfaces with the heritage industry and there is thus a need to consider conservation, reconstruction, management and presentation all of which raise quite difficult technical and ethical issues – issues of authenticity, the need for unbiased story lines and the all-too-frequent conflict between preservation and redevelopment especially where this impacts on the interests of minority groups. In this way historical archaeology merges into the continuum of contemporary life.

Anyone who comes afresh to historical archaeology through this volume cannot fail to be impressed by the range of the discipline, its high academic standards and the integrity and commitment of its practitioners. It is a vibrant and innovative branch of the mother discipline – archaeology – a discipline which carries the awesome responsibility of researching and communicating the entire history of humankind.

References

Abraham, T. and P. Wegars 2003. Urns, bones and burners: overseas Chinese cemeteries. *Australasian Historical Archaeology* 21: 58–69.

Adams, J. 1985. *Sea Venture*: a second interim report, part one. *International Journal of Nautical Archaeology* 14 (4): 275–300.

2001. Ships and boats as archaeological source material. *World Archaeology* 32 (3): 292–310.

Adams, P. C. 2001. Peripatetic imagery and peripatetic sense of place. In P. C. Adams, S. Hoelscher and K. E. Till (eds.) *Textures of Place: Exploring Humanist Geographies*. Minneapolis, MN: University of Minnesota Press, pp. 186–206.

Adams, W. H. 2003. Dating historical sites: the importance of understanding time lag in the acquisition, curation, use and disposal of artefacts. *Historical Archaeology* 37: 38–64.

Alcock, N. W., M. W. Barley, P. W. Dixon and R. A. Meeson 1996. *Recording Timber-Framed Buildings: An Illustrated Glossary*. York: Council for British Archaeology (Practical Handbook in Archaeology 5).

Alcock, S., T. D'Altroy, K. Morrison and C. Sinopoli (eds.) 2001. *Empires: Perspectives from Archaeology and History*. Cambridge: Cambridge University Press.

Alexander, R. 1999. Mesoamerican house lots and archaeological site structure: problems of inference in Yaxcaba, Yucatan, Mexico, 1750–1847. In P. Allison (ed.) *The Archaeology of Household Activities: Gender, Ideologies, Domestic Spaces, and Material Culture*. New York: Routledge, pp. 78–100.

Alexandria Archaeology Museum nd. *Publications about Archaeology in Alexandria*. Online bibliography held at http://oha.ci.alexandria.va.us/ archaeology/ar-research-biblio.html (accessed 4 April 2005).

Alfrey, J. and C. Clark 1993. *The Landscape of Industry*. London: Routledge.

Ali, M. 2003. *Brick Lane*. London: Doubleday.

Allan, J. P. 1984. *Medieval and Post-Medieval Finds from Exeter, 1971–1980*. Exeter: Exeter City Council and University of Exeter.

1999. Producers, distributors and redistributors: the role of the south western ports in the seventeenth century ceramics trades. In G. Egan and R. L. Michael (eds.) pp. 278–288.

Allan, J. P. and P. Pope 1990. A new class of south-west English pottery in North America. *Post-Medieval Archaeology* 24: 51–59.

Althusser, L. 1969. *For Marx*. New York: Pantheon.

1971a. *Lenin and Philosophy*. New York: Monthly Review Press.

1971b. Ideology and ideological state apparatuses. In L. Althusser (ed.) *Lenin and Philosophy and Other Essays*. New York: Monthly Review Press, pp. 27–86.

Anderson, E. B. 1984. *Annapolis: A Walk Through History*. Centreville, MD: Tidewater Publishers.

Anderton, M. and J. Schofield 1999. Anti-aircraft gunsites – then and now. *Conservation Bulletin* 36: 11–13.

Andrews, D., B. Blake, M. Clowes and K. Wilson 1995. *The Survey and Recording of Historic Buildings*. Oxford: Association of Archaeological Illustrators and Surveyors (Technical paper No. 12).

Anon 1999. *National Heritage Resources Act, Republic of South Africa* (Act No. 25). www.info.gov.za/gazette/acts/1999/a25-99.pdf (Accessed 3 March 2005).

Appadurai, A. (ed.) 1986. *The Social Life of Things: Commodities in Cultural Perspective*. Cambridge: Cambridge University Press.

Archaeologia Polona 2000. Archaeological heritage management: theory and practice. *Archaeologia Polona* 38.

Armstrong, D. and E. M. Armstrong 1991. *The Great Medicine Show: Being an Illustrated History of Hucksters, Healers, Health Evangelists, and Heroes from Plymouth Rock to the Present*. New York: Prentice Hall.

Armstrong, D. V. 2003. *Creole Transformation from Slavery to Freedom: Historical Archaeology of the East End Community, St. John, Virgin Island*. Tallahassee, FL: University Press of Florida.

Arnold, D. 1998. The country house: form, function and meaning. In D. Arnold (ed.) *The Georgian Country House: Architecture, Landscape and Society*. Stroud: Sutton, pp. 1–19.

Arnold, J. B. 1993. Matagorda Bay surveys. *International Journal of Nautical Archaeology* 22(1): 79–87.

Arnold, J. B., T. J. Oertling and A. J. Hall 2001. The Denbigh Project: test excavations at the wreck of an American Civil War blockade-runner. *World Archaeology* 32(3): 400–412.

Ascher, R. and C. H. Fairbanks 1971. Excavation of a slave cabin: Georgia, USA. *Historical Archaeology* 5: 3–17.

Ashmore, O. 1969. *The Industrial Archaeology of Lancashire*. Newton Abbot: David & Charles.

Atterbury, P. 2003. Architects and ceramics in Victorian Britain. In T. Walford and H. Young (eds.) *British Ceramic Design: 1600–2002*. Beckenham, Kent: English Ceramic Circle, pp. 138–144.

Ayre, J. and R. Wroe-Brown 2003. *The London Millennium Bridge: Excavation of the Medieval and Later Waterfronts at Peter's Hill, City of London, and Bankside, Southwark*. London: Museum of London Archaeology Service.

Ayris, I. and S. Gould 1994. *Colliery Landscapes: An Aerial Survey of the Deep-Mined Coal Industry in England*. London: English Heritage.

Badcock, A. and B. Malaws 2004. Recording people and processes at large industrial structures. In D. Barker and D. Cranstone (eds.) pp. 269–290.

Baker, D. 1991. *Potworks: The Industrial Architecture of the Staffordshire Potteries*. London: Royal Commission on Historical Monuments.

Baker, F., S. Taylor and J. Thomas 1990. Writing the past in the present: an introductory dialogue. In F. Baker and J. S. Thomas (eds.) *Writing the Past in the Present*. Lampeter: St. David's University College, pp. 1–11.

Baker, P. and G. Henderson 1979. *James Matthew* excavation. *International Journal of Nautical Archaeology* 8(3): 225–231.

Bakhtin, M. M. 1981. *The Dialogic Imagination: Four Essays*. (trans. C. Emerson and M. Holquist, ed. M. Holquist). Austin, TX: University of Texas Press.

1986. *Speech Genres and Other Late Essays*. (trans. V. W. McGee, ed. C. Emerson and M. Holquist). Austin, TX: University of Texas Press.

Ballard, R. D. 1985. *The Discovery of the Titanic*. London: Simon and Schuster.

1990. *The Discovery of the Bismarck*. London: Simon and Schuster.

Ballard, R. D., A. M. McCann, D. Yoerger, L. Whitcomb, D. Mindell, J. Oleson, H. Singh, B. Foley, J. Adams, D. Piechota and G. Giangrande 2000. The discovery of ancient history in the deep sea. *Deep Sea Research* 1 (47): 1591–1620.

Bapty, I. 1989. The meanings of things, writing, and archaeology. *Archaeological Review from Cambridge* 8: 175–184.

1990. The agony and the ecstasy: the emotions of writing the past, a tragedy in one act for three voices. *Archaeological Review from Cambridge* 9: 233–242.

Barile, K. S. and J. C. Brandon (eds.) 2004. *Household Chores and Household Choices: Theorizing the Domestic Sphere in Historical Archaeology*. Tuscaloosa, AL: University of Alabama Press.

Barka, N. F. 2004. Archaeology of a colonial pottery factory: the kilns and ceramics of the 'Poor Potter' of Yorktown. In R. Hunter (ed.) *Ceramics in America 2004*. Milwaukee: Chipstone Foundation, pp. 15–47.

Barker, D. 1991. *William Greatbatch – A Staffordshire Potter*. London: Jonathan Horne.

1993. *Slipware*. Princes Risborough: Shire.

1999. The ceramic revolution 1650–1850. In G. Egan and R. L. Michael (eds.) pp. 226–234.

2001. 'The usual classes of useful articles': Staffordshire ceramics reconsidered. In R. Hunter (ed.) *Ceramics in America 2001*. Milwaukee, WI: Chipstone Foundation, pp. 72–93.

2004. The industrialization of the Staffordshire potteries. In D. Barker and D. Cranstone (eds.) pp. 203–221.

2005. Pottery usage in a crofting community: an overview. In K. Branigan (ed.) *From Clan to Clearance – History and Archaeology on the Isle of Barra c. 850 to 1850 AD*. Oxford: Oxbow, pp. 111–122.

Barker, D. and D. Cranstone (eds.) 2004. *The Archaeology of Industrialization*. Leeds: Maney (Society for Post-Medieval Archaeology).

Barnatt, J. and R. Penny 2004. *The Lead Legacy: The Prospects for the Peak District's Lead Mining Heritage*. Bakewell: Peak District National Park Authority with English Heritage and English Nature.

Barrett, J. C. 2000. Comments on Laurie A. Wilkie and Kevin M. Bartoy, A critical archaeology revisited. *Current Anthropology* 41(5): 761–762.

Bartels, M. 1999. *Steden in Scherven, Vondsten uit beerputten in Deventer, Dordrecht, Nijmegen en Tiel (1250-1900).* Zwolle: Stichting Promotie Archeologie.

Barton, K. J. 1967. The origins of the Society for Post-Medieval Archaeology. *Post-Medieval Archaeology* 1: 1–3.

Bass, G. F. 1966. *Archaeology Under Water.* London: Thames and Hudson.

1979. The shipwreck at Serçe Limani, Turkey. *Archaeology* 32(1): 36–43.

1982. *Yassiada, Vol. I: A Seventh Century Byzantine Shipwreck.* College Station: Texas A&M University Press.

1983. A plea for historical particularism in nautical archaeology. In R. A. Gould (ed.) *Shipwreck Anthropology.* Albuquerque, NM: University of New Mexico Press, pp. 91–104.

Bass, G. F. and C. Pulak 1989. The Bronze Age shipwreck at Ulu Burun. *American Journal of Archaeology* 93(1): 1–29.

Basu, P. 2001. Hunting down home: reflections on homeland and the search for identity in the Scottish diaspora. In B. Bender and M. Winer (eds.) pp. 333–348.

Beaudry, M. C. 1984. Archaeology and the historical household. *Man in the Northeast* 28: 27–38.

1987. Opinion – analytical scale and methods for the archaeological study of urban households. *Society for Historical Archaeology Newsletter* 20(1): 22–25.

1988a. Introduction. In M. C. Beaudry (ed.) pp. 1–3.

Beaudry, M. C. (ed.) 1988b. *Documentary Archaeology in the New World.* Cambridge: Cambridge University Press.

Beaudry, M. C. 1989a. Household structure and the archaeological record: examples from New World historical sites. In S. MacEachern, D. Archer, and R. Garvin (eds.) *Households and Communities.* Calgary, Alberta: University of Calgary, pp. 84–92

1989b. The Boott Mills complex and its housing: material expressions of corporate ideology. *Historical Archaeology* 23(1): 18–32.

1995. Introduction: ethnography in retrospect. In M. E. D'Agostino, E. Prine, E. Casella and M. Winer (eds.) *The Written and the Wrought: Complementary Sources in Historical Archaeology.* Berkeley, CA: Kroeber Anthropological Society Papers 79, pp. 1–16.

1996. Reinventing historical archaeology. In Lu Ann De Cunzo and Bernard L. Herman (eds.) pp. 473–497.

1998. Farm journal: first person, four voices. *Historical Archaeology* 32(1): 20–33.

1999. House and household: the archaeology of domestic life in early America. In G. Egan and R. L. Michael (eds.) pp. 117–126.

2004. Doing the housework: new approaches to the archaeology of households. In K. S. Barile and J. C. Brandon (eds.) pp. 254–262.

2006. *Findings: The Material Culture of Needlework and Sewing.* New Haven, CT: Yale University Press.

Beaudry, M. C. nd. Stories that matter: material lives in 19th-century Boston and Lowell, Massachusetts, USA. In A. Green and R. Leech (eds.) *Cities in the World, 1500–2000*. London: Maney (Society for Post-Medieval Archaeology Monograph No. 3), pp. 249–268.

Beaudry, M. C. and S. A. Mrozowski (eds.) 1987a. *Interdisciplinary Investigations of the Boott Mills, Lowell, Massachusetts, Vol. I: Life at the Boardinghouses*. Cultural Resources Management Study no. 18, Division of Cultural Resources, Boston, North Atlantic Regional Office, National Park Service, United States Department of the Interior.

(eds.) 1987b. *Interdisciplinary Investigations of the Boott Mills, Lowell, Massachusetts, Vol. II: The Kirk Street Agent's House*. Cultural Resources Management Study no. 19, Division of Cultural Resources, Boston, North Atlantic Regional Office, National Park Service, United States Department of the Interior.

(eds.) 1989. *Interdisciplinary Investigations of the Boott Mills, Lowell, Massachusetts, Vol. III: The Boardinghouses System as a Way of Life*. Cultural Resources Management Study no. 21, Division of Cultural Resources, Boston, North Atlantic Regional Office, National Park Service, United States Department of the Interior.

Beaudry, M. C. and J. White 1994. Cowgirls with the blues? a study of women's publication and the citation of women's work in *Historical Archaeology*. In C. Claassen (ed.) *Women in Archaeology*. Philadelphia, PA: University of Pennsylvania Press, pp. 138–158.

Beaudry, M. C., L. Cook and S. Mrozowski 1991. Artifacts and active voices: material culture as social discourse. In R. McGuire and R. Paynter (eds.) *The Archaeology of Inequality*, Oxford: Blackwell, pp. 150–191.

Beaudry, M. C., K. J. Goldstein and C. Chartier 2003. Archaeology of Plymouth colony in Massachusetts. *Avalon Chronicles* 8: 155–183 (Special issue: The English in America, 1497–1696, ed. J. Tuck).

Beaudry, M. C., J. Long, H. M. Miller, F. D. Neiman and G. W. Stone 1983. A vessel typology for early Chesapeake ceramics: the Potomac typological system. *Historical Archaeology* 17: 18–39.

1988. A vessel typology for early Chesapeake ceramics: the Potomac typological system. In M. C. Beaudry (ed.) pp. 51–67.

Becher, B. and H. Becher 2004. *Typologies of Industrial Buildings*. Cambridge, MA: MIT Press.

Beck, C. M., H. Drollinger and J. Schofield nd. Archaeology of dissent: landscape and symbolism at the Nevada Peace Camp. In J. Schofield and W. D. Cocroft (eds.) *A Fearsome Heritage: Diverse Legacies of the Cold War*. London: Routledge (One World Archaeology).

Bederman, G. 1995. *Manliness and Civilization*. Chicago, IL: University of Chicago Press.

Behar, R. and D. A. Gordon (eds.) 1995. *Women Writing Culture*. Berkeley, CA: University of California Press.

Belford, P. 2003. Forging ahead in Coalbrookdale: historical archaeology at the Upper Forge. *Industrial Archaeology Review* 25(1): 59–62.

Bell, A. 2002. Emulation and empowerment: material, social, and economic dynamics in eighteenth- and nineteenth-century Virginia. *International Journal of Historical Archaeology* 6(4): 253–298.

Bell, M. 1997. The ghosts of place. *Theory and Society* 26: 813–836.

Bell, P. 1998. The fabric and structure of Australian mining settlements. In A. B. Knapp, V. Piggott and E. Herbert (eds.) *Social Approaches to an Industrial Past*. London: Routledge, pp. 27–38.

Bender, B. (ed.) 1993. *Landscape Politics and Perspectives*. Oxford: Berg.

Bender, B. 1998. *Stonehenge: Making Space*. Oxford: Berg.

2001. Introduction. In B. Bender and M. Winer (eds.) pp. 1–18.

2002. Landscape and politics: Introduction. In V. Buchli (ed.) pp. 135–140.

Bender, B. and M. Winer (eds.) 2001. *Contested Landscapes: Movement, Exile and Place*. Oxford: Berg.

Bender, G. 1968. A refinement of the concept of household: families, co-residence and domestic functions. *American Anthropologist* 69: 493–503.

Benjamin, W. 1969. The work of art in the age of mechanical reproduction. In H. Arendt (ed.) *Illuminations*. New York: Schocken, pp. 217–252.

Bennett, J. 2001. *The Enchantment of Modern Life: Attachments, Crossings and Ethics*. Princeton and Oxford: Princeton University Press.

Beresford, M. 1971. An historian's appraisal of archaeological research. In M. Beresford and J. Hurst (eds.) pp. 169–181.

Beresford, M. and J. Hurst (eds.) 1971. *Deserted Medieval Villages: Studies*. Woking: Lutterworth Press.

Beresford, M. and J. Hurst 1990. *Wharram Percy: Deserted Medieval Village*. London: Batsford.

Berkeleyan 1880. *Description of Housing and Amenities on Campus*. Microfilm on file at Bancroft Library, University of California, Berkeley.

Betts, I., N. Crowley and J. Keily 1991. Recent work on medieval and later building materials in London. *Medieval Ceramics* 15: 37–41.

Biddle, M. 1983. The study of Winchester: archaeology and history in a British town. *Proceedings of the British Academy* 69: 83–135.

Biddle, M., J. Hiller and I. Scott 2001. *Henry VIII's Coastal Artillery Fort at Camber Castle, Rye, East Sussex: An Archaeological, Structural and Historical Investigation*. Oxford: Oxbow Books.

Biko, S. and A. Stubbs 1978. *I Write What I Like*. London: Bowerdean Press.

Binford, L. R. 1962. Archaeology as anthropology. *American Antiquity* 28(2): 217–225.

1967. Smudge pits, and hide smoking: the use of analogy in archaeological reasoning. *American Antiquity* 32(1): 1–2.

1978. A new method of calculating dates from Kaolin pipe stem samples. In R. L. Schuyler (ed.) pp. 66–67.

Birmingham, J., I. Jack and D. Jeans 1979. *Australian Pioneer Technology: Sites and Relics*. Richmond: Heinemann Educational Australia.

1983. *Industrial Archaeology in Australia: Rural Industry*. Richmond: Heinemann Publishers Australia.

Blake, H. 1987. Archaeology and maiolica. In T. Wilson (ed.) *Ceramic Art of the Italian Renaissance*. London: British Museum Publications, pp. 15–16.

Blair, J. and C. Pyrah (eds.) 1996. *Church Archaeology: Research Directions for the Future*. York: Council for British Archaeology (Research Report 104).

Blaut, J. M. 2000. *Eight Eurocentric Historians*. New York: Guilford Press.

Bloch, M. 1983. *Marxism and Anthropology: The History of a Relationship*. Oxford: Clarendon Press.

Bloice, B. J. 1971. Norfolk House, Lambeth: excavations at a delftware kiln site, 1968. *Post-Medieval Archaeology* 5: 99–159.

Blue and Gold 1880–1920. *Year Book of the University of California*, Volumes 7–47. Berkeley, CA: University of California Press.

Boivin, N. 2000. Life rhythms and floor sequences: excavating time in rural Rajasthan and Neolithic Çatalhöyük. *World Archaeology* 31(3): 367–388.

2004. Mind over matter? Collapsing the mind–matter dichotomy in material culture studies. In E. DeMarrais, C. Gosden and C. Renfrew (eds.) *Rethinking Materiality: the Engagement of Mind with the Material World*. Cambridge: McDonald Institute for Archaeological Research (McDonald Institute Monographs), pp. 63–71.

Bound, M. (ed.) 1995. *The Archaeology of Ships of War*. London: Anthony Nelson.

Bourdieu, P. 1977. Structures and the habitus. In P. Bourdieu *Outline of a Theory of Practice* (trans. R. Nice). Cambridge: Cambridge University Press, pp. 72–95.

1990 [1970]. The Kabyle house, or the world reversed. In P. Bourdieu *The Logic of Practice*. Stanford, CA: Stanford University Press, pp. 271–283.

Bowen, J. 1992. Faunal remains and urban household subsistence in New England. In A. E. Yentsch and M. C. Beaudry (eds.) pp. 267–282.

Bowsher, J. 1998. *The Rose Theatre: an Archaeological Discovery*. London: Museum of London.

Bradley, A., V. Buchli, G. Fairclough, D. Hicks, J. Miller and J. Schofield 2004. *Change and Creation: Historic Landscape Character 1950–2000*. London: English Heritage.

Bradley, R. 1997. *Rock Art and the Prehistory of Atlantic Europe*. London: Routledge.

2000. *An Archaeology of Natural Places*. London: Routledge.

2002. *The Past in Prehistoric Societies*. London: Routledge.

Brand, S. 1997. *How Buildings Learn: What Happens After They're Built* (revised edition). London: Phoenix.

Brandon, J. C. and K. S. Barile 2004. Introduction: household chores; or, the chore of defining the household. In K. S. Barile and J. C. Brandon (eds.) pp. 1–12.

Brashler, J. G. 1991. When daddy was a shanty boy: the role of gender in the organization of the logging industry in highland West Virginia. *Historical Archaeology* 25(4): 54–68.

Braudel, F. 1972. *The Mediterranean and the Mediterranean World at the Time of Philip II*. London: Collins.

1980. *On History*. London: Weidenfeld and Nicolson.

Brauner, D. (ed.) 2000. *Approaches to Material Culture Research for Historical Archaeologists* (second edition). Tucson, AZ: The Society for Historical Archaeology.

Brears, P. 1967. Excavations at Potovens, near Wakefield. *Post-Medieval Archaeology* 1: 3–43.

Broadwater, J. D. 1985. The Yorktown shipwreck archaeological project. *International Journal of Nautical Archaeology* 14(4): 301–314.

1992. Shipwreck in a swimming pool: an assessment of the methodology and technology utilized on the Yorktown shipwreck archaeological project. *Historical Archaeology* 26(4): 36–46.

Broeze, F. 1998. *Island Nation: A History of Australians and the Sea*. London: Allen and Unwin.

Brooks, A. 1997. Beyond the fringe: transfer-printed ceramics and the internationalisation of Celtic myth. *International Journal of Historical Archaeology* 1: 39–55.

1999. Building Jerusalem: transfer-printed finewares and the creation of British identity. In S. Tarlow and S. West (eds.) pp. 51–65.

2005. *An Archaeological Guide to British Ceramics in Australia, 1788–1901*. Sydney: Australasian Society for Historical Archaeology.

Brooks, R. H. 1968 *Archaeological Report on the Central Nevada Test Site, Nye County, Nevada*. Las Vegas, NV: Nevada Archaeological Survey, Desert Research Institute and University of Nevada.

Brown, B. 2001. Thing theory. *Critical Inquiry* 28 (1): 1–22.

Brown, D. 1998. Domestic masonry architecture in 17th-century Virginia. *Northeast Historical Archaeology* 27: 85–120.

Brown, M. R. 1988. The behavioral context of probate inventories. In M. Beaudry (ed.) pp. 79–82.

Brown, M. R. and P. Samford 1994. Current archaeological perspectives on the growth and development of Williamsburg. In P. A. Shackel and B. J. Little (eds.) *Historical Archaeology of the Chesapeake*. Washington, DC: Smithsonian Institutional Press, pp. 231–245.

Brumfiel, E. 1991. Weaving and cooking: women's production in Aztec Mexico. In J. M. Gero and M. W. Conkey (eds.) pp. 224–251.

Brunskill, R. W. 1974. *Vernacular Architecture of the Lake Counties: a Field Handbook*. London: Faber.

Bruseth, J. E. and T. S. Turner 2005. *From A Watery Grave: The Discovery And Excavation Of La Salle's Shipwreck, La Belle*. College Station: Texas A&M University Press.

Buchanan, R. A. 1972. *Industrial Archaeology in Britain*. London: Penguin.

1978. Industrial archaeology: retrospect and prospect. In R. L. Schuyler (ed.) pp. 53–56.

2000. The origins of industrial archaeology. In N. Cossons (ed.) *Perspectives on Industrial Archaeology*. London: Science Museum, pp. 18–38.

Buchanan, T. 1983. *Photographing Historic Buildings*. London: HMSO.

Buchli, V. 1995. Interpreting material culture: the trouble with text. In I. Hodder et al. (eds.) pp. 181–193.

    1997. Khruschev, modernism and the fight against *petit-bourgeois* consciousness in the Soviet home. *Journal of Design History* 10: 187–202.

    1999. *An Archaeology of Socialism*. Oxford: Berg.

Buchli, V. (ed.) 2002a. *The Material Culture Reader*. Oxford: Berg.

Buchli, V. 2002b. Towards an archaeology of the contemporary past. *Cambridge Archaeological Journal* 12 (1): 132–134.

    2002c. Architecture and the domestic sphere. In V. Buchli (ed.) *The Material Culture Reader*. Oxford: Berg, pp. 207–213.

    2004. Material culture: current problems. In L. Meskell and R. Preucel (eds.) *A Companion to Social Archaeology*. Oxford: Blackwell, pp. 179–184.

Buchli, V. and G. Lucas (eds.) 2001a. *Archaeologies of the Contemporary Past*. London: Routledge.

    2001b. The archaeology of alienation: a late twentieth-century British council house. In V. Buchli and G. Lucas (eds.) pp. 158–167.

    2001c. The absent present: archaeologies of the contemporary past. In V. Buchli and G. Lucas (eds.) pp. 3–18.

    2001d. Presencing absence. In V. Buchli and G. Lucas (eds.) pp. 171–174.

Buchli, V., A. Clarke and D. Upton 2004. Editorial. *Home Cultures* 1: 2–4.

Buckham, S. 2003. Commemoration as an expression of personal relationships and group identities: a case study of York Cemetery. *Mortality* 8 (2): 160–175.

Burke, C. A. 2000. Nineteenth century ceramics from a seasonally occupied fishing station on the Labrador coast. Paper presented at the Council for Northeast Historical Archaeology Conference, Halifax, Nova Scotia.

Burke, H. 1999. *Meaning and Ideology in Historical Archaeology: Style, Social Identity and Capitalism in an Australian Town*. New York: Kluwer.

Burley, D. 1989. Function, meaning and context: ambiguities in ceramic use by the *Hivernant* Metis of the northwestern Plains. *Historical Archaeology* 23 (1): 97–106.

Burman, B. and C. Turbin (eds.) 2003. *Material Strategies: Dress and Gender in Historical Perspective*. Oxford: Blackwell.

Burns, J. A., 1989. *Recording Historic Structures*. Washington: The American Institute of Architects Press.

Burton, A. and D. Pratt 2002. *Anatomy of Canals: The Mania Years*. Stroud: Tempus.

Butler, B. 2001. Egypt: constructed exiles of the imagination. In B. Bender and M. Winer (eds.) pp. 303–318.

Butler, J. 1993. *Bodies that Matter: On the Discursive Limits of 'Sex'*. London: Routledge.

Byrne, D. 1999. Traces of '65: sites and memories of the post-coup killings in Bali. *UTS Review* 5 (1): 36–52.

Byrne, D., H. Brayshaw and T. Ireland 2001. *Social Significance: A Discussion Paper*. Hurstville, NSW: New South Wales National Parks and Wildlife Service.

Cabak, M. and S. Loring 2000. 'A set of very fair cups and saucers': stamped ceramics as an example of Inuit incorporation. *International Journal of Historical Archaeology* 4: 1–34.

Cadw 2003. *Guide to Good Practice on Using the Register of Landscapes of Historic Interest in Wales in the Planning and Development Process.* Cardiff: Cadw.

Caffyn, L. 1983 *Workers' Housing in West Yorkshire.* London: HMSO.

Cain, E. 1983. *Ghost Ships: Hamilton and Scourge Historical Treasures from the War of 1812.* New York: Olympic.

Callandine, A. and J. Fricker 1993. *East Cheshire Textile Mills.* London: HMSO.

Cameron, C. M. and S. A. Tomka (eds.) 1996. *The Abandonment of Settlements and Regions: Ethnoarchaeological and Archaeological Approaches.* Cambridge: Cambridge University Press.

Campbell, C. 1986. *The Romantic Ethic and the Spirit of Modern Consumerism.* Oxford: Blackwell.

Campbell, F. and J. Hansson (eds.) 2000. *Archaeological Sensibilities.* Gothenburg: Gotarc Series C.

Campbell, W. A. 1971. *The Chemical Industry.* London: Longman.

Cantwell, A. and D. di Zerega Wall 2001. *Unearthing Gotham, The Archaeology of New York City.* New Haven, CT: Yale University Press.

Carillo, R. 1974. English wine bottles as revealed by a statistical study: a further approach to evolution and horizon in historical archaeology. *Historical Archaeology* 7: 290–317.

Carr, L. G., L. S. Walsh and R. Menard 1991. *Robert Cole's World.* Chapel Hill, NC: University of North Carolina Press.

Carson, B. 1990. *Ambitious Appetites: Dining, Behavior, and Patterns of Consumption in Federal Washington.* Washington, DC: American Institute of Architects.

Carson, C., N. Barka, W. Kelso, G. W. Stone and D. Upton 1981. Impermanent architecture in the Southern American colonies. *Wintherthur Portfolio* 16 (2–3): 135–196.

Carsten, J. and S. Hugh-Jones 1995. Introduction. In J. Carsten and S. Hugh-Jones (eds.) *About the House: Levi-Strauss and Beyond.* Cambridge: Cambridge University Press, pp. 1–46.

Carver, M. 1987. *Underneath English Towns: Interpreting Urban Archaeology.* London: Batsford.

Casella, E. C. 2001a. Landscapes of punishment and resistance: a female convict settlement in Tasmania, Australia. In B. Bender and M. Winer (eds.) pp. 103–120.

2001b. To watch or restrain: female convict prisons in nineteenth-century Tasmania. *International Journal of Historical Archaeology* 5 (1): 45–72.

2002. *Archaeology of the Ross Female Factory: Female Incarceration in Van Diemen's Land, Australia.* Launceston, Tasmania: Records of the Queen Victoria Museum No. 108.

Casella, E. C. and J. Symonds (eds.) 2005. *Industrial Archaeology: Future Directions.* New York: Springer.

Casey, E. S. 1996. How to get from space to place in a fairly short stretch of time: phenomenological prolegomena. In S. Feld and K. H. Basso (eds.) *Senses of Place*. Santa Fe: School of American Research Press, pp. 13–52.

Cattell, J. and K. Falconer 1995. *Swindon: Legacy of a Railway Town*. London: HMSO.

Cattell, J., S. Ely and B. Jones 2002. *The Birmingham Jewellery Quarter: An Architectural Survey of the Manufactories*. London: English Heritage.

Celoria, F. A. S. and J. H. Kelly 1973. *A Post-Medieval Pottery Site with a Kiln Base Found off Albion Square, Hanley, Stoke-on-Trent*. Stoke-on-Trent: City of Stoke-on-Trent Museum Archaeological Society Report 4.

Chadwick, A. 2003. Post-processualism, professionalization and archaeological methodologies. Towards reflective and radical practice. *Archaeological Dialogues* 10 (1): 97–117.

Chaney, E. E. 1999. *Archaeological Excavations at Mattapany-Sewall (18ST390), Naval Air Station Patuxent River, St. Mary's County, Maryland*. Report prepared for Natural Resources Branch, Environmental Support Division, Naval Air Station Patuxent River, Maryland.

Chapman, J. 1997. Places as timemarks – the social construction of prehistoric landscapes in Eastern Hungary. In G. Nash (ed.) *Semiotics of Landscape: Archaeology of Mind*. Oxford: Archaeopress (British Archaeological Reports, International Series 661), pp. 31–45.

  2000. *Fragmentation in Archaeology: People, Places and Broken Objects in the Prehistory of South-eastern Europe*. London: Routledge.

Chappell, E. A. 1986 [1980]. Acculturation in the Shenandoah Valley: Rhenish houses of the Massanutten settlement. In D. Upton and J. M. Vlach (eds.) *Common Places: Readings in American Vernacular Architecture*. Athens, GA: University of Georgia Press, pp. 27–57.

Cheek, C. (ed.) 1998. Perspectives in the archaeology of Colonial Boston: the archaeology of the Central Artery/Tunnel Project, Boston, Massachusetts. *Historical Archaeology* 32 (3).

Cheek, C. 1999. An evaluation of regional differences in colonial English foodways. In G. Egan and R. Michael (eds.) pp. 349–357.

Cherry, J. and H. Tait 1980. Excavations at the Longton Hall porcelain factory. Part II. The kiln furniture. *Post-Medieval Archaeology* 14: 1–21.

Childe, V. G. 1944. *Progress and Archaeology*. London: Corbett.

Chippendale, C. 2004. *Stonehenge Complete* (third edition). London: Thames and Hudson.

Chisholm, D. and R. Brazeau 2002. Introduction (Special issue: the Other city: (de) mystifying urban culture). *Journal of Urban History* 29: 3–5.

Chudacoff, H. P. 1999. *The Age of the Bachelor: Creating an American Subculture*. Princeton, NJ: Princeton University Press.

Cipolla, C. 1967. *Clocks and Culture*, London: Collins.

City of Berkeley Liaison Committee 1957. *Report on the Master Plan for the University of California. City of Berkeley, California*. Report on file at the Bancroft Library, University of California, Berkeley.

Claney, J. P. 2004. *Rockingham Ware in American Culture, 1830–1930: Reading Historical Artifacts*. Hanover: University Press of New England.

Clark, J., J. Darlington and G. Fairclough 2004. *Using Historic Landscape Characterisation*. London: English Heritage and Lancashire County Council.

Clark, C. 1987. Trouble at t' mill: industrial archaeology in the 1980s. *Antiquity* 61(232): 169–179. [NB from the mid 1990s, Kate Clark published as K. Clark, rather than C. Clark].

Clark, K. (ed.) 1999. *Conservation Plans in Action: Proceedings of the Oxford Conference*. London: English Heritage.

Clark, K. 2001. *Informed Conservation: Understanding Historic Buildings and their Landscapes for Conservation*. London: English Heritage.

2005. From valves to values: industrial archaeology and heritage practice. In E. C. Casella and J. Symonds (eds.) pp. 95–120.

Cleland, C. E. 1992. From ethnohistory to archaeology: Ottawa and Ojibwa band territories of the northern Great Lakes. In B. J. Little (ed.) pp. 97–102.

2001. Historical archaeology adrift? *Historical Archaeology* 35 (2): 1–8.

Clements, J. M. 1997. The cultural creation of feminine gender: an example from 19th-century military households at Fort Independence, Boston. *Historical Archaeology* 27(4): 39–64.

Clifford, J. and G. Marcus (eds.) 1986. *Writing Culture: the Poetics and Politics of Ethnography*. Berkeley, CA: University of California Press.

Cloke, P. and O. Jones 2004. Turning in the graveyard: trees and the hybrid geographies of dwelling, monitoring and resistance in a Bristol cemetery. *Cultural Geographies* 11: 313–341.

Clough, R. 1991. The archaeology of the historic copper industry on Kawau Island. *Australian Journal of Historical Archaeology* 9: 45–48.

Coad, J. 1989. *The Royal Dockyards 1690–1850*. London: HMSO.

Cocroft, W. D. 2001. *Cold War Monuments: An Assessment by the Monuments Protection Programme*. London: English Heritage (also available in CD format from English Heritage).

Cocroft, W. D. and R. J. C. Thomas 2003. *Cold War: Building for Nuclear Confrontation 1946–1989*. London: English Heritage.

Cocroft, W. D., D. Devlin, J. Schofield and R. J. C. Thomas 2006. *War Art: Murals and Graffiti: Military Life, Power and Subversion*. York: Council for British Archaeology.

Cohen, G. A. 1978. *Karl Marx's Theory of History: A Defence*. Oxford: Oxford University Press.

Coleman-Smith, R. and T. Pearson 1988. *Excavations in the Donyatt Potteries*. Chichester: Phillimore.

Collard, E. 1984. *Nineteenth-Century Pottery and Porcelain in Canada* (second edition). Kingston: McGill-Queen's University Press.

Collingwood, R. G. 1994 [1946]. *The Idea of History*. Oxford: Oxford University Press.

Colloredo-Mansfeld, J. 2003. Introduction: matter unbound. *Journal of Material Culture* 8(3): 245–254.

Comaroff, J. and J. Comaroff 1992. *Ethnography and the Historical Imagination.* Boulder, CO: Westview Press.

Connah, G. 1988. '*Of the Hut I Builded': The Archaeology of Australia's History.* Cambridge: Cambridge University Press.

1994. *The Archaeology of Australia's History.* Cambridge: Cambridge University Press.

Connah, G. and D. Pearson 2002. Artifact of empire: the tale of a gun. *Historical Archaeology* 36(2): 58–70.

Connell, J. and C. Gibson 2003. *Sound Tracks: Popular Music, Identity and Place.* London: Routledge.

Connerton, P. 1989. *How Societies Remember.* Cambridge: Cambridge University Press.

Cook, L. J. 1998a. 'Katherine Nanny, alias Naylor': a life in Puritan Boston. *Historical Archaeology* 32(1): 15–19.

1998b. The construction of a slum: a visual archeology of Five Points. In R. Yamin (ed.) pp. 460–499.

Cook, L. J., R. Yamin and J. P. McCarthy 1996. Shopping as meaningful action: toward a redefinition of consumption in historical archaeology. *Historical Archaeology* 30(4): 50–65.

Cooney, G. 2003. Introduction: seeing the land from the sea. *World Archaeology* 35(3): 323–328.

Cooper, M. 2005. Exploring Mrs Gaskell's legacy. In E. C. Casella and J. Symonds (eds.) pp. 155–173.

Coppack, G. 2003. *Fountains Abbey: The Cistercians in Northern England.* Stroud: Tempus.

Cossons, N. 1987 [1975]. *The BP Book of Industrial Archaeology.* Newton Abbot: David & Charles.

2000. *Perspectives on Industrial Archaeology.* London: Science Museum.

Cossons, N. and K. Hudson (eds.) 1969. *Industrial Archaeologists' Guide 1969–70.* Newton Abbott: David and Charles.

Costello, J. G. 1998. Bread fresh from the oven: memories of Italian breadbaking in the California mother-lode. *Historical Archaeology* 32 (1): 66–73.

2000. Red light voices: an archaeological drama of late nineteenth-century prostitution. In R. A. Schmidt and B. L. Voss (eds.) *Archaeologies of Sexuality.* London: Routledge, pp. 160–175.

Costello, J. G. and M. L. Maniery 1988. *Rice Bowls in the Delta: Artifacts Recovered from the 1915 Asian Community of Walnut Grove, California.* Los Angeles: University of California (Institute of Archaeology Occasional Paper No. 16)

Cotter, J. L. 1957. Excavations at Jamestown, Virginia. Site of the first permanent English settlement in America. *Antiquity* 31(121): 19–24.

1958. *Archaeological Excavations at Jamestown, Virginia.* Washington, DC: National Park Service (Archaeological Research Series 4).

Cottman, M. H. 1999. *The Wreck of the Henrietta Marie: An African-American's Spiritual Journey to Uncover a Sunken Slave Ship's Past.* New York: Harmony.

Couper-Smartt, J. 2003. *Port Adelaide: Tales from a 'Commodious Harbour'.* Adelaide: South Australian Maritime Museum.

Courtney, P. 1997. The tyranny of constructs: some thoughts on periodisation and change. In D. Gaimster and P. Stamper (eds.) pp. 9–23.

1999. 'Different strokes for different folks': the trans-Atlantic development of historical and post-medieval archaeology. In G. Egan and R. Michael (eds.) pp. 1–9.

Coysh, A. W. and R. K. Henrywood 1982. *The Dictionary of Blue and White Printed Pottery 1780–1880.* Woodbridge: Antique Collectors' Club.

1989. *The Dictionary of Blue and White Printed Pottery 1780–1880, Vol. II.* Woodbridge: Antique Collectors' Club.

Cranstone, D. 2001. Industrial archaeology – manufacturing a new society. In R. Newman (ed.) pp. 183–210.

Crehan, K. 2002. *Gramsci, Culture and Anthropology.* Berkeley, CA: University of California Press.

Crossick, G. (ed.) 1997. *The Artisan and the European Town, 1500–1900.* Aldershot: Scolar Press.

Crossland, Z. 2002. Violent spaces: conflict over the reappearance of Argentina's disappeared. In J. Schofield, C. M. Beck and W. G. Johnson (eds.) pp. 115–131.

Crossley, D. 1990. *Post-Medieval Archaeology in Britain.* Leicester: Leicester University Press.

Crumlin-Pedersen, O. and B. Munch-Thye (eds.) 1995. *The Ship as Symbol.* Copenhagen: Danish National Museum.

Cummings, A. L. 1979. *The Framed Houses of Massachusetts Bay, 1625–1675.* Cambridge, MA: Harvard University Press.

2004. Recent tree-ring studies of early New England. *Vernacular Architecture* 35: 66–72.

Cunliffe, B. 1975. *Excavations at Portchester Castle. Vol. I: Roman.* London: Society of Antiquaries of London (Reports of the Research Committee of the Society of Antiquaries of London 32).

1976. *Excavations at Portchester Castle. Vol. II: Saxon.* London: Society of Antiquaries of London (Reports of the Research Committee of the Society of Antiquaries of London 33).

1977. *Excavations at Portchester Castle. Vol. III: Medieval.* London: Society of Antiquaries of London (Reports of the Research Committee of the Society of Antiquaries of London 34).

2001. *Facing the Ocean.* Oxford: Oxford University Press.

Cunliffe, B. and B. Garratt 1994. *Excavations at Portchester Castle. Vol. V: Post Medieval, 1609–1819.* London: Society of Antiquaries of London (Reports of the Research Committee of the Society of Antiquaries of London 52).

Cunliffe, B. and J. Munby 1985. *Excavations at Portchester Castle. Vol. IV: Medieval, the Inner Bailey.* London: Society of Antiquaries of London (Reports of the Research Committee of the Society of Antiquaries of London 43).

Curl, J. 1980. *Death and Architecture.* Stroud: Sutton.

Currie, C. 1988. Time and chance: modelling the attrition of old houses. *Vernacular Architecture* 19: 1–9.

Curtis, J. B. 1985. Sherd and shipwrecks: the Dutch and the China Trade 1600–1650. In P. F. Johnston (ed.) *Underwater Archaeology: Proceedings of the 1985 SHA Conference*. Rockville: Society for Historical Archaeology, pp. 26–29.

Daily Californian 1900. A woman's gymnasium (April 11).

1902. Distinguished ladies will speak (November 14).

Dalglish, C. 2003. *Rural Society in the Age of Reason: An Archaeology of the Emergence of Modern Life in the Southern Scottish Highlands*. New York: Plenum/Kluwer.

Daniels, I. M. 2001. The 'untidy' Japanese house. In D. Miller (ed.) *Home Possessions: Material Culture Behind Closed Doors*. Oxford: Berg, pp. 201–229.

Darby, W. J. 2000. *Landscape and Identity: Geographies of Nation and Class in England*. Oxford: Berg.

Dash, M. 2002. *Batavia's Graveyard*. London: Weidenfeld and Nicholson.

Davidoff, L. and C. Hall 2002. *Family Fortunes. Men and Women of the English Middle Class 1780–1850*. Routledge: London.

Davis, D. L. 2002. *When Smoke Ran Like Water*. New York: Basic Books.

DCMS 1999. *World Heritage Sites: the Tentative List of the United Kingdom of Great Britain and Northern Ireland*. London: Department of Culture, Media and Sport. www.culture.gov.uk/global/publications/archive_1999/

2001. *The Historic Environment: A Force for Our Future*. London: Department for Culture, Media and Sport. www.culture.gov.uk/global/publications/archive_2001/

DCMS 2001. *The Historic Environment: a Force for our Future*. London: Department for Culture, Media and Sport.

De Cunzo, L. A. 1995. Reform, respite, ritual: an archaeology of institutions. The Magdalen Society of Philadelphia, 1800–1850. *Historical Archaeology* 29(3) (Special Issue).

1996. Introduction: people, material culture, context, and culture in historical archaeology. In L. A. De Cunzo and B. L. Herman (eds.) pp. 1–18.

1998. A future after freedom. *Historical Archaeology* 32(1): 42–54.

2001. On reforming the 'fallen' and beyond: transforming continuity at the Magdalen Society of Philadelphia, 1845–1916. *International Journal of Historical Archaeology* 5(1): 19–43.

2004. *A Historical Archaeology of Delaware: People, Contexts and the Cultures of Agriculture*. Knoxville, TN: University of Tennessee Press.

2006. Exploring the institution: reform, confinement, social change. In M. Hall and S. Silliman (eds.) *Historical Archaeology*. Oxford: Blackwell, pp. 167–189.

De Cunzo, L. A. and Bernard L. Herman (eds.) 1996. *Historical Archaeology and the Study of American Culture*. Winterthur, DE: Henry Francis du Pont Winterthur Museum.

De Vries, J. 1993. Between purchasing power and the world of goods: understanding the household economy in early modern Europe. In J. Brewer and R. Porter (eds.) *Consumption and the World of Goods*. London: Routledge, pp. 85–132.

Deagan, K. A. 1973. Mestizaje in Colonial St. Augustine. *Ethnohistory* 20(1): 55–65.

(ed.) 1983. *Spanish St. Augustine: The Archaeology of a Colonial Creole Community.* New York: Academic Press.

1985. Spanish–Indian interaction in sixteenth-century Florida and Hispaniola. In W. Fitzhugh (ed.) *Cultures in Contact.* Washington, DC: Smithsonian Institution Press and the Anthropological Society of Washington, pp. 281–318.

1987. *Artifacts of the Spanish Colonies of Florida and the Caribbean, 1500–1800. Vol. I: Ceramics, Glassware and Beads.* Washington, DC: Smithsonian Institution Press.

1996. Colonial transformations: Euro-American cultural genesis in the early Spanish-American colonies. *Journal of Anthropological Research* 52(2): 135–160.

2002. *Artifacts of the Spanish Colonies of Florida and the Caribbean 1500–1800. Vol. II: Portable Personal Possessions.* Washington, DC: Smithsonian Institution Press.

2003. Colonial origins and colonial transformations in Spanish America. *Historical Archaeology* 37(4): 3–13.

Deagan, K. A. and J. Cruxent 2002. *Columbus's Outpost among the Taínos: Spain and America at La Isabela, 1493–1498.* New Haven, CT: Yale University Press.

DeCorse, C. R. 1996. Documents, oral histories, and the material record: historical archaeology in West Africa. *World Archaeological Bulletin* 7: 40–50.

Deetz, J. F. 1968. Late man in North America: archaeology of European Americans. In B. J. Meggers (ed.) *Anthropological Archaeology in the Americas.* Washington, DC: Anthropological Society of Washington, pp. 121–130. (Reprinted in J. Deetz (ed.) 1971 *Man's Imprint from the Past: Readings in the Method of Archaeology.* Boston, MA: Little, Brown.)

1977. *In Small Things Forgotten: An Archaeology of Early American Life.* New York: Anchor Books.

1982. Households: a structural key to archaeological interpretation. *American Behavioral Scientist* 25(6): 717–724.

Delgado, J. P. 1991. *To California by Sea.* New York: Columbia University Press.

Delle, J. A. 1998. *An Archaeology of Social Space: Analyzing Coffee Plantations in Jamaica's Blue Mountains.* New York: Plenum.

2000a. Gender, power, and space: negotiating social relations under slavery on coffee plantations in Jamaica, 1790–1834. In J. A. Delle et al. (eds.) pp. 168–201.

2000b. The material and cognitive dimensions of creolization in nineteenth-century Jamaica. *Historical Archaeology* 34(3): 56–72.

Delle, J. A., S. A. Mrozowski and R. Paynter (eds.) 2000. *Lines That Divide: Historical Archaeologies of Race, Class, and Gender.* Knoxville: University of Tennessee Press.

Denning, K. 2003. Drawing the dark: the evolution of captivity. Paper presented at World Archaeological Congress, Washington DC (25 June 2003). Online at www.logomancer.com/aoz

DeSilvey, C. 2005. Salvage Rites making memory on a Montana homestead. Unpublished Ph.D. thesis, Open University (Geography Discipline).

Diamond, S. 1974. *In Search of the Primitive: A Critique of Civilisation*. New Brunswick: Transaction Books.

Dietler, M. 1998. A tale of three sites: the monumentalization of Celtic oppida and the politics of collective memory and identity. *World Archaeology* 30(1): 72–89.

Diole, P. 1952. *Four Thousand Years Under the Sea*. London: Sidgwick and Jackson.

Divers, D. 2002. The post-medieval waterfront development at Adlards Wharf, Bermondsey, London. *Post-Medieval Archaeology* 36: 39–117.

Dobinson, C. 2001. *AA Command: Britain's Anti-Aircraft Defences of the Second World War*. London: Methuen.

Dobinson, C., J. Lake and J. Schofield 1997. Monuments of war: defining England's twentieth century defence heritage. *Antiquity* 71: 288–299.

Donley, L. 1982. House power: Swahili space and symbolic markers. In I. Hodder (ed.) *Symbolic and Structural Archaeology*. Cambridge: Cambridge University Press, pp. 63–73.

Doolittle, C. J. and T. Majewski (eds.) 1997. *Archaeological Investigations at the Superblock Site (CA-SBR-7975H), San Bernardino, California*. Tucson, AZ: Statistical Research (Technical Series 62).

Douglas, A. 1999. Excavations at Rainbow Quay, an 18th-century whale rendering plant, Rotherhithe, London. *Post-Medieval Archaeology* 33: 179–193.

Douglas, M. and B. Isherwood 1979. *The World of Goods: Towards an Anthropology of Consumption*. New York: W. W. Norton.

Douglass, W. 1998. The mining camp as community. In A. B. Knapp, V. C. Pigott and E. W. Herbert (eds.) *Social Approaches to an Industrial Past*. London: Routledge, pp. 97–108.

Dubrow, G. and D. Graves 2002. *Sento at Sixth and Main: Preserving Landmarks of Japanese American Heritage*. Seattle: University of Washington Press.

Duke, P. and D. Saitta 1998. An emancipatory archaeology for the working class. *Assemblage* 4 www.shef.ac.uk/assem/4/4duk_sai.html (accessed 27 March 2005).

Duncan, J. F. and D. Sanford 2005. Stratford's changing landscape: coming to terms with complexity in a Unified Space. Paper presented at the annual meeting of the Society for Historical Archaeology, York, England.

Dyer, A. 1981. Urban housing: a documentary study of four Midland towns 1530–1700. *Post-Medieval Archaeology* 15: 207–218.

Dyson, S. L. 1982. Material culture, social structure, and changing cultural values: the ceramics of eighteenth- and nineteenth-century Middletown, Connecticut. In R. S. Dickens (ed.) *Archaeology of Urban America: The Search for Pattern and Process*. New York: Academic Press, pp. 361–380.

Eagleton, T. 1976. *Marxism and Literary Criticism*. Berkeley, CA: University of California Press.

Edensor, T. 2005a. *Industrial Ruins: Aesthetics, Materiality and Memory*. Oxford: Berg.

2005b. Waste matter: the debris of industrial ruins and the disordering of the material world. *Journal of Material Culture* 10(3): 311–332.

Edgeworth, M. 2003. *Acts of Discovery: An Ethnography of Archaeological Practice.* Oxford: Archaeopress (British Archaeological Reports International Series 1131).

Edwards, B. 2000. Avebury and other not-so-ancient places: the making of the English heritage landscape. In H. Kean, P. Martin and S. Morgan (eds.) *Seeing History: Public History in Britain Now.* London: Francis Boutle, pp. 65–79.

Edwards, E. 2002. Material beings: objecthood and ethnographic photographs. *Visual Studies* 17(1): 67–75.

Edwards, S. R. and W. G. Johnson 1994. *A Status Report on the Hot Creek Archaeological Collection (Project Faultless Area, Nye County, Nevada).* Las Vegas: Desert Research Institute, Quaternary Sciences Center Technical Report.

Edwards-Ingram, Y. 2001. African American medicine and the social relations of slavery. In C. E. Orser (ed.) *Race and the Archaeology of Identity.* Salt Lake City, UT: University of Utah Press, pp. 34–53.

Egan, G. 1990. Leaden seals: evidence for East India Company trade in textiles. In V. Fenwick and M. Redknap (eds.) *Ships, Cargoes and the East India Trade.* Dorchester: Dorset Press, pp. 87–90.

Egan, G. and R. L. Michael (eds.) 1999. *Old and New Worlds: Historical/Post-Medieval Archaeology Papers from the Societies' Joint Conferences at Williamsburg and London 1997 to mark Thirty Years of Work and Achievement.* Oxford: Oxbow Books.

Engels, F. 1954. *Anti-Dühring.* Moscow: Foreign Language Publishers.

  1992 [1882]. Engels to Eduard Bernstein in Zurich (Letter). *Marx and Engels Collected Works* (Vol. 46). New York: International Publishers, p. 353.

English Heritage 2000. *Power of Place: the Future of the Historic Environment.* London: English Heritage.

  2004. *Military Wall Art: Guidelines on its Significance, Conservation and Management.* London: English Heritage. Also available at www.english-heritage.org/military

  2005. *Conservation Bulletin 47: Characterisation.* London: English Heritage.

English, W. 1969. *The Textile Industry.* London: Longman.

Epperson, T. W. 2000. Panoptic plantations: the garden sights of Thomas Jefferson and George Mason. In J. A. Delle et al. (eds.) pp. 58–77.

  2001. 'A separate house for the Christian slaves, one for the negro slaves': the archaeology of race and identity in late seventeenth-century Virginia. In C. E. Orser (ed.) *Race and the Archaeology of Identity.* Salt Lake City, UT: University of Utah Press, pp. 54–70.

Ernstein, J. H. 1998. Shifting land use, shifting values, and the reinvention of Annapolis. In P. A. Shackel, P. R. Mullins, and M. S. Warner (eds.) *Annapolis Pasts: Historical Archaeology in Annapolis, Maryland.* Knoxville, TN: University of Tennessee Press, pp. 147–168.

  2000. Landscape archaeology and the recent past: a view from Bowie, Maryland. In D. L. Slaton and W. G. Foulks (eds.) *Preserving the Recent Past Vol. II.* Washington, DC: Preservation Education Foundation, National Park Service, and Association for Preservation International, pp. 97–103.

2004. Constructing context: historical archaeology and the pleasure garden in Prince George's county, Maryland, 1740–1790. Unpublished Ph.D. dissertation, Boston University. (Ann Arbor: University Microfilms International).

Ernstein, J.H., A. M. Hartig and L. G. Hoyos 2005. Setting the bar: the pros and cons of holding the recent past to a higher standard. *Preservation Forum* 20(1) 23–29. At http://forum.nationaltrust.org/PDF/Fall_2005_Journal.pdf

Erwin, T. 1994. The *Lady Elgin*: A nineteenth century palace steamer in Lake Michigan. In R. P. Woodward and C. D. Moore (eds.) *Underwater Archaeology: Proceedings of the 1994 SHA Conference, Vancouver*. Rockville: Society for Historical Archaeology, pp. 90–95.

Ewins, N. 1997. 'Supplying the present wants of our Yankee cousins . . .': Staffordshire ceramics and the American market 1775–1880. *Journal of Ceramic History* 15: 1–154.

Fairclough, G. 2003. Cultural landscape, sustainability and living with change. In J. M. Teutonico and F. Matero (eds.) *Managing Change: Sustainable Approaches to the Conservation of the Built Environment*. Los Angeles The Getty Conservation Institute, pp. 23–46.

Fairclough, G. and S. Rippon (eds.) 2002. *Europe's Cultural Landscape: Archaeologists and the Management of Change*. Brussels and London: Europae Archaeologiae Consilium (Occasional Paper No. 2).

Falk, P. and C. B. Campbell (eds.) 1997. *The Shopping Experience*. London: Sage.

Fennell, C. 2005. *The African Diaspora Archaeology Network*. Webpages online at http://diaspora.uiuc.edu/ (Accessed 1 April 2005).

Fenwick, V. and M. Redknap (eds.) 1990. *Ships, Cargoes and the East India Trade*. Dorchester: Dorset Press.

Ferguson, L. (ed.) 1977. *Historical Archaeology and the Importance of Material Things*. Tucson, AZ: Society for Historical Archaeology (Society for Historical Archaeology Special Publication 2).

Ferguson, L. 1991. Struggling with pots in South Carolina. In R. McGuire and R. Paynter (eds.) *The Archaeology of Inequality*. Oxford: Blackwell, pp. 28–39.

1992. *Uncommon Ground: Archaeology and Early African America, 1650–1800*. Washington, DC: Smithsonian Institution Press.

Finamore, D. (ed.) 2004. *Maritime History as World History*. Gainesville, FL: University Press of Florida.

Finch, J. 2003. A reformation of meaning: commemoration and remembering the dead in the parish church, 1450–1640. In D. Gaimster and R. Gilchrist (eds.) pp. 437–449.

Fine, B. 2004. Debating production–consumption linkages in food studies. *Sociologia Ruralis* 44(3): 332–342.

Finlay, N. 1999. Outside of life: traditions of infant burial in Ireland from *cillín* to cist. *World Archaeology* 31(3): 407–422.

Finn, C. A. 2001. *Artifacts: An Archaeologist's Year in Silicon Valley*. Cambridge, MA: MIT Press.

2004. *Past Poetic: Archaeology in the Poetry of W. B. Yeats and Seamus Heaney.* London: Duckworth.

Finn. C. A. and M. Henig (eds.) 2001. *Outside Archaeology: Material Culture and the Poetic Imagination.* Oxford: Archaeopress (British Archaeological Reports International Series 999).

Fischer, D. H. 1989. *Albion's Seed: Four British Folkways in America.* New York: Oxford University Press.

Fitts, R. K. 2000. The rhetoric of reform: the Five Points Missions and the cult of domesticity. *Historical Archaeology* 35: 115–132.

2002. Becoming American: the archaeology of an Italian immigrant. *Historical Archaeology* 36(2): 1–17.

Fitzgerald, R. S. 1980. *Liverpool Road Station, Manchester.* Manchester: Manchester University Press in association with the RCHME and the Greater Manchester Council.

Flannery, K. V. 1976. The Early Mesoamerican house. In K. V. Flannery (ed.) *The Early Mesoamerican Village.* New York: Academic Press, pp. 16–25.

Flatman, J. 2003. Cultural biographies, cognitive landscapes and dirty old bits of boat. *International Journal of Nautical Archaeology* 32(2): 143–157.

Fleming, A. 1998. *Swaledale: Valley of the Wild River.* Edinburgh: Edinburgh University Press.

Fleming, E. M. 1974. Artifact study: a proposed model. *Winterthur Portfolio* 9: 153–173.

Flemming, N. C. 2004. Submarine prehistoric archaeology of the Indian continental shelf. *Current Science* 86(9): 1225–1230.

Fletcher, R. 1995. *The Limits of Settlement Growth: A Theoretical Outline.* Cambridge: Cambridge University Press.

Foot, W. 2004. *Defence Areas: A National Study of Second World War Anti-Invasion Landscapes in England.* York: Council for British Archaeology and English Heritage. (Typescript report available on CD from Council for British Archaeology.)

Ford, H. 1929. *My Philosophy of Industry.* New York: Coward-McCann Inc.

Ford, J. 2004. *The Archaeology of Aircraft Losses in Water in Victoria, Australia During World War II.* Adelaide: Flinders University Press (Maritime Archaeology Monographs and Reports Series 1).

Formanek-Brunell, M. 1993. *Made to Play House: Dolls and the Commercialization of American Girlhood, 1830–1930.* New Haven, CT: Yale University Press.

Forty, A. and S. Küchler (eds.) 2001. *The Art of Forgetting.* Oxford: Berg.

Fotiadis, M. 1992. Units of data as deployment of disciplinary codes. In J.-C. Gardin and C. S. Peebles (eds.) *Representations in Archaeology.* Bloomington, IN: Indiana University Press, pp. 132–148

Foucault, M. 1979. *Discipline and Punish: The Birth of the Prison* (trans. A. Sheridan). New York: Vintage.

1983. On the genealogy of ethics: an overview of work in progress. In H. Dreyfus and P. Rabinow (eds.) *Michel Foucault: Beyond Structuralism and Hermeneutics.* Chicago, IL: University of Chicago Press, pp. 340–372.

1986a. Space, knowledge, and power. In P. Rabinow (ed.) *The Foucault Reader: An Introduction to Foucault's Thought*. London: Harmondsworth Press, pp. 239–256.

1986b. Of other spaces. *Diacritics* 16: 22–27.

Fox, C. F. and Baron R. S. Raglan 1951–4. *Monmouthshire Houses: A Study of Building Techniques and Smaller House-Plans in the Fifteenth to Seventeenth Centuries*. Three volumes. Cardiff: National Museum of Wales and Welsh Folk Museum.

Fox, G. L. 1999. *The Archaeology of the Clay Tobacco Pipe XV: The Kaolin Clay Tobacco Pipe Collection from Port Royal, Jamaica* (ed. P. Davey). Oxford: Archaeopress. British Archaeological Reports (International Series 809).

2002. Interpreting socioeconomic changes in 17th-century England and Port Royal, Jamaica, through analysis of the Port Royal kaolin clay pipes. *International Journal of Historical Archaeology* 6(1): 61–78.

Fox, H. 2001. *The Evolution of the Fishing Village: Landscape and Society Along the South Devon Coast, 1086–1550*. London: Leopard's Head Press.

Francis, P. 2001. *A Pottery by the Lagan. Irish Creamware from the Downshire Pottery, Belfast 1787–c. 1806*. Belfast: The Institute of Irish Studies.

Frankel, D. 2000. Migration and ethnicity in prehistoric Cyprus: technology as habitus. *European Journal of Archaeology* 3: 167–187.

Frankel, D. and J. M. Webb 1998. Three faces of identity: ethnicity, community and status in the Cypriot Bronze Age. *Mediterranean Archaeology* 11: 58–80.

Franklin, M. 2004. Foreword. In K. S. Barile and J. C. Brandon (eds.) pp. xiii–xiv.

Frazer, B. 1999a. Reconceptualizing resistance in the historical archaeology of the British Isles: an editorial. *International Journal of Historical Archaeology* 3(1): 1–10.

1999b. Common recollections: resisting enclosure 'by Agreement' in seventeenth-century England. *International Journal of Historical Archaeology* 3(2): 75–100.

Friedman, J. and M. Rowlands (eds.) 1978. *The Evolution of Social Systems*. London: Duckworth.

Friel, I. 1995. *The Good Ship*. London: British Museum Press.

Frost, A. 2003. *The Global Reach of Empire: Britain's Maritime Expansion in the Indian and Pacific Oceans, 1764–1815*. Melbourne: Miegunyah Press.

Froud, D. 2004. Thinking beyond the homely: countryside properties and the shape of time. *Home Cultures* 1: 211–234.

Funari, P. P. A. 2000. Comments on Laurie A. Wilkie and Kevin M. Bartoy, a critical archaeology revisited. *Current Anthropology* 41(5): 764–765.

2003. Conflict and the interpretation of Palmares, A Brazilian runaway polity. *Journal of Historical Archaeology* 37(3): 81–92.

Funari, P. P. A., S. Jones and M. Hall 1999. Introduction: archaeology in history. In P. P. A. Funari, S. Jones and M. Hall (eds.) *Historical Archaeology: Back from the Edge*. London: Routledge (One World Archaeology), pp. 1–20.

Gable, E. and R. Handler 2000. Public history, private memory: notes from the ethnography of Colonial Williamsburg, Virginia, USA. *Ethnos* 65(2): 237–252.

Gaimster, D. R. M. 1997. *German Stoneware 1200–1900*. London: British Museum Press.

1999a. The post-medieval ceramic revolution in southern Britain c. 1450–1650. In G. Egan and R. L. Michael (eds.) pp. 214–225.

Gaimster, D. R. M. (ed.) 1999b. *Maiolica in the North. The Archaeology of Tin-Glazed Earthenwares in North-West Europe c. 1500–1600*. London: British Museum.

Gaimster, D. R. M. nd. 'An embarrassment of riches? Post-medieval archaeology in northern Europe. In T. Majewski and D. Gaimster (eds.) *International Handbook of Historical Archaeology*. New York: Springer.

Gaimster, D. R. M. and R. Gilchrist (eds.) 2004. *The Archaeology of the Reformation*. Oxford: Oxbow Books.

Gaimster, D. R. M. and P. Stamper (eds.) 1997. *The Age of Transition. The Archaeology of English Culture 1400–1600*. Oxford: Oxbow Books (Society for Medieval Archaeology Monograph 15; Oxbow Monograph 98).

Gale, W. K. V. 1969. *Iron and Steel*. London: Longman.

Gard'ner, J. 2001. Heritage protection and social inclusion: a case study from the Bangladeshi community of East London. Unpublished Masters thesis, University of London (Architectural Association of London).

Gardiner, J. (ed.) 2005. *Before the Mast: Life and Death Aboard the Mary Rose*. Portsmouth: Mary Rose Trust *(The Archaeology the Mary Rose Vol. IV)*.

Garman, J. C. 2005. *Detention Castles of Stone and Steel: Landscape, Labor, and the Urban Penitentiary*. Knoxville, TN: University of Tennessee Press.

Gass, W. H. 1970. *Fiction and the Figures of Life*. New York: Knopf.

Gates, W. C. and D. E. Ormerod 1982. The East Liverpool, Ohio, pottery district: identification of manufacturers and marks. *Historical Archaeology* 16: 1–2.

Gaughwin, D. 1995. Chinese settlement sites in north-east Tasmania. In P. Macgregor (ed.) *Histories of the Chinese in Australasia and the South Pacific*. Melbourne: Museum of Chinese Australian History, pp. 230–248.

Gawronski, J. H. G. 1997. The *Hollandia* and the *Amsterdam*: ships and the economic network of the VOC. In D. C. Lakey (ed.) *Underwater Archaeology*. Corpus Christi: Society for Historical Archaeology, pp. 1–8.

Gawronski, J. H. G. and H. H. Van Rooiji 1989. *East Indiaman Amsterdam*. Amsterdam: Amsterdam Foundation.

Geertz, C. 1973. *The Interpretation of Cultures*. New York: Basic Books.

Gell, A. 1996. Vogel's net: traps and artworks and artworks as traps. *Journal of Material Culture* 1(1): 15–38.

1998. *Art and Agency: An Anthropological Theory*. Oxford: Clarendon.

Genette, G. 1988. *Narrative Discourse Revisited* (trans. J. E. Lewin). Ithaca, NY: Cornell University Press.

Gero, J. M. 1985. Socio-politics of archaeology and the woman-at-home ideology. *American Antiquity* 50: 342–350.

Gero, J. M. and M. W. Conkey (eds.) 1991. *Engendering Archaeology: Women in Prehistory*. Oxford: Blackwell.

Gibb, J. G. 2000. Imaginary, but by no means unimaginable: storytelling, science, and historical archaeology. *Historical Archaeology* 34(2): 1–6.

Gibbins, D. and J. Adams 2001. Shipwrecks and maritime archaeology. *World Archaeology* 32(3): 279–291.

Gibbon, G. 1993. O'Shea on Hodder's domestication. *American Anthropologist* 95(3): 711–714.

Gibbs, M. 2003. The archaeology of crisis. *Historical Archaeology* 37(1): 128–145.

Giddens, A. 1979. *Central Problems in Social Theory: Action, Structure, and Contradiction in Social Analysis*. Berkeley, CA: University of California Press.

Gilchrist, R. 1994. *Gender and Material Culture: The Archaeology of Religious Women*. London: Routledge.

   2000. Archaeological biographies: realizing human lifecycles, -courses and -histories. *World Archaeology* 31(3): 325–328.

   2005. Introduction: scales and voices in world historical archaeology. *World Archaeology* 37(3): 339–336.

Gilchrist, R. and J. Blair 1996. Continuity, reaction and revival: church archaeology in England 1600–1800. In J. Blair and C. Pyrah (eds.) pp. 112–126.

Giles, C. and I. H. Goodhall 1992. *Yorkshire Textile Mills: the Buildings of the Yorkshire Textile Industry 1770–1930*. London: HMSO.

Giles, K. 1999. The 'familiar' fraternity: the appropriation and consumption of medieval guildhalls in early modern York. In S. Tarlow and S. West (eds.) pp. 87–102.

Gillespie, S. D. 2000. Beyond kinship: an introduction. In R. A. Joyce and S. D. Gillespie (eds.) *Beyond Kinship: Social and Material Reproduction in House Societies*. Philadelphia, PA: University of Pennsylvania Press, pp. 1–21.

Gillespie, W. B. and M. M. Farrell 2002. Work camp settlement patterns: landscape-scale comparisons of two mining camps in southeastern Arizona. *Historical Archaeology* 36(3): 59–68.

Gilman, A. 1998. The communist manifesto 150 years later. *Antiquity* 72: 910–913.

   2001. Assessing political development in Copper and Bronze Age southeast Spain. In J. Hass (ed.) *From Leaders to Rulers*. New York: Kluwer/Plenum, pp. 59–81.

Giorgi, J. 1999. Archaeobotanical evidence from London on aspects of post medieval urban economies. In G. Egan and R. L. Michael (eds.) pp. 342–348.

Givens, D. R. 1992. The role of biography in writing the history of archaeology. In J. Reyman (ed.) *Rediscovering our Past: Essays on the History of American Archaeology*. Aldershot: Avebury Press (Worldwide Archaeology Series), pp. 51–56.

Glassie, H. 1968. The types of the Southern mountain cabin. In J. Van Brunvand (ed.) *The Study of American Folklore*. New York: Norton, pp. 338–370.

   1975. *Folk Housing in Middle Virginia: A Structural Analysis of Historic Artifacts*. Knoxville, TN: University of Tennessee Press.

   1977. Archaeology and folklore: common anxieties, common hopes. In L. Ferguson (ed.) pp. 23–35.

   1999. *Material Culture*. Bloomington, IN: Indiana University Press.

2000. *Vernacular Architecture*. Bloomington, IN: Indiana University Press.

Goddard, R. A. 2002. Nothing but tar paper shacks. *Historical Archaeology* 36(3): 85–93.

Godden, G. A. 1964. *Encyclopaedia of British Pottery and Porcelain Marks*. London: Barrie & Jenkins.

Godelier, M. 1977. *Perspectives in Marxist Archaeology*. Cambridge: Cambridge University Press.

Goings, K. W. and R. A. Mohl (eds.) 1996. *The New African American Urban History*. Thousand Oaks, CA: Sage Publications.

Gojak, D. and C. Allen 2000. The Fighting Ground Creek quartz roasting pits and the early importation of gold processing technology into Australia 1850–1860. *Australasian Historical Archaeology* 18: 29–38.

Goldenberg, N. G. and C. M. Beck 1991a. *Historic Building Inventory and Evaluation: Underground Parking Garage, Nevada Test Site, Nye County, Nevada*. Las Vegas: Desert Research Institute (Cultural Resources Reconnaissance Short Report No. SR092691–1).

1991b. *Historic Structure Inventory and Evaluation: BREN Tower, Area 25, Nevada Test Site, Nye County, Nevada*. Las Vegas: Desert Research Institute (Cultural Resources Reconnaissance Short Report No. SR092791–1).

Goody, J. 1971. *The Developmental Cycle in Domestic Groups*. Cambridge: Cambridge University Press.

2000. *The Power of the Written Tradition*. Washington, DC: Smithsonian Institution Press.

Gosden, C. 1994. *Social Being and Time*. London: Routledge.

1999. *Anthropology and Archaeology: A Changing Relationship*. London: Routledge.

2004. *Archaeology and Colonialism: Cultural Context from 5000 BC to the Present*. Cambridge: Cambridge University Press.

Gosden, C. and Y. Marshall 1999. The cultural biography of objects. *World Archaeology* 31(2): 169–178.

Gould, R. A. 1983. Looking below the surface: shipwreck archaeology as anthropology. In R. A. Gould (ed.) *Shipwreck Anthropology*. Albuquerque, NM: University of New Mexico Press, pp. 3–22.

1990. Underwater construction at the Royal Naval Dockyard, Bermuda. *Bermuda Journal of Archaeology and Maritime History* 2: 71–86.

1997. Shipwreck anthropology. In J. P. Delgado (ed.) *Encyclopaedia of Underwater and Maritime Archaeology*. London: British Museum Press, pp. 377–380.

2000. *Archaeology and the Social History of Ships*. Cambridge: Cambridge University Press.

Gould, R. A. and M. Schiffer (eds.) 1981. *Modern Material Culture: the archaeology of us*. New York: Academic Press.

Gould, R. A. and D. J. Souza 1995. History and archaeology of HM Floating Dock Bermuda. *Bermuda Journal of Archaeology and Maritime History* 7: 157–185.

Gould, S. 1999. Planning, development and social archaeology. In S. Tarlow and S. West (eds.) pp. 140–154.

2001. Review of N. Cossons (2000) 'Perspectives on Industrial Archaeology'. *Industrial Archaeology Review* 23 (1): 67.

Gradwohl, D. M. and N. M. Osborn 1984. *Exploring Buried Buxton*. Ames, IA: The Iowa State University Press.

Grant, A. 1983. *North Devon Pottery: The Seventeenth Century*. Exeter: University of Exeter Press.

Graves-Brown, P. 2000. Introduction. In P. Graves-Brown (ed.) *Matter, Materiality and Modern Culture*. London: Routledge, pp. 1–9.

Greeley, J. M. 2005. *Watery Highways: Trade and Travel in the Colonial Chesapeake*. St Mary's City, MD: Historic St Mary's City.

Green Carr, L. and L. S. Walsh 1988. The standard of living in British North America. *William and Mary Quarterly* 45(1): 135–159.

Green, C. 1999. *Fulham Pottery Excavations, 1971–1979*. London: HMSO.

Green, E. R. R. 1963. *The Industrial Archaeology of County Down*. Belfast: HMSO.

Green, H. 1986. *Fit for America*. New York: Pantheon Books.

Green, J. N. 1989. *Loss of the Verenigde Oostindische Compagnie Retourschip 'Batavia', Western Australia, 1629*. Oxford: British Archaeological Reports (BAR International Series 489).

Greenhill, B. 1995. *The Archaeology of Boats and Ships*. London: Conway Maritime Press.

Greenhill, B. and S. F. Manning 1988. *The Evolution of the Wooden Ship*. London: Batsford.

Greer, G. 1981. *American Stonewares: The Art and Craft of Utilitarian Potters*. Exton: Schiffer.

Gregory, R. A. 2004. Rediscovering the Denaby Pottery: archaeological investigations at Denaby Main, Conisbrough, South Yorkshire. *Post-Medieval Archaeology* 38: 133–179.

Grele, R. 1985. *Envelopes of Sound: The Art of Oral History* (revised second editing). Chicago: Precedent Publishing.

Grenier, R. and J. A. Tuck 1981. A sixteenth century Basque whaling station in Labrador. *Scientific American* 254(5): 180–188.

Grenville, J. 1997. *Medieval Housing*. London: Leicester University Press.

Griggs, H. J. 1999. *Go gCuire Dia Rath Blath Ort* (God Grant that You Prosper and Flourish): Social and Economic Mobility Among the Irish in Nineteenth-Century New York. *Historical Archaeology* 33 (1): 87–101.

Groover, M. D. 2001. Linking artifact assemblages to household cycles. *Historical Archaeology* 35(4): 38–57.

2003. *An Archaeological Study of Rural Capitalism and Material Life: The Gibbs Farmstead in Southern Appalachia*. New York: Plenum.

Gundaker, G. 1996. What goes around comes around: circles, cycles and recycling in African-American yard work. In C. Cerny and S. Seriff (eds.) *Recycled Re-seen: Folk Art from the Global Scrap Heap*. New York: Harry N. Abrams, pp. 72–81.

1998. *Signs of Diaspora/Diaspora of Signs: Literacies, Creolization, and Vernacular Practice in African America*. Oxford: Oxford University Press.

Gwyn, D. 2004. Landscape, economy and identity: a study of the archaeology of industrialisation. In D. Barker and D. Cranstone (eds.) pp. 35–52.

Gye, L. 2005. *Half Lives* http://halflives.adc.rmit.edu.au/ (accessed 9 May 2005).

Habermas, J. 1984. *The Theory of Communicative Action.* (trans. T. McCarthy). Boston, MA: Beacon.

Haggarty, G. and A. McIntyre 1996. Excavation and watching brief at Newbigging Pottery, Musselburgh, East Lothian. *Proceedings of the Society of Antiquaries of Scotland* 126: 943–962.

Halbwachs, M. 1992. The legendary topography of the gospels in the Holy Land: conclusion. In M. Halbwachs *On Collective Memory.* (edited, translated, and introduced by L. A. Coser). Chicago, IL: University of Chicago Press, pp. 191–235.

Hall, M. 1992. Small things and mobile, conflictual fusion of power, fear, and desire. In A. E. Yentsch and M. C. Beaudry (eds.) pp. 373–399.

    2000. *Archaeology and the Modern World: Colonial Transcripts of South Africa and the Chesapeake.* London: Routledge.

    2005. The industrial archaeology of entertainment. In E. C. Casella and J. Symonds (eds.) pp. 261–278.

Hall, M. and P. Bombardella 2005. Las Vegas in Africa. *Journal of Social Archaeology* 5(1) : 5–24.

Hall, P. 1998. *Cities in Civilization.* London: Weidenfeld and Nicolson.

Hamer, D. 1990. *New Towns in the New World: Images and Perceptions of the Nineteenth Century Urban Frontier.* New York: Columbia University Press.

Hamilton, D. 1978. *Architectural Ceramics.* London: Thames and Hudson.

Hamilton, D. L. 1991. A decade of excavations at Port Royal, Jamaica. In J. D. Broadwater (ed.) *Underwater Archaeology: Proceedings from the SHA Conference, Richmond, Virginia, 1991.* Rockville, MD: Society for Historical Archaeology, pp. 90–94.

Hamilton, N. 2000. The conceptual archive and the challenge of gender. In I. Hodder (ed.) *Towards a Reflexive Method in Archaeology: The Example at Çatalhöyük.* Cambridge: McDonald Institute for Archaeological Research (British Institute of Archaeology at Ankara Monograph 28), pp. 95–99.

Hammel, E. A. 1984. On the *** of studying household form and function. In R. M. Netting, R. R. Wilk and E. J. Arnould (eds.) *Households Comparative and Historical Studies of the Domestic Group.* Berkeley: University of California Press, pp. 29–43.

Hammond, G. B. 1993. *Conscience and Its Recovery: From the Frankfurt School to Feminism.* Charlottesville, VA: University Press of Virginia.

Handler, J. S. and F. W. Lange 1978. *Plantation Slavery in Barbados: An Archaeological and Historical Investigation.* Cambridge, MA: Harvard University Press.

Hands off Committee 2003a. South African Heritage Resources Agency public consultation process: transcript of meeting held on the 29th August 2003 at St Andrew's Presbyterian Church, Somerset Road, Green Point. Cape Town: South African Heritage Resources Agency.

2003b. Submission to SAHRA's Appeal Committee, and substantiation of appeal. Cape Town: Hands Off Prestwich Street Ad Hoc Committee. Ms on file at Department of Archaeology, University of Cape Town.

Handsman, R. G. 1983. Historical archaeology and capitalism, subscriptions and separations: the production of individualism. *North American Archaeologist* 4(1): 63–79.

Handsman, R. G. and M. P. Leone 1989. Living history and critical archaeology in the reconstruction of the past. In V. Pinsky and A. Wylie (eds.) *Critical Traditions in Contemporary Archaeology: Essays in the Philosophy, History, and Socio-politics of Archaeology*. Cambridge: Cambridge University Press, pp. 117–135.

Hannaford, I. 1996. *Race: The History of an Idea in the West*. Baltimore, MD: Johns Hopkins University Press.

Haraway, D. J. 1991. Situated knowledges: the science question in feminism and the privilege of a partial perspective. In D. J. Haraway *Simians, Cyborgs, and Women: The Reinvention of Nature*. London: Free Association Books, pp. 183–201.

Hardesty, D. 1988. *The Archaeology of Mining and Miners*. Society for Historical Archaeology Special Publication Series, Number 6. Pleasant Hill, CA: Society for Historical Archaeology.

1994. Class, gender strategies, and material culture in the Mining West. In E. Scott (ed.) *Those of Little Note*. Tucson, AZ: University of Arizona Press, pp. 129–148.

Harré, R. 1990. Some narrative conventions of scientific discourse. In C. Nash (ed.) *Narrative in Culture: the Uses of Storytelling in the Sciences, Philosophy, and Literature*. London: Routledge, pp. 81–101.

Harreld, D. J. 2003. Trading places: the public band private spaces of merchants in sixteenth-century Antwerp. *Journal of Urban History* 29: 657–669.

Harrington, F. 1992. Deepwater fishing from the Isles of Shoals. In A. E. Yentsch and M. C. Beaudry (eds.) pp. 249–266.

Harrington, J. C. 1978. Dating stem fragments of seventeenth and eighteenth century clay tobacco pipes. In R. L. Schuyler (ed.) pp. 63–65.

Harris, E. 1989. Bermuda defences at the end of the American Revolutionary War. *Bermuda Journal of Archaeology and Maritime History* 1: 81–108.

Harrison, Harrod & Co. 1861. *Gazetteer and Directory of Staffordshire, with Dudley, in Worcestershire*. London: Harrison, Harrod & Co.

Hart, T. 2003. Heritage Impact Assessment of West Street and Erf 4721 Green Point, Cape Town. Cape Town: Archaeology Contracts Office. (Ms on file at Department of Archaeology, University of Cape Town.)

Hawley, G. 1995. *Treasures of the Steamboat Arabia*. Kansas City: Arabia Steamboat Museum.

Hayden, D. 1994. The power of place, claiming urban landscapes as people's history. *Journal of Urban History* 20: 466–485.

1995. *The Power of Place: Urban Landscapes as Public History*. Cambridge, MA: MIT Press.

2004. *A Field Guide to Sprawl*. New York: W. W. Norton & Co.

Haywood, J. and W. Lee 1848. Report on the sanitary condition of the borough of Sheffield. Sheffield: Manuscript, Sheffield Archives.

Heath, B. J. nd. Landscape archaeology at Thomas Jefferson's Poplar Forest. In A. Malek (ed.) *Dumbarton Oaks Handbook for Garden Archaeology*. Washington, DC: Dumbarton Oaks.

Heidegger, M. 1962. *Being and Time* (trans. J. Macquarrie and E. Robinson). Oxford: Blackwell.

Henderson, G. 1976. *James Matthews* excavation. *International Journal of Nautical Archaeology* 5(3): 245–251.

1986. *Maritime Archaeology in Australia*. Nedlands: University of Western Australia Press.

Hendon, J. A. 1996. Archaeological approaches to the organization of domestic labor: household practice and domestic relations. *Annual Review of Anthropology* 25: 45–61.

Henry, S. 1987. Factors influencing consumer behaviour in turn-of-the-century Phoenix, Arizona. In S. Spencer-Wood (ed.) *Consumer Choice in Historical Archaeology*. New York: Plenum, pp. 359–382.

Henrywood, R. K. 2002. *Staffordshire Potters 1781–1900*. Woodbridge: Antique Collectors' Club.

Hepp, J. H. 2003. *The Middle-Class City: Transforming Space and Time in Philadelphia, 1876–1926*. Philadelphia, PA: University of Pennsylvania Press.

Heritage Lottery Fund 1998. *Conservation Plans for Historic Places*. London: Heritage Lottery Fund.

Hess, A. 1995. Fast food culture: the archaeology of McDonald's. In M. Leone and N. A. Silberman (eds.) *Invisible America: Unearthing our Hidden History*. New York: Henry Holt, pp. 258–259.

Hewison, R. 1987. *The Heritage Industry*. London: Routledge.

Hewitt, T. 2002. Half a century of development. In T. Allen and A. Thomas (eds.) *Poverty and Development in the 21st Century*. Oxford: Oxford University Press, pp. 289–308.

Hicks, B. and S. Kropf 2003. *Raising the Hunley: The Remarkable History and Recovery of the Lost Confederate Submarine*. Novato, CA: Presidio Press.

Hicks, D. 2000. Ethnicity, race and the archaeology of the Atlantic slave trade. *Assemblage* 5, www.shef.ac.uk/assem/5/hicks.html (accessed 12 February 2005).

2003. Archaeology unfolding: diversity and the loss of isolation. *Oxford Journal of Archaeology* 22(3): 315–329.

2004. From the 'Questions that count' to the stories that 'matter' in historical archaeology. *Antiquity* 78: 934–939.

2005. 'Places for thinking' from Annapolis to Bristol: situations and symmetries in 'world historical archaeologies'. *World Archaeology* 37(3): 373–391.

Hicks, D. and N. Jeffries 2004. *Biographies of London Life: The Archaeology of Londoners and their Things, AD 1600–2000*. London: Museum of London ('Research Matters' Occasional Publication 3).

Higgs, D. (ed.) 1999. *Queer Sites: Gay Urban Histories Since 1600*. London: Routledge.

Higman, B. W. 1998. *Montpelier Jamaica: A Plantation Community in Slavery and Freedom, 1739–1912*. Bridgetown: University of the West Indies Press.

Hill, S. H. 1982. An examination of manufacture-deposition lag for glass bottles from late historic sites. In R. S. Dickens (ed.) *Archaeology of Urban America*. New York: Academic Press, pp. 291–327.

Hillier, B. and J. Hanson 1985. *The Social Logic of Space*. Cambridge: Cambridge University Press.

Hingley, R. 1999. The imperial context of Romano-British studies and proposals for a new understanding of social change. In P. P. Funari, M. Hall and S. Jones (eds.) *Historical Archaeology: Back from the Edge*. London: Routledge, pp. 137–150.

2000. *Roman Officers and English Gentlemen: The Imperial Origins of Roman Archaeology*. London: Routledge.

Historical Records of Australia 1921. *Series III Despatches and Papers Relating to the Settlement of the States*. Sydney: Library Committee of the Commonwealth Parliament.

Hocker, F. and C. Ward (eds.) 2004. *Towards a Philosophy of Ancient Shipbuilding*. College Station: Texas A&M University Press.

Hodder, I. 1982. *Symbols in Action*. New York: Cambridge University Press.

1986. *Reading the Past: Current Approaches to Interpretation in Archaeology*. Cambridge: Cambridge University Press.

1989. Writing archaeology. *Antiquity* 63: 268–274.

1990. *The Domestication of Europe*. Oxford: Blackwell.

1992. Towards radical doubt: a dialogue. In I. Hodder *Theory and Practice in Archaeology*. London: Routledge, pp. 155–159.

1993. Narrative and rhetoric of material culture sequences. *World Archaeology* 25: 268–282.

1995. Material culture in time. In I. Hodder et al. (eds.) pp. 164–168.

1999. *The Archaeological Process: An Introduction*. Oxford: Blackwell.

2004. Dialogical archaeology and its implications. In I. Hodder *Archaeology Beyond Dialogue*. Salt Lake City, UT: University of Utah Press, pp. 1–7.

Hodder, I., M. Shanks, A. Alexandri, V. Buchli, J. Carman, J. Last and G. Lucas (eds.) 1995. *Interpreting Archaeology: Finding Meaning in the Past*. London: Routledge.

Holland, A. J. 1985. *Buckler's Hard: A Rural Shipbuilding Centre*. London: Mason.

Holman, R. G., C. J. Martin and P. F. Martin 1977. The *Dartmouth*, a British Frigate Wrecked off Mull. *International Journal of Nautical Archaeology* 6(3): 219–223.

Holtorf, C. 2000–2005. *Monumental Past: The Life-histories of Megalithic Monuments in Mecklenburg-Vorpommern (Germany)*. Electronic monograph. University of Toronto: Centre for Instructional Technology Development. http://hdl.handle.net/1807/245 (accessed 10 April 2005).

2002. Notes on the life history of a pot sherd. *Journal of Material Culture* 7 (1): 49–72.

2005. *From Stonehenge to Las Vegas. Archaeology as Popular Culture.* Walnut Creek, CA: Altamira.

nd. The zoo as a site of memories. In Archaeology of Zoo Collective (eds.) *The Archaeology of Zoos.* Charlottesville, VA: University of Virginia Press.

Holyoak, V. 2002. Out of the blue: assessing military aircraft crash sites in England, 1912–45. *Antiquity* 76: 657–663.

Honychurch, L. 1997. Crossroads in the Caribbean: a site of encounter and exchange on Dominica. *World Archaeology* 28(3): 291–304.

hooks, b. 2000. *Feminism is for Everybody.* Cambridge, MA: South End Press.

Horning, A. 1995. 'A verie fitt place to erect a great citie': comparative contextual analysis of archaeological Jamestown. Unpublished Ph.D. dissertation, University of Pennsylvania (Ann Arbor: University Microfilms).

2000. Urbanism in the Colonial South: the development of seventeenth-century Jamestown. In A. Young (ed.) *Urban Archaeology in the South.* Tuscaloosa, AL: University of Alabama Press, pp. 52–68.

2002. Myth, migration, and material culture: archaeology and the Ulster influence on Appalachia. *Historical Archaeology* 36(4): 129–149.

Hoshower-Leppo, L. 2002. Missing in action: searching for America's war dead. In J. Schofield *et al.* (eds.) pp. 80–90.

Hoskins, J. 1998. *Biographical Objects. How Things tell the Stories of People's Lives.* London: Routledge.

Hoskins, W. G. 1953. The rebuilding of rural England, 1570–1640. *Past and Present* 4: 44–59.

1955. *The Making of the English Landscape.* London: Hodder and Stoughton.

1967. *Fieldwork in Local History.* London: Faber.

2004 [1960] *Two Thousand Years in Exeter.* Chichester: Phillimore.

Houston, S. D. 2004. Overture to *The First Writing.* In S. D. Houston (ed.) *The First Writing: Script Invention as History and Process.* Cambridge: Cambridge University Press, pp. 3–15.

Hudson, K. 1963. *Industrial Archaeology: An introduction.* London: John Baker.

1967. *Handbook for Industrial Archaeologists.* London: John Baker.

Hughes, S. R. 2000. *Copperopolis.* Aberystwyth: Royal Commission on the Ancient and Historical Monuments of Wales.

Hume, J. R. 1976. *The Industrial Archaeology of Scotland: Vol. I. The Lowlands and Borders.* London: Batsford.

Hunter, J. and I. Ralston (eds.) nd. Archaeological resource management in the UK: an introduction. Stroud: Sutton/Institute of Field Archaeologists (revised second edition).

Hunter, R. 2001. Introduction. In R. Hunter (ed.) *Ceramics in America 2001.* Milwaukee: Chipstone Foundation, pp. xi–xiv.

Hurst, J. G., D. S. Neal and H. J. E. Van Beuningen 1986. *Pottery Produced and Traded in North-West Europe 1350–1650.* Rotterdam: Museum Boymans-van Beuningen (Rotterdam Papers, VI).

Huxley, M. 1997. Gentrification, densification and the inner city. *Historic Environment* 13(1): 47–53.

Hymes, D. (ed.) 1972. *Reinventing Anthropology*. New York: Pantheon.

Ingelman-Sundberg, C. 1977. The VOC Ship *Zeewijk*. *International Journal of Nautical Archaeology* 6(3): 225–231.

Ingold, T. 2000a [1993]. The temporality of landscape. In J. S. Thomas (ed.) *Interpretive Archaeology: A Reader*. London: Leicester University Press, pp. 510–530.

    2000b. Building, dwelling, living: how animals and people make themselves at home in the world. In T. Ingold *The Perception of the Environment: Essays on Livelihood, Dwelling and Skill*. London: Routledge, pp. 172–188.

Insoll, T. 1999. *The Archaeology of Islam*. Oxford: Blackwell.

International Commission for the History of Towns. 2005. Historia Urbium web pages. www.historiaurbium.org (accessed 12 June 2005).

Iota Chapter. 1890–1893. Photographic album. University Archives, Bancroft Library, University of California, Berkeley.

Ireland, T. 2003. 'The absence of ghosts': landscape and identity in the archaeology of Australia's settler culture. *Historical Archaeology* 37(1): 56–72.

Jack, I. 1995. Joadja, New South Wales; the paragon of early oil-shale communities. *Australasian Historical Archaeology* 13: 31–40.

Jackson, L. M. 1991. Nineteenth century British ceramics: a key to cultural dynamics in southwestern Alaska. Unpublished Ph.D. thesis, University of California at Los Angeles (Ann Arbor, University Microfilms).

Jackson, P. 2000. Rematerializing social and cultural geography. *Social and Cultural Geography* 1: 9–14.

Jameson, F. 1997. Five theses on actually existing Marxism. In E. M. Wood and J. B. Foster (eds.) *In Defence of History: Marxism and the Post-Modern Agenda*. New York: Monthly Review Press, pp. 175–183.

Jameson, J. H. (ed.) 1997. *Presenting Archaeology to the Public: Digging for Truths*. Walnut Creek, CA: Altamira Press.

Jameson, J. H., C. A. Finn and J. E. Ehrenhard (eds.) 2003. *Ancient Muses: Archaeology and the Arts*. Tuscaloosa, AL: University of Alabama Press.

Jarman, N. 1997. *Material Conflicts: Parades and Visual Displays in Northern Ireland*. Oxford: Berg.

Jasinski, M. 1993. The maritime cultural landscape. *Archaeologia Polski* 38(1): 7–21.

Jeffrey, B. 2004. WWII underwater cultural heritage sites in Truk Lagoon: considering a case for World Heritage Listing. *International Journal of Nautical Archaeology* 33(1): 106–121.

Jennings, S. 1981. *Eighteen Centuries of Pottery from Norwich*. Norwich: The Norwich Survey (East Anglian Archaeology Report 13).

Jeppie, S. and C. Soudien (eds.) 1990. *The Struggle for District Six: Past and Present*. Cape Town: Buchu Books.

Johnson, A. W. 2003. Showdown in the Pacific: a remote response to European power struggles in the Pacific, Dawes Point Battery, Sydney, 1791–1925. *Historical Archaeology* 37(1): 114–127.

Johnson, M. H. 1990. The Englishman's home and its study. In R. Samson (ed.) *The Social Archaeology of Buildings*. Edinburgh: Edinburgh University Press, pp. 245–258.

    1992. Meanings of polite architecture in sixteenth-century England. *Historical Archaeology* 26: 45–56.

    1993a. *Housing Culture: Traditional Architecture in an English Landscape*. London: University College London Press.

    1993b. Rethinking the Great Rebuilding. *Oxford Journal of Archaeology* 12(1): 117–125.

    1996. *An Archaeology of Capitalism*. Oxford: Blackwell.

    1997. Vernacular architecture: the loss of innocence. *Vernacular Architecture* 13–19.

    1999a. *Archaeological Theory: An Introduction*. Oxford: Blackwell.

    1999b. Rethinking historical archaeology. In P. P. A. Funari, M. Hall and S. Jones (eds.) *Historical Archaeology. Back from the Edge*. London: Routledge, pp. 23–36.

    2005. On the particularism of English landscape archaeology. *International Journal of Historical Archaeology* 9(2): 112–122.

Johnson, W. G. and S. R. Edwards 2000. *Survival Town: The Apple II Historic District, Nevada Test Site, Nye County, Nevada*. Las Vegas: Desert Research Institute (Division of Earth and Ecosystem Sciences Cultural Resources Technical Report No. 99).

Johnson, W. G., B. A. Holz and R. Jones 2000. *A Cold War Battlefield: Frenchman Flat Historic District, Nevada Test Site, Nye County, Nevada*. Las Vegas: Desert Research Institute (Division of Earth and Ecosystem Sciences Cultural Resources Technical Report No. 97).

Jones, A. 2002. *Archaeological Theory and Scientific Practice*. Cambridge: Cambridge University Press.

    2004. Archaeometry and materiality: materials-based analysis in theory and practice. *Archaeometry* 46(3): 327–338.

Jones, D. (ed.) 2002. *20th Century Heritage: Our Recent Cultural Legacy*. Adelaide: University of Adelaide and Australia ICOMOS Secretariat (School of Architecture, Landscape Architecture and Urban Design).

Jones, M. O. 1989. *Craftsman of the Cumberlands: Tradition and Creativity*. Lexington, KY: University Press of Kentucky.

    1993. Why take a behavioral approach to folk objects? In S. Lubar and W. D. Kingery (eds.) *History from Things: Essays on Material Culture*. Washington, DC: Smithsonian Institution Press, pp. 182–196.

Jones, N., M. Walter and P. Frost 2004. *Mountains and Orefields: Metal Mining Landscapes of Mid and North-East Wales*. York: Council for British Archaeology in association with Cadw (CBA Research Report 142).

Jones, O. 1986. *Cylindrical English Wine and Beer Bottles 1735–1850*. Ottowa: Parks Canada.

Jones, S. 1997. *The Archaeology of Ethnicity: Constructing Identities in the Past and Present*. New York: Routledge.

Jordan, S. and C. Schrire 2002. Material culture and the roots of colonial society at the South African Cape of Good Hope. In C. L. Lyons and J. K. Papadopoulos (eds.) *The Archaeology of Colonialism*. Los Angeles: Getty Research Institute, pp. 241–272.

Jordan, T. G. 1980. Alpine, Alemannic, and American architecture. *Annals of the Association of American Geographers* 70: 154–180.

Jordan, T. G., M. Kaups and R. M. Lieffort 1986. New evidence on the European origin of Pennsylvania V-Notching. *Pennsylvania Folklife* 36: 20–31.

Joyce, P. 2001. A quiet victory: the growing role of postmodernism in history. *Times Literary Supplement* 26 October: 15.

Joyce, R. A. 2000. Heirlooms and houses: materiality and social memory. In R. A. Joyce and S. D. Gillespie (eds.) *Beyond Kinship: Social and Material Reproduction in House Societies*. Philadelphia, PA: University of Pennsylvania Press, pp. 189–212.

2002. *The Languages of Archaeology: Dialogue, Narrative and Writing*. Oxford: Blackwell.

Junker, L. L. 1998. Integrating history and archaeology in the study of contact period Philippine chiefdoms. *International Journal of Historical Archaeology* 2: 291–320.

Karklins, K. (ed.) 2000. *Studies in Material Culture Research*. Tucson, AZ: Society for Historical Archaeology.

Karlsson, H. (ed.) 2001. *It's About Time. The Concept of Time in Archaeology*. Gothenburg: Bricoleur Press.

Karskens, G. 1997. *The Rocks: Life in Early Sydney*. Parkville: Melbourne University Press.

1999. *Inside the Rocks: The Archaeology of a Neighbourhood*. Sydney: Hale and Iremonger.

2002. Small things, big pictures: new perspectives from the archaeology of Sydney's Rocks neighbourhood. In A. Mayne and T. Murray (eds.) pp. 69–88.

2003. Revisiting the worldview: the archaeology of convict households in Sydney's Rocks neighborhood. *Historical Archaeology* 37(1): 34–55.

Kassiem, A. E. 2003. Slaves' skeletons to be relocated. *Cape Times* (2 September).

Kelso, W. M. 1984. *Kingsmill Plantation, 1619–1800: Archaeology of Country Life in Colonial Virginia*. New York: Academic Press.

1997. *Archaeology at Monticello: Artifacts of Everyday Life in the Plantation Community*. Charlottesville, VA: Thomas Jefferson Memorial Foundation.

Kelso, W. M. and R. Most (eds.) 1990. *Earth Patterns: Essays in Landscape Archaeology*. Charlottesville, VA: University Press of Virginia.

Kent, S. 1987. *Method and Theory for Activity Area Research: An Ethnoarchaeological Approach*. New York: Columbia University Press.

Kent, S. (ed.) 1990. *Domestic Architecture and the Use of Space: An Interdisciplinary Cross-Cultural Study*. Cambridge: Cambridge University Press.

Kerr, J. S. 2000. *Conservation Plans* (Fifth Edition). Sydney: National Trust of New South Wales.

Khan, I. 2004. Every . . . *Next Level Magazine* 2(3).

Kidd, C. 1999. *British Identities before Rationalism: Ethnicity and Nationhood in the Atlantic World, 1600–1800.* Cambridge: Cambridge University Press.

Killock, D., J. Brown and C. Jarrett 2003. The industrialisation of an ecclesiastical hamlet: stoneware production in Lambeth and the sanitary revolution. *Post-Medieval Archaeology* 37: 29–78.

King, J. A. 1994. Rural landscape in the mid-nineteenth-century Chesapeake. In B. J. Little and P. A. Shackel (eds.) *Historical Archaeology of the Chesapeake Region.* Washington, DC: Smithsonian Institution Press, pp. 283–299.

1997. Tobacco, innovation and economic persistence in nineteenth century southern Maryland. *Agricultural History* 71(2): 207–236.

King, J. A. and E. E. Chaney 2003. Lord Baltimore's neighborhood: standards of living on the seventeenth-century Patuxent Frontier. *Avalon Chronicles* 8: 261–283.

King, J. A. and H. M. Miller 1987. The view from the midden: an analysis of midden distribution and composition at the van Sweringen site, St. Mary's City, Maryland. *Historical Archaeology* 21(2): 37–59.

King, J. A. and D. H. Ubelaker (eds.) 1996. *Living and Dying on the 17th Century Patuxent Frontier.* Crownsville, MD: Maryland Historical Trust Press.

King, T. F. 2003. *Places that Count: Traditional Cultural Properties in Cultural Resource Management.* Walnut Creek, CA: Altamira Press.

Kiser, T. 2001. Seventeenth-century Donyatt Pottery in the Chesapeake. In R. Hunter (ed.) *Ceramics in America 2001.* Milwaukee, WI: Chipstone Foundation, pp. 220–222.

Kist, J. B. 1990. Integrating archaeological and historical records in Dutch East India Company research. In V. Fenwick and M. Redknap (eds.) *Ships, Cargoes and the East India Trade.* Dorchester: Dorset Press, pp. 49–52.

Klein, T. 1991. Nineteenth-century ceramics and models of consumer behavior. *Historical Archaeology* 25(2): 77–91.

Klejn, L. S. 1991. A Russian lesson for theoretical archaeology: a reply. *Fennoscandia Archaeologica* 8: 67–71.

Knappett, C. 2002. Photographs, skeuomorphs and marionettes: some thoughts on mind, agency and object. *Journal of Material Culture* 7(1): 97–117.

Kniffen, F. B. 1936. Louisiana house types. *Annals of the Association of American Geographers* 26: 179–193.

Knight, H. 2002. *Aspects of Medieval and Later Southwark: Archaeological Excavations (1991–98) for the London Underground Limited Jubilee Line Extension Project.* London: Museum of London Archaeology Service.

Kobylinski, Z. 1988. Things as symbols: the boat in the early medieval culture of Northern Europe. *Archaeologia Polona* 27: 185–190.

Kopytoff, I. 1986. The cultural biography of things: commoditization as process. In A. Appadurai (ed.) pp. 64–91.

Koslofsky, C. 2002. Court culture and street lighting in seventeenth-century Europe. *Journal of Urban History* 28: 743–768.

Kostoff, S. 1991. *The City Shaped: Urban Patterns and Meanings Through History*. Boston, MA: Bulfinch.

 1992. *The City Assembled: The Elements of Urban Form through History*. Boston, MA: Bulfinch.

Kryder-Reid, E. 1994. 'With manly courage:' reading the construction of gender in a nineteenth-century religious community. In E. M. Scott (ed.) *Those of Little Note: Gender, Race, and Class in Historical Archaeology*. Tucson, AZ: University of Arizona Press, pp. 97–114.

Küchler, S. 2002. *Malanggan: Art, Memory and Sacrifice*. Oxford: Berg.

Küchler, S. and D. Miller (eds.) 2005. *Clothing as Material Culture*. Oxford: Berg.

Küchler, S. and G. Were (eds.) 2005. *The Art of Clothing: A Pacific Example*. London: UCL Press.

Kurlansky, M. 2002. *Salt: A World History*. London: Cape.

Kybalová, J. 1989. *European Creamware*. London: Hamlyn.

Lahiri, N. 2003. Commemorating and remembering 1857: the revolt in Delhi and its afterlife. *World Archaeology* 35(1): 35–60.

Lally, E. 2002. *At Home with Computers*. Oxford: Berg.

Lamphere, L., H. Ragone and P. Zavella 1997. *Situated Lives: Gender and Culture in Everyday Life*. London: Routledge.

Landers, J. 2000. *Colonial Plantations and Economy in Florida*. Gainesville, FL: University Press of Florida.

Landscapes circum-*Landnám* Project 2005. http://tsunami.geo.ed.ac.uk/~ajn/leverhulme/ (Consulted 3 March 2005).

Landström, B. 1980. *The Royal Warship Vasa*. Stockholm: Vasa Museet.

Lanier, G. M. and B. L. Herman 1997. *Everyday Architecture of the Mid-Atlantic*. Baltimore, MD: Johns Hopkins University Press.

LaRoche, C. J. and M. L. Blakey 1997. Seizing intellectual power: the dialogue at the New York African Burial Ground. *Historical Archaeology* 31: 84–106.

Laslett, P. and R. Wall (eds.) 1972. *Household and Family in Past Time*. Cambridge: Cambridge University Press.

Latour, B. 1993. *We Have Never Been Modern*. Brighton: Harvester Wheatsheaf.

 1996. *Aramis, or the Love of Technology*. Cambridge, MA: MIT Press.

 2000a. When things strike back: a possible contribution of 'science studies' to the social sciences. *British Journal of Sociology* 51(1): 107–123.

 2000b. The Berlin key or how to do words with things. In P. M. Graves-Brown (ed.) *Matter, Materiality and Modern Culture*. London: Routledge, pp. 10–21.

Latour, B. and S. Woolgar 1979. *Laboratory Life: The Social Construction of Scientific Facts*. London: Sage.

Lawler, E. 2002. The President's house in Philadelphia: the rediscovery of a lost landmark. *The Pennsylvania Magazine of History and Biography* 126: 5–95.

Lawrence, S. 2000. *Dolly's Creek: An Archaeology of a Victorian Goldfields Community*. Melbourne: Melbourne University Press.

 2003. Introduction. In S. Lawrence (ed.) *Archaeologies of the British: Explorations of Identity in Great Britain and its Colonies, 1600–1945*. London: Routledge (One World Archaeology 46), pp. 1–13.

Lawrence, S. and M. Staniforth 1998. Introduction. In S. Lawrence and M. Staniforth (eds.) *The Archaeology of Whaling in Southern Australia and New Zealand*. Gundaroo: Australasian Society for Historical Archaeology, pp. 7–10.

Lawson, A. 1983. *The Archaeology of Witton, near North Walsham, Norfolk*. Dereham: Norfolk Archaeological Unit (East Anglian Archaeology Report No. 18).

Lay, K. E. 1982. European antecedents of seventeenth-century and eighteenth-century Germanic and Scots-Irish architecture in America. *Pennsylvania Folklife* 32(1): 2–43.

LeRoy Ladurie, E. 1979. The 'event' and the 'long term' in social history: the case of the Chouan Uprising. In E. LeRoy Ladurie *The Territory of the Historian*. Hassocks: Harvester Press, pp. 111–124.

1980. *Montaillou: the Promised Land of Error*. Harmondsworth: Penguin.

Leacock, E. B. 1972. Introduction. In F. Engels (ed.) *The Origins of the Family, Private Property and the State*. New York: International Publishers, pp. 7–67.

1981. *Myths of Male Dominance: Collected Articles*. New York: Monthly Review Press.

Leech, R. 1981. *Industrial Housing in the Trinity Area of Frome*. London: HMSO.

Lefebvre, H. 1991. *The Production of Space*. (trans. D. Nicholson-Smith). Oxford: Blackwell.

Legendre, J-P. 2001. Archaeology of World War II: the Lancaster bomber of Fléville (Meurthe et Moselle, France). In V. Buchli and G. Lucas (eds.) pp. 126–137.

Lehner, L. 1988. *Lehner's Encyclopedia of U.S. Marks on Pottery, Porcelain, and Clay*. Paducah: Collector Books.

Lemon, J. T. 1996. *Liberal Dreams and Nature's Limits: Great Cities of North America Since 1600*. Oxford: Oxford University Press.

Lenihan, D. J. (ed.) 1989. *USS Arizona Memorial and Pearl Harbour National Historic Landmark*. Santa Fe, NM: National Parks Service.

Leone, M. P. 1973. Archaeology as the science of technology: Mormon town plans and fences. In C. L. Redman (ed.) *Research and Theory in Current Archaeology*. New York: John Wiley and Sons pp. 125–150.

1977. The new Mormon temple in Washington DC. In L. Ferguson (ed.) pp. 43–61.

1978. Time in American archaeology. In C. Redman (ed.) *Social Archaeology: Beyond Subsistence and Dating*. London: Academic Press, pp. 25–36.

1981a. Archaeology's relationship to the present and the past. In R. A. Gould and M. Schiffer (eds.) pp. 5–13.

1981b. The relationship between artefacts and the public in outdoor history museums. *Annals of the New York Academy of Sciences* 376: 301–313.

1982. Some opinions about recovering mind. *American Antiquity* 47: 742–760.

1988a. The relationship between archaeological data and the documentary record: eighteenth-century gardens in Annapolis, Maryland. *Historical Archaeology* 22: 29–35.

1988b. The Georgian order as the order of merchant capitalism in Annapolis, Maryland. In M. P. Leone and P. B. Potter (eds.) pp. 235–261.

1995. A historical archaeology of capitalism. *American Anthropologist* 97(2): 251–268.

1996 [1984]. Interpreting ideology in historical archaeology: using the rules of perspective in the William Paca Garden in Annapolis, Maryland. In C. Orser (ed.) *Images of the Recent Past*. Walnut Creek, CA: Altamira Press, pp. 371–391 (originally published in *Ideology, Power and Prehistory* (eds. D. Miller and C. Tilley). Cambridge: Cambridge University Press, pp. 25–35.

1999. Setting some terms for historical archaeologies of capitalism. In M. P. Leone and P. B. Potter (eds.) *Historical Archaeologies of Capitalism*. New York: Plenum, pp. 3–20.

2005. *The Archaeology of Liberty in an American Capital: Excavations in Annapolis*. Berkeley, CA: University of California Press.

Leone, M. P. and S. D. Hurry 1998. Seeing: the power of town planning in the Chesapeake. *Historical Archaeology* 32(4): 34–62.

Leone, M. P. and P. B. Potter (eds.) 1988. *The Recovery of Meaning in Historical Archaeology*. Washington, DC: Smithsonian Institution Press.

Leone, M. P. and P. B. Potter 1996 [1984]. Archaeological Annapolis: a guide to seeing and understanding three centuries of change. In R. W. Preucel and I. Hodder (eds.) *Contemporary Archaeology in Theory*. Oxford: Blackwell, pp. 570–598.

Leone, M. P. and P. B. Potter (eds.) 1999. *Historical Archaeologies of Capitalism*. New York: Kluwer/Plenum.

Leone, M. P. and P. A. Shackel 1990. Plane and solid geometry in colonial gardens in Annapolis, Maryland. In W. M. Kelso and R. Most (eds.) pp. 153–167.

Leone, M. P., J. H. Ernstein, E. Kryder-Reid and P. A. Shackel 1989. Power gardens of Annapolis. *Archaeology* 42(2): 34–37, 74–75.

Leone, M. P., P. B. Potter and P. A. Shackel 1987. Toward a critical archaeology. *Current Anthropology* 28(3): 283–302.

Lepine, A. 1983. Discovery of a nineteenth century barge laden with iron ore near the village of St. Antoine. *International Journal of Nautical Archaeology* 12(2): 101–112.

Leslie, D. and S. Reimer 1999. Spatialising commodity chains. *Progress in Human Geography* 23(3): 401–420.

Levi, G. 2001. On microhistory. In P. Burke (ed.) *New Perspectives in Historical Writing*. University Park, PA: Pennsylvania State University Press, pp. 97–119.

Levi-Strauss, C. 1987. The concept of 'house'. In C. Levi-Strauss *Anthropology and Myth*. Oxford: Blackwell, pp. 151–152.

Lewis, K. E. 2000. Imagination and archaeological interpretations: a methodological tale. *Historical Archaeology* 34(2): 7–9.

Lewis, M. E. 2002. Impact of industrialisation: comparative study of child health in four sites from medieval and postmedieval England (AD 850–1859). *American Journal of Physical Anthropology* 119(3): 211–223.

Little, B. J. 1988. Craft and culture change in the eighteenth-century Chesapeake. In M. P. Leone and P. B. Potter (eds.) pp. 263–292.

1992a. Text-aided archaeology. In B. J. Little (ed.) pp. 1–8.

Little, B. J. (ed.) 1992b. *Text-Aided Archaeology*. Boca Raton, FL: CRC Press.

Little, B. J. 1994. People with history: an update on historical archaeology. *Journal of Archaeological Method and Theory* 1(1): 5–40.

1998. Cultural landscapes of printers and the 'Heav'n-taught art' in Annapolis, Maryland. In P. A. Shackel, P. R. Mullins and M. S. Warner (eds.) *Annapolis Pasts: Historical Archaeology in Annapolis, Maryland.* Knoxville, TN: University of Tennessee Press, pp. 225–243.

2000. Compelling images through storytelling: comment on 'Imaginary, but by no means unimaginable: storytelling, science, and historical archaeology'. *Historical Archaeology* 34(2): 10–13.

Little, B. J. (ed.) 2002. *The Public Benefits of Archaeology.* Gainesville, FL: University Press of Florida.

Little, B. J. and P. A. Shackel 1989. Scales of historical anthropology: an archaeology of colonial Anglo-America. *Antiquity* 63: 495–509.

Lloyd, G. E. R. 1990. *Demystifying Mentalités.* New York: Cambridge University Press.

Locock, M. (ed.) 1994a. *Meaningful Architecture: Social Interpretations of Buildings.* Aldershot: Avebury Press.

Locock, M. 1994b. Meaningful architecture. In M. Locock (ed.) *Meaningful Architecture: Social Interpretations of Buildings.* Aldershot: Avebury Press, pp. 1–13.

Loren, D. D. 2001. Social skins: orthodoxies and practices of dressing in the early colonial lower Mississippi valley. *Journal of Social Archaeology* 1(2): 172–189.

Loren, D. D. and M. C. Beaudry 2006. Becoming American: small things remembered. In M. Hall and S. Silliman (eds.) *Historical Archaeology.* Oxford: Blackwell (Studies in Global Archaeology). pp. 251–271.

Lorimer, H. and K. Lund 2003. Performing facts: finding a way over Scotland's mountains. In B. Szerszynski, W. Heim and C. Waterton (eds.) *Nature Performed: Environment, Culture, and Performance.* London: Blackwell *The Sociological Review* 51 (s2): 130–144.

Low, S. M. 1993. Cultural meaning of the plaza: The history of the Spanish American gridplan-plaza urban design. In R. Rotenberg and G. McDonogh (eds.) *The Cultural Meaning of Urban Space.* Westport: Bergin and Garvey, pp. 75–94.

2003. *Behind the Gates: Life, Security and the Pursuit of Happiness in Fortress America.* London: Routledge.

Lowenthal, D. 1985. *The Past Is a Foreign Country.* Cambridge: Cambridge University Press.

2005. Natural and cultural heritage. *International Journal of Heritage Studies* 11(1): 81–92.

Lowry, B. 1995. *Twentieth-Century Defences in Britain.* York: Council for British Archaeology.

Lubar, S. and W. D. Kingery (eds.) 1993. *History from Things: Essays on Material Culture.* Washington, DC: Smithsonian Institution Press.

Lucas, G. 1995. The changing face of time: English domestic clocks from the seventeenth to nineteenth century. *Journal of Design History* 8: 1–9.

1999. The archaeology of the workhouse: the changing use of the workhouse buildings at St. Mary's, Southampton. In S. Tarlow and S. West (eds.) pp. 125–139.

2001. *Critical Approaches to Fieldwork: Contemporary and Historical Archaeological Practice.* London: Routledge.

2003. Reading pottery: literature and transfer-printed pottery in the early nineteenth century. *International Journal of Historical Archaeology* 7: 127–143.

2004. Modern disturbances. On the ambiguities of archaeology. *Modernism/Modernity* 11(1): 109–120.

2005. *The Archaeology of Time.* London: Routledge.

Lucas, G. and R. Roderick 2003. The changing vernacular: archaeological excavations at Temple End, High Wycombe, Buckinghamshire. *Post-Medieval Archaeology* 37 (2): 165–206.

Ludlow Collective 2001. Archaeology at the Colorado Coal Field War, 1913–1914. In V. Buchli and G. Lucas (eds.) pp. 94–107.

Lydon, J. 1999a. *Many Inventions: The Chinese in the Rocks, 1890–1930.* Clayton, Victoria: Monash University (Monash Publications in History).

1999b. Pidgin English: historical archaeology, cultural exchange and the Chinese in the Rocks. 1890–1930. In P. P. A. Funari, M. Hall and S. Jones (eds.) *Historical Archaeology: Back from the Edge.* London: Routledge, pp. 255–283.

2003. Seeing each other: the colonial vision in nineteenth-century Victoria. In S. Lawrence (ed.) *Archaeologies of the British: Explorations of Identity in Great Britain and its Colonies 1600–1945.* London: Routledge, pp. 174–190.

Lynch, K. 1972. *What Time Is This Place?* Cambridge, MA: MIT Press.

Lyons, C. and J. Papadopoulos (eds.) 2002. *The Archaeology of Colonialism.* Oxford: Oxford University Press.

Maarleveld, T. 1995. Some thoughts on boat and ship finds as indicative of cultural traditions. *International Journal of Nautical Archaeology* 24(1): 3–7.

Macey, D. 2001. *The Penguin Dictionary of Critical Theory.* London: Penguin.

Machan, P. 1999. John Watts, Lambert Street: a surviving Sheffield firm with over 200 years' history. In M. Jones (ed.) *Aspects of Sheffield Vol. 2: Discovering Local History.* Sheffield: Wharncliffe Publishing Limited, pp. 79–96.

Machin, R. 1977. The great rebuilding: a reassessment. *Past and Present* 77: 33–56.

Macintyre, S. and A. Clark 2003. *The History Wars.* Melbourne: Melbourne University Press.

MacKnight, C. 1998. *Low Head to Launceston: The Earliest Reports of Port Dalrymple and the Tamar.* Launceston: Historical Survey of Northern Tasmania.

Madox Ford, F. 2000. *The Cinque Ports: A Historical and Descriptive Record.* London: Classic Books.

Main, G. L. 1975. Probate records as a source for early American history. *William and Mary Quarterly* 32: 89–99.

1982. *Tobacco Colony: Life in Early Maryland.* Princeton, NJ: Princeton University Press.

Majewski, T. 2000. 'We are all storytellers': comments on storytelling, science, and historical archaeology. *Historical Archaeology* 34(2): 17–19.

2002. Makers' marks. In C. E. Orser (ed.) *Encyclopaedia of Historical Archaeology*. London: Routledge, pp. 323–325.

Majewski, T. and M. J. O'Brien 1987. The use and misuse of nineteenth-century English and American ceramics in archaeological analysis. In M. B. Schiffer (ed.) *Advances in Archaeological Method and Theory* Vol. XI. New York: Academic Press, pp. 97–209.

Majewski, T. and M. B. Schiffer 2001. Beyond consumption: toward an archaeology of consumerism. In V. Buchli and G. Lucas (eds.) pp. 26–50.

Malan, A. 2003. *Prestwich Place Public Consultation Process*. Cape Town: Cultural Sites and Resources Forum.

Manders, M. R., W. M. Chandraratne, A. M. A. Dayananda, R. Muthucumarana, K. B. C. Weerasena and K. P. D. Weerasingha 2004. The physical protection of a 17th century VOC shipwreck in Sri Lanka. *Current Science* 86(9): 1251–1255.

Mangan, P. H. 2000. Building biographies: spatial changes in domestic structures during the transition from feudalism to capitalism. In J. A. Delle et al. (eds.) pp. 205–238.

Maniery, M. L. 2002. Health, sanitation, and diet in a twentieth-century dam construction camp: a view from Butt Valley, California. *Historical Archaeology* 36(3): 69–84.

Manley, J. E. and B. Foley 2004. Deep frontiers: ocean exploration in the 20th century. In D. Finamore (ed.) *Maritime History as World History*. Gainesville, FL: University Press of Florida, pp. 82–101.

Manning-Sterling, E. 2000. Antietam: the cultural impact of battle on an agrarian landscape. In C. R. Geier and S. R. Potter (eds.) *Archaeological Perspectives on the American Civil War*. Tallahassee, FL: University Press of Florida, pp. 188–216.

Marcus, G. 1995. The emergence of a multi-sited ethnography. *Annual Review of Anthropology* 24: 95–117.

Marcus, G., and M. M. J. Fischer 1986. *Anthropology as Cultural Critique: An Experimental Moment in the Human Sciences*. Chicago, IL: University of Chicago Press.

Markell, A., M. Hall and C. Schrire 1995. The historical archaeology of Vergelegen, an early farmstead at the Cape of Good Hope. *Historical Archaeology* 29(1): 10–34.

Marken, M. W. 1994. *Pottery from Spanish Shipwrecks 1500–1800*. Gainesville, IL: University Press of Florida.

Marsden, P. 1981. Early shipping and the waterfronts of London. In G. Milne and B. Hobley (eds.) *Waterfront Archaeology*. London: Council for British Archaeology, pp. 10–16.

Marshall, D. 2004. Making sense of remembrance. *Social and Cultural Geography* 5(1): 37–54.

Martin, A. S. 1989. The role of pewter as missing artifact: consumer attitudes toward tablewares in late eighteenth century Virginia. *Historical Archaeology* 23: 1–27.

1993. Makers, buyers, and users: consumerism as a material culture framework. *Winterthur Portfolio* 28: 141–157.

Martin, A. S. and J. R. Garrison (eds.) 1997. *American Material Culture: The Shape of the Field*. Knoxville, TN: University of Tennessee Press.

Martin, C. J. M. 1997. Ships as integrated artifacts: the archaeological potential. In M. Redknap (ed.) *Artefacts from Wrecks*. Oxford: Oxbow, pp. 1–13.

1998. *Scotland's Historic Shipwrecks*. Edinburgh: Historic Scotland.

2001. De-particularising the particular: approaches to the investigation of well-documented post-medieval shipwrecks. *World Archaeology* 32(3): 383–399.

Marx, K. 1906. *Capital: A Critique of Political Economy*. New York: The Modern Library.

1978. *The Eighteenth Brumaire of Louis Bonaparte*. Peking: Foreign Language Press.

Marx, K. and F. Engels 1970. *The German Ideology*. New York: International Publishers.

1977. *Selected Letters*. Peking: Foreign Language Press.

Marx, R. F. 1973. *Port Royal Rediscovered*. New York: Doubleday.

Matthews, C. N. 2002. *An Archaeology of History and Tradition: Moments of Danger in the Annapolis Landscape*. New York: Kluwer/Plenum.

Matthews, C. N., M. P. Leone and K. A. Jordan 2002. The political economy of archaeological cultures. *Journal of Social Archaeology* 2(1): 109–134.

Mauk, D. C. 1997. *The Colony that Rose from the Sea – Norwegian Maritime Migration and Community in Brooklyn, 1850–1910*. New York: Norwegian-American Historical Association and University of Illinois Press.

Mayne, A. 1993. *The Imagined Slum, Newspaper Representation in Three Cities 1870–1914*. Leicester: Leicester University Press.

Mayne, A. and S. Lawrence 1998. An ethnography of place: imagining 'Little Lon'. *Journal of Australian Studies* 57: 93–107.

Mayne, A. and T. Murray (eds.) 2001. *The Archaeology of Urban Landscapes, Explorations in Slumland*. Cambridge: Cambridge University Press.

Mayne, A. and T. Murray 2003. (Re)Constructing a lost community: 'Little Lon', Melbourne, Australia. *Historical Archaeology* 37: 87–107.

McAtackney, L. 2005. What can archaeology tell us about the Maze site? *Archaeology Ireland* 19: 22.

McAuley, J. 2001. The trouble with capitalism in one-country theories. *Against the Current* 16(4): 445–447.

McCann, A. M. and J. P. Oleson (eds.) 2004. *Deep-Water Shipwrecks off Skerki Bank: The 1997 Survey*. Portsmouth: Journal of Roman Archaeology (Supplementary Series 58).

McCarthy, M. 2001. *Iron and Steamship Archaeology: Success and Failure on the SS Xantho*. New York: Plenum.

McCormack, J. and N. Jarman 2005. Death of a mural. *Journal of Material Culture* 10(1): 49–71.

McCracken, C. 1990. *Culture and Consumption*. Bloomington, IN: University of Indiana Press.

McDavid, C. 1997. Descendants, decisions, and power: the public interpretation of the archaeology of the Levi Jordan plantation. *Historical Archaeology* 31(3): 114–131.

McDavid, C. and D. W. Babson (eds.) 1997. In the realm of politics: prospects for public participation in African-American and plantation archaeology. *Historical Archaeology* 31(3).

McDonald, J. D., L. J. Zimmerman, A. L. McDonald, W. Tall Bull and T. Rising Sun 1991. The Northern Cheyenne Outbreak of 1879: using oral history and archaeology as tools of resistance. In R. Paynter and R. McGuire *The Archaeology of Inequality*. Oxford: Blackwell, pp. 64–78.

McErlean, T. 2004. Fish and fishing in Strangford Lough. In T. McErlean, R. Conkey and W. Forsythe (eds.) *The Maritime Cultural Landscape of Strangford Lough*. Belfast: Backstaff Press, pp. 132–143.

McEwan, B. 1991. The archaeology of women in the Spanish New World. *Historical Archaeology* 25(4): 33–41.

McGhee, F. 1997. Towards a postcolonial nautical archaeology. *Assemblage* 3, www.shef.ac.uk/assem/3/3mcghee.htm (Accessed 1 March 2005).

McGovern, G. S. and L. F. Guttridge 1972. *The Great Coalfield War*. Boston, MA: Houghton Mifflin.

McGowan, B. 2003. The archaeology of Chinese alluvial mining in Australia. *Australasian Historical Archaeology* 21: 11–17.

McGrail, S. (ed.) 1977. *Sources and Techniques in Boat Archaeology*. Oxford: British Archaeological Reports Supplementary Series No. 29).

McGrail, S. 1978. *Logboats of England and Wales with Comparative Material from European and Other Countries*. Oxford: British Archaeological Reports (British Series, BAR 51).

1984a. Boats, ethnography and maritime archaeology. *International Journal of Nautical Archaeology* 13(1): 149–150.

McGrail, S. (ed.) 1984b. *Aspects of Maritime Archaeology and Ethnography*. London: National Maritime Museum.

McGrail, S. 2001. *Boats of the World*. Oxford: Oxford University Press.

McGuire, R. H. 1988. Dialogues with the dead, ideology and the cemetery. In M. P. Leone and P. B. Potter (eds.) pp. 435–480.

1991. Building power in the cultural landscape of Broome County, New York 1880 to 1940. In R. H. McGuire and R. Paynter (eds.) pp. 102–124.

1992. *A Marxist Archaeology*. Orlando: Academic Press.

McGuire, R. H. and R. Paynter (eds.) 1991. *The Archaeology of Inequality*. Oxford: Blackwell.

McGuire, R. H. and P. Reckner 2002. The unromantic West: labor, capital and struggle. *Historical Archaeology* 36(3): 44–58.

2003. Building a working-class archaeology: the Colorado Coal Field War Project. *Industrial Archaeology Review* 25(2): 83–96.

McGuire, R. H. and M. Walker 1999. Class confrontations in archaeology. *Historical Archaeology* 33(1): 159–183.

McGuire, R. H. and L. Wurst 2002. Struggling with the past. *International Journal of Historical Archaeology* 6(2): 85–94.

McKee, B. R. 1999. Household archaeology and cultural formation processes: examples from the Cerén site, El Salvador. In P. M. Allison (ed.) *The Archaeology of Household Activities: Gender, Ideologies, Domestic Spaces, and Material Culture*. New York: Routledge, pp. 30–42.

McKee, J. E. G. 1983. *Working Boats of Britain*. London: Conway.

McKee, L. and J. Galle 2000. Scientific creativity and creative science: looking at the future of archaeological storytelling. *Historical Archaeology* 34(2): 14–16.

McKendrick, N., J. Brewer and J. H. Plumb 1982. *The Birth of a Consumer Society*. Bloomington: University of Indiana Press.

McNeil, I. 1972. *Hydraulic Power*. London: Longman.

Meillassoux, C. 1981. *Maidens, Meal and Money*. Cambridge: Cambridge University Press.

Meniketti, M. 1998. The port of St. George project: reconnaissance and assessment of a sugar plantation/harbour site in Nevis, West Indies. In L. E. Babits, C. Fach and R. Harris (eds.) *Underwater Archaeology: Proceedings of the 1998 SHA Conference*. Rockville: Society for Historical Archaeology, pp. 88–95.

Mercer, E. 1975. *English Vernacular Houses: A Study of Traditional Farmhouses and Cottages*. London: HMSO.

Mercer, H. 1976 [1924]. The origin of log houses in the United States. Doylestown, PA: Bucks County Historical Society (reprinted from *A Collection of Papers Read before the Bucks County Historical Society, Volume 5*). Online at www.libraries.psu.edu/do/digitalbookshelf/28988620/ (Part 105) (accessed 14 June 2005).

Merleau-Ponty, M. 1969. *The Essential Writings of Merleau-Ponty*. New York: Harcourt, Brace & World.

Meskell, L. M. 1996. The somatization of archaeology: institutions, discourses, corporeality. *Norwegian Archaeological Review* 29(1): 1–16.

1999. *Archaeologies of Social Life: Age, Sex, Class, et cetera in Ancient Egypt*. Oxford: Blackwell.

2000. Writing the body in archaeology. In A. E. Rautman (ed.) *Reading the Body: Representations and Remains in the Archaeological Record*. Philadelphia, PA: University of Pennsylvania Press, pp. 13–21.

2004. *Object Worlds in Ancient Egypt: Material Biographies in Past and Present*. Oxford: Berg.

Meskell, L. M., C. Gosden, I. Hodder, R. Joyce and R. Preucel 2001. Editorial statement. *Journal of Social Archaeology* 1(1): 5–12.

Miller, D. 1984. Appropriating the state from the council estate. *Man* 23: 353–372.

1987. *Material Culture and Mass Consumption*. Oxford: Blackwell.

1995. Consumption studies as the transformation of anthropology. In D. Miller (ed.) *Acknowledging Consumption: A Review of New Studies*. London: Routledge, pp. 264–295.

1998a. Coca-cola: a black sweet drink from Trinidad. In D Miller (ed.) *Material Cultures: Why Some Things Matter*. London: UCL Press, pp. 169–187.

Miller, D. (ed.) 1998b. *Material Cultures: Why Some Things Matter*, London: UCL Press.

Miller, D. 1998c. *A Theory of Shopping*. New York: Cornell University Press.

1998d. Why some things matter. In D. Miller (ed.) *Material Cultures: Why Some Things Matter*. London: UCL Press, pp. 3–21.

2001a. *The Dialectics of Shopping*. Chicago: University of Chicago Press.

Miller, D. (ed.) 2001b. *Home Possessions: Material Culture Behind Closed Doors*. Oxford: Berg.

Miller, D. and C. Tilley (eds.) 1984. *Ideology, Power and Prehistory*. Cambridge: Cambridge University Press.

1996. Editorial. *Journal of Material Culture* 1: 5–14.

Miller, D., M. Rowlands, and C. Tilley 1989. Introduction. In. D. Miller, M. Rowlands and C. Tilley (eds.) *Domination and Resistance*. London: Unwin Hyman, pp. 1–26.

Miller, D., P. Jackson, N. Thrift, B. Holbrook and M. Rowlands 1998. *Shopping, Place and Identity*. London: Routledge.

Miller, G. L. 1980. Classification and economic scaling of 19th century ceramics. *Historical Archaeology* 14: 1–40.

1987. Origins of Josiah Wedgwood's pearlware. *Northeast Historical Archaeology* 16: 80–92.

1991. A revised set of CC index values for classification and economic scaling of English ceramics from 1787 to 1880. *Historical Archaeology* 25(1): 1–25.

Miller, G. L., A. S. Martin and N. S. Dickinson 1994. Changing consumption patterns: English ceramics and the American market 1770 to 1840. In C. E. Hutchins (ed.) *Everyday Life in the Early Republic*. Winterthur: Henry Francis du Pont Winterthur Museum, pp. 219–248.

Miller, H. M. 1988a. An archaeological perspective in the evolution of diet in the colonial Chesapeake, 1620–1745. In L. G. Carr, P. Morgan, and J. Russo (eds.) *Colonial Chesapeake Society*. Chapel Hill, NC: University of North Carolina Press, pp. 176–199.

1988b. Baroque cities in the wilderness: archaeology and urban development in the colonial Chesapeake. *Historical Archaeology* 22: 57–73.

Miller, M. and O. V. Ridout (eds.) 1998. *Architecture in Annapolis*. Crownsville, MD: Vernacular Architecture Forum and the Maryland Historical Trust Press.

Milne, G. 1987. Waterfront archaeology in British towns. In J. Schofield and R. Leech (eds.) *Urban Archaeology in Britain*. London: Council for British Archaeology (Research Report 61), pp. 192–200.

2003. *The Port of Medieval London*. Stroud: Tempus.

Mirkin, A. (ed.) 1970. *The 1927 Edition of the Sears, Roebuck Catalogue*. New York: Crown Publishers.

Montgomery Ward 1924. *Winter Catalog*. Oakland, California: Montgomery Ward.

Moore, J. A. and A. S. Keene (eds.) 1983. *Archaeological Hammers and Theories*. New York: Academic Press.

Moore, P. R. and N. A. Ritchie 1998. In-ground ore-roasting kilns on the Hauraki Goldfield, Coromandel Peninsula, New Zealand. *Australasian Historical Archaeology* 16: 45–59.

Moorhouse, S. and I. Roberts (eds.) 1992. *Wrenthorpe Potteries*. Leeds: West Yorkshire Archaeology Service (Yorkshire Archaeology 2).

Moose, K. 2001. *Annapolis: The Guide Book*. Annapolis, MD: Conduit.

Moreland, J. 2001. *Archaeology and Text*. London: Duckworth.

Morley, B. 1977. *Henry VIII and the Development of Coastal Defence*. London: HMSO.

Morris, A. E. J. 1979. *History of Urban Form: Before the Industrial Revolution*. London: George Godwin.

Morris, M. 1994. Towards an archaeology of navvy huts and settlements of the industrial revolution. *Antiquity* 68: 573–584.

Morris, R. 1989. *Churches in the Landscape*. London: Dent.

Morris, W. 1877. *Manifesto*. London: Society for the Protection of Ancient Buildings.

Morriss, R. 2000. *The Archaeology of Buildings*. Stroud: Tempus.

Mouer, L. D. 1998. Thomas Harris, Gent., as related by his second sonne. *Historical Archaeology* 32(1): 4–14.

Mrozowski, S. A. 2000. The growth of managerial capitalism and the subtleties of class analysis in historical archaeology. In J. A. Delle et al. (eds.) pp. 276–305.

Mrozowski, S. A., E. L. Bell, M. C. Beaudry, D. B. Landon and G. K. Kelso 1989. Living on the Boott: health and well being in a boardinghouse population. *World Archaeology* 21(2): 298–319.

Mrozowski, S. A., G. H. Zeising and M. C. Beaudry 1996. *Living in the Boott. Historical Archaeology of the Boott Mills Boarding Houses, Lowell, Massachusetts*. Amherst, MA: University of Massachusetts Press.

Muckelroy, K. 1976. The integration of historical and archaeological data concerning an historic wreck site. *World Archaeology* 7(3): 280–290.

1978. *Maritime Archaeology*. Cambridge: Cambridge University Press.

Muckelroy, K. and R. Price 1979. The *Kennemerland* site: the fifth season. *International Journal of Nautical Archaeology* 8(4): 311–320.

Muir, R. 2000. Conceptualising landscape. *Landscapes* 1(1): 4–21.

Mukerji, C. 1997. *Territorial Ambitions and the Gardens of Versailles*. Cambridge: Cambridge University Press.

Mullins, P. R. 1999. *Race and Affluence: An Archaeology of African-American Consumer Culture*. New York: Plenum Press.

2000. Comments on Laurie A. Wilkie and Kevin M. Bartoy, a critical archaeology revisited. *Current Anthropology* 41(5): 767–768.

Mumford, L. 1961. *The City in History: its Origins, its Transformations, and its Prospects*. New York: Harcourt Brace Jovanovich.

Murphy, L. E. and D. J. Lenihan 1994. *Shipwrecks of Isle Royale National Park*. Lake Superior: Port Cities Foundation.

Murray, T. (ed.) 1999. *Time and Archaeology*. London: Routledge.

2003. *Exploring the Modern City: Recent Approaches to Urban History and Archaeology*. Sydney: Historic Houses Trust of New South Wales.

Mytum, H. 2003. A comparison of nineteenth- and twentieth-century Anglican and Nonconformist memorials in North Pembrokeshire. *Archaeological Journal* 159: 194–241.

2004a. Rural burial and remembrance: changing landscapes of commemoration. In D. Barker and D. Cranstone (eds.) pp. 223–240.

2004b. *Mortuary Monuments and Burial Grounds of the Historic Period*. New York: Kluwer/Plenum.

nd. Monuments and memory in the estate landscape: Castle Howard and Sledmere. In J. Finch and K. Giles (eds.) *Post-Medieval Estate Landscapes: Design, Improvement and Power*. Leeds: Maney.

Nash, C. 2000. Progress reports, performativity in practice: some recent work in cultural geography. *Progress in Human Geography* 24(4): 653–664.

Nash, G. B. 2001. *First City: Philadelphia and the Forging of Historical Memory*. Philadelphia, PA: University of Pennsylvania Press.

Nash, J. 1979. *We Eat The Mines And The Mines Eat Us: Dependency And Exploitation In Bolivian Tin Mines*. New York: Columbia University Press.

Nash, M. 2001. *Cargo for the Colony: the 1797 Wreck of the Merchant Ship Sydney Cove*. Canberra: Navarine.

2003. *The Bay Whalers: Tasmania's Shore-based Whaling Industry*. Canberra: Navarine.

2004. *Investigation of a Survivors Camp from the Sydney Cove Shipwreck*. Adelaide: Flinders University Press.

Neich, R. 1994. *Painted Histories: Early Maori Figurative Painting*. Auckland: Auckland University Press.

Neiman, F. 1993. Temporal patterning in house plans from the seventeenth century Chesapeake. In T. R. Reinhart and D. J. Pogue (eds.) *The Archaeology of Seventeenth Century Virginia*. Richmond, VA: Dietz Press (Archaeological Society of Virginia Special Publication 30), pp. 251–284.

Nelson, S. M. 2004. *Gender in Archaeology: Analyzing Power and Prestige*. Second Edition. Walnut Creek, CA: Altamira Press.

Netting, R.McC. 1993. *Smallholders, Householders: Farm Families and the Ecology of Intensive, Sustainable Agriculture*. Stanford, CA: Stanford University Press.

Nevell, M. and J. Walker 1999. *Tameside in Transition*. Tameside: Tameside Metropolitan Borough Council.

Newman, R. (ed.) 2001. *The Historical Archaeology of Britain, c. 1540–1900*. Stroud: Sutton Publishing.

Neyland, R. S. and D. Grant 1999. Navy aircraft as artefacts. In A. A. Neidinger and. M. A. Russell (eds.) *Underwater Archaeology: Proceedings of the 1999 SHA Conference*. Rockville: Society for Historical Archaeology, pp. 46–51.

Nijhof, E. 2004. Snail and shell: industrial heritage and the reconstruction of a lost world. In D. Barker and D. Cranstone (eds.) pp. 299–312.

Noël Hume, I. 1962. An Indian ware of the colonial period. *Archaeological Society of Virginia Quarterly Bulletin* 17(1): 1–12.

1964. Archaeology: handmaiden to history. *North Carolina Historical Review* 41(2): 215–225.

1969. *A Guide to Artifacts of Colonial America.* New York: Knopf.

1983. *Martin's Hundred: the Discovery of a Lost Colonial Virginia Settlement.* New York: Delta.

1997. *The Virginia Adventure: Roanoke to James Towne – An Archaeological and Historical Odyssey.* Charlottesville, VA: University of Virginia Press.

Nora, P. (ed.) 1984–1992. *Les Lieux de Mémoire.* 7 Vols. Paris: Editions Gallimard. (Abbreviated English Edition: P. Nora and L.Kritzman (eds.) 1996–1998. *Realms of Memory: Rethinking the French Past.* 3 Vols. New York: Columbia University Press.)

North, J. D. 1975. Monasticism and the first mechanical clocks. In J. T. Fraser and N. Lawrence (eds.) *The Study of Time* (volume II). New York: Springer Verlag, pp. 381–398.

Norton, M. B. 1996. *Founding Mothers and Fathers: Gendered Power and the Founding of American Society.* New York: Alfred A. Knopf.

Novick, P. 1988. *That Noble Dream: The 'Objectivity Question' and the American Historical Profession.* New York: Cambridge University Press.

O'Sullivan, A. 2001. *Foragers, Farmers and Fishers in a Coastal Landscape.* Dublin: Royal Irish Academy.

Oakland Tribune 1910. Cornerstone is laid for new Zeta Psi house (February 5).

Olivier, L. 2001. The archaeology of the contemporary past. In V. Buchli and G. Lucas (eds.) pp. 175–188.

Olivier, L. and B. Ollman 1971. *Alienation.* London: Cambridge University Press. 1993. *Dialectical Investigations.* New York: Routledge.

Olsen, B. 2003. Material culture after text: re-membering things. *Norwegian Archaeological Review* 36(2): 87–104.

Oosting, R. 1991. Preliminary results of the research on the 17th century merchantman found at lot E81. In R. Reinders and K. Paul (eds.) *Carvel Construction Technique.* Oxford: Oxbow, pp. 72–76.

Oosting, R. and A. Van Holk 1994. The excavation of a peat barge found at Lot LZ1 in Zuidelijk Flevoland. In C. Westerdahl (ed.) *Crossroads in Ancient Shipbuilding.* Oxford: Oxbow, pp. 215–221.

Orr, D. G. 1992. The City Point headquarters cabin of Ulysses S. Grant. In C. Wells (ed.) *Perspectives in Vernacular Architecture 1.* Annapolis, MD: Vernacular Architecture Forum.

Orser, C. E. 1988. Toward a theory of power for historical archaeology: plantations and space. In M. P. Leone and P. B. Potter (eds.) pp. 313–343.

1996. *A Historical Archaeology of the Modern World.* New York: Plenum.

2000. Comments on Laurie A. Wilkie and Kevin M. Bartoy, a critical archaeology revisited. *Current Anthropology* 41(5): 768–769.

Orser, C. E. and B. Fagan 1995. *Historical Archaeology.* New York: Harper-Collins.

Orser, C. E. and P. P. A. Funari 2001. Archaeology and slave resistance and rebellion. *World Archaeology* 33(1): 61–72.

Osborne, M. 2004. *Defending Britain: Twentieth-Century Military Structures in the Landscape*. Stroud: Tempus.

Ottaway, P. 1992. *Archaeology in British Towns: From the Emperor Claudius to the Black Death*. London: Routledge.

Otto, J. S. 1977. Artifacts and status differences – a comparison of ceramics from planter, overseer, and slave sites on an antebellum plantation. In S. South (ed.) *Research Strategies in Historical Archaeology*. New York: Academic Press, pp. 91–118.

1980. Race and class on antebellum plantations. In R. L. Schuyler (ed.) *Archaeological Perspectives on Ethnicity in America*. Farmingdale, NY: Baywood, pp. 3–13.

1984. *Cannon's Point plantation, 1794–1860: Living Conditions and Status Patterns in the Old South*. New York: Academic Press.

Outlaw, M. A. 2002. Scratched in clay: seventeenth-century North Devon slipware at Jamestown, Virginia. In R. Hunter (ed.) *Ceramics in America 2002*. Milwaukee, WI: Chipstone Foundation, pp. 17–38.

Owen, J. V. and J. Sandon 2003. A rose by any other name: a geochemical comparison of Caughley (*c*.1772–99), Coalport (John Rose & Co.; *c*. 1799–1837), and rival porcelains based on sherds from the factory sites. *Post-Medieval Archaeology* 37: 79–89.

Oxford Dendrochronology Laboratory 2005. Dated buildings in the USA. www.dendrochronology.com (accessed 12 April 2005).

Palmer, M. 1990. Industrial archaeology: a thematic or period discipline? *Antiquity* 64 (243): 275–282.

2005. Industrial archaeology: constructing a framework of inference. In E. C. Casella and J. Symonds (eds.) pp. 59–76.

Palmer, M. and P. Neaverson 1987. *The Basset Mines: their History and Industrial Archaeology* Sheffield: Northern Mines Research Society.

1998. *Industrial Archaeology: Principles and Practice*. London: Routledge.

Palus, M. 2005. Building an architecture of power: electricity in Annapolis, Maryland. In L. M. Meskell (ed.) *Archaeologies of Materiality*. Oxford: Blackwell, pp. 162–189.

Parker Pearson, M. 1982. Mortuary practices, society and ideology: an ethnoarchaeological study. In I. Hodder (ed.) *Symbolic and Structural Archaeology*. Cambridge: Cambridge University Press, pp. 99–114.

Parker Pearson, M. and C. Richards (eds.) 1994. *Architecture and Order*. London: Routledge.

Parker, A. J. 2001. Maritime landscapes. *Landscapes* 1: 22–41.

Parker, J. 1980. Invincible amphibian. *American West* 17(6): 48–53.

Pastron, A. G. and E. M. Hattori (eds.) 1990. *The Hoff Store Site and Gold Rush Merchandise from San Francisco, California*. Rockville, MD: Society for Historical Archaeology.

Pastron, A. G. and J. P. Delgado 1991. Archaeological investigations of a mid-nineteenth-century ship-breaking yard, San Francisco, California. *Historical Archaeology* 25(3): 61–77.

Patterson, T. 2003. *Marx's Ghost: Conversations With Archaeologists.* Oxford: Berg.

Pawson, M. and D. Buisseret 2000. *Port Royal, Jamaica.* Kingston, Jamaica: University of the West Indies Press.

Paynter, R. 1982. *Models of Spatial Inequality: Settlement Patterns in Historical Archaeology.* New York: Academic Press.

1985. Surplus flow between frontiers and homelands. In S. W. Green and S. Perlman (eds.) *Archaeology of Frontiers and Boundaries.* Orlando, FL: Academic Press, pp. 125–137.

1988. Steps to an archaeology of capitalism: material culture and class analysis. In M. P. Leone and P. B. Potter (eds.) pp. 407–433.

1989. The archaeology of equality and inequality. *Annual Review of Anthropology* 18: 369–399.

Pearce, J. 1992. *Border Wares.* London: HMSO.

Pearson, M. and M. Shanks 2001. *Theatre/Archaeology: Disciplinary Dialogues.* London: Routledge.

Pearson, W. 1996. Water power in a dry continent: the transfer of watermill technology from Britain to Australia in the nineteenth century. *Australasian Historical Archaeology* 14: 46–62.

Pels, D., K. Hetherington and F. Vandenberghe 2002. The status of the object: performances, mediations and techniques. *Theory, Culture and Society* 19(5/6): 1–21.

Pels, P. 1998. The spirit of matter. In P. Spyer (ed.) *Border Fetishisms: Material Objects in Unstable Spaces.* London: Routledge, pp. 91–121.

Perks, R. and A. Thomson (eds.) 1998. *The Oral History Reader.* London: Routledge.

Petsche, J. E. 1974. *The Steamboat Bertrand.* Washington, DC: Naval Institute Press.

Pfaffenberger, B. 1998. Mining communities, *chaînes opératoires* and socio-technical systems. In A. B. Knapp, V. C. Pigott and E. W. Herbert (eds.) *Social Approaches to an Industrial Past.* London: Routledge, pp. 1–6.

Phillips, W. D. 2004. Maritime exploration in the Middle Ages. In D. Finamore (ed.) *Maritime History as World History.* Gainesville, FL: University Press of Florida, pp. 47–61.

Piddock, S. 2001. 'An irregular and inconvenient pile of buildings': the destitute asylum of Adelaide, South Australia and the English workhouse. *International Journal of Historical Archaeology* 5(1): 73–95.

Pinney, C. 2002. *Camera Indica: The Social Life of Indian Photographs.* Chicago, IL: University of Chicago Press.

Platt, C. 1990. *The Architecture of Medieval Britain: A Social History.* New Haven: Yale University Press.

1994. *The Great Rebuildings of Tudor and Stuart England: Revolutions in Architectural Taste.* London: UCL Press.

Pluciennik, M. 1999. Archaeological narratives and other ways of telling. *Current Anthropology* 40: 653–678.

Pogue, D. J. 1996. Grant in the earth: George Washington, landscape designer. In R. Yamin and K. B. Metheny (eds.) pp. 52–69.

Pointon, M. 1999. Funerary and sexual topographies: the death and commemoration of Diana, Princess of Wales. *New Formations* 37: 114–129.

Pollard, J. 2004. The art of decay and the transformation of substance. In C. Renfrew, C. Gosden and E. DeMarrais (eds.) *Substance, Memory, Display: Archaeology and Art*. Cambridge: Cambridge McDonald Institute Monographs, pp. 47–62.

Pollard, S. 1959. *A History of Labour in Sheffield*. Liverpool: Liverpool University Press.

Pollard, T. 1999. The drowned and the saved: archaeological perspectives on the sea as grave. In J. Downes and T. Pollard (eds.) *The Loved Body's Corruption: Archaeological Contributions to the Study of Human Mortality*. Glasgow: Cruithne, pp. 30–51.

Pope, P. 2004. *Fish into Wine: The Newfoundland Plantation in the Seventeenth Century*. Chapel Hill, NC: University of North Carolina Press.

Potter, P. B. 1991. What is the use of plantation archaeology? *Historical Archaeology* 25(3): 94–107.

    1992. Critical archaeology: in the ground and on the street. *Historical Archaeology* 26(3): 116–129.

    1994. *Public Archaeology in Annapolis, A Critical Approach to History in Maryland's Ancient City*. Washington, DC: Smithsonian Institution Press.

Praetzellis, A. 1998. Introduction: why every archaeologist should tell stories once in a while. *Historical Archaeology* 32(1): 1–3.

    2000. *Death by Theory: A Tale of Mystery and Archaeological Theory*. Walnut Creek, CA: Altamira.

    2003. *Dug to Death: A Tale of Archaeological Method and Mayhem*. Walnut Creek, CA: Altamira.

Praetzellis, A. and M. Praetzellis 1987. Artifacts as symbols of identity: an example from Sacramento's Gold Rush era Chinese community. In E. Staski (ed.) *Living in Cities: Current Research in Urban Archaeology*. Tucson, AZ: Society for Historical Archaeology (Special Publication 5), pp. 75–99.

    1992. Faces and facades: Victorian ideology in early Sacramento. In A. E. Yentsch and M. C. Beaudry (eds.) pp. 75–100.

    1998. A Connecticut merchant in Chinadom: a play in one act. *Historical Archaeology* 32(1): 86–93.

Praetzellis, M. (ed.) 2001. *Block Technical Report: Historical Archaeology I-880 Cypress Replacement Project*. 7 Volumes. Rohnert Park, CA: Anthropological Studies Center, Sonoma State University.

Praetzellis, M. and A. Praetzellis 1998. Further tales of the Vasco. *Historical Archaeology* 32(1): 55–65.

Praetzellis, M. and A. Praetzellis (eds.) 2004. *Putting the 'There' There: Historical Archaeologies of West Oakland: I-880 Cypress Replacement Project*. Rohnert Park, CA: Anthropological Studies Center, Sonoma State University. www.sonoma.edu/asc/cypress/finalreport/ (accessed 21 February 2005).

Pryor, S. and K. Blockley 1978. A seventeenth-century kiln site at Woolwich. *Post-Medieval Archaeology* 12: 30–85.

Psota, S. 2002. Boss of the road: early 20th century consumer selections of work clothing from Alabama Gates work camp, Owens Valley, California. *Historical Archaeology* 36(4): 111–128.

Purser, M. 1991. 'Several paradise ladies are visiting in town:' gender strategies in the early industrial West. *Historical Archaeology* 25(4): 6–16.

1992. Oral history and historical archaeology. In B. Little (ed.) pp. 25–38.

Qualman, K. E., H. Rees, G. D. Scobie and R. Whinney (eds.) 2004. *Oram's Arbour. The Iron Age Enclosure at Winchester. Vol. I: Investigations 1950–1999.* Winchester: Winchester Museums Service.

Quimby, I. M. G. (ed.) 1973. *Ceramics in America.* Charlottesville: University Press of Virginia.

Rabinow, P. and W. M. Sullivan (eds.) 1987. *Interpretive Social Science: A Second Look.* Berkeley, CA: University of California Press.

Rahtz, P. and L. Watts 2003. *Glastonbury: Myth and Archaeology.* Stroud: Tempus.

Raistrick, A. 1972. *Industrial Archaeology: An Historical Survey.* London: Eyre Methuen.

Rajchman, J. 2000. *The Deleuze Connections.* Boston, MA: MIT Press.

Ramos, M. and D. Duganne 2000. *Exploring Public Perceptions and Attitudes about Archaeology.* Rochester, NY: Harris Interactive and the Society for American Archaeology. www.saa.org/pubEdu/nrptdraft4.pdf (accessed 12 June 2005).

Rappoport, A. 1982. *The Meaning of the Built Environment: A Nonverbal Communication Approach.* London: Sage.

Rathje, W. H. 1981. A manifesto of modern material culture studies. In R. Gould and M. Schiffer (eds.) pp. 51–56.

2001. Integrated archaeology: a garbage paradigm. In V. Buchli and G. Lucas (eds.) pp. 63–76.

Rathje, W. H. and C. Murphy 1992. *Rubbish! The Archaeology of Garbage.* New York: HarperCollins.

RCHME 1996. *Thesaurus of Monument Types.* London: HMSO (Royal Commission on the Historical Monuments of England).

Read, P. 1996. *Returning to Nothing: The Meaning of Lost Places.* Cambridge: Cambridge University Press.

Reckner, P. 2002. Remembering Gotham: urban legends, public history, and representations of poverty, crime, and race in New York City. *International Journal of Historical Archaeology* 6(2): 95–112.

Redknap, M. (ed.) 1997. *Artefacts from Wrecks: Dated Assemblages from the Late Middle Ages to the Industrial Revolution.* Oxford: Oxbow.

Read, T. C. 2004. *At the Abyss: An Insider's History of the Cold War.* New York: Presidio Press.

Rees, D. M. 1975. *The Industrial Archaeology of Wales.* Newton Abbot: David & Charles.

Reeves, M. (ed.) nd. *Montpelier: The Archaeology of the Madison Family Plantation 1723–1844.* Gainesville, FL: University Press of Florida.

Reid, A. M. and P. J. Lane (eds.) 2004. *African Historical Archaeologies.* New York: Springer.

Reilly, P. and S. Rahtz (eds.) 1992. *Archaeology and the Information Age*. London: Routledge (One World Archaeology 21).

Reinders, R. 1979. Medieval ships: recent finds in the Netherlands. In S. McGrail (ed.) *Medieval Ships and Harbours*. Oxford: British Archaeological Reports (BAR International Series 66), pp. 35–44.

Reitz, E. J. and C. M. Scarry 1985. *Reconstructing Historic Subsistence with an Example from Sixteenth-Century Spanish Florida*. Tucson, AZ: Society for Historical Archaeology.

Richards, N. 1998. Inferences from the study of iron and steamship abandonment: a case study from Garden Island ships' graveyard, South Australia. *Bulletin of the Australasian Institute for Maritime Archaeology* 22(1): 75–80.

Riess, W. C. 1991. Design and construction of the Ronson ship. In R. Reinders and K. Paul (eds.) *Carvel Construction Technique*. Oxford: Oxbow, pp. 176–183.

Ritchie, N. A. 2003. Traces of a Chinese past: archaeological insights into the New Zealand Chinese experience in southern New Zealand. In M. Ip (ed.) *Unfolding History, Evolving Identity*. Auckland: Auckland University Press, pp. 31–48.

Ritchie-Noakes, N. 1984. *Liverpool's Historic Waterfront: The World's First Mercantile Dock System*. London: HMSO.

Rix, M. 1955. Industrial archaeology. *The Amateur Historian* 2(8): 225–226.

Roberts, T. 2004. *Archaeological Survey of Machinery at the John Watts Works, Lambert Street, Sheffield*. Sheffield: Archaeological Research Consultancy at the University of Sheffield (ARCUS) Report 780b.

Robinson, D. M. 2002. *Neath Abbey*, Cardiff: Cadw.

Robson, L. 1983. *A History of Tasmania: Vol. I, Van Diemen's Land from the Earliest Times to 1855*. Oxford: Oxford University Press.

Rodgers, B. A., N. Richards and W. R. Lusardi 2005. Ruling theories linger: questioning the identity of the Beaufort Island shipwreck. *International Journal of Nautical Archaeology* 34(1): 24–37.

Rodman, M. C. 1992. Empowering place: multilocality and multivocality. *American Anthropologist* 94(3): 640–656.

Rodwell, W. 1989. *Church Archaeology* (revised edition). London: Batsford.

Rogers, E. B. 2001. *Landscape Design. A Cultural and Architectural History*. New York: Harry N. Abrams.

Rogge, A. E., D. L. McWatters, M. Keane and R. P. Emanuel 1995. *Raising Arizona's Dams*. Tucson, AZ: University of Arizona Press.

Rogic, T. 2004. Industrial buildings and their evaluation. In D. Barker and D. Cranstone (eds.) pp. 291–298.

Rolt, L. T. C. 1969. *Navigable Waterways*. London: Longman.

Roseberry, W. 1989. *Anthropologies and Histories*. New Brunswick: Rutgers University Press.

Rowlands, M. 2001. Remembering to forget: sublimation in war memorials. In A. Forty and S. Küchler (eds.) pp. 129–145.

2002. Heritage and cultural property. In V. Buchli (ed.) pp. 105–114.

Rule, J. 1986. *The Labouring Classes in Early Industrial England 1750–1850*. Harlow: Longman Group Limited.

Rule, M. 1983. *The Mary Rose: the Excavation and Raising of Henry VIII's Flagship*. London: Conway.

Ruskin, J. 1849. *The Seven Lamps of Architecture*. London: Smith Elder and Company.

Ryan, L. 1996. *The Aboriginal Tasmanians*. Sydney: Allen and Unwin.

Ryder, R. L. 1998. 'Why I continue to live across the tracks from sister Sue,' as told by William Monroe. *Historical Archaeology* 32(1): 34–41.

Rynne, C. 1999. *The Industrial Archaeology of Cork City and Its Environs*. Dublin: Stationery Office.

Sahlins, M. 1985. *Islands of History*. Chicago, IL: University of Chicago Press.

SAHRA 2003. *Prestwich Place Burial Ground: Minutes of Meeting Between SAHRA, HWC, City Council and Department of Public Works*. Cape Town: South African Heritage Resources Agency.

Salinger, S. V. 1992. The phoenix of the 'new urban history' in Old Philadelphia. *Journal of Urban History* 18: 330–337.

Samford, P. M. 1997. Response to a market: dating English underglaze transfer-printed wares. *Historical Archaeology* 31(2): 1–30.

Samson, R. (ed.) 1990. *The Social Archaeology of Houses*. Edinburgh: Edinburgh University Press.

Samuel, R. 1994. *Theatres of Memory, Vol. I: Past and Present in Contemporary Culture*. London: Verso.

Sandercock, L. (ed.) 1998. *Making the Invisible Visible: A Multicultural Planning History*. Berkeley, CA: University of California Press.

Sansom, I., P. Barwick, K. Evans and P. Kostoglou 2004. *York Town Conservation Management Plan, Third Draft*. Hobart: Ian Sansom for the West Tamar Historical Society.

Santley, R. S. and K. G. Hirth (eds.) 1993. *Prehispanic Domestic Units in Mesoamerica: Studies of the Household Compound and Residence*. Boca Raton, FL: CRC Press.

Saunders, N. J. 1999. Biographies of brilliance: pearls, transformations of matter and being, c. AD 1492. *World Archaeology* 31(2): 243–257.

2003a. *Trench Art: Materialities and Memories of War*. Oxford: Berg.

2003b. Crucifix, calvary, and cross: materiality and spirituality in Great War landscapes. *World Archaeology* 35(1): 7–21.

Saunders, T. 1991. Marxism and archaeology: the origins of feudalism in early medieval England. Unpublished Ph.D. Dissertation, Department of Archaeology, University of York.

Sayer, D. 1987 *The Violence of Abstraction: The Analytical Foundations of Historical Materialism*. Oxford: Blackwell.

Scháevelzon, D. 1999. *The Historical Archaeology of Buenos Aires: A City at the End of the World*. New York: Plenum.

Schama, S. 1995. *Landscape and Memory*. London: HarperCollins.

Schiffer, M. B. 1987. *Formation Processes of the Archaeological Record*. Albuquerque: University of New Mexico Press.

Schlecker, M. and E. Hirsch 2001. Incomplete knowledge: ethnography and the crisis of context in studies of media, science and technology. *History of the Human Sciences* 14(1): 69–87.

Schmidt, P. 1978. *Historical Archaeology: A Structural Approach in an African Culture*. Westport, CT: Greenwood Press.

Schoenauer, N. 2000. *6,000 Years of Housing* (third edition). London: W. W. Norton & Company.

Schofield, J. 2002a. Monuments and the memories of war: motivations for preserving military sites in England. In J. Schofield et al. (eds.) pp. 143–158.

2002b. The role of aerial photographs in national strategic programmes: assessing recent military sites in England. In R. H. Bewley and W. Raczkowski (eds.) *Aerial Archaeology: Developing Future Practice*. Amsterdam: IOS Press, pp. 269–282.

2004a. *Modern Military Matters: Studying and Managing the Twentieth-Century Defence Heritage in Britain: A Discussion Document*. York: Council for British Archaeology (with contributors).

2004b. New urban frontiers and the will to belong. In G. Dolff-Bonekaemper (ed.) *Dividing Lines, Connecting Lines – Europe's Cross-Border Heritage*. Strasbourg: Council of Europe Publishing, pp. 69–92.

2005a. *Combat Archaeology: Material Culture and Modern Conflict*. London: Duckworth (Debates in Archaeology Series).

2005b. Discordant landscapes: managing modern heritage at Twyford Down, Hampshire (England). *International Journal of Heritage Studies* 11 (2): 143–159.

Schofield, J. and M. Anderton 2000. The queer archaeology of Green Gate: interpreting contested space at Greenham Common Airbase. *World Archaeology* 32(2): 236–251.

Schofield, J. and W. D. Cocroft (eds.) nd. *A Fearsome Heritage: Diverse Legacies of the Cold War*. London: Routledge (One World Archaeology).

Schofield, J., C. Beck and H. Drollinger 2003. The archaeology of opposition: Greenham Common and Peace Camp, Nevada. *Conservation Bulletin* 44: 47–49.

Schofield, J., W. M. Johnson and C. M. Beck (eds.) 2002. *Matériel Culture: The archaeology of twentieth century conflict*. London: Routledge (One World Archaeology 44).

Schrager, S. 1983. What is social in oral history? *International Journal of Oral History* 4(2): 76–98.

Schrire, C. 1995. *Digging Through Darkness: Chronicles of an Archaeologist*. Charlottesville, VA: University Press of Virginia.

Schuyler, R. L. (ed.) 1978. *Historical Archaeology: A Guide to Substantive and Theoretical Contributions*. New York: Baywood Publishing Co., Inc.

Scott, J. C. 1985. *Weapons of the Weak: Everyday Forms of Peasant Resistance*. New Haven, CT: Yale University Press.

Sealy, J. 2003. *A Proposal for the Future of the Prestwich Street Remains*. Cape Town: University of Cape Town.

Seifert, D. J. (ed.) 1991a. Introduction: gender in historical archaeology. *Historical Archaeology* 25(4): 1–4.

Seifert, D. J. 1991b. Within sight of the White House: the archaeology of working women. *Historical Archaeology* 25(4): 82–108.

  1994. Mrs Starr's profession. In E. Scott (ed.) *Those of Little Note: Gender, Race, and Class in Historical Archaeology*. Tucson, AZ: University of Arizona Press, pp. 149–173.

Serle, P. 1949. *Dictionary of Australian Biography*. Sydney: Angus and Roberston.

Shackel, P. A. 1993. *Personal Discipline and Material Culture. An Archaeology of Annapolis, Maryland 1695–1870*. Knoxville, TN: University of Tennessee Press.

  1996. *Culture Change and the New Technology: An Archaeology of the Early American Industrial Era*. New York: Plenum Press.

  2000a. *Archaeology and Created Memory: Public History in a National Park*. New York: Kluwer/Plenum.

  2000b. Comment on Wilkie and Bartoy. *Current Anthropology* 41(5): 769.

Shackel, P. A. (ed.) 2001. *Myth, Memory and The Making of The American Landscape*. Gainesville: University Press of Florida.

Shackel, P. A. 2004. Labor's heritage: remembering the American industrial landscape. *Historical Archaeology* 38(4): 44–58.

Shackel, P. A., P. R. Mullins and M. S. Warner (eds.) 1998. *Annapolis Pasts: Historical Archaeology in Annapolis, Maryland*. Knoxville, TN: University of Tennessee Press.

Shammas, C. 1990. *The Pre-Industrial Consumer in England and America*. Oxford: Clarendon Press.

Shanks, M. 2004a. Archaeology and politics. In J. Bintliff (ed.) *A Companion to Archaeology*. Oxford: Blackwell, pp. 409–508.

  2004b. Three rooms: archaeology and performance. *Journal of Social Archaeology* 4: 147–180.

Shanks, M. and R. H. McGuire 1996. The craft of archaeology. *American Antiquity* 61: 75–88.

Shanks, M. and C. Tilley 1982. Ideology, symbolic power and ritual communication: a reinterpretation of Neolithic mortuary practices. In I. Hodder (ed.) *Symbolic and Structural Archaeology*. Cambridge: Cambridge University Press, pp. 129–154.

  1987. *Re-Constructing Archaeology: Theory and Practice*. Cambridge: Cambridge University Press.

Shanks, M., D. Platt and W. Rathje 2004. The perfume of garbage: modernity and the archaeological. *Modernism/Modernity* 11(1): 61–83.

Shennan, S. J. 1989. Cultural transmission and cultural change. In S. E. Van der Leeuw and R. Torrence (eds.) *What's New? A Closer Look at the Process of Innovation*. London: Unwin Hyman, pp. 330–346.

  1991. Tradition, rationality, and cultural transmission. In R. W. Preucel (ed.) *Processual and Postprocessual Archaeologies: Multiple Ways of Knowing the Past*.

Carbondale, IL: Southern Illinois University (Center for Archaeological Investigations Occasional Paper Number 10), pp. 197–208.

Sherlock, R. 1976. *The Industrial Archaeology of Staffordshire*. Newton Abbot: David & Charles.

Sherratt, A. G. and E. S. Sherratt 1991. From luxuries to commodities: the nature of Mediterranean Bronze Age trading systems. In N. Gale (ed.) *Bronze Age Trade in the Mediterranean*. Jonsered: Paul Aströms Förlag, pp. 351–386.

Shull, C. D. and B. L. Savage 1995. Trends in recognising places for significance in the recent past. In D. Slaton and R. A. Shiffer (eds.), pp. 3–13.

Silliman, S. W. 2004. *Lost Laborers In Colonial California: Native Americans and the Archaeology of Rancho Petaluma*. Tucson, AZ: University of Arizona Press.

Sinclair, A. 1989. This is an article about archaeology as writing. *Archaeological Review from Cambridge* 8: 212–231.

Sinclair, P. J. J., I. Pikirayi, G. Pwiti and R. Soper 1993. Urban trajectories on the Zimbabwe plateau. In T. Shaw, P. Sinclair, B. Andah and A. Okpodo (eds.) *The Archaeology of Africa: Food, Metals and Towns*. London: Routledge, pp. 705–731.

Singleton, T. A. 1990. The archaeology of the plantation South: a review of approaches and goals. *Historical Archaeology* 24(4): 70–77.

    1991. The archaeology of slave life. In E. Campbell and K. Rice (eds.) *Before Freedom Came: African-American Life in the Antebellum South*. Charlottesville, VA: Museum of the Confederacy, Richmond and University Press of Virginia, pp. 155–191.

Sinopoli, C. 1994. The archaeology of empires. *Annual Review of Anthropology* 23: 159–180.

    1995. The archaeology of empires: a view from South Asia. *Bulletin of the American Schools of Oriental Research* 299/300: 3–12.

Slaton, D. and R. A. Shiffer (eds.) 1995. *Preserving the Recent Past: Vol. II*. Washington, DC: Historic Preservation Education Foundation.

Slemon, S. 1995. The scramble for post-colonialism. In B. Ashcroft, G. Griffiths and H. Tiffen (eds.) *The Post-Colonial Studies Reader*. London: Routledge, pp. 45–52.

Smith, D. M. 1965. *The Industrial Archaeology of the East Midlands*. Newton Abbot: David & Charles.

Smith, J. T. 1965. Timber-framed building in England, its development and regional differences. *Archaeological Journal* 122: 133–158.

Smith, S. O. (ed.) 1993. *Underwater Archaeology: Proceedings of the 1993 SHA Conference, Kansas City*. Rockville, MD: Society for Historical Archaeology.

Sofaer Deverenski, J. (ed.) 2000. *Children and Material Culture*. London: Routledge.

Soja, E. W. 1989. *Postmodern Geographies: The Reassertion of Space in Critical Social Theory*. London: Verso.

    1996. *Thirdspace: Journeys to Los Angeles and Other Real-And-Imagined Places*. Oxford: Blackwell.

2000. *Postmetropolis: Critical Studies of Cities and Regions*. Oxford: Basil Blackwell.

Somerville, M., W. Beck, C. Brown, D. Murphy, T. Perkins and A. Smith 1999. *Arrawarra: Meeting Place*. Armidale, NSW: University of New England and Yarrawarra Aboriginal Corporation.

Soop, H. 1992. *The Power and the Glory*. Stockholm: Vasa Museet.

Sørensen, M. L. S. 2000. *Gender Archaeology*. Cambridge: Polity Press.

Souter, C. 2003. Archaeology and oral history of WWII flying boat wrecks in Broome. *Bulletin of the Australasian Institute for Maritime Archaeology* 27: 115–120.

South, S. 1977a. *Method and Theory in Historical Archaeology*. New York: Academic Press.

South, S. (ed.) 1977b. *Research Strategies in Historical Archaeology*. New York: Academic Press.

South, S. 1993. *The Search for John Bartlam at Cain Hoy: America's First Creamware Potter*. Columbia: University of South Carolina (South Carolina Institute of Archaeology and Anthropology Research Manuscript Series 219).

Spector, J. 1993. *What This Awl Means: Feminist Archaeology at a Wahpeton Dakota Village*. St. Paul: Minnesota Historical Society Press.

Spencer-Wood, S. M. (ed.) 1987. *Consumer Choice in Historical Archaeology*. New York: Plenum Press.

Spencer-Wood, S. M. 1996. Feminist historical archaeology and domestic reform. In L. A. De Cunzo and B. L. Herman (eds.) pp. 397–446.

1999. The world their household: changing meanings in the domestic sphere in the nineteenth century. In P. M. Allison (ed.) *The Archaeology of Household Activities: Gender, Ideologies, Domestic Spaces, and Material Culture*. New York: Routledge, pp. 162–189.

2001. Introduction and historical context to the archaeology of seventeenth and eighteenth century almshouses. *International Journal of Historical Archaeology* 5(2), 115–122.

2003. Gendering the creation of green urban landscapes in America at the turn of the century. In D. L. Rotman and E.-R. Savulis (eds.) *Shared Spaces and Divided Places*. Knoxville, TN: University of Tennessee Press, pp. 24–61.

2004. What difference does feminist theory make in researching households? In K. S. Barile and J. C. Brandon (eds.) pp. 235–253.

Spicksley, J. 2003. Conference report: The social and cultural history of early modern England: new approaches and interpretations. University of East Anglia 24 April 2002. *Social History* 28(1): 83–87.

Stahl, A. B. 2001. *Making History in Banda: Anthropological Visions of Africa's Past*. Cambridge: Cambridge University Press.

2002. Colonial entanglements and the practices of taste: an alternative to logocentric approaches. *American Anthropologist* 104(3): 827–845.

Stanbury, M. (ed.) 1975. *Batavia Catalogue*. Perth: Western Australian Maritime Museum.

Staniforth, M. 2003. *Material Culture and Consumer Society: Dependent Colonies in Colonial Australia*. New York: Kluwer Academic/Plenum Publishers.

Staniforth, M., S. Briggs and C. Lewczak 2001. Archaeology unearthing the invisible people: European women and children and aboriginal people at South Australian shore-based whaling stations. *Mains'l Haul: A Journal of Pacific Maritime History* 37(3/4): 12–19.

Stankowski, K. 2004. A pole apart? Polish and German material culture in South Australia. *Australasian Historical Archaeology* 22: 4–14.

Star, S. L. 1983. Simplification in scientific work: an example from neurosciences research. *Social Studies of Science* 15: 205–228.

Starbuck, D. R. 1994. The identification of gender at northern military sites of the late eighteenth century. In E. M. Scott (ed.) *Those of Little Note: Gender, Race, and Class in Historical Archaeology*. Tucson, AZ: University of Arizona Press, pp. 115–128.

    1999. Military archaeology of America's Colonial Wars. In G. Egan and R. L. Michael (eds.) pp. 195–202.

Stave, B. M. 1974. A conversation with Sam Bass Warner, Jr. *Journal of Urban History* 1: 85–110.

STAS 2003. Excavations at the Minton factory *Stoke-on-Trent Archaeology Newsletter* 1: 1–2.

Stone, G. W. 1988. Artifacts are not enough. In M. C. Beaudry (ed.) pp. 68–77.

Stone, J. (ed.) 2002. *Voices from the Waterways*. Stroud: Sutton.

Strathern, M. 1991. *Partial Connections*. Savage, MD: Rowman and Littlefield.

    2004. Laudible aims and problematic consequences, or: the flow of knowledge is not neutral. *Economy and Society* 33(4): 550–561.

Stratton, M. and B. Trinder 2000. *Twentieth Century Industrial Archaeology*. London: E & FN Spon.

Stropin, F. and S. Marsden (eds.) 2001. *Twentieth Century Heritage: Marking the Recent Past*. Adelaide: Australian Heritage Information Network.

Sturken, M. 1999. The image as memorial: personal photographs in cultural memory. In M. Hirsch (ed.) *The Familial Gaze*. Hanover, CT: University Press of New England, pp. 178–195.

Sullivan, G. 1994. *Slave Ship: The Story of the Henrietta Marie*. New York: Cobblehill.

Sundaresh, A., A. S. Guar, S. Tripati and K. H. Vora 2004. Underwater investigations off Mahabalipuram, Tamil Nadu, India. *Current Science* 86(9): 1231–1237.

Sweezy, P. (ed.) 1976. *The Transition From Feudalism To Capitalism*. London: Humanities Press.

Symonds, J. 1999. Toiling in the Vale of Tears: everyday life and resistance in South Uist, Outer Hebrides, 1760–1860. *International Journal of Historical Archaeology* 3(2): 101–122.

    2000. The dark island revisited: an approach to the historical archaeology of Milton, South Uist. In J. A. Atkinson, I. Banks and G. MacGregor (eds.) *Townships to Farmsteads. Rural Settlement Studies in Scotland, England and*

Wales. Oxford: British Archaeological Reports (BAR British Series 293), pp. 197–210.

Symonds, J. (ed.) 2002. *The Historical Archaeology of the Sheffield Cutlery and Tableware Industry 1750–1900.* Sheffield: ARCUS Studies in Historical Archaeology 1.

Symonds, J. 2003. Beyond the industrial revolution. *British Archaeology* 72: 19–23.

2004. Historical archaeology and the recent urban past. *International Journal of Heritage Studies* 10: 33–48.

Syracuse China 1918. Order form and price list. Syracuse China Archive, Syracuse China Center for the Study of American Ceramics, Everson Museum of Art, Syracuse, New York.

Tacchi, J. 1998. Radio Texture: Between self and others. In D. Miller (ed.) *Material Cultures: Why Some Things Matter.* London: UCL Press, pp. 25–45.

Tait, H. and J. Cherry 1978. Excavations at the Longton Hall porcelain factory. Part I. *Post-Medieval Archaeology* 12: 1–29.

Tarlow, S. 1999a. Strangely familiar. In S. Tarlow and S. West (eds.) pp. 263–272.

1999b. Capitalism and critique. *Antiquity* 73: 467–470.

1999c. *Bereavement and Commemoration. An Archaeology of Mortality.* Oxford: Blackwell.

2000a. Emotion in archaeology. *Current Anthropology* 41(5): 713–746.

2000b. Landscapes of memory: the nineteenth-century garden cemetery. *European Journal of Archaeology* 3(2): 217–240.

2002. Excavating Utopia: why archaeologists should study 'ideal' communities of the nineteenth century. *International Journal of Historical Archaeology.* 6(4): 299–323.

Tarlow, S. and S. West (eds.) 1999. *The Familiar Past? Archaeologies of Later Historical Britain.* London: Routledge.

Taylor, S., M. Cooper and P. Barnwell 2002. *Manchester: The Warehouse Legacy.* London: English Heritage.

Terrell, J. 1990. Storytelling and prehistory. *Archaeological Method and Theory* 2: 1–29.

Terrell, M. M. 2004. *The Jewish Community of Early Colonial Nevis: A Historical Archaeological Study.* Gainesville, FL: University of Florida Press.

Thijssen, J. 1991. *Tot de Bodem Uitgezocht, glas en ceramiek uit een beerput van 'Hof van Batenburg' te Nijmegen, 1375–1850.* Nijmegen: Stichting Stadsarcheologie Nijmegen.

Thomas, B. W. 1998. Power and community: the archaeology of slavery at the Hermitage Plantation. *American Antiquity* 63: 531–551.

Thomas, C. 2003. *London's Archaeological Secrets: A World City Revealed.* New Haven, CT: Yale University Press.

Thomas, D. H. (ed.) 1990. *Columbian Consequences: Archaeological and Historical Perspectives on the Spanish Borderlands East. Vol. II.* Washington, DC: Smithsonian Institution Press.

Thomas, J. 1971. *The Rise of the Staffordshire Potteries.* Bath: Adams & Dart.

Thomas, J. S. 1992. Gender politics and American archaeology. *Anthropology Today* 8(3): 12–13.

1996. *Time, Culture and Identity: An Interpretive Archaeology*. London: Routledge.

2000a. Comments on Laurie A. Wilkie and Kevin M. Bartoy, A critical archaeology revisited. *Current Anthropology* 41(5): 770.

2000b. Introduction: the polarities of post-processual archaeology. In J. S. Thomas (ed.) *Interpretive Archaeology: A Reader*. London: Leicester University Press, pp. 1–20.

Thomas, K. 1971. *Religion and the Decline of Magic*. New York: Scribners Sons.

Thomas, M. 2001. *A Multicultural Landscape: National Parks and the Macedonian Experience*. Hurstville, NSW: New South Wales National Parks and Wildlife Service and Pluto Press, Australia.

Thomas, N. 1991. *Entangled Objects: Exchange, Material Culture and Colonisation in the Pacific*. Cambridge, MA: Harvard University Press.

Thomas, R. M. 2004. Archaeology and authority in England. In N. Merriman (ed.) *Public Archaeology*. London: Routledge, pp. 191–201.

Thompson, E. P. 1966. *The Making of the English Working Class*. New York: Vintage Books.

1967. Time, work-discipline and industrial capitalism. *Past and Present* 38: 56–97.

1978. The poverty of theory. In E. P. Thompson (ed.) *The Poverty of Theory*. New York: Monthly Review Press, pp. 1–210.

Thornton, J. 1997. *Africans and Africans in the Making of the Atlantic World, 1400 – 1800*. Second Edition. Cambridge: Cambridge University Press.

Thrift, N. 1996. *Spatial Formations*. London: Sage.

2000. With child to see any strange thing: everyday life in the city. In G. Bridge and S. Watson (eds.) *A Companion to the City*. Oxford: Blackwell, pp. 398–409.

Tilley, C. (ed.) 1990. *Reading Material Culture: Structuralism, Hermeneutics and Post-Structuralism*. Oxford: Blackwell.

Tilley, C. 1994. *A Phenomenology of Landscape: Places, Paths, and Monuments*. Oxford: Berg.

1999. *Metaphor and Material Culture*. Oxford: Blackwell.

2004. *The Materiality of Stone: Studies in Landscape Phenomenology*. Oxford: Berg.

Trigger, B. 1990. *A History of Archaeological Thought*. Cambridge: Cambridge University Press.

1995. Archaeology and the integrated circus. *Critique of Anthropology* 15(4): 319–335.

Tringham, R. 1991. Households with faces: the challenge of gender in prehistoric architectural remains. In J. M. Gero and M. W. Conkey (eds.) pp. 93–131.

Tripati, S., A. Sundaresh, A. S. Gaur, P. Gudigar and S. N. Bandodker 2003. Exploration of Basel Mission Company shipwreck remains at St. George's Reef, Goa, west coast of India: impact of the Basel Mission Co. on Society and Culture. *International Journal of Nautical Archaeology* 32(1): 111–123.

Tripati, S., A. S. Gaur, A. Sundaresh and K. H. Vora 2004. Shipwreck archaeology of Goa. *Current Science* 86(9): 1228–1245.

Trouillot, M.-R. 2003. *Global Transformations. Anthropology and the Modern World.* New York: Palgrave Macmillan.

Tuck, J. A. 1996. Archaeology at Ferryland, Newfoundland 1936–1995. *Avalon Chronicles* 1: 21–42.

Tuck, J. A. and R. Grenier 1989. *Red Bay, Labrador: World Whaling Capital, AD 1550–1600.* St. John's, Newfoundland: Atlantic Archaeology.

Tuck, J. A., B. Gaulton and M. Carter 1999. A glimpse of the colony of Avalon. In G. Egan and R. L. Michael (eds.) pp. 147–154.

Turnbaugh, S. P. (ed.) 1985. *Domestic Pottery of the Northeastern United States, 1625–1850.* New York: Academic Press.

Tyler, K. 1999. The production of tin-glazed ware on the north bank of the Thames: excavations at the site of the hermitage pothouse, Wapping. *Post-Medieval Archaeology* 33: 127–163.

Tyler, K. and R. Stephenson 2000. *The Limehouse Porcelain Manufactory.* London: Museum of London Archaeology Service.

Upton, D. 1986. Vernacular domestic architecture in 18th century Virginia. In D. Upton and J. Vlach (eds.) *Common Places: Readings in American Vernacular Architecture.* Athens, GA: University of Georgia Press, pp. 315–335.

1992. The city as material culture. In A. E. Yentsch and M. C. Beaudry (eds.) pp. 51–74.

1996. Keynote address 1996: ethnicity, authenticity and invented traditions. *Historical Archaeology* 30(2): 1–7.

Vaeth, G. J. 1992. *USS Macon* lost and found. *National Geographic* 181(1): 114–127.

Van Bueren, T. M. 2002a. The changing face of work in the West: some introductory comments. *Historical Archaeology* 36(3): 1–7.

2002b. Struggling with class relations at a Los Angeles aqueduct construction camp. *Historical Archaeology* 36(3): 28–43.

Van Der Hoorn, M. 2003. Exorcizing remains: architectural fragments as intermediaries between history and individual experience. *Journal of Material Culture* 8: 189–213.

Van der Pijl-Ketel, A. (ed.) 1982. *Ceramic Load of the Witte Leeuw.* Amsterdam: Rijksmuseum.

Van Doorninck, F. H., G. F. Bass and J. Steffy 1988. The glass wreck at Serçe Limani. *Institute for Nautical Archaeology Quarterly* 15(3): 1–31.

Van Dyke, R. and S. E. Alcock (eds.) 2003. *Archaeologies Of Memory.* Oxford: Blackwell.

Vansina, J. 1985. *Oral Tradition as History.* Madison, WI: University of Wisconsin Press.

Veeckman, J. 1999. Maiolica in sixteenth- and early seventeenth-century Antwerp: the archaeological evidence. In D. Gaimster (ed.) pp. 113–123.

Veth, P. and M. McCarthy 1999. Types of explanation in maritime archaeology: the case of the *SS Xantho. Australian Archaeology* 48(1): 12–15.

Vlach, J. M. 1986 [1976]. The shotgun house: an African architectural legacy. In D. Upton and J. M. Vlach (eds.) *Common Places: Readings in American Vernacular Architecture*. Athens, Georgia: University of Georgia Press, pp. 58–78 (reprint of 'The shotgun house: an African legacy'. *Pioneer American* 8: 47–80).

    1993. *Back of the Big House: The Architecture of Plantation Slavery*. Chapel Hill, NC: University of North Carolina Press.

Waddell, P. J. A. 1986. The disassembly of a 16th century galleon. *International Journal of Nautical Archaeology* 15(2): 135–148.

Wade Martins, S. 1991. *Historic Farm Buildings*. London: Batsford.

Waldie, D. J. 2004. Facing the facts. In D. J. Waldie *Close to Home: An American Album*. Los Angeles: J. Paul Getty Trust, pp. 6–16.

Walker, M. and D. Saitta 2002. Teaching the craft of archaeology: theory, practice, and the field school. *International Journal of Historical Archaeology* 6: 199–207.

Wall, D. diZ. 1991. Sacred dinners and secular teas: constructing domesticity in mid-nineteenth century New York. *Historical Archaeology* 25(4): 69–81.

    1994. *The Archaeology of Gender: Separating the Spheres in Urban America*. New York: Plenum.

    2000. Family meals and evening parties: constructing domesticity in nineteenth-century middle-class New York. In J. A. Delle et al. (eds.) pp. 109–141.

Wallerstein, I. 1974. *The Modern World System. Vol. I: Capitalist Agriculture and the Origins of the European World Economy in the Sixteenth Century*. New York: Academic Press.

    1995. *Historical Capitalism*. London: Verso.

Ward, I. A. K., P. Larcombe and P. Veth 1999. A new process-based model for wreck site formation. *Journal of Archaeological Science* 26(5): 561–570.

Watkins, C. M. 1960. *North Devon Pottery and its Export to America in the Seventeenth Century*. Washington, DC: US National Museum Bulletin 225. (Contributions from the Museum of History and Technology Paper 13.)

Watson, B. 2004. Digging up a post-medieval English prison: resolving the conflict between documents and archaeology. In G. Carver (ed.) *Digging in the Dirt: Excavation in the New Millennium*. Oxford: British Archaeological Reports (International Series 1256), pp. 79–85.

Weatherill, L. 1988. *Consumer Behaviour and Material Culture in Britain 1660–1760*. London: Routledge.

Webster, A. D. 1998. Excavation of a Vietnam-era aircraft crash site: use of cross-cultural understanding and dual forensic recovery methods. *Journal of Forensic Science* 43(2): 277–283.

Wells, C. 1993. Interior designs: room furnishings and historical interpretations at Colonial Williamsburg. *Southern Quarterly* 31(3): 89–111.

West, S. 1999. Introduction. In S. Tarlow and S. West (eds.) pp. 1–15.

Westerdahl, C. 1992. The maritime cultural landscape. *International Journal of Nautical Archaeology* 21(1): 5–14.

    1994. Maritime cultures and ship types. *International Journal of Nautical Archaeology* 23(4): 265–270.

Whatmore, S. 2002. *Hybrid Geographies*. London: Sage.

White, C. L. 2004. What the warners wore: an archaeological investigation of visual appearance. *Northeast Historical Archaeology* 33: 39–66.

2005. *American Items of Personal Adornment 1680–1820: A Guide to Identification and Interpretation*. Walnut Creek, CA: AltaMira Press.

White, C. L. and M. C. Beaudry nd. Artifacts and Personal Identity. In T. Majewski and D. Gaimster (eds.) *The International Handbook of Historical Archaeology*. New York: Springer.

White, H. 1987. *The Content of the Form: Narrative Discourse and Historical Representation*. Baltimore: Johns Hopkins University Press.

Whitehorne, J. W. A., C. E. Geier and W. R. Hofstra 2000. The Sheridan Field Hospital, Winchester, Virginia, 1864. In C. R. Geier and S. R. Potter (eds.) *Archaeological Perspectives on the American Civil War*. Gainesville, FL: University Press of Florida, pp. 148–165.

Whyte, N. 2003. The deviant dead in the Norfolk landscape. *Landscapes* 1: 24–39.

Wilbanks, R. L. and W. Hall 1996. The discovery of the Confederate submarine *H. L. Hunley*. In S. R. James and C. Stanley (eds.) *Underwater Archaeology: Proceedings of the 1996 SHA Conference*. Rockville: Society for Historical Archaeology, pp. 82–88.

Wilk, R. R. and W. Ashmore (ed.) 1988. *Household and Community in the Mesoamerican Past*. Albuquerque, NM: University of New Mexico Press.

Wilk, R. R. and W. L. Rathje (eds.) 1982. Household archaeology. *American Behavioral Scientist* 25(6): 617–639.

Wilkie, L. A. 2000. *Creating Freedom: Material Culture and African-American Identity at Oakley Plantation, Louisiana, 1840–1950*. Baton Rouge: Louisiana State University Press.

2001. Results of archaeological excavations at 2251 College Ave., the Zeta Psi Fraternity. Report on File, Capital Projects, University of California, Berkeley.

2003. *The Archaeology of Mothering: An African-American Midwife's Tale*. London: Routledge.

Wilkie, L. A. and K. M. Bartoy 2000. A critical archaeology revisited. *Current Anthropology* 41(5): 747–777.

Williams, H. (ed.) 2003. *Archaeologies of Remembrance: Death and Memory in Past Societies* New York: Kluwer/Plenum.

Williamson, T. 1993. Gardens and society in eighteenth-century England. In S. Lubar and W. Kingery (eds.) *History from Things: Essays on Material Culture*. Washington, DC: Smithsonian Institution Press, pp. 94–114.

1995. *Polite Landscapes: Gardens and Society in Eighteenth-Century England*. Baltimore, MD: Johns Hopkins University Press.

1998. *The Archaeology of the Landscape Park: Garden Design in Norfolk, England 1680–1840*. Oxford: Archaeopress (British Archaeological Reports, British Series 268).

2005. *The Transformation of Rural England: Farming and the Landscape, 1700–1870*. Exeter: University of Exeter Press.

Williamson, T. and L. Bellamy 1987. *Property and Landscape: A Social History of Land Ownership and the English Countryside.* London: George Philip.

Wilson, E. O. 1998. *Consilience: The Unity of Knowledge.* London: Little, Brown and Company.

Wingood, A. J. 1982. *Sea Venture*: an interim report on an early 17th century shipwreck lost in 1609. *International Journal of Nautical Archaeology* 11(4): 333–349.

1986. The *Sea Venture* (1609): second interim report. *International Journal of Nautical Archaeology* 15(2): 149–159.

Wolf, E. 1982. *Europe and the People Without History.* Berkeley, CA: University of California Press.

2001. *Pathways of Power: Building an Anthropology of the Modern World.* Berkeley, CA: University of California Press.

Wood, E. M. 2002. *The Origin of Capitalism: A Longer View.* London: Verso.

Wood, J. (ed.) 1994. *Buildings Archaeology: Applications in Practice.* Oxford, Oxbow.

Wood, M. C. 2002. Women's work and class conflict in a working-class coal-mining community. In M. O'Donovan (ed.) *The Dynamics of Power.* Carbondale: Southern Illinois University, (Center for Archaeological Investigations, Occasional Paper No. 30.), pp. 66–87.

Woodall, J. N., S. T. Trage and R. W. Kirchen 1997. Gunflint production in Monti Lessini, Italy. *Historical Archaeology* 31(4): 15–27.

Wood-Jones, R. B. 1963. *Traditional Domestic Architecture of the Banbury Region.* Manchester: Manchester University Press.

World Archaeological Congress 1989. Vermillion accord on human remains. www.wac.uct.ac.za/archive/content/vermillion.accord.html (accessed 15 June 2005).

1991. First codes of ethics. www.wac.uct.ac.za/archive/content/ethics.html (accessed 15 June 2005).

Worman, F. C. V. 1969. *Archaeological Investigations at the U.S. Atomic Energy Commission's Nevada Test Site and Nuclear Rocket Development Station.* Los Alamos, NM: Los Alamos National Laboratory publications LA4125.

Worth, D. 2005. Gas and grain: the conservation of networked industrial landscapes. In E. C. Casella and J. Symonds (eds.) pp. 135–154.

Wray, N., B. Hawkins and C. Giles 2001. *'One Great Workshop': The Buildings of the Sheffield Metals Trades.* London: English Heritage.

Wright, P. 1985. *On Living in an Old Country.* London: Verso.

Wurst, L. 1999. Internalizing class in historical archaeology. *Historical Archaeology* 33(1): 7–21.

2002. 'For the means of your subsistence . . . look under God to your own industry and frugality': Life and labor in Gerrit Smith's Peterboro. *International Journal of Historical Archaeology* 6(3): 159–172.

Wurst, L. and R. K. Fitts 1999. Introduction: why confront class? *Historical Archaeology* 33(1): 1–6.

Wurst, L. and R. H. McGuire 1999. Immaculate consumption: a critique of the 'shop till you drop' school of human behavior. *International Journal of Historical Archaeology* 3(3): 191–199.

Wylie, A. 1982. An analogy by any other name is just as analogical. *Journal of Anthropological Archaeology* 1: 382–401.

1985. Putting Shakertown back together: critical theory in archaeology. *Journal of Anthropological Archaeology* 4: 133–147.

1989. Archaeological cables and tacking: the implications of practice for Bernstein's 'options beyond objectivism and relativism.' *Philosophy of Social Sciences* 19: 1–18.

1991. Gender theory and the archaeological record: why is there no archaeology of gender? In J. Gero and M. Conkey (eds.) pp. 31–56.

2002. *Thinking from Things: Essays in the Philosophy of Archaeology*. Berkeley: University of California Press.

Wylie, J. 2002. An essay on ascending Glastonbury Tor. *Geoforum* 33: 441–454.

Yalouri, E. 2001. *The Acropolis: Global Fame, Local Claim*. Oxford: Berg.

Yamin, R. 1997. 'New York's mythic slum, digging lower Manhattan's infamous Five Points'. *Archaeology Magazine* 50: 44–53.

1998a. Lurid tales and homely stories of New York's Notorious Five Points. *Historical Archaeology* 32: 74–85.

Yamin, R. (ed.) 1998b. *Tales of Five Points: Working-Class Life in Nineteenth-Century New York*. West Chester, PA: John Milner Associates.

Yamin, R. 1998c. The rediscovery of Five Points. In R. Yamin (ed.) pp. 1–14.

2001. Alternative narratives: respectability at New York's Five Points. In A. Mayne and T. Murray (eds.) pp. 154–170.

2002. Children's strikes, parents' rights: Paterson and Five Points. *International Journal of Historical Archaeology* 6: 113–126.

Yamin, R. and K. B. Metheny (eds.) 1996. *Landscape Archaeology: Reading and Interpreting the American Historical Landscape*. Knoxville, TN: University of Tennessee Press.

Yanagisako, S. J. 1979. Family and household: the analysis of domestic groups. *Annual Review of Anthropology* 8: 161–205.

Yarrow, T. 2003. Artefactual persons: the relational capacities of persons and things in the practice of excavation. *Norwegian Archaeological Review* 36(1): 65–73.

Yentsch, A. E. 1991. Engendering visible and invisible ceramic artifacts, especially dairy vessels. *Historical Archaeology* 25(4): 132–155.

1992. Gudgeons, mullet, and proud pigs: historicity, Black fishing, and Southern myth. In A. E. Yentsch and M. C. Beaudry (eds.) pp. 283–314.

1994. *A Chesapeake Family and their Slaves: A Study in Historical Archaeology*. Cambridge: Cambridge University Press.

Yentsch, A. E. and M. C. Beaudry (eds.) 1992. *The Art and Mystery of Historical Archaeology: Essays in Honor of James Deetz*. Boca Raton, FL: CRC Press.

Yentsch, A. E. and M. C. Beaudry 2001. American material culture in mind, thought, and deed. In I. Hodder (ed.) *Archaeological Theory Today*. Cambridge: Polity Press, pp. 214–240.

Young, D. J. B. 2004. The material value of color: the estate agent's tale. *Home Cultures* 1: 5–22.

Zarzynski, J. W. and D. K. Abbass 1998. The Rhode Island ship *Gem*: slaver of propaganda. In L. E. Babits, C. Fach and R. Harris (eds.) *Underwater Archaeology: Proceedings of the 1998 SHA Conference*. Rockville: Society for Historical Archaeology, pp. 74–78.

Zenzen, M. and S. Restivo 1982. The mysterious morphology of immiscible liquids: a study of scientific practices. *Social Science Research* 21: 447–473.

Index

Tower Hamlets 112
Westminster Abbey 246
Woolwich 210
see also shopping
Loren, Diana DiPaolo 199
Los Angeles, California 20, 90, 153
Los Vaqueros Reservoir, California 63
Louis XIV 94
Louisa County, Virginia 278
Low, Sandra 94
Lowell, Massachusetts 136, 262, 306
see also Boott Cotton Mills
Lowland Gorilla Alfred 250
Lucas, Gavin 47, 231
Ludlow, Colorado 137, 141
strike camp, archaeology of 138
see also massacre
Lydon, Jane 283

Maarleveld 171
McCann, Anna Marguerite 177
McDonald, J. Douglas 19
Macedonian community of Australia 112
McGhee, Fred 186
McGrail, Seán 171
McGuire, Randall 148
McGuire, Randall, and Mark Walker 136
Machin, Robert 275
Macon, wreck of 178
Madiba, Pumla 82
Majewski, Teresita, and Michael J. O'Brien 208
Majewski, Teresita, and Michael B. Schiffer 226
makers' marks 216, *218*
Malan, Antonia 81
'Malanggan' figures 198
Manchester, England 143
Maori, North Island, New Zealand, figurative
painting of 288, *289*
maps, use of in historical archaeology 17
Sanborn Fire Insurance maps 17, 99
Ordnance Survey maps 161
marbles, analysis of 59–60
marine archaeology 168
Maritime Archaeology 171
maritime historical archaeology
of aircraft 177–178
of colonialism 188
development of 169–172
ethical issues 187
focuses of 168
of globalisation 188
of maritime culture 171, 187
of maritime landscapes 172–174
of military sites 187
regional traditions in 178–183
Australia 180–181

Britain 182
North America 179–180
remotely operated vehicles 175
remote-sensing technology 175
submersibles 175
of trade and exchange 187
types of sites 172–178
watercraft, excavations of 174–177
see also ceramic studies
Marken, Mitchell W. 210
maroons 137
Martin, Ann Smart 43, 225
Martin, Colin 171
Marx, Karl 123, 135
analysis of class 123
theory of capitalism 123
Marx, Karl, and Friedrich Engels 256
Marxism 123–125, 257, 301
in archaeology 5, 141–142, 192, 195, 287
critiques, Marxist 124, 131
definition of labour 127–128
Frankfurt School of 130, 256, 257
goals of 124
holistic approach 127
notion of ideology 130
political economy, logic, theory, and method
of 125–129
radical concept of history 127
structural 6, 130–131
theory of capitalism 126–128
totalising theory of 123, 124–125, 130
Mary Rose, wreck of 175, 177, 318
Maryland Gazette 259
masculine identity *see* masculinity
masculinity 25–32, 200
Mason, George 260
massacre
of Cheyenne in Nebraska 19
Ludlow Massacre 137, 141, 151
Matagorda Bay, Texas 174
Material Culture and Mass Consumption 194
material culture
agency of 195, 196
anthropological material culture
studies 196–199
of architecture and the home 197, 198
of art and visual culture 197, 198–199
of consumption 197
of heritage 197, 198
of landscape 197–198
'artefact studies', definition of 193
of Atlantic world 174
connoisseurship approaches 194
contextual approaches 194, 195
foundational studies 193
Hegelian studies of 131